MĪRZĀ MALKUM KHĀN

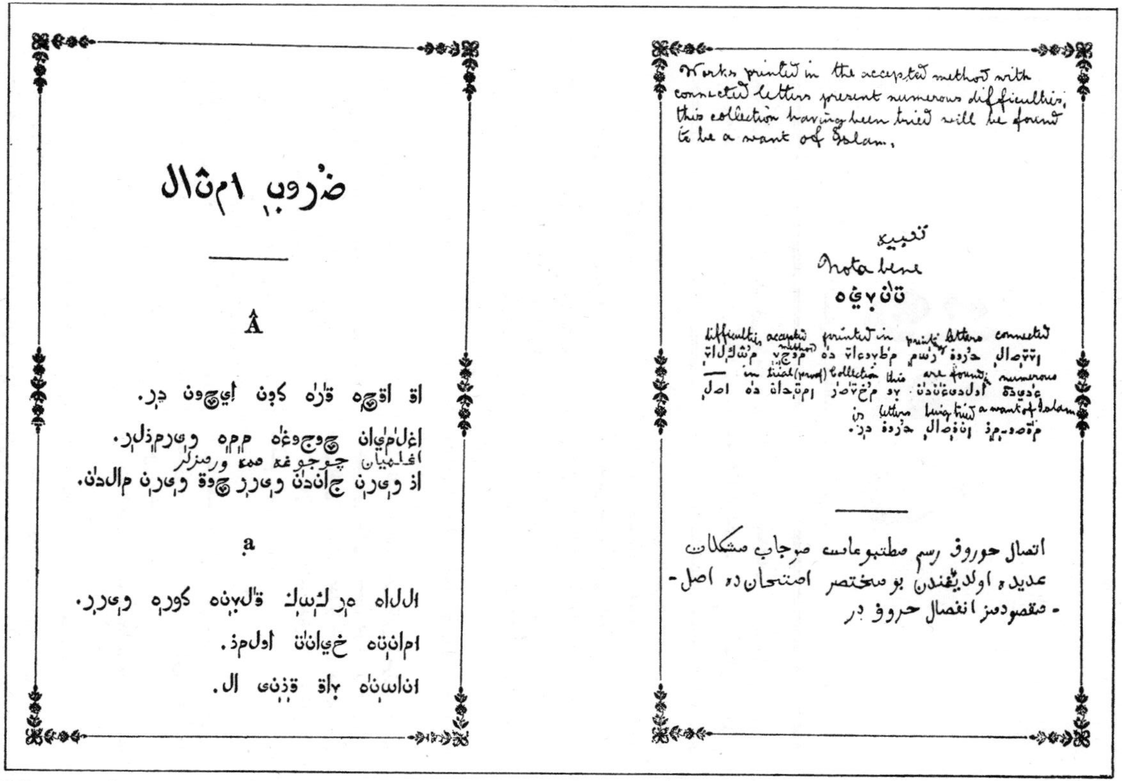

The opening pages of Malkum's *Dürûb-u Emsâl-i Müntehabe*. The handwritten annotations are by E. H. Whinfield, to whom this copy of the book belonged.

قانون

اتفاق . عدالت . ترقی .

نمرهٔ اول غرهٔ رجب ۱۳۰۷	محل صدور این جریده در دفترخانهٔ کمپانی انطباعات شرقی در کوچهٔ لومبارد نمرهٔ ۳۸ در لندن .	قیمت اشتراک سالیانه یک لیرهٔ انگلیس

بسم الله الرحمن الرحیم .

اللهم بدأنا باسمک العظیم . بعد الاتکال علی عونک الکریم . بنشر صحیفة "القانون" قانوناً لعبادک المومنین . ودستوراً یهتدی بامو‌له خیر المهتدین . فارشدنا وایاهم الی سراط الرشاد المستقیم وانر عقولنا بنبراس العلم السلیم . لنسلک فی منهاج العدل والاستقامه . ونحظی بخاتمة الصالحین یوم القیامه .

جمع کثیر از خلق ایران به چندین سبب خودرا از وطن مألوف بیرون کشیده در ممالک خارجه متفرق شده اند . در میان این مهاجرین متفرقه ان اشخاص باشعور که ترقی خارجه را با اوضاع ایران تطبیق میکنند سالها در این فکر بودند که ایا بچه تدبیر می‌توان بآن بیچارگان که در ایران گرفتار مانده اند جزئی امدادی برسانند . پس از تفحص و تفکر زیاد براین عقیده متفق شدند که بجهة نجات وترقی خلق ایران بهتر از یک روزنامهٔ ازاد هیچ اسباب نمی‌توان تصور کرد .

ان چند نفر اشخاص وطن‌پرست که معنی و قدرت روزنامه جات را درست فهمیده اند در این چهار پنج سال بیک عزم مردانه افتادند باطراف دنیا و بهر وسیله چه باصرار چه بالتماس و چه بگدائی از دولتخواهان ایران وارباب کرم و طالبان ترقی اعانه‌های وافر جمع نمودند و بعون الهی این روزها یک کمپانی معتبری ترتیب دادند باین عزم مبارک که از اطراف ایران بقدری که بتوانند روزنامه‌جات و کتابچه‌های مفید انتشار بدهند که از ان جمله یکی همین جریدهٔ قانون است .

ایران مملوّ است از نعمات خداداد .

چیزی که همهٔ این نعمات را باطل گذاشته نبودن قانون است .

هرچکس در ایران مالک هیچ چیز نیست زیراکه قانون نیست .

حاکم تعیین میکنیم بدون قانون . سرتیپ معزول میکنیم بدون قانون . حقوق دولت را میفروشیم بدون قانون . بندگان خدا را حبس میکنیم بدون قانون . خزانه می‌بخشیم بدون قانون . شکم پاره میکنیم بدون قانون .

در هند در پاریس در تفلیس در مصر در اسلامبول حتی در میان ترکمن هرکس میداند که حقوق و وظایف او چیست .

در ایران احدی نیست که بداند تقصیر چیست و خدمت کدام .

فلان مجتهد را بچه قانون اخراج کردند .

مواجب فلان سرتیپ را بچه قانون قطع نمودند .

فلان وزیر بکدام قانون مغضوب شد .

فلان سفیه بچه قانون خلعت پوشید .

هیچ امیر و هیچ شاهزادهٔ نیست که از شرط زندگی خود بقدر غلامان سفرای خارجه اطمینان داشته باشد .

The front page of the first issue of *Qānūn*.

MĪRZĀ MALKUM KHĀN

A Study in the History of Iranian Modernism

HAMID ALGAR

UNIVERSITY OF CALIFORNIA PRESS

Berkeley Los Angeles London

University of California Press
Berkeley and Los Angeles, California
University of California Press, Ltd.
London, England

ISBN 0–520–02217–3
Library of Congress Catalog Card Number: 78–187750
Printed in the United States of America
Designed by Dave Comstock

CONTENTS

Preface	vii
Chapter One	1
Chapter Two	20
Chapter Three	56
Chapter Four	78
Chapter Five	101
Chapter Six	127
Chapter Seven	163
Chapter Eight	185
Chapter Nine	206
Chapter Ten	228
Chapter Eleven	238
Conclusion	260
Appendix A	264
Appendix B	278
Appendix C	300
Bibliography	309
Index	319

PREFACE

THE HISTORY OF NINETEENTH-CENTURY IRAN, after a long period of neglect, is beginning to receive concentrated attention both within the country and abroad. Numerous memoirs, travel diaries, and collections of documents are being published, and the spate of material coming off the presses in Tehran shows no signs of abating. Despite all this activity, there is still relatively little concern with a critical analysis of Iranian history in the Qajar period, particularly its intellectual aspects. Iran's diplomatic entanglements and, to a lesser extent, the course of political events within the country, have been made the object of careful study. But beyond a few monographs and articles, the intellectual development of nineteenth-century Iran is still treated in a superficial and all too general manner. The praise or condemnation of controversial figures takes the place of detached and detailed analysis. The present study of Mīrzā Malkum Khān is intended as a contribution to remedying this deficiency. The reader will discern a certain lack of sympathy on the part of the author toward his subject. It is hoped that such lack of sympathy is not equivalent to bias and that the reasons for it will become apparent from the study of Malkum's words and deeds.

The chief interest of Malkum's career lies in his formulation of reformist ideas and tactics and in the role he assigned, in political and social change, to a utilitarian concept of religion promoted in the absence of personal belief. The much vaunted hero of nineteenth-century Islam, Sayyid Jamāl ud-Dīn Asadābādī (Afghānī), also hid rationalist beliefs behind a exterior and the phenomenon of concealed unbelief and political activism discussed in recent writings on Jamāl ud-Dīn is further illuminated in the present study of Malkum Khān. In addition to this manipulation of religious themes, numerous political and ideological motifs important in later Iranian history were first adumbrated by

Malkum. Indeed, some have considered him the intellectual progenitor of the Constitutional Revolution.

Malkum was a versatile figure. His career included masonic activity, journalism, diplomacy, and concession-mongering as well as political agitation and the demand for reform. In view of this variety, his life possesses an inherent interest; it also constitutes an important part of the total history of Iran for more than seventy years. This biography should then furnish a source for further investigation of several aspects of Qajar history and is intended, after my *Religion and State in Iran: The Role of the Ulama in the Qajar Period,* as a second contribution to the overall history of nineteenth-century Iran.

Part of the research for the present work was carried out with the support of the Humanities Institute of the University of California in the summer of 1967. Thanks are also due to Professor Nikki R. Keddie of the University of California, Los Angeles, who read the book while in manuscript and made several useful suggestions for its improvement; and to Dr. Soheil Afnan, who, many years ago in Istanbul, first suggested to me the interest of the topic.

H. A.

CHAPTER 1

Mīrzā Malkum Khān was born in the Armenian settlement at Julfā. This suburb, facing the city of Isfahan from the opposite shore of the Zāyanda Rūd, was the fruit of royal planning no less than the mosques, palaces, and gardens of the Safavid capital itself. Shah ʿAbbās, in moving the capital of Iran from its exposed westerly site at Qazvin to a position more centrally situated on the Iranian plateau, had made of Isfahan, through his lavish care and patronage, a true center of Iranian life, religious, cultural, and political. Associated with that center but separated from it by the waters of the Zāyanda Rūd, was a concentration of commercial and economic talent gathered in Julfā by Shah ʿAbbās almost as a supplement to the glories of the Safavid capital.

The Armenians of Julfā had come to Iran in the wake of Shah ʿAbbās's campaign against the Ottomans which began with the recapture of Tabriz in 1603 and ended with his tactical retreat from Kars in 1605. There are indications that the Armenians of eastern Anatolia and the southern Caucasus thought the advent of Iranian rule desirable and a welcome substitute for that of the Ottomans, and that David, a claimant to the Catholicate of Echmiadzin, expected Iranian support in the displacement of his rival, Srapion.[1] The actions of Shah ʿAbbās in the Armenian populated lands, however, were to be guided by his own strategic and other considerations. He attempted to turn the area between Nakhjavān and Kars into an unusable and barren buffer zone between Anatolia and Azerbayjan, where the Ottomans would no longer be able to create a base of activity and obtain supplies for southeasterly thrusts into the Safavid realm. To this end, the Armenian population of the

1. See the chronicle of Vartabied Arakel of Tabriz in *Collection d'Historiens Arméniens*, translated and edited by M. Brosset (St. Petersburg, 1874), I: 271–275.

area was gathered together and prepared for removal to Iran, and many villages and towns were wholly or partially destroyed.

Among the towns thus destroyed was Julfā on the Aras river, a settlement of largely Armenian population. Through its favorable geographical situation, Julfā had commanded a dominant position on the trade routes between Iran, the Caucasus, Anatolia and Arab Iraq. This position was reinforced by the prominence of Armenians in other centers of Near Eastern trade—such as Izmir and Aleppo—who were engaged in commerce with Europe, either independently or as the "factors" of British, French, and Dutch merchants.[2] In 1604, the troops of Shah ʿAbbās destroyed Julfā and compelled the inhabitants to emigrate southeastward into Iran. On the bank of the Zāyanda Rūd facing the royal capital, land was allotted to the Armenians, and "New Julfā" (Nor Julfa in Armenian) arose.

The transference of name from the old to the new settlement was not merely a pious remembrance of the former homeland. New Julfā was to fulfill essentially the same function as Old Julfā: that of a mercantile center with a place in the extensive network of the Armenian commercial diaspora. It was true that the center of the Iranian plateau was not, perhaps, so favorable a location as the point where the Caucasus, Anatolia and Azerbayjan converge, but Shah ʿAbbās took care that the community he had transplanted should flourish. The silk crop of the Caspian provinces constituted the chief commodity in the Iranian export trade, and its marketing in Europe was entrusted by Shah ʿAbbās to the Armenians of Julfā.[3] The French traveler Jean-Baptiste Tavernier relates that he "chose from among them those whom he judged most suitable and intelligent in matters of commerce, and gave to each of them, according to his capacity, bales of silk, for which they were to pay a reasonable sum on their return. The excess of the price they were able to attain was to be a reward for their troubles, and to cover the expenses of travel."[4] So successful and prolonged was this venture in state capitalism that another traveler, the Italian Pietro della Valle, found cause to remark: "The Armenians are in relation to the king of Persia as the Genovese are in relation to the king of Spain: they cannot live without the king, nor he without them."[5]

2. A. K. Sanjian, *The Armenian Communities in Syria under the Ottoman Dominion* (Cambridge, Mass., 1965), p. 46.

3. Jean Chardin, *Voyages en Perse et Autres Lieux de l'Orient* (Amsterdam, 1711), II: 88; III: 77.

4. Jean-Baptiste Tavernier, *Voyages en Perse*, ed. Vincent Monteil (Paris, 1964), pp. 76–77.

5. *Viaggi di Petro della Valle il Pellegrino, Descritti da Lui Medesimo in Lettere Familiari all'Erudito suo Amico, Mario Schipano* (Rome, 1668), p. 244.

The importation of European goods into Iran and their passage across Iran to India and Central Asia, were also secured largely by Armenian commercial enterprise. Among the objects brought back by the Armenians from Europe, partly for exchange en route against provisions and partly for sale in the bazaars of Isfahan, was not only the celebrated Dutch and English broadcloth, but also items such as clocks, mirrors, imitation pearls, and, in general, "things light in weight but heavy in price."[6] It is probable that the turkey was first introduced to Iran by Armenian traders returning from Europe,[7] and it may also be noted that, in 1641, in Isfahan, a certain Hagopian set up one of the earliest printing presses in Iran on the model of one he had seen in Venice.[8] Thus it was that the Armenians came gradually to be not only commercial, but also, to a certain extent, cultural intermediaries between Iran and Europe. In this they were helped by their acquaintance with numerous tongues, Near Eastern and European, and their mobility across a network of communities extending from Amsterdam to Batavia.

With the downfall of the Safavid state and its capital, the prosperity and significance of Julfā too went into inevitable decline. Julfā was sacked by the invading Ghilzai Afghans in 1722, and the Armenian suburb, like Isfahan itself, was not to recover throughout the eighteenth century. Incessant warfare rendered the trade routes between Iran, Anatolia and Syria only intermittently usable, and although some traffic with Europe was rerouted across the Caspian, down the Volga and through Russia,[9] Julfā was unable to regain its commercial importance. Many of its inhabitants left to join Armenian mercantile communities abroad, particularly in India.[10]

When in the late eighteenth century Iran recovered a measure of stability and security under the rule of the Qajar dynasty, the conditions governing trade between Iran and Europe were radically different from those that had prevailed in the Safavid period. On the one hand, the cultivation of silk, the chief Iranian export good, had declined, and on the other, European, particularly Russian, commercial ambition was now supported by military force of threatening proximity. A new relation of preoccupying intensity came into being between Iran and the West—more specifically, Britain and Russia—and in its elaboration the

6. Chardin, *op. cit.*, III: 24.

7. Tavernier, *op. cit.*, p. 40.

8. *Ibid.*, p. 237. See too Ismāʿīl Rāʾīn, *Īrānīān-i Armanī* (Tehran, 1349 solar/1970), p. 155f.

9. Jonas Hanway, *An Historical Account of the British Trade over the Caspian Sea* (London, 1762), I: 28–29.

10. See Mesrob J. Seth, *History of the Armenians in India* (London, 1897), pp. 27, 34.

Armenians participated as they had in the more desultory and primarily commercial contacts of the Safavid period.

This Armenian role in Iran paralleled a rise to prominence of Armenians elsewhere in the nineteenth-century Islamic world, a phenomenon everywhere attributable to the impact of European power and the beginnings of westernization. In Egypt, Muḥammad ʿAlī Pāshā, with whom the modern history of that country is generally held to begin, staffed his cabinets with a number of Armenians. One such was Boghos Yusufian, the minister of trade and foreign affairs, whose nephew, the celebrated Nūbār Pāshā, came in turn to occupy a number of government posts almost continuously until 1885.[11] In Syria, many Armenians found positions in the civil service or acted as consuls for European powers.[12] In the life of the Ottoman capital itself, the Armenian community, honored with the title of *millet-i sâdike* (the faithful people), played a role of some importance throughout the Tanzimat period.[13]

In Iran, Armenians continued to be active in foreign commerce, and were much used by the Russians to promote their trade in the northern part of the country.[14] More significant, however, was the Armenian share in the development of diplomatic relations between Iran and the outside world. Acquaintance with the languages and conditions of Europe made Armenians useful as interpreters and messengers, particularly at a time when Iranian Muslims with experience of European travel were an extreme rarity. Thus, in 1828, we find ʿAbbās Mīrzā, the crown prince, dispatching an Armenian with a message to Metternich seeking his intervention at the Russian court to prevent the impending renewal of hostilities between Iran and Russia.[15] Some twenty years later, when Mīrzā Taqī Khān went to Erzerum to negotiate a new border settlement with the Ottoman Empire under the auspices of Britain and Russia, he was accompanied as interpreter and mentor in protocol by another Armenian, Mīrzā Dāʾūd Khān.[16] On the basis of precedents such as these, when permanent Iranian diplomatic representation abroad came to be established, Armenians were allotted a large

11. See Otto F. A. Meinhardus, *Christian Egypt, Ancient and Modern* (Cairo, 1965), p. 402.

12. Sanjian, *op. cit.* (n. 2, above), p. 68.

13. See Y. Çark, *Türk Devleti Hizmetinde Ermeniler* (Istanbul, 1953), pp. 110 ff., and Sadi Koçaş, *Tarih Boyunca Ermeniler ve Türk-Ermeni İlişkileri* (Ankara, 1967), pp. 94–113.

14. James Greenfield, *Die Verfassung des persischen Staates* (Berlin, 1904), p. 68.

15. On the course of his mission, see Sharaf ud-Dīn Qahramān Mīrzā, "Yak Silsila Asnād-i Tārīkhī yā ʿIlal-i Vāqiʿī-yi Jang-i Duvvum-i Rūs-Īrān," *Sharq*, I (1310 solar/1931–1932): 253–257, 318–331, 439–440, 564–567, 625–632, 669–672.

16. Greenfield, *op. cit.*, p. 4, quoting from *Yereveli Haikazunk i Parskastan* [Prominent Armenians of Iran] (Tiflis, 1891), p. 242.

number of posts, together with members of another Christian community, the Assyrians. Undoubtedly the most important of the Armenians thus employed is the subject of this study, Mīrzā Malkum Khān.

The life of Malkum's father, Mīrzā Yaᶜqūb Khān, well illustrates the continuing role of the Armenians of Julfā as in some sense intermediaries between Europe and Iran. Born in 1815, he claimed descent from a French grandmother who bore some relation to Jean-Jacques Rousseau. Although the account of his life in which this claim occurs contains a number of untruths, the assertion appears plausible.[17] In about 1707, a cousin of Jean-Jacques Rousseau, Jacob, came to settle in Isfahan, spending the rest of his life working there as jeweler and clockmaker. He married Reine de l'Estoile, daughter of another French clockmaker, and although their male offspring went to Europe and entered the French diplomatic service, it is conceivable that their daughter should have married a local Armenian and become Mīrzā Yaᶜqūb's grandmother.[18]

He received his education among the Armenian community in India, where many emigrants from Julfā—among them, possibly, his relatives—had settled.[19] From India, he is reputed to have continued eastward to Java, joining for a time the ranks of the Armenian merchants of Batavia.[20] In the course of his travels, he evidently acquired a knowledge of French, for when he returned to Iran in about 1845, he entered the service of the Russian embassy in Tehran as interpreter and translator.[21] He also tutored a number of the Qajar princes in French, including Masᶜūd Mīrzā Ẓill us-Sulṭān, later governor of Isfahan, and thereby gained a useful friend not only for himself, but also for Malkum.[22]

Mīrzā Yaᶜqūb's position at the Russian embassy enabled him to establish links with Iranian officialdom and to make himself generally available and useful as informant and messenger. Thus, with varying

17. Charles Mismer, *Souvenirs du Monde Musulman* (Paris, 1892), p. 133.

18. See L. Lockhart, *The Fall of the Safavid Dynasty and the Afghan Occupation of Persia* (Cambridge, 1958), p. 433.

19. Mismer, *op. cit.*, p. 133; and ᶜAbbās Iqbāl, *Mīrzā Taqī Khān Amīr Kabīr* (Tehran, 1340 solar/1961), p. 326, n. 1.

20. *Ibid.*

21. *Ibid.*; Khān Malik Sāsānī, *Siyāsatgarān-i Daura-yi Qājār* (Tehran, 1337 solar/1958), I: 5, 127; Firīdūn Ādamīyat, *Fikr-i Āzādī va Muqaddima-yi Nihḍat-i Mashrūṭiyat* (Tehran, 1340 solar/1961), p. 94; and introduction of Muḥīṭ Ṭabāṭabāʾī to *Majmūᶜa-yi Āthār-i Mīrzā Malkum Khān* [hereafter referred to as *Majmūᶜa-yi Āthār*] (Tehran, 1327 solar/1948), p. i.

22. Masᶜūd Mīrzā Ẓill us-Sulṭān, *Sargudhasht-i Masᶜūdī* (Tehran, 1325 lunar/1907), p. 136; see also the collection of correspondence addressed to Malkum by Ẓill us-Sulṭān (Bibliothèque Nationale, Supplément Persan, 1990) and pp. 144–146 and 156–157 below.

degrees of cordiality, he came to enjoy the acquaintance of Ḥājjī Mīrzā Āqāsī, prime minister to Muḥammad Shāh (1834–1848), and the first two ministers of Nāṣir ud-Dīn Shāh, Mīrzā Taqī Khān Amīr Kabīr (in office from 1848 to 1851) and Mīrzā Āqā Khān Nūrī. Mīrzā Yaᶜqūb's contacts with these three men permitted him the exercise of an important role only on one occasion—the death of Amīr Kabīr. He has been accused of helping to bring about the end of this reform-minded and energetic minister in order to gain the gratitude of his successor in office, Mīrzā Āqā Khān Nūrī, for whom the disgrace and dismissal of his rival were not enough. Nāṣir ud-Dīn Shāh hesitated to take the final step of execution, for Amīr Kabīr was, after all, his brother-in-law, and had committed no offence beyond the use of a certain brusque straightforwardness in addressing the monarch. While Mīrzā Āqā Khān Nūrī was pressing the shah to conclude the affair as quickly as possible, the Russians were concerned to keep Amīr Kabīr alive, if not in power, as a preferable alternative to his anglophile successor. Hence Dolgorukiy, the ambassador in Tehran, wrote to the tsar suggesting he communicate directly with Nāṣir ud-Dīn Shah to obtain his pardon. Mīrzā Yaᶜqūb Khān is reputed to have conveyed news of this initiative to Mīrzā Āqā Khān Nūrī, who was then able, together with his associates, to precipitate the execution of Amīr Kabīr before the arrival of the tsar's letter of intercession.[23] The account appears plausible: it is certain that Mīrzā Yaᶜqūb Khān stood close to Mīrzā Āqā Khān Nūrī and continued to enjoy his favor.

The remainder of Mīrzā Yaᶜqūb's career is closely linked with the activities of his son, Malkum, and is best related in connection with them. It is appropriate here, however, to consider the probable nature of Mīrzā Yaᶜqūb's political and religious attitudes and beliefs and the degree to which they exercised an influence upon Malkum. Mīrzā Yaᶜqūb is recorded outwardly to have professed Islam,[24] and although it has not proved possible to find any direct evidence for the depth or shallowness of his beliefs, the sparse information that is available suggests strongly an opportunistic conversion. Suspicion of Mīrzā Yaᶜqūb's motives is in the first place aroused by the fact that his profession of Islam took place after his return to Iran and entry to official circles: it is unlikely that he should have turned to Islam while among the Armenians of India and Java. He may well have seen the adoption of Islam as an expedient step for the furtherance of his career. This was not a

23. Sāsānī, *op. cit.*, pp. 5, 38–39. He gives as references the manuscript memoirs of Ḥājjī ᶜAlī Khān Iᶜtimād us-Salṭana and another work of his own, entitled *Dast-i Panhān-i Siyāsat-i Inglīs dar Īrān*, to which I do not have access.

24. *Majmūᶜa-yi Athār*, p. i; Sāsānī, *op. cit.*, p. 127.

unique occurrence, for Yahya Naci Efendi, the Greek grandfather of his Istanbul acquaintance, Ahmet Vefik Paşa, found his position as interpreter at the Bâb-ı Âlî strengthened by conversion to Islam.[25]

The opportunistic nature of Mīrzā Yaᶜqūb's profession of Islam, however, went far beyond mere personal interest. This is clear from the record left by a French journalist, Charles Mismer, of his impressions of both Mīrzā Yaᶜqūb and Malkum, whose acquaintance he made during their Istanbul exile in the 1860s. His highly colored work, *Souvenirs du Monde Musulman* (Paris, 1892), contains certain autobiographical details supplied by Mīrzā Yaᶜqūb which, for the most part, may be discounted, but are of interest for indicating a trait common to father and son: a delight in the spinning of conceited fancies for the benefit of credulous foreigners. Mīrzā Yaᶜqūb claimed to have been the "arbiter of Persia" during the reign of Muḥammad Shāh and to have secured the succession to the throne of Nāṣir ud-Dīn Shāh in 1848.[26] More significant than these baseless assertions is what Mismer relates of Mīrzā Yaᶜqūb's outlook and beliefs.

> From his youth onwards, he had been struck by the marvellous benefit an intelligent government could derive from Islam. In his eyes, Islam was not merely a religion, but an entire system of social organisation, easier to reconcile with civilisation than to suppress or replace. . . . His plan consisted of preparing an Islamic renaissance, similar to the Christian renaissance which accompanied the reform of Luther. In order to effect it, he set himself up as a defender of the religion deriving from the Koran. Let me add that he died poor, in order to keep his memory clear of any suspicion of personal interest. Having converted his family and his entourage, he found adepts among the sheikhs, the mollahs and the high officials of state.[27]

In addition to this plan for an "Islamic renaissance," Mismer records other preoccupations of Mīrzā Yaᶜqūb, similarly of interest for their probable influence on Malkum. He considered the primary cause of the backwardness and weakness of the Muslims, made apparent by their confrontation with Europe, to be the inadequacy and complexity of the Arabic alphabet which did not permit "the popular acquisition of science, indispensable to progress."[28] Impressed by Mīrzā Yaᶜqūb's arguments, Mismer took it upon himself to submit a memorandum on the subject to Âlî Paşa, the grand vizier, entitling it "The Cause of Oriental

25. See Sadrettin Celal Antel, "Tanzimat Maarifi," in *Tanzimat I: Yüzüncü Yıldönümü Münasebetile* (Istanbul, 1940), p. 448.

26. Mismer, *op. cit.*, p. 133.

27. *Ibid.*, pp. 134–135.

28. *Ibid.*, p. 139.

Immobility." Malkum, too, devoted prolonged if fruitless attention to the question of alphabet reform.[29]

Further indications of Mīrzā Yaᶜqūb's outlook are contained in an earlier work of Mismer, *Les Soirées de Constantinople* (Paris, 1870), which, he says, was the fruit of his discussions with Mīrzā Yaᶜqūb.[30] The chief interest of this rather banal book lies in the view of Islam it sets forth: strictly utilitarian and well suited to Mīrzā Yaᶜqūb's plan for an "Islamic renaissance," "reconciling" Islam with "civilization." It views revealed religion as coeval with the necessity for government and to have originated when mere force was no longer adequate for maintaining the social order (p. 66). Religion is essentially a response to social need (p. 330) and therefore all religions will correspond "more or less, depending upon the faculties of observation and common sense of their authors, to the demands of the age in which they are born" (p. 74). Islam, then, is the creation of the Prophet Muhammad and the Qur᾽ān his work. Islam has continuing social utility because "a profound study of the human heart and human nature inspired the legal prescriptions of Muhammad" (p. 106). The essence of Islam is seen to lie in its social and communal aspect: the mosque is "above all a temple of equality" (p. 123), and Islam itself is "a kind of freemasonry, intended to unite all men in the worship of a single God and the practice of a morality based on observation" (p. 206).

This view of religion in general and Islam in particular may be assumed to be that held by Mīrzā Yaᶜqūb, even though the formulations are not his. It appears unlikely that he should have evolved such a view independently, or that he should have acquired it only during his Istanbul exile: his involvement in Malkum's pseudomasonic foundation in Tehran suggests some previous awareness of a relativist and utilitarian attitude to religion. It is of interest to determine how Mīrzā Yaᶜqūb came to hold these attitudes in an age when the Near East was still largely untouched by skepticism in matters of belief. The view of the Prophet as the author of the Qur᾽ān and the architect of its prescriptions, as a fundamentally rational man bound by the circumstances of his age to don the mask of religion, is essentially the modified European view of Islam produced by the Enlightenment and best exemplified, perhaps, by Voltaire's play *Mahomet*.[31] Conceivably, Mīrzā Yaᶜqūb was in corre-

29. The text of the memorandum is reproduced in full in Mismer's *Soirées de Constantinople* (Paris, 1870), pp. 341–363.

30. Mismer, *Souvenirs du Monde Musulman*, p. 138. Mismer's views on Islam are also to be found in two articles: "L'Islamisme et la Science," *Revue de la Philosophie Positive*, XXX (May–June 1883): 432–438; and "La Régénération de l'Islam," *Revue de la Philosophie Positive*, XXXI (September–October 1883): 283–289.

31. Voltaire, *Le Fanatisme ou Mahomet le Prophète*, in *Oeuvres Complètes* (Paris, 1877) IV: 106–167.

spondence with his somewhat distant relatives in France, themselves descended from the same family as one of the chief representatives of the European Enlightenment, and thereby gained acquaintance with this view of Islam. More probably, his study of French had entailed some reading of the classics of the Enlightenment and furnished him with a view of religion he found acceptable and attractive. It is also likely that he had had some contact with freemasonry; many Iranians early in the century had a vague concept of freemasonry as superseding and transcending positive religion.[32] He may also have encountered it in the lodges of British India during his residence there. Finally, we may speculate that his position as an Armenian enjoying continuous intercourse with Muslims as well as Christians, Armenian and foreign, and the resulting close acquaintance with both communities, induced in him a relativism in matters of belief. This relativism was not contradicted by his profession of Islam, but made it possible in the first place. Mīrzā Yaᶜqūb believed that Islam was founded by "a wise lawgiver," and therefore had more social utility than other faiths, both for himself in his career and for society in general. Such an attitude permitted outward affiliation with Islam and even contained a measure of intellectual appreciation for some of its aspects. It lacked, however, any basis of spiritual conviction, and it is not surprising to hear the suspicion raised that Mīrzā Yaᶜqūb reverted to the faith of his ancestors for purposes of burial. He is said to have been laid to rest in an Armenian cemetery in Istanbul, until disinterred and reburied by Malkum, for whom the preservation of a Muslim exterior was still of importance.[33]

This skeptical and utilitarian view of religion was transmitted to Malkum, who elaborated upon it and made of it an effective weapon for the promotion of westernization in Iran. Malkum once declared that he was born an Armenian Christian, though raised among Muslims, and this would seem to suggest that Mīrzā Yaᶜqūb's profession of faith took place some time after Malkum's birth in 1249/1833–1834.[34] Malkum's statements of religious affiliation, however, are so confused and contradictory that this cannot be taken as decisive evidence. Throughout his Persian writings, and particularly in the celebrated newspaper *Qānūn* (Law), great care is taken to show respect for and belief in Islam, the eternal adequacy and perfection of its laws, and the wisdom and piety of its scholars. These affirmations will be examined in the context of the political situations that produced them as a tactical response. Here we

32. Hamid Algar, "An Introduction to the History of Freemasonry in Iran," *Middle Eastern Studies*, VI (1970): 276–296.

33. *Majmūᶜa-yi Āthār*, p. xxii.

34. W. S. Blunt, *Secret History of the English Occupation of Egypt* (London, 1903), p. 83.

will only note evidence for Malkum's general insincerity in personal profession of Islam as a religious belief.

It is first of all remarkable that Malkum throughout his life retained his Armenian, and hence Christian, name.[35] His father's name, Yaʿqūb, was one common to both Muslims and Christians, and hence there would have been no occasion for a change upon profession of Islam. At the most, it might have been necessary to translate Hagop into Yaʿqūb. Although Malkum showed little tendency to associate with Armenians, either in Iran or abroad, or to demonstrate, in any other way, a sense of Armenian identity,[36] his retention of an Armenian name may be taken as evidence of a less than total conversion to Islam. His two brothers, whom he took with him on the staff of his embassy in London, were called Iskandar and Mikāʾīl, and it is not known whether they made any profession of Islam.[37]

Second, during his Istanbul exile in 1864, Mīrzā Malkum Khān married the daughter of Arakel, a prominent Armenian, and the ceremony took place in an Armenian church. Malkum's participation in this ceremony was taken by his protector, Mīrzā Huṣayn Khān, the Iranian ambassador, to imply apostasy, and he reproached him for hypocrisy in his previous profession of Islam.[38]

Lastly, it may be noted that a British ambassador in Iran at the turn of the nineteenth century saw fit to refer to Malkum in a dispatch as "a professed Christian."[39]

More enlightening than these fragments of circumstantial evidence are the statements of Malkum himself on matters relating to religion.

35. In some recent works, such as Firuz Kazemzadeh's *Russia and Britain in Persia, 1864–1914* (Yale, 1968) and Nikki R. Keddie's *An Islamic Response to Imperialism* (Berkeley and Los Angeles, 1968), the name is spelled "Malkam." "Malkum" is, however, a preferable spelling, reflecting the Armenian pronunciation. Malkum himself when writing in French or English used to sign himself "Malcom" (see, for example, his "Persian Civilisation," *Contemporary Review*, LIX [February 1891]: 244). In an Ottoman Turkish document relating to his removal from Baghdad to Istanbul, his name is spelled "Malqūn," evidently the form used by Armenians in the Ottoman Empire (see below, p. 61).

36. He did maintain some contact with relatives in Julfā, as is demonstrated by a letter from Masʿūd Mīrzā Ẓill us-Sulṭān concerning one of them (Bibliothèque Nationale, Supplément Persan 1990, ff. 20–21).

37. Iskandar is both a Muslim and a Christian name, and Mīkāʾīl exclusively Christian. According to a Tuscan adventurer, Enrico Andreini, who served in the Iranian army, all of Malkum's family professed Islam. See Angelo Piemontese, "Per una biografia di Mirza Malkom Xān," *Annali, Istituto Orientale di Napoli*, new series, XIX (1969) : 375.

38. Sāsānī, *op. cit.* (n. 21, above), p. 129, quoting Mīrzā Ḥusayn Khān's dispatch to the Iranian Ministry of Foreign Affairs, dated 7 Jumādī I 1281/8 October 1864.

39. Confidential report of Sir Arthur Hardinge to Lord Lansdowne, dated 6 September 1901, Public Records Office, London, F. O. 60/637.

We may first refer to a remarkable pseudo-autobiographical statement delivered in London and recorded by the British publicist, Wilfred Scawen Blunt, who was also a non-Muslim believer in an "Islamic renaissance."[40] The statement is highly reminiscent of the fantasies with which Mīrzā Yaᶜqūb impressed Mismer. In both cases we find the same false claims to past political prominence and to a huge and devoted following in Iran, and the same fairly frank admission of his intention to use Islam for promoting westernization.

> Perhaps it would interest you to hear of the story of a religion which was founded some years ago in Persia, and of which I was at one time the head. It will exemplify the manner in which religions are produced, and you will see that the doctrine of Humanity is one at least as congenial to Asia as to Europe. Europe, indeed, is incapable of inventing a real religion, one which shall take possession of the souls of men; as incapable as Asia is of inventing a system of politics. The mind of Asia is speculative, of Europe practical. In Persia we every day produce "new Christs." We have "sons of God" in every village, martyrs for their faith in every town.[41] I have myself seen hundreds of Babis suffer death and torture for their belief in a prophet whose teachings were identical with those of Jesus Christ, and who, like him, was crucified. Christianity is but one of these hundred Asiatic preachings, brought into notice through its adoption by the Greek mind and given a logical form and a material complexion. If it had remained an Asiatic faith, it would long ago have perished, as a hundred moral and mystic teachings have perished before and after it. When I was a young man, I, too, as I told you, founded a religion which at one time numbered 30,000 devotees. I was born an Armenian Christian, but I was brought up among Mohammedans, and my tone of thought is theirs. I was foster-brother to the Shah,[42] and when he came to the throne he made me his Prime Minister. At the age of twenty I was practically despotic in Persia. I saw the abuses of government,

40. Blunt was an early British proponent of Arab separatism and of the establishment of an Arab pseudocaliphate under British tutelage. See his *The Future of Islam* (London, 1882).

41. Compare this passage with these remarkably similar sentences from Mismer's *Soirées de Constantinople* (pp. 68–69): "At all times, Asia has been a laboratory of religions. Every day men are born who believe themselves called upon to regenerate humanity. . . . In Asia there have been thousands of Zoroasters, of Confucius's, of Jesus's, of Muhammads. At the very moment we are writing these lines, throughout Asia Minor, Persia and Central Asia there is not a single group of men without its 'son of God.' "

42. The slight grain of truth which has blossomed into this fantasy is possibly that Malkum lost his mother at an early age, for nowhere do we find mention of her. If she had remained alive, it is highly probable that some clue to her whereabouts after the expulsion from Iran of Mīrzā Yaᶜqūb and Malkum would have been made in the accounts of their exile. When Yaᶜqūb died in Istanbul in 1881, he appears to have been alone. See letter of Iqbāl ud-Daula dated 22 April (1881?), Supplément Persan, 1995, f. 74; and *Majmūᶜa-yi Āthār*, p. xxii.

the decline of material prosperity in the country, and I was bitten with the idea of reform. I went to Europe and studied there the religious, political and social systems of the West. I learned the spirit of the various sects of Christendom, and the organisation of the secret societies and freemasonries, and I conceived a plan which should incorporate the political wisdom of Europe with the religious wisdom of Asia. I knew that it was useless to attempt a remodelling of Persia in European forms, and I was determined to clothe my material reformation in a garb my people would understand, the garb of religion. I therefore on my return called together the chief persons of Teheran, my friends, and spoke to them in private of the need which Islam had of purer doctrine. I appealed to their moral dignity and pride of birth. There are in Persian two words each signifying man—*insan*, from the Arabic, and *adhem* [*sic*], more strictly Persian in derivation.[43] The second signifies man as a genus, a particular kind of animal—the first, man as an intellectual and distinguished being (the *homo* and *vir* of Latin). You all, I said, pride yourselves that you are more than *adhem*, you are also *insan*. And it is to enable you to justify that pretension that I will advise you to do this and that. They all found my reasoning good, and in a short time I had got together 30,000 followers under the name of a Reformation of Islam. I thus introduced what material reforms I could. To my doctrine is due the telegraph, the reorganisation of the administrative departments, and many another attempted improvement since gone to ruin. I had, however, no intention at the outset of founding a religion. The character of saint and prophet was forced on me by my followers. They gave me the title of "Holy Ghost," and the Shah, that of "Reformer of Islam." I wrote a book, a bible of my creed, and enthusiasts maintained that I worked miracles.[44]

Fully to untangle this web of distortion, mendacity, and charlatanry would require a minute commentary on every sentence. The claims to have been foster-brother to Nāṣir ud-Dīn Shāh and later to have been his prime minister with despotic powers are among the most obvious absurdities contained in the passage. As for the claim to have founded a new religion and to have gathered thousands of followers, its only basis in fact is provided by the episode of the pseudomasonic *farāmūshkhāna* (house of oblivion), founded in Tehran by Malkum in 1858. The tenuous relation between the exaggerated claims to sainthood and grandeur made in this passage and the actual career of the *farāmūshkhāna* will receive separate consideration below. It is relevant here to note the highly relativist view of religion which Malkum freely admits. Religion

43. In fact, of course, both words are of Arabic derivation. Malkum evidently changed his mind about the precise implications of *insān* and *ādam*, for it was the latter to which he gave great prominence in the columns of *Qānūn* as signifying a "true human being." The concept was also enshrined in the *Majmaᶜ-i Ādamīyat* (The League of Humanity), the successor to the proscribed *farāmūshkhāna*. See below, pp. 228–235.

44. Blunt, *Secret History of the English Occupation of Egypt*, pp. 82–84.

is something to be "invented," to be "founded." Asia is the continent of religion and endless speculation par excellence, where, it appears, anyone might try his luck with a freshly invented religion, as Malkum did. It would follow then that any successful plan of action for the introduction of reform must take account of this aspect of "Asiatic" character and cloak its intention in the respectability of religion. For Iran, that cloak had to be Islam, and beneath it was hidden "a material reformation." Here, then, is stated that same intention of an "Islamic reform" or "Islamic renaissance" put forward by Mīrzā Yaᶜqūb to Mismer.

Malkum further expounded his views on the subject in the course of a lecture entitled "Persian Civilisation," and delivered in London in 1891. He began his remarks by denying the alleged responsibility of Islam for the backwardness of the Muslims. Islam, he said, was not generally understood in Europe, for the Qurʾān was in reality nothing more than "a sort of revised bible," and did not constitute "the whole of Islamism." "Islam is the accumulated wisdom of the East. It is an ocean where you can find everything which is good to be known, and it offers all kinds of facilities, not in the Khoran [*sic*] alone, but in the traditions,[45] for the progress of the people."[46] This being the case, the greatest obstacle to progress in the Muslim East was not Islam, but rather that the "principles of civilisation" were presented as essentially European, and by association Christian, in origin. The only way to secure their acceptance was to divest them of their European aspect and to present them as the long-forgotten achievement of the Muslims themselves.[47]

> As to the principles which are found in Europe, which constitute the root of your civilisation, we must get hold of them somehow, no doubt; but instead of taking them from London or Paris, instead of saying that this comes from such an ambassador, or that it is advised by such a Government (which will never be accepted), it would be very easy to take the same principle, and to say that it comes from Islam, and that this can be soon proved. We have had some experience in this direction. We found that ideas which were by no means accepted when coming from your agents in Europe, were

45. Malkum does not make it clear whether he is referring to the *ḥadīth*, the Traditions of the Prophet (and, in a Shiᶜi context, of the Imams also), or simply to social and cultural traditions and conventions. If it is the former he intends, he joins the long line of those who have sought to fabricate or manipulate Prophetic tradition for the sake of preconceived aims.

46. Prince Malcom Khan, "Persian Civilisation," *Contemporary Review*, LIX (February 1891): 239.

47. This tactic had been used in Iran for the first time by the Crown Prince ᶜAbbās Mīrzā in justification of his military reforms in the 1820s. See the present writer's *Religion and State in Iran: The Role of the Ulama in the Qajar Period* (Berkeley and Los Angeles, 1969), pp. 75–79.

accepted at once with the greatest delight when it was proved that they were latent in Islam.[48]

It appeared to Malkum that the Shiᶜi school of Islamic law, that dominant in Iran, was particularly suitable for the promotion of westernization with the sanction of religion. Shiᶜi jurisprudence provides for the guidance of the believer in matters of practice by a *mujtahid,* a scholar competent to deliver judgment on the legality of a course of action, in accordance with the Qurʾān, the Traditions of the Prophet, and those of the Twelve Imams of the Shiᶜa. Unless the believer himself has attained the qualifications necessary for the rank of *mujtahid,* it is incumbent upon him to follow such judgment without independent investigation of its accuracy. Since this guidance must, moreover, be dispensed by a living *mujtahid,* there is the possibility for constant reassessment of the duties and obligations of the community under the changing circumstances to which they are subject.[49] From this closely defined legal principle, Malkum saw fit to deduce the following:

> Persian Islamism [*sic*], rejecting the Caliphate and all immovable orthodoxy, is based on the open examination of living scholars, an admirable principle which opens the door to the broadest interpretations and the most novel ideas. The Persians, forming a secular nationality, independent of any religious idea, can adopt without difficulty the most advanced principles of modern society.[50]

It is true that many in the nineteenth-century Islamic world refused to see European civilization as a phenomenon free of debt to them (or their ancestors). Some indeed went so far as to identify the nineteenth-century European values of parliamentary democracy and material progress with the essential teachings of Islam. The justification of these attitudes is not here in question (although we may note in passing that the role of Islamic civilization, and particularly centers in Spain and Sicily, in fecundating, if not originating the European renaissance, is receiving increasing recognition). What should be remarked, in connection with Malkum's attitudes, is that his facile identification of west-

48. Malcom Khan, "Persian Civilisation," p. 243. See too H. R. Haweis, "Talk with a Persian Statesman," *Contemporary Review,* LXX (1896): 76, where Malkum is similarly reported to have said: "The rapidity of communication, the facility of travel, the circulation of thought, have at last suggested to Persian thinkers a system founded on sound principles of modern civilisation; but their programme had to be carefully drawn up under Mussulman formulas. We must admit no Western nomenclature, no 'Christian' civilisation—everything must be Mussulman!"

49. For a recent and concise statement of the principle, see Ḥājj Āqā Ḥusayn Ṭabāṭabāʾī Burūjirdī, *Tauḍiḥ ul-Masāʾil* (Tehran, n.d.), pp. 4–5.

50. "Papers submitted by Malkum Khan to Nasiruddin Shah and communicated to the Marquess of Salisbury (February 13, 1888)," F. O. 60/497.

ernization with the spirit and dictates of Islam was a purely tactical device, based neither on detailed argumentation nor upon personal conviction. One suspects that Malkum, in reality, wished not only to "open the door to the broadest interpretations and most novel ideas," but ultimately to break down and destroy the door altogether. Although, in the last quarter of the century, the identification justified itself as an expedient political device for enlisting a segment of the ulama (the religious scholars) on the side of reform, in the long run it only added to the confusion surrounding the Iranian encounter with the West and its civilization. Selectivity and care in cultural borrowing, already difficult because of the intensity of external pressure, were further discouraged by this facile identification of two civilizations which were, after all, fundamentally different.

We see, then, that Malkum held in common with his father, Mīrzā Yaᶜqūb, certain attitudes to religion in general and to Islam in particular, and a belief in the tactical desirability of the use of Islam for the promotion of westernizing reform. While Malkum was a more prolific exponent of these attitudes and of the plan for "an Islamic renaissance" than his father, it is likely that Mīrzā Yaᶜqūb was the earliest source of his ideas. Mismer, who knew both father and son, wrote that Malkum supplemented and extended the ideas of Mīrzā Yaᶜqūb, while still remaining his disciple.[51] This is probably a fair statement of the matter.

Malkum undoubtedly owed his ability to supplement and extend his father's ideas to his European education. Mīrzā Yaᶜqūb had used his influence with Mīrzā Āqā Khān Nūrī to have Malkum sent to France for his education at government expense, together with a number of other selected students.[52] Upon his arrival in Paris at the age of ten, Mal-

51. Mismer, *Souvenirs du Monde Musulman*, p. 135.

52. *Ibid.*; letter of Amīn us-Sulṭān to Mīrzā Ḥasan Shīrāzī dated Rajab 1309 (February 1892), reproduced in *Asnād-i Siyāsī-yi Daurān-i Qājārīya*, ed. Ibrāhīm Safāʾī (Tehran, 1346 solar/1967), p. 314.

In contradiction with all other sources, it has recently been suggested by the Italian scholar, Angelo Piemontese, that Malkum's education took place entirely in Iran and that his first visit to France was when he accompanied the mission of Mīrzā Farrukh Khān Ghaffārī Amīn ud-Daula to Paris in 1856. His denial of Malkum's Parisian education is based on a report dated March 6, 1873 by one Enrico Andreini, a Tuscan adventurer who was a general in the Iranian army and a regular correspondent of the Italian Foreign Ministry. According to Andreini, Malkum was educated at the French Lazarist College set up at Julfā in 1840 and did not even see Tehran until 1848, let alone Paris. It is indeed possible that Malkum began his education at this college, but there is no reason to assume that he did not pursue his studies in France. Andreini appears not to have known Malkum nor his family personally and acknowledges that his information concerning him is limited to what he could learn from the European legations in Tehran. His account contains a number of demonstrable errors. See Piemontese, *op. cit.* (n. 37, above), pp. 368–369, 373–374.

kum was enrolled in an Armenian school and from that time had presumably little contact with the other Iranian students.[53] After graduating from the Armenian *lycée,* Malkum turned initially to natural sciences and engineering[54] but soon transferred his interest to political science, possibly in accordance with advice once given his father by Amīr Kabīr.[55]

There can be little doubt that Malkum found his studies both congenial and absorbing: they later became the basis for most of his numerous memoranda and treatises calling for political, social, and economic reform in Iran. Indeed, he considered his education in Europe to have uniquely qualified him for the dispensation of infallibly correct advice, rejection of which by the shah and his ministers could result only in the total ruin and downfall of the state. On occasion, Malkum went so far as to refuse any elaboration or argumentation in support of his proposals: they were based on his studies in Europe, that part of the globe where thousands of years of human effort had resulted in a civilization worthy of immediate and unquestioning acceptance. Thus he wrote in his *Uṣūl-i Tamaddun* (Principles of civilisation):

> The path of enrichment of a people is none other than this, that they work hard and produce many goods and trade plenteously. The heads of state of Asia are unaware of these simple and useful principles, whereas in Europe five hundred books have been written concerning each of them. It is quite possible to explain the meaning of these principles, but the place for explaining them is called "a school." That which the wise ones of Europe learn with a thousand troubles in twenty lessons, our men of state expect to absorb in a few minutes by way of passing the time and without any trouble.[56]

In another treatise, *Ḥarf-i Gharīb* (Strange words), Malkum concedes that the men of state in Iran are to be excused for their ignorance of the principles of civilization, for they have not studied them.[57] It is not necessary, however, for them to understand what is to be done to reform

53. Ādamīyat, *op. cit.* (n. 21, above), p. 94; *Majmūᶜa-yi Āthār, op. cit.* (n. 21, above), p. i.

54. While in Paris, Malkum evidently managed to come to the attention of Guizot, prime minister to Louis Philippe until the 1848 Revolution, for Guizot praised the progress of his engineering studies to the Iranian envoy, Mīrzā Muḥammad ᶜAlī Khān. See the extract from Mīrzā Muḥammad ᶜAlī Khān's "Rūznāma-yi Safārat-i Īrān Maʾmūr ba Frānsa," quoted in Ādamīyat, *op. cit.*, p. 42.

55. *Majmūᶜa-yi Āthār*, p. ii; Ḥājj Sayyāḥ, *Khāṭirāt yā Daura-yi Khauf va Vaḥshat*, ed. Ḥamīd Sayyāḥ (Tehran, 1346 solar/1967), pp. 551–552.

56. *Kullīyāt-i Malkum*, ed. Hāshim Rabīᶜzāda (Tabriz, 1325 lunar/1908), p. 6. The same treatise has since been republished under the title "Uṣūl-i Taraqqī" [The principles of progress] with an introduction by Firīdūn Ādamīyat in *Sukhan*, XVI (1345 solar/1966): 70–73, 131–135.

57. *Kullīyāt-i Malkum*, p. 36.

the state, but merely to believe in its necessity, much as Muḥammad ʿAlī Pāshā did in Egypt.[58] In effect then, Malkum was asking that they accept him as an oracular authority vested with the secrets of European civilization. It cannot be denied that many Iranian men of state of the time lacked any serious knowledge of economic and political matters, but one cannot escape the feeling that Malkum rejoices in the deficiency of their knowledge as a guarantee of his own status as would-be reformer.

Not only Malkum's supreme self-confidence as reformer of Iran, but also the unconditional and thoroughgoing nature of the westernization he advocated will by now have become apparent. Although for tactical purposes his proposals were usually presented under an Islamic guise, the guise was often extremely thin. He writes, for example, in his treatise *Naum va Yaqẓa* (Slumber and awakening): "To what aim have the strivings of all the Prophets, from the beginning of creation to our time been directed, if not to the establishment of laws and civilization?"[59] He uses here the barbarous loan word *sīvīlīzāsīyūn* instead of the usual *tamaddun*. Moreover, in the eyes of Malkum it was not possible to make a valid distinction between the material and nonmaterial aspects of European civilization, to take the one and leave the other. It was an entity, evolved over thousands of years and had to be adopted as such without delay. Any attempt to develop something independent and indigenous would be, at best, a waste of time and a duplication of effort.

> If you wish to discover the path of progress by your own intelligence, then we will have to wait for three thousand years. The Europeans have discovered the path of progress and the principles of order [*naẓm*—a word much beloved of Malkum] in the course of three thousand years, just as they have discovered the telegraph, and they have reduced them to one well-defined law. Just as we can introduce the telegraph from Europe and set it up in Tehran without any difficulty,[60] so too we can adopt their principles of ordering [the affairs of state].[61]

In view of the comprehensive westernization advocated by Malkum, it is regrettable that we cannot trace the intellectual and political influences to which he was subject while in Paris. He later claimed to have studied there the various sects of Christianity and the organization of the secret societies in Europe.[62] Although he was only fourteen at the time, the events of 1848 may have left some impression on him. Mira-

58. *Ibid.*, p. 40.
59. *Majmūʿa-yi Āthār*, p. 173.
60. Here Malkum is alluding to one of his own achievements. See below, p. 25.
61. "Kitābcha-yi Ghaybī yā Daftar-i Tanẓīmāt" [A pamphlet inspired from the unseen world or the book of reforms] in *Majmūʿa-yi Āthār*, p. 13.
62. Blunt, *op. cit.* (n. 34, above), p. 83.

beau was presumably the special object of his attention at some point, for he translated extracts from his writings into Persian.[63] It should, however, be remembered that Malkum was only eighteen when he completed his studies in France and returned to Iran, and however gifted and precocious a student he may have been, it is probable that the material prosperity and relative political stability he witnessed in France impressed him more profoundly than his readings in political science. To these impressions, and to the harsh contrast provided by the condition of Iran, may be attributed in the final analysis his conviction of the absolute superiority of European civilization and of the imperative need to submit to its model.

This emphatically positive attitude to the West made of Malkum the first coherent advocate of westernization in Iran. So complete, indeed, was his acceptance of the primacy of European civilization and of the universal applicability of its political and social systems, that he may himself be regarded equally as a westerner and an Iranian. Out of the sixty-four years of his life, less than a decade was spent in Iran, and that not continuously. Although he remained well informed of Iranian affairs while in Europe, his involvement in them was always remote and often less than serious. The advice he bestows is essentially that of an outsider, however interested and sympathetic, and his relations with the government are determined more by personal interests than by those of reform. It is particularly noticeable that Malkum subscribes to the nineteenth-century concept of "Asia" as the antithesis of the materially progressive and active West, the inexhaustible breeding ground of religions and speculative philosophies, and of the "Asiatic," an irrational individual firmly caught in a mesh of lifeless and stultifying traditions. Despite his claim that the tone of his thought was that of the Muslims, Malkum's fundamental attitude was one of disengagement from this degenerate "Asia" of which Iran was a part; and, with more pretense than reality, he sought its regeneration from a distance. The combination of his outlook, his Iranian birth, and his involvement in Iranian affairs made of him the foremost Armenian intermediary between the West and Iran in the nineteenth century.

The inspiration for this role Malkum received in part from his father and in larger part from his European education and impressions. Its fulfillment, however, reflected at least as strongly an acute awareness of personal and pecuniary interests, particularly when the regeneration

63. See "Ḥurriyat" [Liberty], translated from Mirabeau (*Majmūᶜa-yi Āthār*, p. 181). There has also been attributed to Malkum the translation of a piece on liberty by John Stuart Mill ("Manāfiᶜ-i Āzādī," *Majmūᶜa-yi Āthār*, pp. 177–178) which in reality is the work of Malkum's friend, Mīrzā Fatḥ ᶜAlī Ākhūndzāda (See M.-F. Akhundov, *Äsärläri* [Baku, 1961], III: 259–261).

of Iran was to involve the granting of commercial concessions. His role was vitiated too by a basic lack of seriousness and an ineradicable penchant to pretense and charlatanry. The combination of these variegated elements made for a peculiar career, which will now be examined in documented detail.

CHAPTER 2

IN 1268/1851–1852, Mīrzā Malkum Khān returned from Paris to Iran,[1] and although only eighteen years old, embarked with characteristic ambitiousness on his program of remaking Iran in the image of the West. The setting for the first stage of his career was the Dār ul-Funūn, The House of Arts. The Dār ul-Funūn, a newly founded college in Tehran, was one of the measures of reform instigated by Amīr Kabīr during his brief tenure of office. Military and administrative reforms were to be supplemented by the training of a new class, acquainted with the rudiments of European science and capable of pursuing the regeneration of the state. When Amīr Kabīr recommended to Mīrzā Yaʿqūb that he encourage Malkum to study political science, it may well have been with the intention of employing him as instructor at the projected institution on his return.[2]

Shortly before his downfall, Amīr Kabīr recruited a number of foreign instructors, chiefly Austrians, to come and teach at the Dār ul-Funūn. On their arrival in Tehran—at approximately the same time as Malkum's return from France—they learned that Amīr Kabīr had fallen from power and had been put to death, so that the execution of his plans for a college appeared doubtful. The new prime minister, Mīrzā Āqā Khān Nūrī, attempted to force the shah do his pleasure by cancelling the inauguration of the Dār ul-Funūn and sending the Austrians back to Europe. Certain contractual obligations, however, had been undertaken with them, and Nāṣir ud-Dīn Shāh, despite his treat-

1. Muḥīṭ Ṭabāṭabāʾī, introduction to *Majmūʿa-yi Āthār-i Mīrzā Malkum Khān* (Tehran, 1327 solar/1948), p. ii [hereafter *Majmūʿa-yi Āthār*]; Khān Malik Sāsānī, *Siyāsatgarān-i Daura-yi Qājār* (Tehran, 1337 solar/1958), I: 128. Firīdūn Ādamīyat, in *Fikr-i Āzādī* (Tehran, 1340 solar/1961), p. 94, gives the date of 1267/1850–1851.

2. *Majmūʿa-yi Āthār*, p. ii.

ment of Amīr Kabīr, was still not totally uninterested in reform. Thus it was that the Dār ul-Funūn was inaugurated, and the Austrians were put to work.[3]

Because they had no knowledge of Persian and their students were initially unacquainted with any European language, it was necessary to employ a number of interpreters for the classroom. These were for the most part Armenians with a command of Russian or French and some knowledge of European science, and Malkum Khān took his place among them.[4] Another of the interpreters was Naẓar Āqā, an Assyrian from the Urumiya region and a protégé of the late Amīr Kabīr, who subsequently occupied a number of diplomatic posts in Europe and was a loyal friend to Malkum for many years.[5]

It is not known to which European instructor Malkum was assigned, or how efficiently and conscientiously he fulfilled his task. It is probable, with his eight years of education in France and the mastery of simple and fluent Persian he soon after demonstrated, that he was well qualified for the post of interpreter. In general, however, the intervention of translator between teacher and student was a serious handicap to the progress of the class, as might indeed be expected.[6] It may be in part for this reason that Malkum himself was entrusted with the teaching of classes in geography and natural science.[7] After all, he had briefly studied engineering and natural science before turning to political science. In any event, the knowledge of these subjects and of geography that he had acquired in the course of his secondary schooling was doubtless adequate for the purposes of the Dār ul-Funūn.

In the course of his teaching, he conducted a number of simple experiments in physics and chemistry, probably for the first time in Iran.[8] One may imagine that these experiments aroused particular interest among the students of the Dār ul-Funūn and that Malkum's purpose in conducting them was not exclusively educational. A few years later, many of the students and graduates of the Dār ul-Funūn joined his newly established *farāmūshkhāna*; it may be assumed then that he

3. J. E. Polak, *Persien, das Land und seine Bewohner* (Leipzig, 1865), I: 301–302.

4. ᶜAbbās Iqbāl, *Mīrzā Taqī Khān Amīr Kabīr* (Tehran, 1340 solar/1961), p. 162.

5. *Ibid.* On his relations with Amīr Kabīr, see Ḥusayn Saᶜādat-Nūrī, "Naẓar Āqā va Amīr Kabīr," *Rāhnamā-yi Kitāb*, VI (1343 solar/1964): 445–450. Naẓar Āqā's friendship with Malkum did not prevent him from cursing him in official correspondence during the years of *Qānūn*. See Humā Nāṭiq, "Naẓar Āqā va Nāmahāʾī az Ū," *Rāhnamā-yi Kitāb*, XII (1348 solar/1969): 672; XIII (1349 solar/1970): 62.

6. Polak, *op. cit.*, I: 303–304.

7. Malkum began by teaching mathematics when Zati, one of the Austrian teachers, suddenly died. See Iqbāl Yaghmāʾī, "Madrasa-yi Dār ul-Funūn," *Yaghmā*, XXIII (1348 solar/1969): 147.

8. *Majmūᶜa-yi Āthār*, p. ii.

was already seeking means to arouse attention and attract a following.[9] It would be interesting to know how complete and detailed were the explanations accompanying the experiments. Malkum for many years retained a reputation for magic and legerdemain,[10] and probably this reputation was not unwelcome to him. He had a constant tendency to depict himself as more powerful and influential than he in fact was, a tendency already exemplified in the pseudo-autobiographical statement quoted above, and which found its fullest expression in the columns of *Qānūn*. He may well have coveted the prestige bestowed upon him by a rumored acquaintance with magic in a country still notable for its interest in alchemy.

It may even have been by means of these experiments that Malkum first brought himself to the notice of Nāṣir ud-Dīn Shāh.[11] The shah's educational background was not such as to permit him any understanding of scientific matters, and his reaction to the wonders of physics and chemistry may have been one of simple amazement. It is in any event certain that Malkum induced in Nāṣir ud-Dīn Shāh a deep belief in his consummate skill, learning and intelligence, a belief that even his anger at Malkum in later years was not able to erase. Once, when wishing to praise extravagantly the intelligence of a certain eunuch at his court, the shah remarked: "This man is even more clever than Malkum Khān," much to the disgust of one of those present.[12] In seeking to impress Nāṣir ud-Dīn Shāh with his talents, Malkum doubtless wished in part simply to gratify his own arrogance, but he may have hoped too to establish a dominance over the monarch which would have permitted him to dictate a program of reform. The previous monarch, Muḥammad Shāh, after all, had abandoned all affairs of state to the control of a dervish to whom he attributed miraculous powers, the celebrated Ḥājjī Mīrzā Āqāsī,[13] and Malkum may have regarded this case as a useful precedent.[14] There were, however, too many pressures on Nāṣir ud-

9. In *ibid.* Ṭabāṭabāʾī, although generally sympathetic to Malkum, writes: "Later when he founded the *farāmūshkhāna*, he evidently made use of his scientific talents to attract the attention of novices."

10. Sir Percy Sykes, in his *History of Persia*, 3rd ed. (London, 1963), II: 397, writes: "He [Malkum] first appeared at Teheran as a conjurer, whose feats of legerdemain excited wonder among the simple Persians."

11. *Majmūʿa-yi Āthār*, p. ii; Nāẓim ul-Islām Kirmānī, *Tārīkh-i Bīdārī-yi Irāniān* (Tehran, n.d.), p. 120.

12. Mīrzā Ḥasan Khān Iʿtimād us-Salṭana, *Rūznāma-yi Khāṭirāt*, ed. Īraj Afshār (Tehran, 1345 solar/1966), p. 180.

13. See Mīrzā Muḥammad Taqī Sipihr Lisān ul-Mulk, *Nāsikh ut-Tavārīkh* (Tehran, n.d.), pp. 333–336.

14. Malkum's claim in his pseudo-autobiographical declaration to have been

Dīn Shāh, both internal and external, for him to remain long under the undisputed influence of Malkum. In any event, Malkum began to spend increasingly long periods outside of Iran, and conjuring had to give way to memoranda and proposals as a means of influencing the shah.

An initial result of Malkum's acquaintance with Nāṣir ud-Dīn Shāh was an additional appointment as personal interpreter to the monarch (*mutarjim-i humāyūn*).[15] The post may have been purely nominal or have involved the translation for the monarch of instructive and diverting items from the European press, a task later fulfilled by the minister of the press, Mīrzā Ḥasan Khān Iᶜtimād us-Salṭana.[16] Malkum's association with the monarch, together with his father's continuing friendship with Mīrzā Āqā Khān Nūrī, enabled Malkum, five years after his return to Iran, to return to Europe for the first phase of his diplomatic career.

Late in 1856, Iran had made a final attempt to reassert its sovereignty over Herat, and an Iranian army under the command of the shah's uncle, Ḥusām us-Salṭana, had succeeded in conquering the city.[17] The conquest, however, was pointless, for British policy still deemed it necessary, despite all treaty obligations, to prevent Herat from coming under the control of a state which was all too vulnerable to a Russian advance in the direction of India.

The Iranian conquest of Herat came at a time when relations with Britain were already strained by the conduct of the ambassador, Charles Augustus Murray, who constantly threatened abrupt departure unless his demands were met.[18] Among his complaints was Mīrzā Āqā Khān Nūrī's use of Malkum Khān as interpreter during their confrontations. Murray charged that the content of their discussions would be immediately conveyed to the Russian representative by Malkum's father, whom he knew was employed at the Russian embassy.[19] In order to satisfy Murray at least on this point, Mīrzā Āqā Khān Nūrī appointed

---

"despotic in Persia" at the age of twenty (W. S. Blunt, *Secret History of the English Occupation of Egypt* [London 1903], p. 83), may reflect what he would have liked to achieve.

15. *Majmūᶜa-yi Āthār*, p. iii.

16. See his *Rūznāma-yi Khāṭirāt, passim.*

17. Riḍā Qulī Khān Hidāyat, *Rauḍat uṣ-Ṣafā-yi Nāṣirī* (Tehran, n.d.), X: 696–701.

18. The most visible cause of friction between the Iranian government and the British embassy was the wife of a certain Mīrzā Hāshim, who was suspected of amatory relations with the British chargé d'affaires, Thompson, and had taken up residence in the British embassy. See Hidāyat, *op. cit.*, X: 685; and Sāsānī, *op. cit.* (n. 1, above), I: 32–35.

19. *Majmūᶜa-yi Āthār*, p. iii.

Malkum to the post of special interpreter at the Iranian embassy in Istanbul.[20]

Before Malkum was able to leave Tehran to assume his post, a final rupture in relations between Britain and Iran took place. One month after the conquest of Herat, British ships bombarded Bushire, and soon after troops from India were landed at Muḥammara (present-day Khurramshahr) at the head of the Persian Gulf. Despite an officially inspired proclamation of *jihād* in the mosques of the capital, and an attempt to arouse popular enthusiasm for resistance to the British,[21] Iranian defeat was swift and complete. Nāṣir ud-Dīn Shāh saw himself obliged to retreat from Herat and finally to foreswear all ambitions in Afghanistan.[22]

The conclusion of a settlement with Britain was entrusted to Mīrzā Farrukh Khān Ghaffārī Amīn ud-Daula, who was dispatched to Paris to negotiate under the auspices of Napoleon III. Instead of being sent to the post in Istanbul, Malkum was attached to Mīrzā Farrukh Khān's mission, doubtless because of his familiarity with the French capital and its language.[23] This was Malkum's first diplomatic experience.

The mission reached Istanbul in October 1856, and Paris three months later. The Iranian and British negotiators soon came to terms, for both sides were eager to settle the matter as quickly as possible: Mīrzā Farrukh Khān because Nāṣir ud-Dīn Shāh had instructed him to accept whatever terms the British put forward, and the British because rebellion had just broken out in India. Malkum appears to have had no part in the political work of the mission, although he was of great use in making practical arrangements. After conclusion of the treaty on 3 March 1857, the Iranian mission paid a brief visit to London,[24] giving Malkum his first glimpse of the country where he was to spend so many years, first as ambassador and then as political exile.

For Malkum, the most important result of his return visit to Paris was without doubt his initiation, together with other members of the Iranian mission, into a masonic lodge, the Sincère Amitié. On 10 December 1857, a mass ambassadorial initiation took place at the headquarters of the Grand Orient, attended by Mīrzā Farrukh Khān, Malkum Khān, Narīmān Khān (later Iranian ambassador in Vienna), Muḥammad ᶜAlī Āqā, Mīrzā Riḍā Khān (later aide-de-camp to Nāṣir

20. *Ibid.*; Muḥammad Ḥasan Khān Iᶜtimād us-Salṭana, *Tārīkh-i Muntaẓam-i Nāṣirī* (Tehran, 1300 lunar/1883), p. 137; Sāsānī, *op. cit.* (n. 1, above), I: 127.

21. Comte Arthur de Gobineau, *Dépêches Diplomatiques*, ed. A. D. Hytier (Geneva, 1959), pp. 46–47, 53.

22. See Sir Henry Rawlinson, *England and Russia in the East* (London, 1875), pp. 93–95.

23. *Majmūᶜa-yi Āthār*, p. iii; Sāsānī, *op. cit.* (n. 1, above), I: 128.

24. Hidāyat, *op. cit.*, X: 767–772; Ḥusayn ibn ᶜAbdullāh Sarābī, *Makhzan ul-Vaqāyiᶜ* (Tehran, 1344 solar/1965), pp. 325–373.

ud-Dīn Shāh), and ᶜAlī Naqī.[25] In the pseudo-autobiographical statement quoted in Chaper One, it was seen that Malkum claimed to have learned while studying in Europe "the organisation of the secret societies and freemasonries."[26] The claim may well be true and suggests that it was Malkum's interest in masonry which led to the initiation of the Iranian embassy. It may also suggest that he had previously established some kind of contact with French masonic authorities. Moreover, it is his name, more than any other, that is associated with the propagation of freemasonry in Iran, and he was the first to establish a lodge in Tehran, although one not affiliated with or recognized by any of the European obediences. One should remember, however, that Iranian travelers to Europe had already made the acquaintance of freemasonry: fifty years earlier, ᶜAskar Khān Afshār, another Iranian envoy, had been initiated into a Paris lodge.[27] Other prominent Iranians had entered both French and British lodges, and something of the curious interest they showed in the masonic institution was current in Iran also.[28] In both London and Paris, the initiations were sponsored by governments eager to forge a powerful but invisible link with those who, they thought, might come to wield influence in their homeland. Malkum's initiation, then, should be placed in the context of general eagerness among Iranians to enter masonic lodges and a corresponding willingness, in both Paris and London, to have them initiated. It remains nonetheless true that Malkum was the first Iranian to take his interest in masonry beyond individual curiosity and to consider the possibilities of the masonic lodge as a basis for political action and agitation for reform.

His return to Iran in 1858 saw him in a new and favorable position to test these possibilities. His useful performance as interpreter and advisor to Mīrzā Farrukh Khān's mission was duly reported to the shah, who expressed his gratification.[29] Nāṣir ud-Dīn's favorable view of Malkum's talents was further increased when in the course of the year he established the first functioning telegraph line in Iran, from the Dār ul-Funūn to the royal palace.[30] Soon after, one of the students at the

25. Mīrzā Farrukh Khān's certificate of initiation is reproduced in Sarābī, *op. cit.*, plate 21. See too Īraj Afshār, "Asnād Marbūṭ ba Farrukh Khān," *Yaghmā*, XVIII (1344 solar/1965): 589. The occasion was recalled two years later in the *Bulletin du Grand Orient de France: Suprême Conseil pour la France et les Possessions Francaises*, XV (5860 = 1860): 396–397.

26. Blunt, *op. cit.* (n. 14, above), p. 83.

27. Hamid Algar, "An Introduction to the History of Freemasonry in Iran," *Middle Eastern Studies*, VI (1970): 276–277.

28. References cited *ibid.*, pp. 278–279.

29. *Majmūᶜa-yi Āthār*, p. iv.

30. Īraj Afshār, "Tiligrāf dar Īrān," *Savād va Bayāḍ* (Tehran, 1344 solar/1965), p. 228.

college, ᶜAlī Qulī Khān, son of the celebrated chronicler, anthologist and poet, Riḍā Qulī Khān Hidāyat, established a line connecting the capital with Tabriz and Sulṭānīyya, where the monarch frequently spent the summer.[31] These technical achievements, combined with Malkum's earlier display of experimental talent, caused a laudatory notice to be inserted in number forty-six of the official gazette, *Sharaf*: "He [Malkum] has brought to Iran from Europe most of the crafts and inventions of the modern age, and it is he who has caused the telegraph to become current in this country."[32]

While Malkum was thus consolidating his position in the eyes of the shah as a capable and learned man, the direction taken by the internal affairs of Iran was making Nāṣir ud-Dīn Shāh unusually attentive to proposals of reform. The Anglo-Iranian War and its humiliating outcome had caused Mīrzā Āqā Khān Nūrī to fall gradually from favor and finally to be dismissed. Nāṣir ud-Dīn Shāh, having in mind not only the inefficiency of Mīrzā Āqā Khān Nūrī, but also, no doubt, the overbearing airs of his predecessor, Amīr Kabīr, decided against the appointment of another *ṣadr-i aᶜẓam* to whom all the affairs of state would be entrusted. Instead, he attempted to divide responsibilities among a number of ministers. Steps were taken in this direction even before the final dismissal of Mīrzā Āqā Khān Nūrī: military and foreign affairs were withdrawn from his control and placed under men directly responsible to the shah.[33] After his dismissal, six ministries were formally instituted to deal respectively with internal affairs, foreign affairs, the army, financial affairs, justice, and the administration of government grants and religious endowments (*auqāf*).[34] The activities of the six ministers were to be loosely coordinated by Mīrzā Jaᶜfar Khān Mushīr ud-Daula, who had been one of the first Iranian students sent to study in England in 1815. They did not, however, constitute a cabinet in the strict sense of the term, for they met together only when the shah demanded that they discuss a particular problem and submit to him their proposals for its solution.[35]

It was approximately at this time, when the apparatus of state appeared to be on the point of reorganization, that Malkum Khān composed and submitted to the shah the first of his celebrated treatises calling for political and administrative reform. Its contents are worth considering at some length, not only because it is the earliest of Mal-

31. ᶜAbdullāh Mustaufī, *Sharḥ-i Zindagānī-yi Man ya Tārīkh-i Ijtimāᶜī va Idārī-yi Daura-yi Qājārīyya* (Tehran, 1341 solar/1962), I: 86; Mīrzā Muḥammad Ḥasan Khān Iᶜtimād us-Salṭana, *al-Maʾāthir va-l-Āthār* (Tehran, 1306 lunar/1889), p. 93.

32. Quoted in Afshār, *op. cit.*, p. 229.

33. Mustaufī, *op. cit.*, I: 87.

34. *Ibid.*, I: 88.

35. *Ibid.*

kum's treatises, but also because most of its chief points are repeated in his later writings with varying degrees of emphasis and adumbration.

The treatise came to be known as the *Kitābcha-yi Ghaybī* (A booklet inspired from the unseen world), and alternatively as *Daftar-i Tanẓīmāt* (The book of reforms).[36] Use of the word *tanẓīmat* in the title of Malkum's treatise is significant as probably the first occurrence of the word in Persian, with the meaning of governmental reform and reorganization.[37] It was a loan word from Ottoman Turkish, and throughout the nineteenth century similar borrowings continued to take place, to such an extent that virtually the whole political vocabulary of Persian in the period may be said to have been derived from Ottoman Turkish.[38] This, of course, is merely the most obvious indication of how, to a considerable extent, events in Iran came to reflect and parallel developments in the Ottoman Empire. Frequently, the influence of the Ottoman model was directly transmitted to Iran, and Malkum, after his Istanbul exile, served as one of its channels of penetration.

Malkum opened the treatise with a typical display of charlatanry. Instead of submitting his proposals directly to the shah, he chose to entrust them to Mīrzā Jaᶜfar Khān Mushīr ud-Daula, who was to bring them to the attention of the shah at a suitable moment. He nonetheless made a show of wishing to remain anonymous, promising to reveal his identity only if Mushīr ud-Daula should consider the contents of the treatise objectionable and its author deserving of punishment.[39] It can hardly have been possible, however, for Malkum to present the treatise to Mushīr ud-Daula for submission to the shah without revealing his identity: possibly the device was intended to impress Nāṣir ud-Dīn Shāh with the disinterested nature of his proposals.

Before proceeding to set them forth, Malkum is astute enough to praise fulsomely Nāṣir ud-Dīn Shāh for his concerned interest in the affairs of the country and his inclination to enact political and administrative reform. Indeed, "without doubt, Iran has never had a better monarch than it does today." In his understanding of matters of state and his awareness of foreign affairs, he surpasses all his ministers, and cannot be considered an obstacle to reform, unlike many European monarchs.[40]

36. *Majmūᶜa-yi Āthār*, pp. 2–52.

37. On the justice of translating the term *tanẓīmāt* as "reforms," see Roderic H. Davison, *Reform in the Ottoman Empire 1856–1876* (Princeton, 1963), p. 5, n. 5.

38. The earliest instance is ᶜAbbās Mīrzā's use of the term *Niẓām-i Jadīd* to designate his military reforms in the 1820s, in imitation of Sultan Selim III (Hamid Algar, *Religion and State in Iran, 1785–1906: the Role of the Ulama in the Qajar Period* [Berkeley and Los Angeles, 1969], pp. 76–78). See also E. G. Browne, *The Press and Poetry of Modern Persia* (Cambridge, 1914), pp. 18–19.

39. *Majmūᶜa-yi Āthār*, p. 3.

40. *Ibid.*, p. 4.

Despite this, he continues, Iran is in a state of weakness and decay. The treasury is empty, natural resources remain unexploited, and two powerful neighbors threaten the very survival of Iran as an independent country: "From Calcutta and St. Petersburg, two awesome tidal waves are rolling towards Iran." Only a few years ago, five thousand Indian soldiers under British command were able to capture all the Persian Gulf ports.[41] In the face of this situation, it is not enough to rely upon the antiquity of Iranian civilization for its continued ability to survive, nor even upon the innate intelligence of the ministers of state. Knowledge and insight into the nature of the problems facing Iran are necessary, for, as far as mere intelligence is concerned, the ministers of Iran may consider themselves equal to their counterparts in Europe.

The first lesson the ministers need to learn is that the progress of the Europeans is primarily due, not to their industries and inventions, but to the "customs of their civilization" (*āʾīn-ī tamaddun*). "For people who have never left Iran, it is impossible to imagine the kind of progress achieved by the Europeans."[42] Europe has advanced by virtue of possessing two kinds of factories: one for producing goods, the other for producing men, where "they take in ignorant children and turn out engineers and accomplished thinkers." It is only the first kind of factory of which the Iranians are more or less aware. Malkum also compares the law courts and stock exchanges of Europe to factories which produce justice and money respectively.[43]

The activities of all these "factories" are coordinated by a wondrous body of subtle functioning known as the government (this appears to be what Malkum intends by the term *dastgāh-i dīvān*). The entire prosperity of Europe depends on this body, and if for some reason it were suddenly to disappear, the entire continent would overnight come to resemble Baluchistan. In fact, it represents "the essence of all achievements of the human intellect."[44] While some progress has been made in the adoption of the material aspects of Western civilization, the principles of European government remain entirely unknown in Iran, and the state goes about its business just as it did three thousand years ago. Unless Iran adopts the European governmental system, just as unquestioningly as it did the telegraph, it will take another three thousand years to evolve a workable basis for the state.[45]

Here, Malkum allows himself to be interrupted by an imaginary listener who objects that the adoption of European laws would be tantamount to the loss of religion and would, in any event, be prevented by the opposition of the ulama. To this Malkum replies that if there is

41. *Ibid.*, pp. 6–7.
42. *Ibid.*, p. 10.
43. *Ibid.*, pp. 10–11.
44. *Ibid.*, pp. 11–12.
45. *Ibid.*, pp. 12–13.

anyone in Iran who understands the principles of European government, he is to be found precisely among the ulama.[46] It is doubtful that Malkum had any member of the religious classes in mind when he made this statement, for not until many years later did any of the ulama gain direct or even indirect acquaintance with Europe. Probably he was concerned here already with presenting his program of westernization as religiously innocuous and with gaining the ulama's support for it, in part by pretending he already had it.

After these preliminaries, Malkum proceeds to set forth some basic notions concerning government. He first divides governments into monarchical and republican, and then states the function of both forms to be the laying down and execution of law.[47] For "law," Malkum uses the word *qānūn*, which, although already existing in Persian with the sense of "regulation, method, principle,"[48] did not answer fully the European concept of law. He therefore deems it advisable to define the sense of the word as follows: "any ordinance issued by the government, tending to the general welfare of the community and equally incumbent upon all its members, is called law."[49] Malkum has been justly credited with the introduction into Persian of the term *qānūn* used in this sense[50] (probably as a loan word from Ottoman Turkish).[51] He failed, however, to clarify the essentially secular nature of the concept of *qānūn* and to discuss seriously the question of its compatibility with the *sharīᶜa*, the divinely sanctioned law based on the immutable foundation of the Qurʾān and the Traditions of the Prophet and the Imams. He preferred instead to present a facile and tactical identification of the two systems of law: that inspired by European example and that derived from the eternal norms of revelation. The method whereby this identification was established and its consequences will be discussed in greater detail in conjunction with Malkum's celebrated journal, which bore the title of *Qānūn*.

Malkum then explains that these two functions—establishment and execution of law—are united in the hands of the sovereign in an absolute monarchy, or in those of a minister when he chooses to delegate his powers. In reality, a separation of the legislative from the executive branch would tend to increase the power of the ruler. Failure so to

46. *Ibid.*, pp. 13–14.

47. *Ibid.*, pp. 14–15.

48. See Muḥammad Ḥusayn ibn Khalaf Tabrīzī, *Burhān-i Qāṭiᶜ*, ed. Muḥammad Muᶜīn (Tehran, 1332–1333 solar/1953–1954), III: 1516.

49. *Majmūᶜa-yi Āthār*, p. 14.

50. Browne, *op. cit.* (n. 38, above), p. 18.

51. The word had long been used in Ottoman Turkish to designate customary law, particularly administrative, financial, and sometimes penal ordinances. See Ömer Lûtfi Barkan, article "Kânûn-Nâme," *İslâm Ansiklopedisi*, VI: 185–196.

separate them has, in Asian states, allowed the minister to gain ascendancy over the king whom he is supposed to serve.[52] It moreover prevents the officials of state from operating within any precisely defined sphere of responsibility, and thus leads to inefficiency and confusion. Although a beginning in the right direction has been made in Iran after the dismissal of Mīrzā Āqā Khān Nūrī, the fundamental necessity of separating the legislative from the executive has still not been grasped, and therefore a further series of reform measures is needed. A minister cannot be expected, on his own initiative, to limit the sphere of his responsibility by enacting relevant legislation, and without such limitation the establishment of ministries is pointless.[53]

In order to present his proposals for an amelioration of the situation, Malkum has recourse to the device of a dream. He imagines himself called upon to submit a comprehensive legislative program to a reform council (*majlis-i tanẓīm*) convened by the shah.[54] Although elsewhere Malkum uses the device of a fictitious dream to good effect,[55] it has little point in the present treatise, other than, possibly, to relieve the tedium of his expository style.

Malkum presents twenty-three separate laws, each containing several articles. The laws are not numbered consecutively, and run from one to seventy-four with many omissions. It may be that Malkum intended to supplement his draft with further provisions, but even as it stood it contained all the basic elements of a constitution. The first law defined the system of government in Iran as absolute monarchy, with law as the basis and method of its operation. The monarch was to exercise his legislative and executive prerogatives through two separate bodies, the reform council (*majlis-i tanẓīmāt*) and the council of ministers (*majlis-i vuzarā*), over both of which he was to preside.[56] The second law laid down certain conditions for legislation, first among them being that "all law must be the expression of the royal will and tend to the welfare of all the people," conditions evidently assumed by Malkum to be permanently and necessarily compatible.[57]

In the third law, the "rights of the people" are listed, and among its articles we may note the equality of all persons before the law and freedom of belief and opinion (Malkum uses the word *ʿaqāʾid*, which might denote either religious belief or any category of opinion).[58]

52. *Majmūʿa-yi Āthār*, pp. 16–17. Malkum doubtless intended here to remind Nāṣir ud-Dīn Shāh of Amīr Kabīr, of whom the monarch once remarked several years after his death: "he was a harsh man" (Polak, *op. cit.* (n. 3, above), II: 302).

53. *Majmūʿa-yi Āthār*, p. 19.

54. *Ibid.*, pp. 22–23.

55. As in *Naum va Yaqẓa* [Slumber and awakening]. See p. 245 below.

56. *Majmūʿa-yi Āthār*, pp. 24–25.

57. *Ibid.*, p. 25.

58. *Ibid.*, p. 26.

The fourth law sets out in some detail rules for the composition and functioning of the proposed reform council, the legislative organ. Apart from the shah, it should contain three princes, fifteen advisors (*mushīr*) and eight ministers. The right to appoint and dismiss its members is to be vested in the shah, and their decisions must be unanimous to become law. It is remarkable that Malkum should have included among the articles of this law one to the effect that members of the council should watch over the execution of the law (article seven), for this contradicts his basic assertion—the necessity of separation of the legislative from the executive. The principle is further violated by the inclusion in the reform council of the eight ministers who are to form the executive organ, the *majlis-i vuzarā*.[59]

The functioning of this body is the subject of laws five and six. Malkum lists eight ministries as necessary: justice, internal affairs, foreign affairs, war, finance, science (*ᶜulūm*), commerce and development, and court affairs. The first five of these had already been brought into being by Nāṣir ud-Dīn Shāh. Malkum omitted the other existing ministry, that of pensions and *auqāf*, presumably because its function was being fulfilled by the ministry of finance.[60] Ministries of science, commerce and development, and court affairs were proposed in Iran for the first time by Malkum.[61]

Equally original was his "Law for the Revival of the Iranian State." It opened by prescribing death as the penalty for treachery, and then proceeded to define treachery to include the acceptance of bribes, the embezzlement of government funds, and circumvention of the law by a government official.[62] In later years when involved in the concession business, Malkum must have been glad not to be subject to the severity of such a law.

His eleventh proposal deals with the codification of the law. Only here is there a slight indication of how he intended existing laws to be reconciled with his *qānūn* of secular basis. He gives essentially the same simple answer to the question that was to be repeated through the years until the Constitutional Revolution—identification without analysis. "The reform council shall collect, within the period of one year, all *sharᶜ* ordinances and those emanating from the state [i.e., customary or *ᶜurf* law] and by subjecting them to the conditions of legality (*qānūnīyat*) incorporate them in the laws of the state."[63]

Among Malkum's remaining proposals, we may note one establishing a standing army of a million troops, together with a levied army (*sipāh-i ᶜāzim*) with a seven-year term of service.[64] Another law pro-

59. *Ibid.*, p. 27.
60. See Mustaufī, *op. cit.* (n. 31, above), I: 88–89.
61. *Majmūᶜa-yi Āthār*, pp. 28–29.
62. *Ibid.*, pp. 29–30.
63. *Ibid.*, p. 30.
64. *Ibid.*, pp. 38–39.

vides for the establishment of separate bodies to assess and collect taxes, and the payment of regular salaries to the members of both out of government funds. This mode of payment is intended to obviate the need of deducting one's salary from the taxes collected on a basis of private initiative.[65]

Law forty-one in the treatise establishes Malkum's place as the earliest advocate of comprehensive educational change in Iran. Three types of school were to be instituted throughout the country: *tarbiya, faḍlīya,* and *ʿāliya.* In the first, the pupils were to learn how to read and write in Persian, and the elements of arithmetic, history, geometry, and the natural sciences. The *faḍlīya* schools were to give instruction in rhetoric, philosophy, mathematics, the natural sciences, history, painting and drawing, and foreign languages. The highest level of education was to involve specialized study of letters, law, medicine, or the fine arts, and to include too a number of colleges devoted to other fields.[66] Although Malkum has here reflected the European division of education into primary, secondary, and advanced, he cannot have hoped to exert any practical influence on the evolution of education in Iran. His proposal is nonetheless remarkable for completely ignoring traditional norms of education, and above all for making no provision for those studies that formed the basis of a traditional Islamic education, whether in Iran or elsewhere: the Qurʾān and the Arabic language.[67]

Just as this proposal anticipated, to a certain extent, later developments in Iran without having any immediate effect, so too was his "Law for the Abolition of Poverty in Iran" prophetic of the days when foreign contractors would descend upon Iran. Its first article demanded emphatically that within ten days of its promulgation an official should be dispatched to France to recruit six highway engineers. They should arrive in Iran within one month of their recruitment and be put to work building roads the day after their arrival. The results of their labors within a year should enable goods to be transported from one end of Iran to the other within twenty days.[68]

Finally, Malkum proposed the establishment of a national bank with an initial capital of one million *tūmāns* to be obtained by selling a portion of the royal lands (*khāliṣa*).[69]

When all these proposals have been enumerated, the tempo of the dream suddenly increases, and Malkum recounts that within six months the reform council enacted no fewer than four thousand laws. The

65. *Ibid.*, p. 42.

66. *Ibid.*, pp. 45–47.

67. In article five of this law, Malkum provides for the establishment of a college of theology. This only emphasizes the thoroughness of the break with tradition he was advocating.

68. *Majmūʿa-yi Āthār*, p. 48.

69. *Ibid.*, p. 50.

dream closes with a minister punished because of an attempt to circumvent the new laws, the old order of anarchy brought to an end, and "the whole land of Iran transformed into a rose garden, as if by magic." Such was the security reigning throughout the realm that there were constantly fifty thousand foreigners traveling back and forth in the utmost safety, and so plentiful was government revenue that "those abject and filthy graveyards they used to call 'towns' had been turned into noble cities that could vie with Paradise itself."[70] And all this had come about from the miraculous effects of a book which was written neither in Arabic nor even in rhymed prose![71]

This treatise, not only the first but also the longest of Malkum's compositions on reform, contains almost all of his most cherished theses. Here is expounded the primacy of European civilization as the culmination of millenia of human development and the necessity to submit unquestioningly to its norms, while the religious problems implied in these assertions are gently passed over. Among the primary desiderata of reform are separation of the legislative from the executive branch, the codification of the law, and the increase of revenue. Malkum was to explain and pursue these aims further, with more or less seriousness of intent, throughout the greater part of his career.

Two treatises intended to supplement the *Kitābcha-yi Ghaybī* also date from this period. The first, *Rafīq va Vazīr* (Our friend and the minister), takes the form of a dialogue in which a reactionary minister raises various objections to the reforms proposed by the friend (*i.e.*, Malkum); it is clearly designed to counter the opposition to reform mounted by a number of the newly appointed ministers. The minister admits initially that he considers any kind of reform inimical to his own interests, but asserts that it is in any event superfluous, for Iran has existed for four thousand years without any adaptation of European governmental systems. In the presence of the shah, he will nonetheless pretend to support reform, in order to conform to the current royal wish and in the confidence that the shah's interest in the doings of his ministers will soon wane. To this the friend replies by affirming the seriousness of the shah's intentions and by promising that the pleasure to be gained from ordering the affairs of state is greater than that afforded by the receipt of gifts and bribes (*madākhil*).[72] The outlook of

70. *Ibid.*, pp. 51–52.

71. *Ibid.*, p. 52. It is difficult not to see here an allusion to the Qurʾān, particularly because in the same sentence Malkum uses the word *iʿjāz* (miraculous inimitability), a quality properly ascribed to no book other than the Qurʾān, to describe the properties of his treatise. It may be significant that Malkum later proclaimed in London that he wrote a book, "a bible of [his] creed" (Blunt, *op. cit.* (n. 14, above), p. 84), doubtless having in mind the *Kitābcha-yi Ghaybī*.

72. *Majmūʿa-yi Āthār*, pp. 53–62.

the ministers in general is narrow and unimaginative: "Truly, how uncivilized, unworthy, and childish a man must be to delight himself, though a minister of the state, with seeing his son ride along with an escort of five horsemen, or his son-in-law adorned with a red sword-belt!"[73] True achievement would lie in building railways, in conquering India, in increasing the income of the state or tearing up the Treaty of Turkumānchāy.[74] The only means for accomplishing these apparently miraculous feats lies in the implementation of the reforms set forth in the *Kitābcha-yi Ghaybī*.[75] The minister's reply is equally straightforward and simple: the strength of a state resides solely in the sword, not in law and administration.[76] And so the argument continues: the friend claiming that application of the contents of the *Kitābcha-yi Ghaybī* constitutes the only path to salvation, while the minister becomes progressively more obtuse and contemptuous of his adversary's pretensions. One passage from the explanations of the friend deserves quotation as a further illustration of Malkum's attitudes toward reform and westernization, and also of his frequently vivid manner of expression.

> We have a house whose very foundation is rotten and unsound. Without even thinking of shoring up and repairing the foundation, we busy ourselves with painting the walls in one of the upper stories, although a wall on the other side of the building is collapsing. Then, when we look at the result of our labors, instead of perceiving the true cause of all this ruin, we begin discussing the paint we have been using, and start to look for other kinds of paint. Our ministers are constantly busy painting the walls in this ruined house of Iran, and all the while they cry out: "Iran can never be put in order!"[77]

It may be worthwhile to consider briefly the contents of a third treatise composed during this period, which, like the second, may be thought of as supplementary to *Kitābcha-yi Ghaybī*. Entitled *Tanẓīm-i Lashkar va Majlis-i Idāra* (Reform of the army and the administrative council),[78] it hardly does justice to either subject and is a less effective affirmation of the *Kitābcha-yi Ghaybī* than the preceding treatise. Rather than discussing the details of military reform, the first topic of his title, Malkum declares the chief weakness of the state to be its inability

73. *Ibid.*, p. 63.

74. The Treaty of Turkumānchāy (1828) brought the Second Russo-Persian War to an end and provided for Russian annexation of Iran's remaining possessions in the Caucasus.

75. *Ibid.*, pp. 63–64.

76. *Ibid.*, p. 65.

77. *Ibid.*, p. 67.

78. Alternatively entitled *Intiẓām-i Lashkar va Majlis-i Tanẓīmāt* [The reorganization of the army and the reform council].

to increase revenue. Without first possessing a well-stocked treasury, it is fruitless to attempt the establishment of a powerful modern army. Indeed, the fact that the income of the state has remained static for two thousand years has still more serious implications. For is it not the ability to progress that distinguishes man from the animals? One might therefore wonder if the Iranians, whose treasury has remained thus static, are members of the human race.[79] Fortunately, however, there is another explanation: the existence of a great obstacle in the path of progress. This is the failure to separate the legislative branch of the government from the executive. Malkum propounds this verity in his frequently assumed oratorical tone: "If they ask me what my proof is for all of this, I will say: my proof is that I went to Europe, that I spent there ten years of my life, and that I learned the science of economics, which is the broadest in scope of all the sciences."[80] He condescends nonetheless to supply some brief explanation of the truths proclaimed. The true function of the monarch should be no more than the issuing of decrees and commands. He should then be able to commit their execution to his ministers with complete confidence. This end, which will result in an increase of the sovereign's power, not in its decrease, can be attained only by the establishment of the two bodies proposed in the *Kitābcha-yi Ghaybī*: the reform council and the council of ministers.[81] A few additional rules are suggested for the former body: no member should interrupt another while speaking; at least half the members should be present at a session; and the council should turn out at least one law per week.[82] Mushīr ud-Daula is put forward as most suitable chairman for the body, for he would soon be able to acquaint its members with their functions.[83] Twenty-five other persons are then listed for membership in the reform council, among them Ḥusayn Khān Ājūdānbāshī and Muḥammad Riḍā Mīrzā, both of whom, like Malkum, had been initiated into freemasonry while in Europe, and the celebrated Riḍā Qulī Khān Hidāyat.[84] Interestingly enough, Malkum also considers it permissible for foreigners to be appointed to the council.[85] All of these additional proposals and suggestions, together with some repeated from the *Kitābcha-yi Ghaybī*, Malkum conveniently puts in the form of a royal decree, which Nāṣir ud-Dīn Shāh had only to have copied by a scribe and affix his seal to for its passage into law. This again indicates how Malkum, in the first flush of his reformist zeal, expected swift and total compliance from Nāṣir ud-Dīn Shāh.

These earliest treatises of Malkum first strike the contemporary

79. *Majmūʿa-yi Āthār*, pp. 98–103.
80. *Ibid.*, p. 103.
81. *Ibid.*, pp. 103–106.
82. *Ibid.*, pp. 107–109.
83. *Ibid.*, p. 110.
84. *Ibid.*, p. 115.
85. *Ibid.*, p. 114.

reader with the gross simplicity—often naïveté—of their tone and content. This defect may be attributed in part to his love of posturing as a uniquely authoritative figure needing only to proclaim the reforms necessary without the obligation to explain in detail the reasons for their necessity. It may also derive from Malkum's lack of seriousness and commitment to the measures he so emphatically recommended. It would be unjust, however, not to take into account the circumstances—political, social, and literary—of the age in which he wrote. His simplicity and straightforwardness of expression are virtues when compared to the bombastic expository style still favored in mid-nineteenth-century prose, particularly in state papers and correspondence. The European concepts of political organization he discussed were, moreover, almost entirely novel to Iran, and it is comprehensible that both simplicity—even oversimplification—and constant repetition should have appeared desirable for their exposition. Above all, one cannot deny the occasional acuteness and insight of his analyses of the condition of Iran, and of the partial and uncoordinated nature of the few reform measures undertaken by the Qajars. Finally, in these treatises appear for the first time flashes of that satirical genius which was to receive its fullest and most uninhibited expression after Malkum's disgrace in 1889, when he seemed to have broken definitively with the existing order in Iran.[86]

If these treatises may be regarded as Malkum's manifesto, directed in the first place to Nāṣir ud-Dīn Shāh and secondarily to the members of his court and the ministers of state, the celebrated *farāmūshkhāna* may be thought of as an organization for putting that manifesto into effect. Invention of the term (meaning house of oblivion or forgetfulness) has frequently been attributed to Malkum, but in fact was in spoken and written use before his return to Iran in 1858.[87] It was doubtless intended to be, as Gobineau pointed out, an approximate mimic rendering of the French *francmaçon*.[88] This imitative form in its literal meaning suggested the secrecy surrounding masonic rites and the deliberate forgetfulness of the initiate concerning his experiences in the lodge. Alternatively, it might refer to the oblivion and freedom from worldly care vouchsafed by the licentious practices at times vaguely imputed to the lodges or even to the forgetting of one's premasonic existence.[89] It was, however, with Malkum's foundation of 1858 that the

86. See Appendix B.

87. References in Algar, "An Introduction to the History of Freemasonry in Iran," p. 279.

88. Comte Arthur de Gobineau, *Les Religions et les Philosophies dans l'Asie Centrale* (Paris, 1865), p. 306.

89. Polak, *op. cit.* (n. 3, above), I: 14.

term came primarily to be associated, and etymological considerations are of little help in understanding the nature and purpose of the farāmūshkhāna.

We have seen that while in Paris Malkum studied "the organization of the secret societies and freemasonries," and conceived "a plan which should incorporate the political wisdom of Europe with the religious wisdom of Asia," i.e., accomplish the westernization of Iran under the guise of an "Islamic reformation" or "renaissance." Although in the course of time his proposals for reform—couched in suitably religious terms—came to be voiced to a broader public through the columns of *Qānūn*, it was necessary to prepare the ground for their implementation by recruiting a select group of highly placed men owing him allegiance and acquainted with the tactics to be used.[90] It is in this sense that we may interpret his statement that "on my return I called together the chief persons of Tehran, my friends, and spoke to them in private of the need which Islam had of purer doctrine."[91] The center for the private discussion of "purer doctrine" was none other than the farāmūshkhāna.

Ostensible leadership of the organization was vested in Mīrzā Ya^cqūb, and meetings were held in the house, in the Masjid-i Ḥauḍ area of Tehran, of Jalāl ud-Dīn Mīrzā, one of the numerous offspring of the second Qajar ruler, Fatḥ ^cAli Shāh (1797–1834).[92] Born in 1242/1826, Jalāl ud-Dīn Mīrzā became early in his life notorious for irreligious tendencies and, paradoxically, once had to take refuge in the shrine of Shāh ^cAbd ul-^cAẓīm to avoid arrest and banishment. The intercession of relatives at court secured his pardon, and in 1852 he was appointed governor of Luristan. His tenure of the post was shortlived: by the time of Malkum's second return from Paris he was again active in the intrigues of Tehran political life, aspiring to replace Nāṣir ud-Dīn Shāh on the throne.[93] He thus had in common with Malkum both irreligion and ambition, and it was only natural for the two men to join forces in the farāmūshkhāna. It is relevant to note that Jalāl ud-Dīn Mīrzā was one of the first writers to attempt the development of a "pure Persian," that is, one unmixed with Arabic loan words. He was too for many years a correspondent of Fatḥ ^cAlī Ākhūndzāda, sharing with him his hatred of the Arabs and of Islam.[94] His association with the farāmūshkhāna may

90. Mas^cūd Mīrzā Ẓill us-Sulṭān remarks that the aim of the farāmūshkhāna was to produce unity among the courtiers (*Sargudhasht-i Mas^cūdī* [Tehran, 1325 lunar/1907], p. 124).

91. Blunt, *op. cit.* (n. 14, above), p. 83.

92. Sāsānī, *op. cit.* (n. 1, above), II: 128; *Majmū^ca-yi Āthār*, p. vii.

93. See ^cAlī Aṣghar Ḥikmat, *Pārsī-yi Naghz* (Tehran, 1323 solar/1944), p. 433; *Majmū^ca-yi Āthār*, p. vii; and Ismā^cīl Rā^ɔīn, *Farāmūshkhāna va Frāmāsūnri dar Īrān* (Tehran, 1348 solar/1969), I: 506–507.

94. Some of his letters to Ākhūndzāda are printed in the collection of letters

thus be regarded as evidence for the existence of an anti-Islamic element in its ideological inspiration, one hardly contradicted by Malkum's plan for an "Islamic renaissance." The only difference was one of emphasis and tactics: Jalāl ud-Dīn was openly hostile to Islam whereas Malkum, as has been shown, preferred a gradualist approach to the elimination of religion.[95]

It is worth examining why Malkum chose the form of a masonic lodge for his organization, particularly since it was not affiliated with any European obedience. First, his aims had something in common with those of masonry: the elevation of progress as the supreme value, and a strictly humanist concept of ethics. Malkum once pronounced the essential duties of man to be the following: to shun evil, to strive to do good, to fight against oppression, to live peacefully with one's fellows, to seek learning, to diffuse learning, and "as far as is possible to strive to maintain harmony among one's compatriots and fellows." These principles, he said, were mentioned in the course of speeches at the farāmūshkhāna.[96]

Second, it may be presumed that he wished to benefit from the prevailing interest in the mysteries of freemasonry to attract attention and a following to himself, in the same way as he had earlier used his experiments in physics and chemistry to gain a reputation for magical power and knowledge. Last and most important, it is probable that the masonic lodge appeared to be the ideal form of political organization under the conditions of inefficient and sporadic tyranny that prevailed in Iran. Its aims, so far as they were known, might be considered harmless, and secrecy would prevent unwelcome intrusion into the functionings of the organization. There were precedents for a secret or semisecret grouping in Iran furnished by the guilds and some of the Sufi orders.[97]

The prevalence of secret societies in the constitutional movement of 1905–1906 later justified, to an extent, Malkum's estimate of "the secret societies and freemasonries" as suitable bodies for organizing political action in Iran. The life of Mīrzā Malkum Khān's own farāmūshkhāna was, however, short, ending with dissolution by royal decree on 18 October 1861. According to one account, he had originally presented the house of oblivion to Nāṣir ud-Dīn Shāh as a device for secur-

---

entitled *Alifbā-yi Jadīd va Maktūbāt*, eds. Ḥamīd Muḥammadzāda and Ḥamid Ārāslī (Baku, 1963), pp. 373, 374, 393, 394. On his *Nāma-yi Khusruvān*, written in "pure Persian," see Malik ush-Shuᶜarā Bahār, *Sabkshināsī* (Tehran, 1337 solar/1958), III: 292.

95. See above, p. 13.

96. Report of conversation with Ākhūndzāda, *Alifbā-yi Jadīd va Maktubāt*, pp. 294–295.

97. See Algar, "An Introduction to the History of Freemasonry in Iran," p. 291.

ing the loyalty of the most important men in the realm: the monarch himself was to be grand master, and his courtiers, ministers, and generals were to be bound to him by the masonic oath.[98] In reality, the monarch was not head of the organization, even in a formal capacity. It has been suggested instead that Nāṣir ud-Dīn Shāh imagined the farāmūshkhāna to be a harmless society for the diffusion of elementary scientific knowledge, a suggestion that is not as implausible as might appear.[99] Malkum had after all been teaching and conducting experiments at the Dār ul-Funūn, and many of the members of the farāmūshkhāna were students and graduates of that institution. To such a scientific association, Nāṣir ud-Dīn Shāh could have had little objection: he had been much impressed by Malkum's telegraphic feats and doubtless wished to see further curiosities introduced to his realm.

Despite initial royal approval, the life of the farāmūshkhāna was brief and surrounded by controversy. It was inevitable that as a secret organization of manifestly Western inspiration the house of oblivion should arouse a varied and complex reaction, ranging from simple curiosity through enthusiastic participation to outright hostility and rejection. The nature of some of this reaction may be deduced from a treatise written by Malkum in defence of the farāmūshkhāna (*Risāla-yi Farāmūshkhāna*), a cleverly argued and worded piece which ranks among the most skillful of his writings.[100] The treatise takes the form of a letter to an unnamed person in reply to objections raised by him against the farāmūshkhāna. Malkum begins by attempting to refute the accusation of *bidᶜat*, that is, reprehensible innovation in matters touching upon the faith.

Freemasonry ("this great secret") is in fact coeval with the world itself, and all the Prophets and saints have been fully aware of it. Indeed, they have made brief and scattered reference to it, though in a form different from that manifested in the *farāmūshkhāna*. It was not, however, in the interest of humanity for the secret to be fully revealed until more recent times. "Because of their perfect wisdom, they [the Prophets] did not wish to disclose in their own age the totality of hidden knowledge, and thus they made no pronouncement concerning the telegraph, the camera, the New World, or a thousand other truths."[101]

Malkum attempts to counter the related objection that the masonic

98. Gobineau, *Les Religions et les Philosophies*, pp. 305–306.

99. *Majmūᶜa-yi Āthār*, p. viii.

100. A manuscript of this treatise is preserved at the Malik Library in Tehran under no. 3116. It has recently been printed in Rāʾīn, *op. cit.*, I: 545–554, and Maḥmūd Katīraʾī, *Frāmāsūnrī dar Īrān* (Tehran, 1347 solar/1968), pp. 160–175. Here, reference will be made to the printing in Rāʾīn.

101. Rāʾīn, *op. cit.*, I: 546.

lodge is of European origin with the argument that truth is universal in scope and that in any event the material inventions of Europe have been accepted in Iran without qualm. The ulama use spectacles to read the Qurʿān; why then should freemasonry be rejected as contrary to the faith?[102] This strange argument is an interesting illustration of Malkum's general contention that the material and nonmaterial aspects of European civilization are inseparable and must be adopted in toto without any attempt at selectivity.

Malkum then proceeds to deal with the secrecy that surrounded the workings of the farāmūshkhāna, a circumstance that evidently led many to proclaim the institution heretical. He first points out that secrecy in itself precluded his accusers from having accurate knowledge of the activities of the lodge, and their judgments were therefore pronounced in ignorance. Moreover, secrecy and the withholding of esoteric truth (*kitmān*) constituted a religiously sanctioned principle, frequently resorted to by various groups throughout Islamic history.[103] Malkum's invocation of kitmān is of great interest, for it demonstrates his awareness of the historical role of clandestine groupings in Iran and the partial resemblance of these to the masonic lodge. Such resemblance may be held in part to account for the widespread interest shown in freemasonry in Iran and also for the popularity of secret and semisecret societies in the period of the Constitutional Revolution. There was, nonetheless, a difference between traditional groupings in Iran and the modern secret society: that between purposes genuinely conceived as religious and aims political in nature with only incidental or expedient invocation of religious themes. The farāmūshkhāna and its successor organizations, discussed below, may be thought of as providing a transition between the two types of groups and motives.

It appears that Malkum's initiative in founding the house of oblivion was also found objectionable on the grounds of his youth and beardlessness. It is understandable that this attempt on the part of a young Armenian recently returned from Europe to recruit the leading men of the capital for an organization led by himself, should have aroused contempt and indignation. By way of response, Malkum again proudly referred to his introduction of the telegraph to Iran: "It is this same abject and beardless person who brought the telegraph to Iran from Europe."[104]

Finally, the objection that the farāmūshkhāna was frequented by persons by no means free of moral defect is pronounced groundless, for

102. *Ibid.*
103. *Ibid.*, I: 547.
104. *Ibid.*

initiation into the secrets of masonry will elevate a man only to the extent of his inborn virtue.[105]

With these objections refuted, Malkum proclaims the true aim of the farāmūshkhāna to be the cultivation and strengthening of fraternity among its members. "Their only sin and irreligious act is this, that they have forgotten their former enmity and spite and now wish to treat each other with love and affection."[106] Because such fraternal unity is the basis of Islam, those who condemn the farāmūshkhāna as irreligious are in reality themselves stepping outside the pale of Islam. Prominent among them are "a group who suppose that God has created them of some special substance. Since they see that their manner of dress is more picturesque than that of others, they imagine that they also enjoy superiority with respect to moral qualities. These complacent gentlemen, who regard all the bounties of the world as their private property, expected our secrets to be vouchsafed exclusively to them."[107] It is clear that by this group Malkum intended the ulama, who probably constituted the most serious opposition to the farāmūshkhāna. These sentences may be taken as indicative of Malkum's true opinion of the ulama, one which he frequently contradicted for purposes of expediency. He concludes the piece by swearing by the Prophet and the Twelve Imams that the farāmūshkhāna is not in any respect contrary to religion.

Malkum's treatise evidently received some attention, for there exists the fragment of an anonymous reply written by someone in Tabriz. By contrast with the treatise, it is badly written and in places barely comprehensible; it is nonetheless valuable as an indication of a contemporary view of the farāmūshkhāna.[108] In a lengthy preamble, the writer declares intercourse with non-Muslims dangerous for the faith and for the religious solidarity (*taᶜaṣṣub-i dīnī*) upon which the existence of the community depends. This solidarity is weakened by the farāmūshkhāna, for contrary to Malkum's assertion, its aim is not to create unity among the Muslims, but rather between Muslims and non-Muslims, on a basis of complete identity. "They wish to establish peace among all religions, whether true or false."[109] In any event, the Prophet Muḥammad has already commanded his followers to regard each other as brothers, and if they disobey his ordinances it is unlikely that Malkum's exhortations will be more effective. "As soon as someone by the

105. *Ibid.*, I: 548.
106. *Ibid.*, I: 550.
107. *Ibid.*, I: 551.
108. The manuscript of this reply is contained in no. 3257, Central Library of the University of Tehran, and has been printed in Rāᵓīn, *op. cit.*, I: 555–560.
109. *Ibid.*, I: 560.

name of Mīrzā Malkum, about whose religion nobody knows anything for sure, comes from Europe and secludes himself with them to teach them the lesson [of fraternity], are they suddenly going to regard obedience to *his* words as a duty? . . . If these people had any sense, they would from the outset follow the words of their Prophet, who is the universal intelligence."[110]

A more informative but again fragmentary and anonymous attack on the farāmūshkhāna was composed soon after its dissolution. The author was a former initiate who, after traversing two degrees, pronounced himself totally disillusioned and desirous of warning his compatriots of the dangers inherent in the organization. From the loyalist tone in which it is written and from the content of several passages, it may be surmised that the piece was presented to Nāṣir ud-Dīn Shāh. The sole copy known to exist is titled "Report of one who traversed two degrees in the farāmūshkhāna" and formerly belonged to the royal library.[111] If the treatise was in fact commissioned by the shah, its reliability becomes questionable; the author might well have been tempted to conform to the shah's obvious mood by portraying the farāmūshkhāna as scandalous and ugly. In particular, the accusations of debauchery practiced in the lodge appear somewhat doubtful. In general, however, the account of the farāmūshkhāna given in the treatise appears plausible enough, and it may be presumed in the absence of contrary evidence to be accurate.

The writer begins with the fundamental objection that the farāmūshkhāna constitutes *bidʿat*. If it were at all legitimate, it would have been explicitly mentioned in the sources of Islamic law—the Qurʾān and the sunna of the Prophet and the Imams. Clear guidance has been given on less significant matters than securing fraternity among believers; how, then, could so important a subject have been neglected? The true means of establishing fraternity is congregational prayer and for the prevention of injustice the *sharīʿa* is more than adequate. The only purpose of the union created by the farāmūshkhāna is fraternity in evil and wickedness. At its meetings, men of religion are humiliated; alcohol is consumed, and the members fornicate at will with foreign women.[112] On one occasion in particular, when, to his credit, Malkum was absent from the proceedings, a number of beardless youths and whores (*amārid*

110. *Ibid.*

111. *Rāpurt-i Shakhṣī ki Dau Daraja az Farāmūshkhāna-ra Ṭayy Karda Ast,* now preserved in the Kitābkhāna-yi Millī, Tehran, under no. 1397. It has recently been printed by Rāʾīn, *op. cit.*, I: 534–545, and Katīrāʾī, *op. cit.*, pp. 176–193. Reference will be made here to the printing in Rāʾīn.

112. Rāʾīn, *op. cit.* (n. 93, above), I: 537.

va ajānida [*sic*]) were put at the disposal of initiates for the modest fee of three tomans.[113]

Apart from these sensual delights, members were attracted by a variety of ways suited to their professions. Ulama, for example, were promised an increased following and prominence over their colleagues once they joined. Their presence in the farāmūshkhāna had a double advantage for its founders: it both tempted other ulama to follow their example and seemed to guarantee the religious innocuity of the organization. Merchants were assured of increased takings once their fellow initiates transferred their custom to them; princes were promised ascendancy over their rivals through the support of their brothers in the lodge. Less exalted folk were tempted with promises of financial aid, either in the form of outright grants or loans given without security.[114]

According to the anonymous report, each member was required to pay a fee of twelve tomans, which went immediately into Malkum's pocket, the sole treasury of the farāmūshkhāna.[115] Malkum himself, in an indiscreet letter written in 1890 after his dismissal from the embassy in London, implicity confirms that he enriched himself by means of the farāmūshkhāna. Addressing himself to the Ministry of Foreign Affairs, he demanded a new position, declaring himself ready to accept anything in preference to idleness. "But if they want me to be both hungry and idle, it won't do. If I resort to trickery I can have a yearly income of seven or eight thousand tomans. If I establish a farāmūshkhāna, I can make twenty or thirty thousand tomans a year."[116]

As for the secrecy which surrounded this immoral and fraudulent organization, the report proceeds, it derived primarily from the shame of initiates at the degrading acts they had committed. What minister or mulla would willingly confess the indignities he had suffered at the hands of common idiots? Men began by desiring to learn a secret which had been the object of curiosity for many years, and once inside the farāmūshkhāna were compelled to silence by embarrassment and regret.[117]

The report then describes in some detail the ceremonies of initiation into the first degree. The candidate is informed that he, like all his compatriots, has hitherto been unaware of the true purpose of life, which he is now about to learn for the first time. It will be a demanding and hazardous experience and he must therefore draw up his testament

113. *Ibid.*, I: 542.

114. *Ibid.*, I: 537.

115. *Ibid.*, I: 538.

116. Quoted by Jahāngīr Qā᾿immaqāmī, "Chand Sanad Marbūṭ ba Tārīkh-i Farāmūshkhāna dar Īrān," *Yaghmā*, XVI (1342 solar/1963): 405.

117. Rā᾿īn, *op. cit.*, I: 539.

to guard against all eventualities and to acquit the lodge of any responsibility for his fate. The purpose of this exercise is to increase the eagerness of the candidate and convince him that great secrets are about to be revealed. After the testament has been drawn up, he is once more told of the dangers that confront him on the path and advised to withdraw before it is too late, again with the purpose of increasing his resolve. He is then blindfolded and led around the courtyard of the house where the ceremony is taking place to the foot of a stairway which he is instructed to mount. This stairway is known as the *falak-i taḥqīq* ("the rack of spiritual realization"). Halfway up it there is a platform referred to as *qāba qawsayn aw adnā* ("the distance of two bowstrings or nearer"), an expression drawn from Qurʾān 9:53, where it refers to the Prophet Muḥammad's distance from the divine presence after his nocturnal ascension from Jerusalem. Upon reaching this platform and learning its name, the candidate imagines himself in heaven.[118]

From the platform he is led toward a door at which he is instructed to knock. From within a voice inquires: "Who is it, and for what purpose have you come?" The candidate is required to answer: "A dweller in the desert wishes to enter the city of knowledge." Question and answer are repeated, and then the door is opened. The candidate enters and is seated. He is again given the possibility of abandoning the whole affair, and upon refusing is told to choose one of three tests to which he must submit: to discharge a pistol at his head, to jump into a fire or hurl himself into a pit. For the sake of verisimilitude, a lamp is placed hissing beside him so that he might imagine a fire to be lit and ready to receive him. Once his choice has been made, he is conducted to a subterranean room to undergo the test. While waiting to begin, he is assailed with a cacophony of noise produced by the swinging of rattles and stones thrown against the wall; these are intended to create an atmosphere of terror. The test is simulated with an empty pistol, a nonexistent fire, or a shallow pit, and the candidate is led to another room, full of people who explain to him in chorus the principles of union (*jamāʿat*), freedom (*ikhtiyār*), and equality (*musāvāt*). His eyes are then unbound, he receives the congratulations of all present, and the strange performance is at an end.[119]

There is no reason to doubt the substantial authenticity of this account of initiation into the first degree. The ceremony bears little resemblance to that enacted by European obediences, and it was doubtless Malkum's genius that substituted the test of pistol, fire, or pit for sword and noose. Of particular interest are those elements in the ceremony which have Islamic references: the *falak-i taḥqīq* with its platform and the "city of knowledge" to which the candidate demands entry. *Taḥqīq*,

118. *Ibid.*, I: 539–540.

119. *Ibid.*, I: 540–541.

in the terminology of the Sufis, denotes "the effort of the servant of God to attain Reality,"[120] and the fruit of his striving will be arrival at that same station of "two bowstrings" which the Prophet attained in an immediate and miraculous manner. The "station of two bowstrings" signifies "proximity to God, with opposite attributes meeting in obedience to divine command,"[121] that is, total integration of the self in harmonious submission to the will of God and in the immediately perceived presence of God. The mystics undertake their journey to this station in the footsteps of the Prophet, and by introducing the term into his ceremony of initiation, Malkum grotesquely suggests that his farāmūshkhāna has the same purpose and effect. Similarly, the expression "the city of knowledge" is an allusion to the celebrated *ḥadīth* of the Prophet: "I am the city of knowledge and ᶜAli is its gate," a *ḥadīth* which has been the object of intense speculation among both Sufis and Shiᶜis.[122] The implication is clearly that the lodge itself is the city of esoteric knowledge referred to in the *ḥadīth.*

Malkum's use of these terms of religious import was not fortuitous. His invocation of the principle of kitmān suggests, as has been noted, awareness of the parallels between freemasonry and traditional secret or closed groupings. Allusions to mystical themes in the ceremony of initiation were doubtless intended both to attract adherents of the Sufi brotherhoods to the farāmūshkhāna and to gain for it a measure of religious legitimacy. There is at least one instance furnished by the father of the poet Abūl Qāsim Lāhūtī suggesting the effectiveness of Malkum's stratagem. The elder Lāhūtī transferred his allegiance from a Sufi order in Kirmanshah to the local branch of the League of Humanity, the successor to the proscribed farāmūshkhāna.[123] When a "regular" lodge, the Reveil de l'Iran, was founded in 1908, it sought to interweave Islamic themes into masonic ideology in a more comprehensive manner than Malkum had done, thus confirming the essential correctness of his initiative.[124]

Having described initiation into the first degree, the report lists the signs of mutual recognition pertaining to it and proceeds briefly to reveal the secrets of the second degree. These consist essentially of ten

120. Sayyid Jaᶜfar Sajjādī, *Farhang-i Muṣṭalaḥāt-i ᶜUrafā, Mutaṣavvifa va Shuᶜarā* (Tehran, 1339 solar/1960), p. 105.

121. *Ibid.*, p. 311.

122. For the symbolic significance of the city in Islamic mysticism, see also the anecdote of the townsman's visit to the countryside in the third book of the *Mathnavī* of Jalāl ud-Dīn Rūmī (ed. R. A. Nicholson, Gibb Memorial Series, Vol. IV: 3, p. 15 f.).

123. See below, pp. 234–235.

124. See the masonic poem of Adīb ul-Mamālik Farāhānī in his *Divan*, ed. Vaḥīd Dastgirdī (Tehran, 1312 solar/1933), pp. 575–593, and Algar, "An Introduction to the History of Freemasonry in Iran," pp. 288–289.

principles upon which public order is based, and are social and political in character—security, equality before the law, freedom of belief and so forth.

Throughout the report there is no mention of Malkum by name; he is referred to simply as "the originator of this affair." His motive in founding the farāmūshkhāna is ambition for supreme power: "The originator of this affair, despite the extreme generosity which, as all can testify, he has received from the sustainer of all Iran, still imagines that he has been treated unfairly. He expresses discontent and wishes the loosening and binding of affairs and all power to be in his hands."[125]

Such an attribution of ambition might safely be dismissed were it not for the following passage from Malkum's own fanciful account of the downfall of the farāmūshkhāna:

> At last the Shah was alarmed at my power, which in truth had become superior to his own. He sought, in spite of our old friendship, to kill me, and my followers sought to kill him. For two months, we both lived in great fear of assassination, and then we came to an explanation. I loved and revered the Shah, and I asked permission to travel. My followers took leave of me with tears, even the Mollahs kissing my feet.[126]

Here it seems that Malkum is implicitly confessing to a desire for supreme power and to the justice of Nāṣir ud-Dīn Shāh's fears for his throne. These fears were fed by a variety of factors. The rise of Babism a few years earlier, and particularly the attempt by four Babis on the shah's life in 1852, had intensified the fear and suspicion that already permeated the political atmosphere of Iran. Those Babis who remained in Iran had recourse to *taqīya*, to prudential concealment of faith, in order to survive unmolested. As a result, accusations of Babism could be easily and damagingly raised against personal enemies and political rivals. It was thus inevitable that the accusation of Babi sympathies should be made against the farāmūshkhāna, which wore the mask of a secret organization.[127] Such accusations were probably groundless, although Malkum, in his curious pseudo-autobiographical statement, showed a certain fascination with the phenomenal rise of Babism and possibly contacted Babi fugitives in Baghdad after his banishment from Iran in 1863.[128]

It has been asserted that the Russians urged Nāṣir ud-Dīn Shāh to proscribe the farāmūshkhāna, fearing that the emergence of a group determined to reform Iran would block the avenues of Russian penetra-

125. Rāʾīn, *op. cit.*, I: 543.
126. Blunt, *op. cit.* (n. 14, above), p. 84.
127. Gobineau, *Les Religions et les Philosophies*, p. 307.
128. Blunt, *op. cit.* (n. 14, above), p. 83; and see below, p. 59.

tion and dominance.[129] Probably, however, certain groups in Iranian society were more actively interested in obtaining its proscription and dissolution. Among these were politicians such as Mīrzā Saᶜīd Khān Muᵓtaman ul-Mulk, minister of foreign affairs, who resented any possible influence of Malkum over the shah.[130] It is likely too that the ulama were opposed to the house of oblivion as an irreligious innovation brought from France. A member of the farāmūshkhāna, Mīrzā Muḥammad Khān Nāẓim-i Daftar, wrote many years after the dissolution that "the leading ulama of Tehran in concert denounced and prohibited it, destroyed and set fire to it, and leveled it to the ground."[131] The farāmūshkhāna, however, had no headquarters, using the house of Jalāl ud-Dīn Mīrzā for its meetings, and it is unlikely that the ulama would have dared to raze to the ground the house of a Qajar prince, even on a religious pretext. Mīrzā Muḥammad Khān's story was probably the product of his imagination and of the passage of time. It may be taken to reflect, in lurid manner, the enmity of the ulama to the farāmūshkhāna. Several years later when Malkum returned to Iran in the capacity of special advisor to the prime minister, this hostility was soon revived and expressed with particular force by Mullā ᶜAlī Kanī, the most influential of the ulama of the capital.[132]

The house of oblivion was suspected above all of propagating republicanism, which, because of the French Revolution, was associated with irreligion and the disruption of the social order. According to a contemporary chronicle: "He [Malkum] used to say that a republican regime should be established in accordance with the system prevailing in most European states, and that individual citizens should participate in the allotment of posts and the assignment of functions in the affairs of the country and the matters of the state."[133] Many years later, Mīrzā Muḥammad Ḥasan Khān Iᶜtimād us-Salṭana, Nāṣir ud-Dīn Shāh's minister of publications, similarly attributed republican tendencies to Malkum: "He created a farāmūshkhāna in Iran and laid the foundations of a republic, one of the concomitants of freemasonry. He thereby for a long time cast into anxiety and tribulation the person of the monarch and thousands of his subjects."[134]

129. See below, pp. 52–53.

130. *Majmūᶜa-yi Āthār*, p. viii.

131. *Ibid.*, p. liii.

132. *Ibid.*, p. x; and Ibrāhīm Taymūrī, *ᶜAṣr-i Bīkhabarī yā Tārīkh-i Imtiyāzāt dar Īrān* (Tehran, 1336 solar/1957), pp. 124–125.

133. Sāsānī, *op cit.* (n. 1, above), I: 146, quoting from Ibrāhīm Navvāb Badāyiᶜ Nagār, *ᶜIbrat un-Nāẓirin va ᶜIbrat ul-Hāḍirin.* See too Mihdī Qulī Khān Hidāyat Mukhbir us-Salṭana, *Khāṭirāt va Khāṭarāt* (Tehran, 1329 solar/1950), p. 75, where he accuses Malkum of republicanism.

134. See his letter to Mīrzā Yūsuf Khān Mustaufī ul-Mamālik quoted in Taymūrī, *op. cit.*, p. 69.

It is unlikely that Malkum was in fact urging the members of his organization to work for the displacement of the monarchy and the institution of a republic. In any event the republican system of government was not that prevailing in most European states of the time. Nonetheless, the distinctions between courses of action such as legal and administrative reform, the constitutional limitation of royal power, and the institution of a republic, were not generally appreciated in Iran, either in the middle of the nineteenth century or for a long time thereafter. In his *Kitābcha-yi Ghaybī*, Malkum was at pains to stress that his aim was the increase, not the diminution, of royal power, and his treatises enjoyed some circulation around the capital. Malkum's unfamiliar theme and manner of expression probably served, however, to arouse an indiscriminate repugnance to innovation. This, together with his display of "magical" powers, makes it comprehensible that the monarch, his suspicions suitably aroused, should have feared the existence of a republican conspiracy working to depose him and centered on Malkum's secret organization. The presence at the head of the organization of Jalāl ud-Dīn Mīrzā, a prince known to be coveting the throne, probably served to intensify rather than contradict these fears.

Nāṣir ud-Dīn Shāh began his moves against the farāmūshkhāna by sending one of the ulama associated with his court to investigate the society and to submit a report on his findings. Having obtained access to the lodge on the recommendation of Shaykh Hādī Najmābādī, one of its prominent clerical members, he attended only a few meetings before reporting to Nāṣir ud-Dīn Shāh that what he had seen was "the prelude to the downfall of the monarchy."[135]

Understandably alarmed, Nāṣir ud-Dīn then turned to his French doctor, Tholozan, for his opinion on freemasonry as a native of the country whence it had sprung. Sensing the atmosphere at court, Tholozan confirmed the subversive nature of the movement and warned his royal employer to guard himself against it.[136]

Thus it was that on 18 October 1861, the following decree was published in the official gazette:

> It has recently come to our knowledge that certain of the lowly ruffians of the city have spoken of founding and organizing European houses of oblivion, and expressed a desire to establish such. Therefore a clear imperial decree is issued that if henceforth anyone utter the expression and phrase house of oblivion, let alone attempt to establish such, he will be subject to the full wrath and chastisement of the state. Let use of this word be

135. Rā'īn, *op. cit.* (n. 93, above), I: 524.
136. *Ibid.*, I: 526.

completely abandoned, and let none concern himself with these absurdities, for he shall without doubt receive thoroughgoing punishment.[137]

It is difficult to form a precise idea of the membership of the farāmūshkhāna during its brief life. Malkum's claim to have attracted 30,000 followers reasonably may be ignored.[138] As mentioned above, many members of the farāmūshkhāna were students or graduates of the Dār ul-Funūn. Beyond these, it may be assumed that many were attracted to the lodge by the air of secrecy surrounding it and by the mysterious reputation previously enjoyed by freemasonry in Iran. The serious involvement of such persons in the reformist aims of the organization may be doubted. On the other hand, a number of figures who attained prominence in Iranian history were also members of the farāmūshkhāna. Among these may be mentioned Majd ul-Mulk, author of one of the earliest reformist treatises, the *Risāla-yi Majdīya.*[139] He was the father of Mīrzā ᶜAlī Khān Amīn ud-Daula, a faithful associate of Malkum who held various ministerial posts under Nāṣir ud-Dīn Shāh and was prime minister to his successor, Muẓaffar ud-Dīn Shāh, from mid-1897 to June 1898. Another prominent initiate was Riḍā Qulī Khān Hidāyat, the celebrated littérateur and chronicler and first director of the Dār al-Funūn.[140] His colleagues, Mīrzā Muḥammad Taqī Lisān al-Mulk Sipihr and Mīrzā Jaᶜfar Ḥaqāʾiqnagār, also glimpsed the masonic light in Malkum's house of oblivion, as did the poet laureate, Mīrzā Maḥmūd Khān Ṣabā.[141] Among other men of learning drawn to the farāmūshkhāna were Mīrzā Jaᶜfar Ḥakim-Ilāhī and Mīrzā Ḥasan Jilva, both prominent exponents of *ḥikmat,* that fusion of mysticism, neo-

137. Quoted in *Majmūᶜa-yi Āthār,* p. viii; and Iᶜtimād us-Salṭana, *al-Maʾāthir va-l-Āthār,* p. 118.

138. Blunt, *op. cit.* (n. 14, above), p. 83. Lists of members are given by Rāʾīn, *op. cit.,* I: 513–514 and Katīrāʾī, *op. cit.* (n. 100, above), p. 69. The former enumerates thirty-eight persons, the latter sixteen. Neither list is reliable, nor supported by reference to primary sources, and that of Rāʾīn in particular contains a number of obvious errors. Thus Mīrzā Ḥusayn Khān Sipahsālār, presumably on the basis of his later association with Malkum, is reckoned among the members of the farāmūshkhāna, even though he was throughout its lifetime Iranian minister in Istanbul.

139. See Mīrzā Yūsuf Khān Rifᶜat ul-Mulk, *Daryā-yi Maᶜrifat,* quoted by ᶜAlī Riḍā Ṣabā in "Iṭṭilāᶜātī dar bāra-yi Maḥmūd Khān Malik ush-Shuᶜarā," *Rāhnamā-yi Kitāb,* XII (1348 solar/1969): 524. Concerning *Risāla-yi Majdīya,* see Malik ush-Shuᶜarā Bahār, *Sabkshināsī* (Tehran, 1337 solar/1958), III: 365–366. The treatise was published in Tehran in 1321 solar/1942 by Saᶜīd Nafīsī.

140. Rifᶜat ul-Mulk, *op. cit.,* p. 524. Concerning Hidāyat, see E. G. Browne, *A Literary History of Persia* (Cambridge, 1924), IV: 344, and Bahār, *op. cit.,* III: 367–369.

141. Rifᶜat ul-Mulk, *op. cit.,* p. 524.

Platonism and Shiʿi speculation which had been evolved in Safavid Iran.[142] Another learned member was Shaykh Hādī Najmābādī, an influential figure who, toward the end of the nineteenth century while wearing the garb of the ulama, gained a reputation for freethinking.[143] In addition to Jalāl ud-Dīn Mīrzā, a number of other princes were associated with the farāmūshkhāna, including Sulṭān Uvays Mīrzā Iḥtishām ud-Daula, a cousin of Nāṣir ud-Dīn Shāh, and Sayfullāh Mīrzā, a grandson of Ẓill us-Sulṭan "ʿAlī Shāh," a prince who had made an unsuccessful bid for the throne in 1834.[144]

Particularly interesting is the membership in the farāmūshkhāna of a number of ulama. Malkum would have us believe that when he was banished from Tehran, "my followers took leave of me with tears, even the Mollahs kissing my feet."[145] The spectacle of the venerable ulama of Tehran falling at the feet of an Armenian youth about to be ignominiously expelled from the city is an unlikely one. It is nonetheless true that a number of the ulama, despite the general hostility of their colleagues to Malkum, joined the farāmūshkhāna, among them Hājjī Mīrzā Zayn ul-ʿĀbidīn, Imām Jumʿa of Tehran,[146] and Sayyid Ṣādiq Ṭabāṭabāʾī. The involvement of the latter in the farāmūshkhāna is of some significance: his son, Sayyid Muḥammad Ṭabāṭabāʾī, became one of the leading figures among the ulama supporting the constitutional movement of 1905–1906 and also had masonic or pseudomasonic connections.[147] According to the account given by Nāẓim ul-Islām Kirmānī, an associate of Sayyid Muḥammad Ṭabāṭabāʾī, Sayyid Ṣādiq Ṭabāṭabāʾī for long shunned any association with Malkum Khān and his farāmūshkhāna. One day, he went to visit a friend in Shemiran, the northern suburb of Tehran; learning of this, Malkum Khān set out in pursuit. There ensued an encounter between the two men as a result of which Sayyid Ṣādiq Ṭabāṭabāʾī became totally converted to Malkum's purposes.[148] Unfortunately, Kirmānī records nothing of the content of

142. *Ibid.* Ḥakīm-Ilāhī retained some interest in Malkum's activities at least until 1871; in that year he asked Ḥasan ʿAlī Khān Amīr Niẓām to persuade Malkum to return from Istanbul. See Amīr Niẓām's letter to Malkum dated Muḥarram 3, 1288/March 27, 1871, in Bibliothèque Nationale, Supplément Persan, 1991, f. 1.

143. Concerning Najmābādī, see Mīrzā Muḥammad Qazvīnī's note in E. G. Browne, *The Persian Revolution of 1905–1909* (Cambridge, 1910), p. 406.

144. Katīrāʾī, *op. cit.* (n.100, above), p. 69.

145. Blunt, *op. cit.* (n.14, above), p. 84.

146. Yaḥyā Daulatābādī, *Tārīkh-i Muʿāṣir yā Ḥayāt-i Yaḥyā* (Tehran, n.d.), I: 337.

147. *Ibid.*, I: 253; Mihdī Malikzāda, *Tārīkh-i Inqilāb-i Mashrūṭīyat* (Tehran, 1327 solar/1948), II: 19; ʿAlī Aṣghar Shamīm, *Īrān dar Daura-yi Salṭanat-i Qājār* (Tehran, 1342 solar/1963), p. 354.

148. Kirmānī, *op. cit.* (n.11, above), p. 120.

their discussion, but it may be suggested that Malkum's eagerness to enroll Ṭabāṭabā'ī proceeded from his tactical identification of reform with religion. For this identification to be credible, it needed the verification and support of prominent ulama. Whether in supplying this verification, first Sayyid Ṣādiq and then Sayyid Muḥammad believed the identification to be true or, like Malkum, merely found it expedient, is a matter of speculation.

The extent to which initiates to the farāmūshkhāna were aware of its lack of affiliation with French masonry is similarly uncertain. Mīrzā Farrukh Khān is reputed to have been among the opponents of the farāmūshkhāna, and his opposition may have been caused in part by the knowledge that Malkum had no authority from the Grand Orient to establish a lodge in Tehran.[149] In general, however, Iranians came to know of Malkum as a mason and probably assumed that his house of oblivion was a regularly constituted lodge. When Mīrzā Āqā Khān Kirmānī first wrote to Malkum from Istanbul offering him his services in the cause of opposition to Nāṣir ud-Dīn Shāh, he felt it necessary to make clear that although he was not a mason, he was still capable of good work.[150] When Sulṭān Uvays Mīrzā, one of Malkum's princely initiates, traveled to Europe in the late 1870s, he wrote to his preceptor (who was then in London) asking for a letter of recommendation to a Berlin lodge. Having traversed the first two degrees in the farāmūshkhāna ("I was a dweller in the desert, but now I live in the city and have spent there two whole years"), he wished to proceed to the third, and possibly beyond, during his stay in Germany.[151] It is evident from this request for an introduction that Uvays Mīrzā assumed the farāmūshkhāna to be regularly affiliated with the European obediences. He did indeed gain entry to a lodge, the Unsterblichkeit,[152] but whether or not this was the result of a recommendation from Malkum Khān is unknown. It cannot in any event be taken as evidence for the "regular and approved" nature of Malkum's foundation. Probably not until the foundation in 1908 of the Reveil de l'Iran, a lodge authorized by the Grand Orient, did the irregularity of the farāmūshkhāna become generally known.[153]

149. Sykes, *op. cit.* (n. 10, above), II: 398; *Majmūʿa-yi Āthār*, vi–vii.

150. Undated letter in Bibliothèque Nationale, Supplément Persan, 1996, ff. 92–93.

151. Undated letter, Supplément Persan, 1989, f. 39.

152. *Internationales Freimaurerlexikon* (Munich, 1956), p. 312.

153. Ignorance of the matter may have persisted even longer. Later in the same year, Yevgeniy Ilyin presented to the Imperial Archeological Society in Moscow a paper on Iranian freemasonry in which he treated the farāmūshkhāna as a legitimate masonic organization and claimed as his source certain unnamed Iranian masons ("Iz

Even though the house of oblivion had no formal ties with the Grand Orient, it is worth noting that it received the sympathetic attention of French diplomatic representatives in Iran. Comte Arthur de Gobineau, envoy in Tehran from 1861 to 1864, briefly discusses the farāmūshkhāna in his *Les Religions et Les Philosophies dans l'Asie Centrale.*[154] He refrains from mentioning Malkum by name and simply refers to "an intelligent and capable Iranian" of progressive outlook as the founder of the organization. According to Gobineau, the aim of the farāmūshkhāna was to create a spirit of unity among courtiers and men of state, and the monarch was offered the position of grand master. The shah's suspicion, however, was aroused not only by the secrecy observed in the lodge, but also by the unconvincing reports brought back by his informants, who assured him that members simply sat there drinking tea and smoking water pipes. Convinced that something of conspiratorial nature was being hidden from him, Nāṣir ud-Dīn Shāh moved to dissolve the organization. Gobineau's account seems to have been based on hearsay and cannot be regarded as authoritative.

Another envoy, Blonnet, reported on the farāmūshkhāna in the course of a dispatch to the French Foreign Ministry in 1861. He too affirmed that the aim of the farāmūshkhāna was to put an end to all discord among courtiers and politicians, to eliminate corruption, and in general to raise the moral tone of political life. Malkum is praised as one who grew up in France and received his education there, and who "well understands what needs to be done for the regeneration of his homeland." All honorable people in the country have joined the organization, and the religious classes in particular have been greatly attracted to it.[155] This report appears to have been directly inspired by Malkum, reflect-

---

Istorii Masonstva v Persii," *Drevnosti Vostochnie: Trudy Vostochnoi Kommissii Imperatorskogo Arkheologicheskogo Obshchestva* [Moscow, 1908], pp. 17–20).

Nāẓim ul-Islām Kirmānī (*op. cit.* [n.11, above], p. 118) denies that Malkum ever had the intention of founding an Iranian branch of freemasonry or that he declared his farāmūshkhāna to be a regularly constituted lodge. According to the anonymous report, however, he did claim to be authorized by the Grand Orient (Rāʾīn, *op. cit.* [n.93, above], I: 543). It is probable that Kirmānī was trying to protect the reputation of Malkum and those associated with him, above all Sayyids Muḥammad and Ṣādiq Ṭabāṭabāʾī, from the accusations of fraud raised by the members of the Reveil de l'Iran. On their attitude to Malkum and his followers in Iran, see below, p. 258.

154. Gobineau, *op. cit.* (n.88, above), pp. 305–306. Gobineau was presumably acquainted with Malkum, for in 1271/1854–1855 it was he who had been entrusted with the presentation to Gobineau of the Order of the Lion and Sun (second class) on behalf of Nāṣir ud-Dīn Shāh, doubtless because of his fluency in French. See Muḥammad Jaʿfar Khūrmūjī, *Ḥaqāʾiq ul-Akhbār-i Nāṣirī*, ed. Ḥusayn Khadīv-i Jam (Tehran, 1344 solar/1965), p. 153.

155. Dispatch quoted by Jahāngīr Qāʾimmaqāmī, *op. cit.* (n.116, above), pp. 404–405.

ing as it does his declared purpose in establishing the farāmūshkhāna. There is, though, no reason to doubt the genuineness of Blonnet's admiration for him as a product of French education, striving diligently to apply lessons learned in France to the problems of his homeland. To the extent that freemasonry was a French institution, its export to Iran, even in a distorted form, was a source of pride and satisfaction.

After the dissolution of the farāmūshkhāna, Nāṣir ud-Dīn Shāh appears to have contemplated punitive action against some of its members, though not, initially, against Malkum. Jalāl ud-Dīn Mīrzā was required to keep prudently to his house,[156] and Mīrzā Jaᶜfar Ḥakīm-Ilāhī thought it wise to take refuge in the shrine at Qum until the royal anger subsided. After a time, he was persuaded to emerge and assured that he could proceed unmolested to the *ᶜatabāt*, the shrine cities of Arab Iraq. Simultaneously, however, orders were given to the governor of Kirmanshah to arrange for his murder while en route to Iraq. Himself an initiate of the farāmūshkhāna, the governor disclosed the danger to Ḥakīm-Ilāhī and helped him return to the security of Qum.

When the shah learned of Ḥakīm-Ilāhī's return to Qum (but not, presumably, of the governor's role), he decided, by way of compensation, to execute Ḥakīm-Ilāhī's cousin, Sayyid Riḍā Shams ul-Aṭibbā, also a member of the farāmūshkhāna, together with three other members of the proscribed organization. The queen mother interceded on Sayyid Riḍā's behalf, telling Nāṣir ud-Dīn Shāh that he would destroy himself if he dared to kill a *sayyid*. When the shah remained adamant, she threatened to ride naked around the capital on an ass. Faced with this danger to his honor, he was obliged to yield.[157]

As nominal head of the farāmūshkhāna, Mīrzā Yaᶜqūb was expelled from Iran immediately after its dissolution, and according to the account of the generally well-informed Khān Malik Sāsānī, took refuge in Central Asia. Here he is alleged to have undertaken espionage on behalf of the British, to whom he had transferred his loyalties after the conclusion of the Treaty of Paris.[158] Sāsānī asserts that the British dressed him in cloak and turban as a mulla and sent him to rouse the

156. Rāʾīn, *op. cit.*, I: 508.

157. *Ibid.*, I: 515–517, quoting the oral account of Ḥakīm-Ilāhī's daughter.

158. Sāsānī, *op. cit.* (n. 1, above), I: 39, quoting from a letter written by Mīrzā Āqā Khān Nūrī to Nāṣir ud-Dīn Shāh. According to another account, that of the Italian Andreini, the Russians were still interested enough in Mīrzā Yaᶜqūb to intervene on his behalf with the shah. As a result of their requests, he received partial payment for the property he was obliged to leave behind in Iran instead of having it confiscated outright. See Angelo Piemontese, "Per una biografia di Malkom Xān," *Annalī, Istituto Orientale di Napoli*, new series, XIX (1969): 371, 375.

Turkomans of Khiva against Iran.[159] According to a contemporary chronicle quoted by the same writer, Mīrzā Yaᶜqūb went as far as Bukhara and incited the Uzbeks to attack Khorasan. From Bukhara, he intended to proceed to Afghanistan, similarly to incite the Afghans against Iran. Before he was able to do so, the Uzbeks became suspicious of his intentions, imprisoned him, and released him only when he undertook to leave the Emirate of Bukhara immediately. This he did, and made his way to Russia.[160] It is certain only that whatever route he took, Mīrzā Yaᶜqūb was in Istanbul by the time Malkum arrived there in 1864.

The evidence supplied by Sāsānī for Mīrzā Yaᶜqūb's alleged Central Asian activities is inconclusive, and it has not proved possible to find any material that would either support or refute his assertions. It is true that after the suppression of the Indian uprising of 1857, the British turned their attention to Central Asia, a region they had for some time neglected, and where the Russians were making signs of resuming their expansionist advance after an interval occasioned by the Crimean War.[161] The British were doubtless sending their agents into Central Asia at the time when Mīrzā Yaᶜqūb was banished from Iran, but it is unlikely that they should have entrusted a mission of any importance to one who had so recently transferred his loyalties from the service of the rival imperialism, that of Russia. It is moreover improbable that British interests would have been served at this point by a Turkoman or Uzbek invasion of Khorasan: Iranian ambitions in Herat had finally been checked, and the maintenance of some semblance of Iranian sovereignty over the Turkomans appeared advisable as at least a legal barrier to further Russian advance into Central Asia.[162]

The circumstances under which Malkum Khān was obliged to leave Iran were also connected, in part, with the affairs of Central Asia. In 1861, a military expedition under Ḥusām us-Salṭana, the frustrated victor of Herat, had set out against Marv, a once great city which had sunk to the rank of a gathering point for the Tekke Turkomans on their plundering raids into Khorasan. His army was defeated by an inferior force, and thousands of Iranian soldiers were taken captive.[163] It appears

159. *Ibid.*, p. 39.

160. *Ibid.*, p. 147.

161. Firuz Kazemzadeh, *Russia and Britain in Persia 1864–1914* (New Haven, 1968), p. 7.

162. According to Ṭabāṭabāʾī (*Majmūᶜa-yi Āthār*, p. i), Mīrzā Yaᶜqūb had gathered information for the Russians in Turkistan before his return to Iran from the Far East and the birth of Malkum. Bozorg Alavi in his *Geschichte und Entwicklung der modernen persischen Literatur* (Berlin, 1964), p. 64, asserts similarly that Mīrzā Yaᶜqūb traveled in Russia and Central Asia, but gives no supporting evidence.

163. Mustaufī, *op. cit.* (n.31, above), I: 93–95.

that Malkum thought himself possessed not only of political, economic, legal, and administrative talent, but also of military skill, for he had offered to command the expedition against Marv. When the expedition failed, he was unsparing in his criticism of those responsible, in particular Mīrzā Muḥammad Khān Sipahsālār. To stifle the criticism, the sipahsālār began agitating for his banishment from Iran.[164]

Malkum was in any event pursuing a course liable to bring about his exile, if not worse. He continued to circulate his writings, and even to maintain, in secret, a successor organization to the proscribed farāmūshkhāna, called the *Jāmiᶜa-yi Ādamīyat* (The Society of Humanity).[165] He may have been even more daring, for, according to a contemporary chronicle, in the same year that he was banished (1278/1861–1862), a number of unidentified persons were found to have formed a conspiracy.[166] This, taken together with Malkum's probably exaggerated statement that some of his followers sought to kill Nāṣir ud-Dīn Shāh,[167] suggests that he may indeed have had a conspiratorial plan to bring himself to immediate prominence and power in the affairs of Iran.

Before any such plan could be executed, Malkum was banished, or, as he put it, "I asked permission to travel."[168] Together with a number of other persons accused of heresy and irreligion, such as Mīrzā Ḥabīb Iṣfahānī, he was put over the Ottoman border at Khanaqin, whence he made his way to Baghdad.[169] His first confident attempts at satisfying personal ambition and at carrying through a comprehensive reform in Iran had failed. Malkum's services to Iran, however, were by no means at an end.

164. *Majmūᶜa-yi Āthār*, p. ix.

165. *Ibid.*, Mirza Kazem Beg, "Bab et les Babis," *Journal Asiatique*, VIII (1866): 339. The author of the treatises circulating in Tehran is not named, but it is obvious that it is Malkum who is intended ("the description of a certain dream written in a captivating style and, we are informed, recently presented to the king by an influential man of state, has elicited a lively reaction in Tehran").

166. Quoted by Sāsānī, *op. cit.* (n. 1, above), I: 146–147.

167. Blunt, *op. cit.* (n. 14, above), p. 84.

168. *Ibid.*

169. Sāsānī, *op. cit.*, p. 128; *Majmūᶜa-yi Āthār*, p. ix.

CHAPTER 3

Baghdad and the surrounding area traditionally known as Arab Iraq have exercised a constant influence on the affairs of Iran. This influence has been due only in part to geographical proximity and to the traditional role of Mesopotamia as a link between the Iranian cultural sphere and the Arab lands to the west. Since the promulgation of Shiᶜism as state religion of Iran at the beginning of the sixteenth century, it has been above all the religious significance of the area that has enabled it both to attract and to influence Iranians. In Iraq are situated the *ᶜatabāt-i ᶜālīyāt*, the sublime thresholds, these being the tombs of ᶜAlī ibn Abī Ṭālib, the first Imam of the Shiᶜa, in Najaf, his martyred son Ḥusayn in Karbalā, and the ninth and eleventh Imams in Kāẓimayn. At Samarra, somewhat to the north, is the cellar where the twelfth and last of the Imams went into occultation, whence he shall emerge to inaugurate a reign of perfect justice before the coming of the apocalypse.

For reasons both religious and strategic the Safavids attempted to gain control of the region and were temporarily successful: the holy places seemed to be safely incorporated into the realm of the sole existing Shiᶜi state, and the westernmost boundaries of the Sasanid empire were more or less reestablished by the first national state to emerge in Iran since the coming of Islam. Even though Ottoman rule reasserted itself and became permanent, the successors of the Safavids made several attempts to conquer the ᶜatabāt for Iran. Nādir Shāh, who sought to end the separation of Shiᶜism from the main body of Islam, may be presumed to have acted primarily for strategic reasons; yet for Karīm Khān-i Zand, the expedition to Iraq had religious significance.[1]

It was precisely the failure of these efforts to wrest the ᶜatabāt from

1. G.A. Olivier, *Voyage dans l'Empire Othoman, l'Egypte et la Perse* (Paris, 1802), III: 335.

the Ottoman Empire that made it possible for them to serve as places of refuge for those fleeing the confusion and anarchy of eighteenth-century Iran. Formerly the ᶜatabāt had been above all places of pilgrimage and only secondarily centers of religious learning: the madrasas of Isfahan and the jurists and theosophists gathered there outshone all the ᶜatabāt could offer. The turbulence of the eighteenth century saw, however, the mainstream of Shiᶜi religious life diverted to the safety and sanctity of the ᶜatabāt. The only scholars to attain prominence during the interregnum between the Safavids and the Qajars lived and worked in Arab Iraq, and it was there too, toward the end of the century, that a theological dispute of some importance took place. The controversy centered on the position and function of the *mujtahid,* the scholar of the religious law who may exercise independent judgment with respect to matters of practice, subject to certain qualifications; obedience to his example is therefore incumbent upon those less learned in the law. A group known as the Akhbārīs disputed the legitimacy of the mujtahid's function, and for a time their view predominated in the ᶜatabāt. They were ultimately defeated by a scholar named Āqā Muḥammad Bāqir Bihbihānī (1705–1803), who established the governing principles of Shiᶜi jurisprudence that were to be followed throughout the nineteenth century.[2] The institution of mujtahid, by the manipulation of which Malkum expected to accomplish so much, was thus preserved and reinforced on the eve of Qajar rule.

Although the Qajars expressed their devotion to the holy places chiefly through the dispatch of costly gifts and ornaments,[3] they too found themselves militarily involved in the area containing the ᶜatabāt. Three wars took place with the Ottomans, in 1804, 1812 and 1818, and hostilities were each time concentrated on Arab Iraq.[4] Iran no longer hoped, however, to gain direct control of the ᶜatabāt. The wars were caused rather by minor frontier disputes and the activities of the Kurdish tribes on both sides of the frontier. The frontier was demarcated and its maintenance hardly in doubt, for the European powers now active in the region reserved to themselves the right of territorial conquest.

Arab Iraq nonetheless remained a point of interaction and on occasion friction between the Ottoman Empire and Iran. Despite the re-

2. On these developments, see Hamid Algar, *Religion and State in Iran, 1785–1906: the Role of the Ulama in the Qajar Period* (Berkeley and Los Angeles, 1969), pp. 33–36.

3. Thus Fatḥ ᶜAlī Shāh (1797–1834) provided for the domes of the shrines at Karbalā and Kazimayn to be gilded. See ᶜImād ud-Dīn Ḥusayn Iṣfahānī, *Tārīkh-i Jughrāfiyāʾī-yi Karbalā-yi Muᶜallā* (Tehran, 1326 solar/1947), p. 130.

4. Algar, *op. cit.,* pp. 53–54.

establishment of security in Iran and the partial revival there of centers of religious learning, the Iranian population of the ᶜatabāt showed no signs of decreasing. Most of the influential ulama continued to reside there, a circumstance particularly important when toward the end of the century they began to oppose actively the Iranian government. It was not only scholars and pilgrims who gathered at the ᶜatabāt: Karbalā in particular had become a refuge for thieves and brigands from both Iran and Arab Iraq. Their warlike independence, together with Iranian predominance in the city, enabled Karbalā to attain the status almost of an Iranian enclave in Ottoman territory. In January 1843, Najīb Pāshā, the governor of Baghdad, forcefully reduced Karbalā to obedience in an operation that claimed over four thousand lives and raised the danger of renewed war with Iran.[5]

When Malkum found himself banished to Baghdad, he was then in an area by no means totally cut off from Iranians and Iranian affairs. Baghdad offered the possibility for continued activity among Iranians subject to interruption only by Ottoman control and supervision. This had been demonstrated shortly before his arrival by the temporary addition of a new element to the Iranian population of the area. Following an attempt on the life of Nāṣir ud-Dīn Shāh by four Babis in 1852 and the succeeding wave of persecution, a number of the leaders of the movement had been pushed across the Ottoman border, among them Mīrzā Ḥusayn ᶜAlī Nūrī, the future "Bahāʾullāh." After an initial period of residence in Sulaymānīya, in 1276/1859–1860 Mīrzā Ḥusayn ᶜAlī came to Baghdad and attempted to spread Babism among the Iranian pilgrims and residents at the ᶜatabāt.[6] When Malkum arrived in Baghdad, late in 1861, the Babis were still active, and in the same way accusations of Babi affiliation have been raised against the farāmūshkhāna, so too Malkum has been suspected of collaboration with the Babis during this first stage of his exile.[7] The suspicion is perhaps well founded, although Malkum himself admits only to having "gained new converts from among the Persian and Bagdad Shiahs."[8] In addition, a letter from the Ottoman Ministry of Foreign Affairs justifying his removal from Baghdad makes no mention of any contact with the Babis. Exiled and disgraced as he was, Malkum, however, could have had few

5. *Ibid.*, pp. 114–115; and ᶜAbbās al-ᶜAzzāwī, *Tārīkh al-ᶜIrāq bayn Iḥtilālayn* (Baghdad, 1383 lunar/1953–1954), VI: 288.

6. Khān Malik Sāsānī, *Yādbūdhā-yi Safārat-i Istānbūl* (Tehran, 1345 solar/1966), pp. 240–242.

7. Ibrāhīm Taymūrī, *ᶜAṣr-i Bīkhabarī yā Tārīkh-i Imtiyāzāt dar Īrān* (Tehran, 1336 solar/1957), p. 64.

8. W.S. Blunt, *Secret History of the English Occupation of Egypt* (London, 1907), p. 84.

reservations about making common cause with the Babis who found themselves in a somewhat similar position. Certainly religious scruples could not have hindered him. Malkum had evidently been impressed with the fortitude of many of the victims of the persecution of 1852, which he had had occasion to witness shortly after his first return from Europe.[9] Moreover, he shared certain important traits with the Babi leaders, notably a marked tendency to messianic pretensions and sacred titles, a tendency he was more successful in muting than was Mīrzā Ḥusayn ᶜAlī Nurī.[10] Babism, as a movement taking its starting point within Islam and then swiftly going beyond its bounds, might also in a certain sense be thought of as a "reform" of Islam, parallel to Malkum's own project of an "Islamic renaissance." Malkum's plan, like Babism, entailed the use of Islamic terminology for purposes fundamentally alien to the Islamic faith. That a certain community of purpose existed between Malkum and the Babis is indicated by the fact that in later years Malkum came to be spoken of approvingly in Babi circles in Istanbul,[11] and received a letter from a Babi leader congratulating him on the publication of *Qānūn*.[12]

The most important piece of circumstantial evidence for collaboration between Malkum and the Babis is the fact that both were expelled from Baghdad at approximately the same time. Malkum's expulsion took place first, probably in April or May 1862. From Baghdad, he went via Diyarbekir to Istanbul, where he found a new and rich field of activity awaiting him. Somewhat later, following repeated representations by the consulate in Baghdad, the Iranian ambassador in Istanbul, Mīrzā Ḥusayn Khān, prevailed on the Ottoman government to have Mīrzā Ḥusayn ᶜAlī and the Babis removed to a place more distant from Iran and less thickly populated with Iranians than Baghdad. They left the city in the autumn of 1862.[13] There may, of course, have been little or no contact between Malkum and the Babis and their expulsion from Baghdad in the same year simply the result of a general decision of the Ottoman government to rid the area of subversive elements.

It is in any event clear that Malkum's activities in Baghdad were severely disturbing to the Ottoman government. This is evident from a long letter justifying his expulsion, written by the Ottoman Ministry of Foreign Affairs to its ambassador in Tehran, Haydar Efendi. The

9. *Ibid.,* p. 83.

10. See below, p. 226.

11. Undated letter of Mīrzā Āqā Khān Kirmānī to Malkum Khān in Bibliothèque Nationale, Supplément Persan 1996, ff. 123–124.

12. Undated and unsigned letter in Supplément Persan 1996, ff. 133–134.

13. Sāsānī, *op. cit.,* pp. 241–242. On links between Babis and freemasonry in general, see Saᶜīd Nafīsī, *Dar Nīma-rāh-i Bihisht* (Tehran, 1344 solar/1965), p. 47.

ambassador, probably at the urging of Malkum's associates in Tehran, had sent on 10 Muḥarram 1279/8 July 1862 the following memorandum to the Bâb-ı Âlî:

> Malkum Khān's forceful expulsion from Baghdad and summoning to the capital have created an impression among the Iranians that the Lofty [Ottoman] State is somewhat weak when faced with the Iranian government. This matter is spoken of openly in the streets, and even some of the foreign ambassadors are saying that it is not fitting for the aforementioned khan, who had resigned from government service and left his country, to be expelled from Baghdad. Anyone who is not a criminal ought normally be allowed to reside anywhere with the utmost freedom. In addition, the consent to this matter of the Lofty State will not have any effect on the policies and actions of the Iranian government. In our opinion, the return of the aforementioned khan to Baghdad will be extremely beneficial.[14]

The implication that the Ottoman authorities had acted in compliance with Iranian demands was resented in Istanbul, and the memorandum received a harsh and explicit reply. The draft of this reply—all that is at our disposal—is not signed. Mehmed Emin Âlî Paşa (1815–1871) was at this time minister of foreign affairs, and since on a later occasion he showed hostility to Malkum, it is almost certain that he was the author of the draft.[15] Haydar Efendi's memorandum of 10 Muḥarram/8 July was evidently not the first he had sent, for the reply opens with a justification of failure to respond earlier:

> By virtue of my sincere regard for you, I chose to remain silent. Your misconceived and erroneous memorandum forces me however to reply. First, it is well known to everyone that through the grace of God Almighty and the fortune of His Majesty the Ottoman State is not so terrified of Iran that it has to agree to every demand made upon it. This most contemptible slave, however much he may be deprived of his share of perspicacity, still imagines that he has not taken leave of his senses so far as to fail to perceive so obvious a truth. As for my submitting to indignity and dishonor, there is without doubt not the least possibility thereof.

The writer then proceeds to admit that he sees no purpose in refusing to settle, peacefully and honorably, any problem raised by the

14. The letter is now in the library of the Hoover Institute at Stanford University (Derelioğlu Collection). I am grateful to Professor Nikki Keddie for drawing my attention to this document.

15. Mehmet Galib seems to have had access to the very same document which, as he says, consists of Haydar Efendi's letter together with the unsigned draft of Âlî Pasa's reply written on the same sheet of paper ("Tarihten bir Sahife: Âlî ve Fuad Paşaların Vasiyetnameleri," *Tarih-i Osmani Encümeni Mecmuası*, I [1329 lunar/1911]: 73).

Iranian government. Even though the perpetual hostility of Iran would not injure the glory of the Ottoman Empire by so much as an atom, nonetheless he cannot deny wishing to bring about an improvement of relations with Iran. On the other hand, Iranian failure to appreciate the conciliatory behavior of the Ottoman government would meet with an appropriate response. With these ponderous preliminaries over, he turns to the question of Malkum Khān:

> As for the matter of Malqūn [Malkum] Khān, this man is an extremely mischievous agitator. In Tehran, he opened masonic lodges [*franmasunhaneler*][16] and engaged in all kinds of evil activity against the state and the monarchy. His father, acting as an agent for certain circles, attempted to disrupt relations between Iran and the Ottoman State. In short, both of them, father and son, are extremely subversive and dangerous persons. This you yourself have written on several occasions, and you will doubtless remember having informed the governor of Baghdad of the matter in a similar vein. Such being the case, by leaving this agitator in a place like Baghdad, populated by different races and religions and situated near the frontier, would we not be neglecting the prime duty of the state, namely farsightedness and caution? Would one who has incited the people to harm the person and the government of a monarch whose kindness and generosity he has himself experienced hesitate to work for the downfall of this government? Who can guarantee that if he were permitted to settle in Baghdad he would not open up a masonic lodge, leading astray empty-headed Arabs, Iranians, and Kurds and causing great disturbance to the state? It is in view of considerations such as these that he has been brought here, and not, as Your Excellency wrongly imagines, out of obedience to some command of the Iranian government. For the reasons set forth, his return to Baghdad can definitely not be regarded as permissible.

The frank and categorical nature of this reply was probably determined by an awareness that Haydar Efendi had been acting at the instigation of Malkum's associates in Tehran. While the letter does not openly accuse him of so doing, its discreet silence on the matter was doubtless inspired by the wish to spare him needless embarrassment. We may accept the assertion that the Ottoman government was not acting out of deference to Iranian requests when it removed Malkum from Baghdad and that it was genuinely concerned about the mischief he might wreak among "empty-headed Arabs, Iranians, and Kurds." The Ottomans were probably more concerned than the Iranian au-

16. It is ironic that Âlî Paşa, who implicitly condemned Malkum for masonic activity, is himself reputed to have been a mason (Roderic H. Davison, *Reform in the Ottoman Empire, 1856–1876* [Princeton, 1963]: pp. 70, 417). This suggests that Âlî Paşa took care to conceal his masonic affiliations. It may also indicate that, as a member of a regular lodge, he scorned Malkum as a charlatan who misused the masonic institution.

thorities with Malkum's activities: shortly before his transfer to Istanbul they informed Mīrzā Ḥusayn Khān that "this man is an agitator and his presence in Arab Iraq will lead to disorder" and requested Iranian agreement for his removal from Baghdad to Istanbul.[17]

Nonetheless, the account given of Malkum's activity in Tehran suggests that the Iranian government had been in contact with the Ottoman Ministry of Foreign Affairs concerning the agitator of whom they had rid themselves. It is particularly interesting to note that Malkum is accused of inciting the people against both "the person and the government" of Nāṣir ud-Dīn Shāh. While this accusation may simply reflect information supplied by the Iranian authorities, it may be another indication of some kind of conspiracy organized by Malkum before his banishment. It is further asserted that Mīrzā Yaᶜqūb, "acting as an agent for certain circles, attempted to disrupt relations between Iran and the Ottoman State." Whether by "certain circles" a foreign power is meant is not clear from the context. If this is the intended meaning, it will not be the first time we have seen Mīrzā Yaᶜqūb accused of acting as agent for a foreign government. Because it has not proved possible to determine the exact date on which Mīrzā Yaᶜqūb entered the Ottoman Empire after his banishment from Iran, nor even to confirm that his supposed adventures in Central Asia took place, we cannot profitably speculate on his attempted disruption of Iranian-Ottoman relations. It seems most likely that his motive would have been to secure his own and Malkum's return to Iran.

Upon his arrival in Istanbul, Malkum displayed his usual resourcefulness and refused to resign himself to a life of obscurity. Undeterred by the fact that the ambassador, Mīrzā Ḥusayn Khān, had been advised of his subversive character, not only by the Ottoman authorities but also—presumably—by the Iranian Ministry of Foreign Affairs, Malkum promptly presented himself at the Iranian embassy. He assured Mīrzā Ḥusayn Khān that he had established the farāmūshkhāna on the explicit instructions of Nāṣir ud-Dīn Shāh and submitted to the monarch a daily report on its activities. Later, however, the shah had changed his mind and ordered the dissolution of the farāmūshkhāna and the exiling of Malkum. Mīrzā Ḥusayn Khān duly reported Malkum's statements to Tehran and was informed in reply that Nāṣir ud-Dīn Shāh had nothing against Malkum and did not regard him as

17. Letter of Mīrzā Ḥusayn Khān to the Iranian Ministry of Foreign Affairs quoted by Firīdūn Ādamīyat in *Fikr-i Āzādī va Muqaddima-yi Nihḍat-i Mashrūṭīyat* (Tehran, 1340 solar/1961), p. 96. The date of the letter given by Ādamīyat, 23 Rābīᶜ ul-Avval 1286/ 3 July 1869, seems to be erroneous. By 1869 Malkum was in the service of the Iranian embassy in Istanbul, and the whole episode of his disgrace and banishment was behind him.

guilty of any offence.[18] It is interesting to speculate on the reasons for this reply. It may be that Nāṣir ud-Dīn Shāh found himself regretting Malkum's departure and that his belief in Malkum's intelligence and capacity had overcome the doubts and suspicions aroused in part by Malkum's enemies. Nāṣir ud-Dīn Shāh appears to have been on occasion a kindly and forgiving person, despite the acts of persecution and cruelty carried out in his name at various times. It may have been this mixture of admiration and generosity that benefited Malkum on this occasion.

Evidently Malkum also succeeded in impressing Mīrzā Ḥusayn Khān, for on receipt of the answer from Tehran clearing Malkum of all guilt in the eyes of the government, he wrote and proposed that some post be allotted to him in order that some use might be made of his talents. In Jumādī uth-Thānī 1279/November-December 1863, he was appointed Iranian Consul-General in Egypt.[19] This post hardly corresponded to his wishes. Egypt, though later in the century one of the centers to which Iranian merchants emigrated in considerable numbers, in the 1860s did not offer a field of activity comparable to Istanbul, where a large Iranian community already existed. Cairo, moreover, could hardly compete at this date with Istanbul as a center of intellectual and political activity, and Malkum clearly came to appreciate the life of the Ottoman capital and the acquaintances he enjoyed with Ottoman notables. Finally, Malkum may well have foreseen that his association with the embassy in Istanbul would enable him to return to position and prominence in Iran, whereas the consulate-general in Cairo was a backwater where he might be stranded for years.[20] Thus it was that he either never assumed his post in Egypt,[21] or returned to Istanbul after an extremely brief period.[22]

Mīrzā Ḥusayn Khān did his best to obtain a more acceptable post for Malkum. He wrote to the Ministry of Foreign Affairs in Tehran that "much benefit may be had of him in the diplomatic service," and that "I know myself that whatever post you bestow upon him, Iran

18. Khān Malik Sāsānī, *Siyāsatgarān-i Daura-yi Qājār* (Tehran, 1337 solar/1958), I: 128–129.

19. *Ibid.*, I: 129; Ādamīyat, *op. cit.*, p. 96.

20. Sir Richard Burton, in his *Personal Narrative of a Pilgrimage to Al-Madinah and Meccah* (New York, 1893), I: 86–87, gives a graphic description of his visit, in 1853, to the "sign of the Lion and Sun" in Cairo.

21. Ādamīyat, *op. cit.*, p. 96.

22. Sāsānī, *Siyāsatgarān-i Daura-yi Qājār*, I: 129. According to Ṭabāṭabāʾi (*Majmūʿa-yi Āthār*, p. x), the accusation has been made that Malkum assumed his post in Egypt but because of an improper gift of 10,000 tūmāns from Ismāʿīl Pāshā was swiftly recalled to Istanbul. He offers no opinion on the justice of the accusation, which does not occur in any other account of Malkum's life.

will have no cause to regret it." He suggested that Malkum be appointed chargé d'affaires in Paris to replace Ḥasan ʿAlī Khān Garrūsī who had been recalled to Tehran, but the suggestion was not adopted. It was finally agreed to the satisfaction of all concerned that Malkum should remain in Istanbul as counsellor at the Iranian embassy. As visible sign of his new status, he took up quarters in the embassy with the blessing of Mīrzā Ḥusayn Khān.[23]

With his livelihood thus assured, Malkum felt himself in a position to marry and in the choice of a wife reverted to the Armenian community whence he and his father had sprung. His bride, Henriette, was the daughter of Arakel Bey Topçubaşı, a prominent member of the Armenian community of Istanbul, and the marriage took place in an Armenian church, Aya Stefanos, on 30 October 1864. According to one account, the marriage was preceded by a ceremony at the Armenian patriarchate in which Malkum formally abjured Islam and declared his allegiance to Christianity.[24]

Mīrzā Ḥusayn Khān came to hear of Malkum's Christian marriage and summoned him to discuss the matter. He reproached him with hypocrisy for having made a show of allegiance to Islam for so many years and in particular for having prayed during a pilgrimage to the ʿatabāt they had shortly before undertaken. Malkum replied that he had always been convinced that the affairs of the world were determined by reason and foresight, but that now he believed fate to be the arbiter of the world, and fate had determined his marriage to the Armenian woman.[25] This ingenious answer certainly has the ring of Malkum's manner of argumentation and seems to have been his polite and discreet way of explaining to Mīrzā Ḥusayn Khān that religious formalities–Muslim or Christian–were of little importance to him. There was, admittedly, nothing unusual in marriages between high-ranking Iranians and Christian women, whether Armenian or Georgian. The custom had been especially prevalent in the Safavid period, and though curtailed somewhat by the loss of the Caucasian provinces to Russia, persisted into the late nineteenth century. It was usual, however, for the women to make a profession of Islam and for the children to be reared as Muslims, rather than for the father to embrace Christianity. Princess Henriette, as she later became, retained her Christian identity throughout her life,[26] and the three daughters born

23. Ādamīyat, *op. cit.*, p. 96.

24. *Majmūʿa-yi Āthār*, p. x; Sāsānī, *Siyāsatgarān-i Daura-yi Qājār*, I: 129.

25. *Ibid.*, quoting a dispatch of Mīrzā Ḥusayn Khān to the Iranian Ministry of Foreign Affairs dated 7 Jumādī ul-Avval 1281/17 September 1864.

26. Ḥājjī Pīrzāda Nāʾīnī, *Safarnāma*, ed. Ḥāfiẓ Farmānfarmāʾīān (Tehran, 1343 solar/1964), I: 294.

of the marriage, Victoria, Lila and Sultane, were raised as Christians.[27] The sole son born of the union, Firīdūn, is reputed to have professed Islam, like his father and grandfather before him.[28]

Malkum's position at the embassy was able to withstand the shock caused by his apostatic marriage, but soon after came to be threatened from another direction. Differences arose between Malkum and the Ministry of Foreign Affairs in Tehran, for which various explanations have been offered. According to the account of Sāsānī, Malkum became dissatisfied with his lowly post in Istanbul and demanded that he be sent as plenipotentiary to London, threatening to reveal state secrets to the Ottomans unless his demands were met.[29] It has, on the other hand, been asserted that Mīrzā Saʿīd Khān Muʾtaman ul-Mulk, Iranian minister of foreign affairs, attempted to deprive Malkum of his post, even going so far as to cut off his salary.[30] Mīrzā Saʿīd Khān had been one of the chief opponents of the administrative reorganization that to some degree was associated with Malkum and also a leading adversary of the farāmūshkhāna. It is thus conceivable that he should now have tried to frustrate Malkum's return to government service, particularly in the sphere of foreign affairs under his control. The offer to Malkum of the undesirable post in Cairo and the refusal to send him as chargé d'affaires to Paris may also be attributed to Mīrzā Saʿīd Khān's continuing hostility. Given Malkum's temperament, it is however equally plausible that he should have suddenly demanded a transfer to London and attached a threat to his demand. Both explanations for his differences with Tehran are probably correct: Malkum's rash behavior gave his antagonist precisely what he desired—a pretext for his dismissal. The pattern was to be repeated with Amīn us-Sulṭān in the case of the celebrated Lottery Concession.

In 1285/1868, Malkum saw himself obliged to quit the service of the Iranian embassy. He moved to a house in Rumeli Hisar on the shore of the Bosphorus and with the help of his Ottoman friends, above all the minister, Fuad Paşa, obtained Ottoman nationality, the rank of colonel, a monthly salary of 120 *tūmāns*, and the offer of a post at the Bâb-ı Âlî.[31] Fuad Paşa evidently offered Malkum a post as counsellor in the ministry he headed, that of foreign affairs, but was overruled by Âlî Paşa who adamantly persisted in his distrust of Malkum. Âlî Paşa had

27. *Majmūʿa-yi Āthār*, p. xxii.

28. *Ibid.*

29. Sāsānī, *Siyāsatgarān-i Daura-yi Qājār*, I: 129.

30. Ādamīyat, *op. cit.*, p. 97.

31. *Ibid.* See too the letter of Mīrzā Yūsuf Khān Mustashār ud-Daula, Iranian ambassador in Paris, to Ākhūndzāda dated May 8, 1868, in *Alifbā-yi Jadīd va Maktūbāt*, eds. Ḥ. Muḥammadzāda and Ḥ. Ārāslī (Baku, 1963), p. 373.

no objection to the employment of Armenians or other non-Muslims. During his own term as minister of foreign affairs, he appears even to have preferred to employ Armenian clerks,[32] and he was once satirically accused of preparing even to appoint a gypsy as prime minister.[33] He evidently saw no reason, however, to revise his original estimate of Malkum as a subversive and dangerous person.

Where the efforts of one influential friend failed, those of another succeeded. Mīrzā Ḥusayn Khān exerted himself, as before, on behalf of Malkum and was soon able to have him reinstated in the embassy, presumably on terms satisfactory to him.[34] Malkum probably had little intention of staying permanently in Ottoman service, and the attempt to join the Ottoman Ministry of Foreign Affairs may have been little more than a manoeuver designed somehow to reinforce his position with regard to Mīrzā Saᶜīd Khān. Having before him at least the possibility of alternative employment, he was able to negotiate with Mīrzā Saᶜīd Khān and, perhaps, to threaten him with the revelation of state secrets to another power. After this episode, Malkum remained undisturbed in his post at the embassy until Mīrzā Ḥusayn Khān's recall to Iran in 1871.

This association in Istanbul of Malkum and Mīrzā Ḥusayn Khān, later continued in Iran, was the expression of a common interest in reform as well as a personal friendship. It is difficult to establish precisely what duties fell to Malkum as counsellor at the Iranian embassy and to what degree he was able to influence Mīrzā Ḥusayn Khān's outlook or was, on the contrary, affected by him. It is likely that Mīrzā Ḥusayn Khān, no less than Malkum, was independently and separately predisposed to the cause of reform and westernization, and it was these common convictions of the two men, strengthened by their experiences in Istanbul, that enabled them to establish a community of interest and outlook.

Born in 1243/1827–1828, Mīrzā Ḥusayn Khān, like Malkum, had studied in Paris in his youth and been the object of Amīr Kabīr's sympathetic attention. When only twenty-three years old, he was appointed Iranian chargé d'affaires in Bombay and three years later transferred to serve as consul-general in Tiflis. In 1275/1858–1859 began his long term of office as ambassador in Istanbul, a period that left a deep impression on him. It was the era of the Tanzimat, those attempts to

32. Mahmud Kemal İnal, *Osmanlı Devrinde Son Sadrıazamlar* (Istanbul, 1940), I: 38.

33. By Ziya Paşa in his "Zafername." See E.J.W. Gibb, *History of Ottoman Poetry* (London, 1907), V: 106–107 (English translation of the poem); VI: 374 (its Turkish text).

34. Ādamīyat, *op. cit.* (n.17, above), p. 97.

reshape the administrative and political structure of the Ottoman Empire that had begun with the military innovations of Sultan Selim III in the late eighteenth century. Mīrzā Ḥusayn Khān arrived in Istanbul some two years after the issue of the *Hatt-ı Hümâyûn,* the Imperial Rescript, a document proclaiming Muslim and non-Muslim subjects of the empire to have certain equal rights and obligations vis-à-vis the state. Largely dictated by British pressure, the Hatt-ı Hümâyûn was in part also the work of two Ottoman statesmen who dominated the second part of the Tanzimat era now inaugurated, Âlî Paşa and Fuad Paşa.[35] The two men occupied alternately the posts of prime minister and foreign minister throughout most of the period of Mīrzā Ḥusayn Khān's embassy in Istanbul, and he appears to have enjoyed their acquaintance. He reported with notable enthusiasm of their various reform measures to the Ministry of Foreign Affairs in Tehran. He approved in particular of the appointment of non-Muslims to government posts (a consequence of the application of the Hatt-ı Hümâyûn), of the foundation of a council of state (*meclis-i şûrâ-yı devlet*), of the establishment of the Mekteb-i Sultani *lycée* (later renamed Galatasaray Lisesi), and of the planned railway line to link Iskenderun with Basra. He recognized too that many of these measures were the result of unrelenting foreign pressure on the Ottoman Empire, and from this realization was later born his own foreign policy for an Iran he thought to be in a similar position.[36]

For Malkum Khān too, the affairs of the Ottoman Empire were full of significance for Iran. Already in his first treatises, composed in Tehran, he had implicitly borne witness to this significance by the use of terms borrowed from Ottoman Turkish such as *tanẓīmāt* and *qānūn*. Elsewhere he gave full recognition to the interest of Ottoman affairs for Iran and invited the Iranian men of state to acquaint themselves with developments in the neighboring empire. In his treatise *Pūlītīkhā-yi Daulatī* (International politics), he claimed that Ottoman affairs were linked to those of Iran in a thousand different ways and lamented that those who could profit by studying them persisted in neglecting them.[37]

While in Istanbul, Malkum composed at least three new treatises: *Mabdaʾ-i Taraqqī* (The principle of progress);[38] *Shaykh va Vazīr* (The

35. On the Hatt-ı Hümayun and the circumstances surrounding it, see Davison, *op. cit.* (n. 16, above), pp. 52–80; on the career of Âlî Paşa, İnal, *op. cit.*, I: 4–58; and on that of Fuad Paşa, the article by Orhan Köprülü in *İslam Ansiklopedisi*, IV: 672–681.

36. Ādamīyat, *op. cit.* (n.17, above), pp. 58–75; and below, pp. 113–114.

37. *Kullīyat-i Malkum*, ed. Hāshim Rabīʿzāda (Tabriz, 1325 lunar/1908), p. 160.

38. Mentioned in *Majmūʿa-yi Āthār*, p. x.

shaykh and the minister), a dialogue on the subject of alphabet reform discussed in the next chapter; and *Dastgāh-i Dīvān* (The organ of state). We will consider here the contents of this last treatise, a somewhat incoherent piece of writing and certainly not among the best of Malkum's production.

There is little in *Dastgāh-i Dīvān* not previously adumbrated in *Kitābcha-yi Ghaybī* and its supplementary treatises. Apart from the impression left on Malkum by the Ottoman reforms, it may be assumed his continuing interest in affecting the affairs of Iran and in resuming participation in a program of reform were the dominant motives for its composition. He begins by justifying his advocacy of reform and by asserting that each individual should regard himself as responsible for the welfare of the state.[39] He then laments that clear qualifications and prerequisites for the various posts of state do not exist and that this in itself discourages the ambitious and talented from pursuing a course of study useful to their future careers. Malkum observes, probably with justice:

> On the one hand, we condemn European learning so thoroughly that we regard our own innate intelligence as superior to all the sciences of Europe, while on the other hand, if anyone spends a few days wandering the streets of Europe, we consider him a compendium of knowledge and an authority for the investigation of all matters. If simply residing in Paris be a proof of intelligence, then all the laborers of that city must be geniuses![40]

Malkum had, of course, clearly resolved the question in his own mind and decided on the absolute primacy of European learning and example. To illustrate his contention that intelligence without European learning is not enough, he points to the case of Reşid Efendi, the newly appointed Ottoman ambassador to Iran, whose innate capacities have not fully developed because of his failure to study European science.[41]

Somewhat abruptly, he then passes to an unconvincing eulogy of Mīrzā Saʿīd Khān.

> I consider him to be the noblest of the truly noble. As for his purity of disposition and clarity of intellect, it is enough to say that despite his proximity to the monarch, he has not wounded the feelings of a single adversary. We must consider the advancement of such persons in Iran to be a matter for self-congratulation. Now the means for his education are available on all sides, and let us see how matters will be determined by the fortune of the state. I sincerely desire the progress of this young man of pure disposition, through the fortune of our auspicious monarch.[42]

39. *Ibid.*, pp. 74–75.
40. *Ibid.*, pp. 75–78.
41. *Ibid.*, p. 79.
42. *Ibid.*, p. 81.

These sentences become comprehensible when we recall that Mīrzā Saᶜīd Khān, at about the time of the composition of the treatise, was attempting to cut off Malkum's salary and to force him out of his post at the embassy. Malkum clearly hoped to placate him with flattery, while at the same time obliquely offering to furnish him with "the means of education," *i.e.*, to dictate policy from his heights of learning and wisdom. Evidently Malkum was caught here between two conflicting desires—to flatter Mīrzā Saᶜīd Khān and to flatter himself.

Having criticized an opponent of Mīrzā Saᶜīd Khān, Mīrzā Yūsuf Mustaufī ul-Mamālik,[43] he proceeds to praise Nāṣir ud-Dīn Shāh, presumably in an effort to erase the last unpleasant memory left behind by the episode of the farāmūshkhāna. Among Nāṣir ud-Dīn Shāh's praiseworthy innovations, he chooses for special mention the *dīvān-ī maẓālim*, a body set up to hear complaints against government officials. The functioning of the body has, however, been hindered by the obstruction and shortsightedness of the ministers. Like other measures of reform, its efficacity is dependent upon the goodwill of individuals, rather than resting upon a firm institutional basis that will enable it to outlive its initiator.[44]

It would be better for Nāṣir ud-Dīn Shāh, who may fittingly be called the Peter the Great of Iran,[45] to turn his attention to truly essential matters. The numerous and largely idle princes should be put to work, the mullas and ulama be made subject to the control of the Ministry of Science, and the Ministries of Foreign Affairs and Justice be expanded. The income of the state should be increased, and the army strengthened. There is indeed no reason why the income of the state should not be increased to six million *tūmāns* a year.[46] As for the army, Iran must stop concentrating its attention on secondary matters such as drill and uniform, and turn instead to more primary considerations. These Malkum does not for the most part specify, asserting, as he did in *Tanẓīm-i Lashkar va Majlis-i Idāra*, that the execution of basic reforms in the structure of the state is a precondition of military reorganization. He does point out, however, that all members of the army should receive regular pay so that they are not obliged to take on additional work to secure their livelihood. Commanders should be acquainted with modern military technique, and some degree of military knowledge and training should be demanded of every officer. Most important, the army should be separately administered, without reference to the ministers and subject only to the shah and the law, and posts in the army should not be bought and sold.[47]

43. *Ibid.*, pp. 81–82.
44. *Ibid.*, p. 83.
45. *Ibid.*, p. 86.
46. *Ibid.*, pp. 84–88.
47. *Ibid.*, pp. 89–92.

Malkum concludes by repeating the need for a thorough reform of the state and by drawing attention to the condition of the Ottoman Empire:

> Profit from the example of the Ottoman Empire. . . . Iran, faced with the onslaught of European conquest, is not in the least different from the Ottoman Empire. Protection of the Christians [in the Ottoman Empire by the European powers] is only a secondary matter. The essential point is that the surging power of Europe has rendered impossible the survival of barbarian states. Henceforth all governments in the world will have to be ordered [*munaẓẓam*] like those of Europe, or to be subjugated and conquered by European power.[48]

Although this treatise points as much to Malkum's continuing concern with Iranian affairs and his future prospects in influencing them as it does to the influence of his Ottoman environment, Malkum regarded his stay in Istanbul as something more than an exile patiently to be endured. Even after returning to the service of the Iranian embassy, he retained his Ottoman nationality at least until his departure for Iran in 1871.[49] His interest in Ottoman affairs was not always passive, and he appears to have involved himself, though not to any great effect, in the politics of Istanbul. His ability to do so was in part due to his position at the Iranian embassy, which throughout the residence of Mīrzā Ḥusayn Khān enjoyed good relations with Ottoman officialdom. According to Sāsānī, these relations were secured largely by an Iranian dervish who had joined the retinue of the embassy, a certain Ḥājjī Mīrzā Ṣafā. He consorted not only with members of the numerous Sufi orders in Istanbul, but also with men of state such as Âlî Paşa and Fuad Paşa, inclining them favorably to Shiᶜism.[50] We have seen, however, that Mīrzā Ḥusayn Khān observed the reforms taking place in the Ottoman Empire with great approval, and it is probable that a shared interest in reform was at least as effective in promoting good relations with the Ottoman government as the activity of Ḥājjī Mīrzā Ṣafā. Malkum, although acquainted with a dervish resident in Istanbul, Sayyid Burhān ud-Dīn Balkhī (known as the pīr of Afghan Turkistan),[51] owed his acquaintances with Ottoman men of state more to masonic than to mystic connections.

Although Malkum's farāmūshkhāna, established in 1858, was the

48. *Ibid.*, p. 95.

49. See Ākhūndzāda's letter to Malkum dated March 8, 1872 in *Alifbā-yi Jadīd va Maktūbāt*, pp. 278–281.

50. See Sāsānī, *Siyāsatgarān-i Daura-yi Qājār,* I: 60–62; the same author's *Yādbūdhā-yi Safārat,* p. 240; and the introduction by Īraj Afshār to Pīrzāda Nāʾīnī, *op. cit.* (n. 26, above), I: xiii-xiv.

51. Sāsānī, *Siyāsatgarān-i Daura-yi Qājār,* II: 283.

first masonic foundation in Iran, freemasonry in the Ottoman Empire had a longer history to which it could point. The first lodge had been founded toward the end of the eighteenth century in the reign of Sultan Selim III, and although it was suppressed as a result of reaction to the French Revolution, other masonic associations came into being to take its place. It was not, however, until the Crimean War and its aftermath that regular lodges emerged with men of political, literary, and social prominence among their members. The foremost of the first generation of Tanzimat statesmen, Mustafa Reşit Paşa (1800–1858) and the British ambassador, Lord Stratford de Redcliffe, cooperated in founding a lodge affiliated with the Scottish obedience.[52] At about the same time, a lodge authorized by the French Grand Orient was established, bearing the name L'Etoile du Bosphore,[53] and such was the development of masonry in the Ottoman Empire that only three years later, in 1861—shortly before Malkum's arrival—a supreme masonic council was instituted in Istanbul.[54]

It has not proved possible to find direct evidence of Malkum's masonic activities during his residence in Istanbul. We may confidently assume, nonetheless, that he contacted the lodges after his arrival in the Ottoman capital in 1862. The dissolution of the farāmūshkhāna had put a temporary end to masonic activity in Iran, but in Europe Iranians continued to frequent the lodges, and the name of Malkum is often encountered in reports of their activity. In 1873, a meeting was held in the Proodos lodge in Istanbul, a mixed Greco-Turkish fraternity, in honor of visiting Iranian masons. The meeting was attended by Malkum, who was then passing through Istanbul on his way from Tehran to London. The grand master, Scalieri, spoke warmly of Malkum's devotion to masonry in terms implying some previous masonically based acquaintance during his residence in Istanbul.[55]

In any event, the four most prominent Ottomans with whom Malkum had dealings of one kind or another were all masons. Ahmet Vefik Paşa (1823–1891), who combined a political career with the pioneering translation into Turkish of sixteen of Molière's comedies, was a member of the Turco-Armenian Ser lodge.[56] He was acquainted

52. *Dünyada ve Türkiyede Masonluk* (Istanbul, 1965), pp. 295–296. Mustafa Reşit Paşa had been initiated to a London lodge in 1835 (see the anonymous article, "Türk Masonluk Âleminin Büyük Simaları," *Türk Mason Dergisi*, I [1951]: 96–97).

53. *Dünyada ve Türkiyede Masonluk*, p. 296.

54. "Masonluk Tarihinden Notlar," *Türk Mason Dergisi*, I (1951): 31. It is not clear whether the Supreme Council embraced lodges of all obediences or only those affiliated with the Grand Orient. It was dissolved by Sultan Abdülhamid II and reestablished in 1908.

55. A report on the meeting in *Le Monde Maçonnique*, XV (1873): 382–386.

56. *Dünyada ve Türkiyede Masonluk*, p. 296.

with both Malkum and his father, sharing a number of their ideas, particularly on alphabet reform, and it was in his house at Rumeli Hisar that Mīrzā Yaᶜqūb died.[57] Münif Paşa (1828–1910), founder of the Ottoman Scientific Society and another proponent of alphabet reform, was a member of the Union d'Orient, a lodge founded in 1858 by the French ambassador. His association with Malkum continued in Tehran, for in 1872, the year of Malkum's return, Münif Paşa was appointed Ottoman ambassador to Iran.[58]

It is, however, Malkum's contacts with Fuad Paşa and Âlî Paşa that deserve the closest attention, for his name is involved in the controversy surrounding the political testaments attributed to the two men. Keçecizade Mehmed Fuad Paşa (1815–1869) was the son of the celebrated poet Keçecizade İzzet Molla and had benefited from a wide education embracing French, medicine and diplomacy.[59] He was a member of the Etoile du Bosphore lodge[60] and reputedly on close terms with Malkum.[61] Shortly before his death in Nice in 1869, he is purported to have composed a political testament, addressed to Sultan Abdülaziz but published soon after in various Istanbul newspapers.[62] The document, the authenticity of which was doubted from its first appearance, was subsequently reprinted a number of times in French, Turkish, and English. The present writer has had access to only one version in each language,[63] but it is likely that all extant versions correspond more or less closely in their content, as do these three.

The purported testament is, in brief, a summary of the internal and external conditions of the Ottoman Empire, together with general proposals and indications for future policy. It proclaims that adherence

57. Charles Mismer, *Souvenirs du Monde Musulman* (Paris, 1892), pp. 143–144. On Ahmet Vefik Paşa's career, see the article by Ahmet Hamdi Tanpınar in *İslam Ansiklopedisi*, I: 207–210.

58. Şerif Mardin, *The Genesis of Young Ottoman Thought* (Princeton, 1962), p. 116, n. 26. On Münif Pasa's career, political and literary, see Mardin, *op. cit.*, pp. 207–208, 234–238; Ali Fuat, "Münif Paşa," *Turk Tarih Encümeni Mecmuası*, I (1930): 1–16; and İbrahim Gövsa, *Turk Meşhurları Ansiklopedisi* (Istanbul, n.d.), p. 267.

59. Davison, *op. cit.* (n. 16, above), pp. 88–90.

60. *Dünyada ve Türkiyede Masonluk*, p. 296.

61. *Majmūᶜa-yi Āthār*, p. x.

62. R. H. Davison, "The Question of Fuad Paşa's 'Political Testament,'" *Türk Tarih Kurumu: Belleten*, XXIII (1959): 122.

63. "Testament Politique de Fouad Pacha," *La Revue de Paris*, III:4 (October–December 1896), 126–135; Mehmet Galib, "Tarihten bir Sahife," pp. 75–84, translated from an unspecified French version; and "The Political Testament of Fuad Pasha," *The Nineteenth Century*, LIII (1903): 190–197. The editor of the last claims erroneously that it has never before been published in English. For previous English editions, see Davison, "The Question of Fuad Paşa's 'Political Testament,'" pp. 121–124.

to ancient methods of government, or the attempt to revive them after falling into disuse, will lead to disastrous consequences. "All our political, all our civil institutions must be changed."[64] Progress, indeed, is the first law of human nature and, moreover, completely in accord with the spirit of Islam. "In all the new institutions which Europe offers to us there is nothing, absolutely nothing, which is contrary to the spirit of our religion."[65] In the field of external affairs, the hostility of Russia should never be forgotten and the friendship of Britain always cultivated.[66] Iran, though weak in itself, might constitute an irritant under certain circumstances and should be guarded against. Similar considerations apply to Greece.[67] The intrigues of foreign powers can be offset only by "unity of the state and the fatherland, based on the equality of all men."[68]

In the controversy surrounding the authenticity of the document, Malkum's name has been put forward as the possible forger. This theory was propounded most strongly in an article by Mehmet Galib published in 1911.[69] Galib argues that the content of the document corresponds closely to the known views of Fuad Paşa and that as one of Fuad Paşa's friends and confidants, Malkum was in a position to summarize his outlook in the form of a testament. We may ask what Malkum would have gained by such a forgery. The answer, according to Galib, is that the testament, containing as it does praise of Âlî Paşa,[70] was a means for placating the hostility he had shown to Malkum ever since his arrival in Ottoman territory.[71] It is true that in 1869, Malkum had temporarily lost his post at the Iranian embassy and may well have wished to eliminate Âlî Paşa's hostility in order to enter Ottoman service. Even so, it seems that he could have found a surer and less tortuous way of gaining Âlî Paşa's goodwill than the insertion of a few laudatory phrases in a forgery his authorship of which might never become known.

The theory of Malkum's authorship of the testament might safely be dismissed as speculation were it not that Malkum himself, in 1896, laid claim to the title of forger. In that year, *Meşveret,* the organ of the Committee of Union and Progress published in Paris, began to publish in serial a Turkish version of the testament. Malkum Khān

64. "The Political Testament of Fuad Pasha," p. 191.

65. *Ibid.*, p. 192.

66. *Ibid.*, pp. 193–194.

67. *Ibid.*, p. 194.

68. *Ibid.*, p. 196.

69. "Tarihten bir Sahife: Fuat ve Ali Paşaların Vasiyetnameleri."

70. This is to be found only in the Turkish translation given by Galib ("Tarihten bir Sahife," p. 78), and in the French version published in *La Revue de Paris* ("Testament Politique de Fouad Pacha," p. 129), but not in the English text appearing in *The Nineteenth Century*.

71. "Tarihten bir Sahife," p. 73.

wrote to the editor, Ahmet Rıza, announcing that he was the author of the original text of the testament, written in French and that it had first been put into Turkish by Ârifi Paşa. If Ahmet Rıza persisted in the serialization of the testament, without mentioning the facts of its origin, he would expose the whole matter in the press.[72] The text of Malkum's letter is not available, and it is therefore difficult to judge the justice of his claim and the motives impelling him to make it. One is obliged to observe that if Malkum had truly forged the document, he would surely have been glad to see it accepted as genuine, or at least to have its true authorship unknown. It may be that after the passage of so many years, when Malkum no longer had a direct interest in Ottoman affairs, he could not bear to be deprived of the fame accruing to him as forger of the testament. It is nonetheless difficult to imagine how he might have justified his forgery. He could conceivably have presented it as a device whereby he, a foreigner, was able to remain anonymous while offering advice to the Ottoman government and simultaneously honoring the memory of Fuad Paşa with an eloquent summary of his opinions.

The question is further complicated by the fact that Malkum, at some time or other, produced a Persian version of the testament.[73] He did not, presumably, preface his translation with a note to the effect that he had forged the testament and attributed it to Fuad Paşa. One wonders, too, whether the hostile references to Iran occurring in the testament were kept in the Persian translation. Like his letter to Ahmet Rıza, the translation does underline Malkum's interest in the testament. It may be that he forged it in order to gain apparent support from a prominent Ottoman for some of his favorite themes or, if he did not forge it, that he thought its contents relevant to Iran and worthy of being made available in Persian. It may be relevant to note that the forgery of "readers' letters" and the attribution to prominent Iranians of statements they never uttered were techniques Malkum often used when composing the numbers of *Qānūn*. If Malkum did in fact forge Fuad Paşa's testament, it would have been for him a preliminary exercise in the art of forgery.

After receiving Malkum's letter, Ahmet Rıza wrote to Mustafa Hikmet, one of the grandsons of Fuad Paşa, asking him to confirm the authenticity of the testament. Mustafa Hikmet, who had shortly before supplied the *Revue de Paris* with a French version of the testament, duly did so, ridiculing Malkum's claims and asserting that the Turkish

72. Köprülü, "Fuad Paşa," p. 678.

73. Mentioned by Ṭabāṭabāʾī in his introduction to *Majmūʿa-yi Āthār*, p. xliii. I have not been able to see a copy of this translation, which has not been included in either of the published collections of Malkum's works.

original of the testament, written in Fuad Paşa's own hand, was in his possession. He argued that Malkum could not have written the testament, since its original language was neither Armenian nor Persian.[74] This argument is inconclusive: Hikmet never displayed the alleged Turkish original, and Malkum was in a position to express himself, with the requisite fluency and correctness, in both French and Turkish. The opinion of another grandson, Reşad Fuad, differed from that of Mustafa Hikmet: he denied the authenticity of the testament.[75]

In the absence of any clear evidence pointing either to the authenticity of the testament or to its forgery by Malkum, we must content ourselves with examination of its text for possible traces of Malkum's authorship. The document contains much that is reminiscent of Malkum's writing. Its praise of Sultan Abdülaziz for his enlightened progressiveness corresponds to Malkum's flattery of Nāṣīr ud-Dīn Shāh as Iran's Peter the Great.[76] As in Malkum's *Rafīq va Vazir,* a warning is made against reliance upon time-worn methods and traditions for the preservation of the state.[77] Perhaps most significant is the assertion of Islam to be identical with "progress," or at least to be fluid and malleable enough for the purposes of reform.

> Islamism comprehends all those true doctrines which acknowledge their essential object to be the progress of the world and of humanity. . . . Every other religion is fettered by dogmas and fixed principles which are so many barriers to the progress of human thought. Islamism alone, unfettered by mysteries, free from all infallible rules, holds it a sacred duty incumbent on us to advance as much as possible all our intellectual faculties. . . . I assert with the deepest conviction that in all the new institutions which Europe offers to us there is nothing, absolutely nothing, which is contrary to the spirit of our religion.[78]

Malkum similarly regarded Islam as a kind of ragbag where useful items might be discovered by the hand of a skillful searcher: "Islam is the accumulated wisdom of the East. It is an ocean where you can find everything which is good to be known, and it offers all kinds of facilities . . . for the progress of the people."[79] He also denied Islam had fixed principles, imagining Shiᶜism in particular to excel in respect of form-

74. Köprülü, "Fuad Paşa," p. 678. The letters exchanged by Ahmet Rıza and Mustafa Hikmet are reproduced in facsimile in Mithat Cemal Kuntay, *Namık Kemal: Devrinin İnsanları ve Olayları Arasında* (Istanbul, 1944), I: 215–217.

75. Davison, "The Question of Fuad Paşa's 'Political Testament,'" p. 134.

76. *Majmūᶜa-yi Āthār*, p. 86.

77. "The Political Testament of Fuad Pasha," p. 191.

78. *Ibid.*, pp. 191, 192.

79. Malkum Khan, "Persian Civilisation," *Contemporary Review*, LIX (1891): 239.

less fluidity: "Persian Islamism [*sic*] rejecting the Caliphate and all immovable orthodoxy, is based on the open examination of living scholars, an admirable principle which opens the door to the broadest interpretations and the most novel ideas."[80] Finally, Malkum thought that European institutions should be imported en bloc.

As regards the section of the testament concerning foreign affairs, in arrangement and manner of presentation it is strongly reminiscent of a memorandum on foreign policy presented by Malkum to Nāṣir ud-Dīn Shāh (*Pūlitīkhā-yi Daulatī*).[81] In the memorandum as in the testament, Russia is presented as the constant peril and Britain as the ally to flatter and attract. The hostile references to Iran in the testament by no means exclude the possibility of Malkum's authorship. Iran is depicted as "a turbulent country always under the domination of Schiite [*sic*] fanaticism." The shah is "entirely dependent on the cabinet of St. Petersburg." For this reason, Iran may become hostile to the Ottoman Empire at Russian bidding. "Fortunately, the Sublime Porte, besides her material strength, is possessed of moral means more than sufficient to keep in awe a country crushed by barbarous despotism, disputed by several pretenders and surrounded on all sides by Sunnites."[82] The year of Fuad's death, 1869, was also the year of Malkum's temporary absence from the service of the Iranian embassy, and it is quite conceivable that he should have found some relief of his frustration in an attack on Iran bearing the signature of Fuad Paşa.

Needless to say, none of this proves that Malkum was the author of the testament. It may do no more than reflect the community of outlook that he shared with Fuad Paşa. The only conclusion possible is that Malkum may have written the testament, not that he did so.[83]

Âlî Paşa, the contemporary and associate of Fuad and another prominent mason, has been attributed with a somewhat lengthier testament, similarly surrounded with controversy and linked with the name of Malkum Khān. According to Mehmet Galib, it was published in the Turkish press soon after Âlî Paşa's death at Bebek in 1871, but he gives no exact references to newspapers or periodicals.[84] A French version was published in 1910 by the *Revue de Paris*.[85] The document reviews the previous decade of Ottoman history and summarizes the

80. "Papers submitted by Malkum Khan to Nasiruddin Shah and communicated to the Marquess of Salisbury" (13 February 1888), F.O. 60/497.

81. See below, pp. 129–134.

82. "The Political Testament of Fuad Pasha," p. 194.

83. Similar conclusions are reached by Köprülü ("Fuad Paşa," p. 678) and Davison ("The Question of Fuad Paşa's 'Political Testament,'" p. 132).

84. "Tarihten bir Sahife," p. 70.

85. Aali Pacha, "Testament Politique," *La Revue de Paris*, XVII:2 (March–April 1910), 505–524; XVII:3 (May–June 1910), 105–124.

views supposedly held by Âlî Paşa on external and internal politics. Galib maintains that the contents of the testament in their general effect tend to bring Âlî Paşa into disrepute and that this indicates another case of forgery by Malkum, who was concerned, in this instance, with wreaking posthumous revenge on his enemy Âlî.[86] The accusation is not developed in any detail and seems much less plausible than the attribution of Fuad Paşa's testament to Malkum. The only part of the document which might be interpreted as damaging to Âlî Paşa's reputation is constituted by those few paragraphs where he admits neglecting relations with vassal principalities such as Serbia, Montenegro, Wallachia, and Tunis.[87] For the rest, the testament accords with Âlî Paşa's known views and hence if not written by Âlî Paşa himself, must have been composed by someone familiar with him.[88] Galib himself points out, however, that Âlî Paşa shunned Malkum and always regarded him with a certain disgust.[89] Relatively few of Malkum's favorite themes are treated in the testament, and their occurrence does not strengthen the case for his authorship.[90] Again, no firm conclusion can be drawn. We can say only that his authorship of the testament, while not impossible, is unlikely.

Despite the contacts, friendly and otherwise, between Malkum on the one hand and Fuad Paşa and Âlî Paşa on the other, and despite the association of their names in the controversies surrounding the purported testaments, it is clear that no profound interaction of mutual influence took place between the Perso-Armenian exile and the Ottoman men of state. With one acquaintance gained in Istanbul, Malkum however did establish a link of true sympathy, reinforced by common interest in a project scorned by all the world and not less by generous mutual admiration. This friend, confidant, and soul mate was Mīrzā Fatḥ ʿAlī Ākhūndzāda.

86. "Tarihten bir Sahife," p. 72.
87. "Testament Politique," pp. 523–524.
88. Davison, *Reform in the Ottoman Empire*, pp. 416–418.
89. "Tarihten bir Sahife," p. 73.
90. E.g., demarcation of ministerial responsibilities (p. 521), and the increase of revenue and reform of the fiscal system (p. 110 f.).

CHAPTER 4

MALKUM'S DEVOTION to the supremacy of Western civilization and his consequent belief in the need for a "reform" of Islam had been acquired largely through immediate contact with the West. Fatḥ ʿAlī Ākhūndzāda, by contrast, worshipped the idol from afar, and his perception of it was filtered through the medium of Russian language and culture. Born in 1812 in the town of Nūkha, in that part of Azerbayjan to be annexed by Russia in 1828, Ākhūndzāda spent his entire life in Azerbayjan and contiguous regions of the Caucasus with the single exception of his journey to Istanbul in 1863.[1] His demand for westernization of the Muslim lands was, however, no less categorical than Malkum's, although in specifically religious matters he preferred outright hostility to the circumspect tactics advocated by Malkum. In this respect, he stands unique among the Russian-inspired westernizers, the majority of whom—such as the Bukharan Ahmad Donish (1827–1897), the Azerbayjani Talibov (1844–1910), and the Crimean Tatar Ismail Gasprinskiy (1851–1914)—sought an amalgam of European and Islamic elements. In relation to Malkum, however, the greater radicality of Ākhūndzāda is merely a nuance, a difference of temper, and does not fundamentally differentiate his attitudes and aspirations from those of the Perso-Armenian.

Initially intended by his family to become a mulla, Ākhūndzāda enjoyed a full traditional education embracing Arabic, Persian, and Turkish literature as well as logic, jurisprudence, and the religious

1. On the life of Ākhūndzāda (Akhundov), see Hüseyin Baykara, *Azerbaycan'da Yenileşme Hareketleri* (Ankara, 1966), pp. 148–170; D. Dzhafarov, *M.-F. Akhundov* (Moscow, 1962); A. Vahap Yurtsever, *Mirza Fethali Ahuntzâdenin Hayatı ve Eserleri* (Ankara, 1950); and introduction by Aziz Sharif to Mirza Fatali Akhundov, *Izbrannoe* (Moscow, 1956), pp. 3–13.

sciences. He was first deflected from his intended career, it seems, by an encounter in 1833 in the city of Ganja with the celebrated Azerbayjani poet Mīrzā Shafīᶜ Vāḍiḥ, who introduced him to Sufism and taught him calligraphy.[2] It may be that a superficial acquaintance with the symbolic mode of expression of the Sufis was, for Ākhūndzāda, a step in the direction of materialism and atheism. This supposition is strengthened by the contents of a letter written by Ākhūndzāda in 1876, in which he subjects the philosophy of Maulānā Jalāl ud-Dīn Rūmī to a grotesque misinterpretation. When Rūmī, in the monistic manner of the Sufis, speaks of the "Unity of Being" (*vaḥdat-i vujūd*), Ākhūndzāda insists that the Being he intends is none other than matter, universal and eternal. The soul is contingent on matter, in the same way that electricity is contingent on the fusion of certain minerals. According to Ākhūndzāda, Rūmī has no belief in the hereafter, nor in the concepts of Prophecy and the Imamate. His unbelief he conceals through various devices, such as a certain deliberate incoherence, but his fundamental materialism is evident to the careful reader. Ākhūndzāda confesses his own inability to express his hostility to religion with similar circumspect skill.[3]

In 1833, Ākhūndzāda was taken by his uncle from Ganja back to Nūkha. There he spent a year learning Russian, evidently with great skill and proficiency, for the following year he was appointed translator into oriental languages in the service of the viceroy of the Caucasus in Tiflis. He retained this post for the rest of his life, ultimately reaching the rank of major, working also in the viceregal archives.[4] He was thus able to enjoy a modest security of livelihood which Malkum, with his more adventurous tendencies, was never able to attain. Continuous residence in Tiflis also served to determine Ākhūndzāda's intellectual development. In the mid-nineteenth century, Tiflis was the cultural center of the Caucasus and even earned the approval of Tolstoy as a "civilised town."[5] There, Ākhūndzāda enjoyed the acquaintance of a wide range of figures, among them the Armenian writer Khachatur Abovyan (1805–1848),[6] the Georgian poet Aleksandr Chavchavadze,[7]

2. Yurtsever, *op. cit.*, pp. 7–9; Baykara, *op. cit.*, p. 150. Mīrzā Shafīᶜ gained a certain fame in the West through the *Nachdichtungen* of the German Romantic poet Friedrich Bodenstedt whose *Die Lieder des Mirza Schaffy* (1851) attained a popularity comparable to that of Fitzgerald's rendering of Khayyam. See Otto Spies, *Der Orient in der deutschen Literatur* (Kevelaer, 1951), p. 22.

3. Mirzä Fätäli Akhundov, "Mollayi-Ruminin vä Onun Tasnifinin Babında," *Äsärläri* (Baku, 1961), II: 204–209.

4. Yurtsever, *op. cit.*, pp. 9, 13; Baykara, *op. cit.*, p. 150.

5. L. Tolstoy, *Sochineniya* (Moscow, 1928), LIX: 59.

6. Dzhafarov, *op. cit.*, p. 21.

7. Dilara Alieva, *Iz Istorii Azerbaydzhansko-Gruzinskikh Literaturnykh Svyazei* (Baku, 1958), pp. 84–85.

the Dekabrist exile A. A. Bestuzhev-Marlinskiy, and the German orientalist Adolf Berge.[8] It was in Tiflis too that Ākhūndzāda gained his first acquaintance with the drama, and he began to compose his plays with the encouragement of the first director of the Tiflis theatre, Vladimir Sollogub.[9] Nor did the cosmopolitan cultural life of Tiflis constitute the limit of Ākhūndzāda's contacts; he corresponded with scholars in St. Petersburg and Moscow, such as Mirza Kazem-Beg, the Azerbayjani convert to Christianity, and Bernard Dorn and, beyond the borders of Russia, with others in Paris and London.[10]

Despite his physical remoteness from Europe, Ākhūndzāda became convinced through these contacts of the primacy of European example and learning no less thoroughly than did Malkum through his residence in Paris. Just as Malkum in various treatises cites as ultimate proof of his contentions the authority of European science, so too does Ākhūndzāda invoke the "learned men of Europe" (*hükämayi Yevropa*) in support of much that he writes. Thus, in his letter concerning Rūmī, he takes issue with the Sufi concept of *fanā*, reabsorption in the source of Being, as "a meaningless concept derived from Buddhism," and immediately adduces as authority for this statement an unnamed Russian book. Similarly, when maintaining the soul to be contingent upon matter, he states flatly: "the learned men of Europe do not recognize an independently existing (*qā'im bi-nafsihi*) soul." When taking issue with certain points of Rūmī's philosophy he says, by way of terminating the discussion: "My attribution of these errors to Rūmī does not represent my own opinion; rather it is the opinion of the learned men of Europe."[11]

Having become convinced of the inherent supremacy of European civilization, Ākhūndzāda turned his full attention to the "reform" of the Islamic world. Like Malkum, he adopted the current nineteenth-century stereotypes of Europe and Asia as two contrasting spheres of science and superstition, enlightenment and backwardness. The contrast is personified in the two main characters of one of his celebrated plays in Azerbayjani Turkish, *The Story of Monsieur Jourdain, the Botanist, and Darvīsh Mast ʿAlī Shāh, the Renowned Magician*, in which science fittingly triumphs over superstition.[12] For Ākhūndzāda, superstition is identical with religion itself, and his career is marked by a clearer and franker hostility to Islam than that displayed by Malkum. Like Malkum, drawing an implicit parallel with European historical

8. Baykara, *op. cit.*, p. 150; Dzhafarov, *op. cit.*, p .21.
9. Dzhafarov, *op. cit.*, p. 32.
10. *Ibid.*, p. 21.
11. Akhundov, *Äsärläri*, II: 205–206.
12. Text in M. F. Akhundov, *Komediyalar* (Baku, 1962), pp. 18–43.

experience, he proclaimed the need for a "reformation" of Islam: "The faith of Islam needs a Prostestantism [*sic*] in conformity with our age and time."[13] Yet he was usually more explicit and made it clear that abolition rather than reform was his aim. "I perceived that the Islamic faith and fanaticism represented an obstacle to the diffusion of civilization among the Muslim peoples. I therefore set myself the task of sundering the foundations of that faith, of extirpating fanaticism and dissipating the dark ignorance of the peoples of the East."[14] The first product of Ākhūndzāda's self-appointed mission was a work composed in 1860, entitled *The Three Letters of the Indian Prince, Kamāl ud-Daula, to his Friend, the Iranian Prince, Jalāl ud-Daula, together with the Reply of Jalāl ud-Daula.*[15] In these letters, authorship of which Ākhūndzāda was at pains to deny to all but the closest associates such as Malkum,[16] the two princes raise certain objections to the Islamic faith—for the most part, those traditional in the European view of Islam—and consider that they amount to a refutation of its claims to validity.

Concerned as he was with his mission of radical antagonism to Islam, Ākhūndzāda had little attention to devote to political matters. Although he was acquainted with a number of Dekabrist exiles in Tiflis, and although his letters were sometimes confiscated by Russian censors,[17] he appears to have shown no interest in Russian revolutionary politics. His denunciations of tyranny are general in tone and are in any event directed only at Muslim monarchs; the tsar was implicitly exempted from criticism as an agent of westernization of Muslim lands. In this respect, Ākhūndzāda anticipates those Soviet historians who justify Russian expansion in the nineteenth century as "a progressive historical phenomenon."[18] His concern with fundamentals and abstention from political activity distinguish Ākhūndzāda's outlook from that of Malkum. Malkum, as has been shown, wished to maintain the structure of religion and a personal pretense of religiosity as a means for the

13. Ākhūndzāda to Jalāl ud-Dīn Mīrzā, June 15, 1870, in Ākhūndzāda, *Alifbā-yi Jadīd va Maktūbāt,* eds. Ḥ. Muḥammadzāda and Ḥ. Ārāslī (Baku, 1963), p. 172.

14. Quoted by M. M. Kasumov, "Mirovozzrenie M.-F. Akhundova," *Trudy Instituta Istorii i Filosofii Akademii Nauk Azerbaydzhanskoi SSR,* VII (1955): 133. See too the same author's "Bor'ba M.-F. Akhundova Protiv Religii Islama," *Trudy Instituta Istorii i Filosofii,* III (1953): 70–101.

15. The letters were originally composed in Persian. Ākhūndzāda's own version in Azerbayjani Turkish is contained in *Äsärläri,* II:99–132. The Persian text was recently printed in Tajikistan in Cyrillic characters, avowedly as an adjunct to atheistic propaganda (M. F. Akhundov, *Maktubho* [Dushanbe, 1962]).

16. See, for example, Ākhūndzāda to ᶜAbd ul-Vahhāb Khān, Muḥarram 1283/ May 1866 in *Alifbā-yi Jadīd va Maktūbāt,* pp. 88–91.

17. Baykara, *op. cit.,* p. 162.

18. See Dzhafarov, *op. cit.,* p. 5.

attainment of westernization. He intended to proceed with strategic caution rather than iconoclastic fervor. He was, moreover, intensely and continuously involved in political life, and the vicissitudes of his political fortunes contrast strongly with Ākhūndzāda's secure and stable post in Tiflis. Nonetheless, the fundamental aims of the two men were in essence the same, and one item from their respective programs of reform was able to bring them together in intense if fruitless cooperation.

This item was the proposed reform of the Arabic alphabet, and, although this concern originated neither with Malkum nor with Ākhūndzāda, they both gave it detailed and prolonged consideration. The question was first raised in Istanbul, by one of the most prominent intellectual representatives of the Tanzimat, Mehmed Münif Paşa, previously mentioned as a masonic acquaintance of Malkum. In a speech delivered to the Ottoman Scientific Society on May 12, 1862, he listed a number of deficiencies of the Arabic alphabet, primarily in relation to the needs of the Turkish language. Many subsequent themes of those who demanded reform, including Malkum, were touched upon in his discussion, and the following may in particular be mentioned: the ambiguity arising from variant readings for the same letters (three for *kāf*, six for *vāv*); the difficulty of rendering accurately foreign proper names; and the problem presented by the conservation, in Turkish, of Persian and Arabic loanwords in their original orthography. It was held that these and similar deficiencies contributed to the high rate of illiteracy in Muslim lands and made the business of printing costly and complicated. To remedy the situation at least partially, two possibilities existed: consistent use of vocalization (*iʿrāb*), supplemented by additional signs to denote those vowel sounds found in Turkish but not in Arabic; or use of the existing letters only in their separate forms, permitting the inclusion of the vowel signs as letters among the consonants and on a level with them. The second course Münif Paşa recommended as manifestly more practical, and he suggested that it be taught experimentally in elementary schools.[19]

It was doubtless in awareness of Münif Paşa's initiative that Ākhūndzāda turned to the question of alphabet reform and came to Istanbul in July 1863 with his own carefully prepared plan of reform. In a treatise on the subject written in Persian, he relates the difficulties he experienced as a child in learning the alphabet, claiming that it took him from three to four years to master the art of reading. Attributing

19. Text of Münif's address given in *Mecmua-ı Fünun*, no. 14, Ṣafar 1280/July 1863, pp. 74–77. See also Fevziye Abdullah Tansel, "Arap Harflerinin Islahı ve Degištirilmesi Hakkında İlk Teşebbüsler ve Neticeleri," *Türk Tarih Kurumu Belleteni*, XVII (1953): 224–225; and Agah Sırrı Levend, *Türk Dilinde Gelişme ve Sadeleşme Safhaları* (Ankara, 1949), pp. 167–169.

the high rate of illiteracy in Muslim countries to the deficiencies of the script, he then proceeds to list some of its weaknesses: the habitual omission of *iʿrāb,* the lack of signs to represent certain vowel sounds found in Turkish (ö, ü, o, e), and the ambiguity of the letter *kāf.*[20] These and all other deficiencies Ākhūndzāda claimed to remedy with his revised alphabet. The basic principles of his alphabet were: the substitution of additional strokes for dots to differentiate letters of identical formation; the invention of letters for short vowels, with forms inspired by the existing vowel signs; and the establishing of a single form for each letter, capable of junction with all other letters, so that each word would correspond to an undivided letter group. Ākhūndzāda's project is impressive as the most serious and elaborate of the proposals for reform made at the time, and he took care to draw up detailed rules of orthography for the writing of Turkish, Arabic, and Persian in his revised script. Like Münif Paşa, he too thought of teaching the modified alphabet first to children, and he evolved a rudimentary method of teaching it.[21]

On his arrival in Istanbul, Ākhūndzāda took up residence in the Iranian embassy as the guest of Mīrzā Ḥusayn Khān whom he had known as Iranian consul-general in Tiflis.[22] Then, equipped with copies of his treatise and specimens of his invention, Ākhūndzāda went to meet in turn Âlî Paşa and Fuad Paşa, at that time minister of foreign affairs and prime minister respectively. Both showed friendly if restrained interest, and the matter was referred for more detailed consideration to Münif Paşa's Ottoman Scientific Society. A meeting of the society to which Ākhūndzāda was invited was convened on July 10, 1863, under the chairmanship of Münif Paşa. Ākhūndzāda presented his plan and expounded its alleged benefits. These are conveniently listed in the previously mentioned Persian treatise. His reformed script would facilitate the acquisition of literacy, particularly by women and children; render possible the accurate transcription of foreign names; and make for greater speed in handwriting, the pen not being lifted from the paper until the completion of each word. To this last point he anticipated the objection that the inclusion of letters for vowel sounds would considerably lengthen the written form of words. His reply was that words in European languages are commonly of great length (doubtless he had Russian in mind, the European tongue with which he was best acquainted). In any event, the greater length of the written form of words resulting from adoption of the revised script could well be offset by the abandonment of useless and ceremonial verbiage and

20. *Alifbā-yi Jadīd va Maktūbāt,* pp. 3–5, 11 f., 41–52.
21. *Ibid.,* pp. 41–52.
22. Dzhafarov, *op. cit.,* p. 172.

by generally attempting a closer approximation of the written to the spoken language.[23]

His arguments were received with general assent, and various members of the society recalled that several years before they had elaborated a plan for an alphabet consisting of separate letters only. Ākhūndzāda replied that his system was more likely to find acceptance as being closer to the existing alphabet. Despite the context of hostility to Islam in which Ākhūndzāda evolved his project, on this occasion he did not hesitate to use specious religious arguments, thus conforming to Malkum's strategy of opportunist use of religious appeal. "I said: to use separate letters from the old alphabet is entirely contrary to Islam. Without doubt the people would be horrified at such letters. It is impossible to write the Qurʾān in separate letters. . . . But in my new alphabet, there occurs not a single form or shape entirely different from the old letters."[24] His real reasons for objecting to unjoined letters Ākhūndzāda was to set forth later in a letter to Malkum Khān.

A week after the first meeting, the Ottoman Scientific Society convened again to discuss the matter, this time without the presence of Ākhūndzāda. As Münif Paşa told him later, their deliberations dealt with three questions: whether the existing form of the alphabet was defective, if so, whether Ākhūndzāda's proposed reform was acceptable, and how any suitable reform might be implemented. The majority of those present agreed that the alphabet, particularly for Turkish, was defective and that Ākhūndzāda's proposal had its merits. It was pointed out, however, that the fact that all its letters were joined presented great problems from the point of view of printing. Moreover, its adoption would ultimately render necessary either the reprinting of all existing literature or its abandonment. On the last question it was concluded that any change would have to be accomplished gradually. Use of a new script in schools and progressively in printing would lead "automatically" to the displacement of the old.[25] Ākhūndzāda had not, at this stage of affairs, intended to replace the existing script with his own invention, but evidently aimed, as a preliminary, to have his script adopted into the corpus of recognized calligraphic styles. It was realized however that he had indeed done more than invent a new style of calligraphy, and he left Istanbul with even his minimum goal unattained.[26]

His failure is in the first place attributable to an understandable reluctance on the part of the Ottoman government to proceed without

23. *Alifbā-yi Jadīd va Maktūbāt,* pp. 5–11.

24. See his notes on the trip to Istanbul in *ibid.*, pp. 79–80; and also Levend, *op. cit.*, p. 170.

25. *Ibid.*; Tansel, *op. cit.*, p. 226; and *Alifbā-yi Jadīd va Maktūbāt,* p. 71.

26. *Ibid.*, pp. 6–7.

delay on so radical a measure as alphabet reform, a measure rich, moreover, in cultural and religious implications. The scheme's rejection may have been partly due also to the negative attitude to Ākhūndzāda and his project adopted by Mīrzā Ḥusayn Khān. Being lodged at the Iranian embassy as his guest, and having enjoyed his previous acquaintance in Tiflis, Ākhūndzāda doubtless hoped that Mīrzā Ḥusayn Khān would exert influence on his behalf in Istanbul.[27] It appears, however, that Mīrzā Ḥusayn Khān came to regret his hospitality and intimated to the Ottoman authorities that his guest was a violent enemy of religion and, moreover, engaged in espionage on behalf of Russia.[28] The first accusation was, of course, true, and the second appears at least plausible. The matter is somewhat clarified in a letter written by Ākhūndzāda to Mīrzā Ḥusayn Khān in September 1868, some five years after his return from Istanbul. Appealing for a reconciliation, he asks the Iranian ambassador to admit that the real cause for their estrangement was not any difference of opinion on the alphabet question, but rather his action in presenting a copy of his Azerbayjani Turkish plays to Fuad Paşa. It seems that Mīrzā Ḥusayn Khān regarded the content of these plays as subversive, as critical of existing political and religious institutions, and was embarrassed at appearing, in the eyes of the Ottoman government, to harbor a guest of pronouncedly heretical views. Ākhūndzāda affirmed, however, that his intention was merely, by medium of the drama, to engage in social criticism, in the analysis of corrupt types such as are found in any society.[29] It was several years before a reconciliation was finally effected between the two men, and Malkum's continuing association with Mīrzā Ḥusayn Khān tended somewhat to cloud his otherwise cordial relationship with Ākhūndzāda.[30]

The general note of bitterness apparent in Ākhūndzāda's memoirs of the trip and in the Persian poem he penned on his return to Tiflis,[31] is of interest: like Malkum Khān shortly afterwards, he conceived of all opposition to his plans as inspired exclusively by blind ignorance or the vested interest of fanatics. This was, for him, inevitable, since he viewed alphabet reform as a necessary part of the eradication of religious influence in the Islamic world. Moreover, the manner in which

27. Ākhūndzāda presented Mīrzā Ḥusayn Khān with a number of his treatises on alphabet reform which are now preserved in the madrasa in Tehran that bears the sipahsālār's name. For a list of them, see Abū Yūsuf Shīrāzī, *Fihrist-i Kitābkhāna-yi Madrasa-yi ᶜĀlī-yi Sipahsālār* (Tehran, 1316 solar/1937), II: 24–28.

28. Dzhafarov, *op. cit.*, pp. 172–173.

29. *Alifbā-yi Jadīd va Maktūbāt*, pp. 108–110.

30. The reconciliation took place in Poti in late 1874. See Ākhūndzāda's letter to Mīrzā ᶜAlī Khān dated December 1874 in *ibid.*, pp. 313–314.

31. Memoirs in *ibid.*, pp. 75–85. The poem is reproduced by Yurtsever in *op. cit.* (n. 1, above), p. 23.

Ākhūndzāda, again like Malkum, brushed aside difficulties and ignored criticism and the speed and ease with which they hoped to change the reading and writing habits of the Muslim world, are indications of the superficial, almost dilettantist nature of much of their thought, not only in regard to alphabet reform.

The first indication of Malkum Khān's interest in the question of alphabet reform occurs in a letter written to him by Ākhūndzāda in September 1868. It cannot be ascertained how and when this interest was first aroused. There is no record of his concern with the question before Ākhūndzāda's visit to Istanbul, and Malkum was attached to the Iranian embassy during Ākhūndzāda's residence there. It is reasonable, therefore, to assume that it was Ākhūndzāda who first directed his attention to the matter.[32] In his memoirs of the visit he records having presented Malkum Khān with a copy of his plays, and, doubtless, the primary reason for Ākhūndzāda's presence in Istanbul was also discussed by the two men.[33] It is also possible that Malkum's essays in alphabet reform were inspired by the example of Münif Paşa, whose acquaintance he enjoyed; although according to Charles Mismer, it was Malkum's own father, Mīrzā Yaᶜqūb, who impressed on him the necessity of reform.[34] It may be noted that Münif Paşa, Ākhūndzāda, Mīrzā Yaᶜqūb, and Malkum Khān had all worked as interpreters and translators, and this common experience was probably of importance in arousing their interest in questions of language and alphabet reform. Malkum Khān's interest in alphabet reform, therefore, may be parallel to that of Münif Paşa and Ākhūndzāda, rather than necessarily influenced by either or both of them.

Allowing, then, for an independent interest in the matter on the part of Malkum Khān, it is nonetheless in conjunction with Ākhūndzāda that we find the earliest record of his active concern for a revised alphabet. For several years the two men remained in close contact, exchanging opinions on each other's projects, seeking the adoption of their schemes, separately or in conjunction, in both the Ottoman Empire and Iran, and consoling each other for the failure they both encountered.

By September 1868, whether independently or as a result of Ākhūndzāda's example, Malkum had taken the first step in formulating a revised alphabet. Although the present writer has been unable to find a sample of this prototype, it appears to have enshrined the prin-

32. The assumption is made by A. M. Shoitov in "Rol' M.-F. Akhundova v Razvitii Persidskoi Progressivnoi Literatury," *Kratkie Soobshcheniya Instituta Vostokovedeniya*, IX (1953): 61.

33. *Alifbā-yi Jadīd va Maktūbāt*, p. 78.

34. Charles Mismer, *Souvenirs du Monde Musulman* (Paris, 1892), p. 142.

ciple underlying Malkum's final version of a modified script: reduction of all letters to a single form (the existing isolated form) to be employed without junction. This reform had in common with the proposals of Ākhūndzāda only the elimination of the varying forms of the letter. In other respects, it represented a complete antithesis. Hence Ākhūndzāda's criticisms, all based on practical considerations and not on that repugnance to Islam which he had alleged in front of the Ottoman Scientific Society:

> I object to your retention of the dots; your failure to include *iʿrāb* [i.e., as letters, together with the consonants]; your failure to invent special signs for all vowel signs, nine in number; and to your retention of the existing ugly signs of iʿrāb. You say that the dots will gradually disappear, and that iʿrāb will gradually become included among the letters. But there are dots in use throughout your alphabet, and iʿrāb, apart from two or three of the existing ugly signs, is nonexistent. So when will the dots disappear, and when will iʿrāb be included among the letters? Presumably your intention is that with the passage of time the dots should automatically disappear as the forms of the letters become differentiated, and iʿrāb too will be included among the letters. If this is really your intention, I cannot regard it as sound; it will result in interminable delay. If reform is to take place at all, let it be a thoroughgoing reform, now, this very hour.[35]

Indeed Malkum's assertion that the dots used to differentiate letters of identical formation could "gradually" and "automatically" disappear and that the signs of iʿrāb could gradually attain the status of letters is vague in the extreme: one has the mental picture of dots shrinking and fading away, as *ḥarakāt* (vowel signs) swell forth and insert themselves between the consonants. Here is not only a proof of Ākhūndzāda's more serious concern with the question, but also an instance of his preference for radical and immediate measures, in contrast to Malkum's inclination to more subtle and gradual tactics.

Proceeding with his evaluation of Malkum Khān's proposal, he further points out the difficulty that would be experienced in the use of separate letters for handwriting. At the very least, junction of each consonant with its following vowel would be a requirement in any ideally reformed alphabet. Ākhūndzāda suspects, however, that Malkum's purpose in his initial project may be to prepare the way for a script running from left to right (assumed, without discussion, to be an improvement on an alphabet running in the opposite direction). Perhaps recalling criticisms of his own script by the Ottoman Scientific Society, he also conceded that Malkum's invention might be useful for

35. Ākhūndzāda to Malkum, September 1868 in *Alifbā-yi Jadīd va Maktūbāt*, pp. 115–118.

purposes of printing. Even for such a limited purpose, his objections to the retention of dots and to the failure to invent letters for the vowels would have to be met.[36]

These considerations and suggestions, together with copies of his own and Malkum's revised alphabets, Ākhūndzāda forwarded via the Iranian consul in Tiflis, Mīrzā ʿAli Khān, to the foreign ministry in Tehran. Considering the wide divergence between their two schemes, it is probable that Malkum Khān and Ākhūndzāda coordinated their efforts primarily in order to keep the issue of alphabet reform alive, rather than to secure the immediate application of either proposed reform. Thus, in 1870, when Mīrzā ʿAli Khān was returning to Iran, Ākhūndzāda entrusted him with additional copies of Malkum's alphabet, which he had criticized so strongly, and requested him to propagate energetically the cause of alphabet reform in Iran.[37]

In return for Ākhūndzāda's efforts directed from Tiflis toward Iran, Malkum campaigned for the adoption of their projects in Istanbul. Thus Ākhūndzāda sent to Malkum his comments on the proposed reform of Ali Suavi, requesting him to translate them into Turkish and to forward them for consideration to the Ottoman Scientific Society.[38] Malkum also appears to have furnished a channel of communication between Ākhūndzāda and Münif Paşa in their further exchanges on the alphabet question, apart from undertaking himself the propagation of Ākhūndzāda's proposals. In this, he followed tactics similar to those used by Ākhūndzāda on his visit to Istanbul in 1863, by suggesting that the new script be allotted a recognized place among the alphabets used in the Ottoman Empire. "I do not say that they should accept this script. I say only: just as your language is printed in the Armenian, Greek and Roman scripts, we wish to print it in this new script."[39] This argument appears to have had little effect, and early in 1871 Malkum Khān was

36. *Ibid.*, p. 118.

37. *Ibid.*, p. 178.

38. Ākhūndzāda to Malkum, September 1868, in *ibid.*, p. 117. The text of his comments can be found in *ibid.*, pp. 124–136.

39. Malkum to Ākhūndzāda, May 27 (no year), in *ibid.*, p. 408. A number of books and periodicals were printed in the Armenian script for Turcophone Armenians. For a list see *Catalogue de la Librairie des Pères Méchitaristes* (Vienna, 1936), pp. 68–75; and H. Adjarian, *History of the Armenian Language* (in Armenian), (Erivan, 1951), II: 263. (References owed to Dr. Paul Essabal). The printing of Turkish in the Greek script was for the benefit of the small Turkish-speaking Orthodox community, above all in Karaman, concerning which see Bernard Lewis, *The Emergence of Modern Turkey* (Oxford, 1961), p. 348, and Gotthard Jäschke, "Die türkisch-orthodoxe Kirche," *Der Islam*, XXXIX (1964): 95–129. By use of the Latin alphabet for Turkish at this date, Malkum is presumably referring to phrasebooks and manuals of the language written for foreigners.

obliged to inform Ākhūndzāda that the Ottoman ministers had finally rejected any alphabet reform.[40]

Malkum Khān's best known contribution to the debate on alphabet reform in the Ottoman Empire came with a letter in Persian (anonymous, but unmistakably his) to the journal of the New Ottoman Society, *Hürriyet,* printed in its number for August 9, 1869. This letter was in the form of a lengthy comment on an article by Namık Kemal in number fifty-four of *Hürriyet* entitled "Hüdâ Kadirdir: Eyler Seng-i Hârâdan Güher Peydâ" (God is omnipotent: from granite He brings forth jewels).[41] The article consisted chiefly of a comprehensive criticism of the state of education in the Ottoman Empire, the progress and attainments of the Muslim children being unfavorably compared with those of Greek, Armenian, and Jewish children of the capital. Even among teachers, only 5 percent were able to read Turkish properly, and this lamentable state extended even to those ulama who gave instruction at the mosques. For this situation, Namık Kemal held the manner of teaching the alphabet (indirectly, through memorization of the Qur'ān) responsible, rather than the shortcomings of the alphabet itself.

In his letter, Malkum Khān by contrast laid emphasis on deficiencies and inadequacies in the Arabic alphabet. The invention of a new script was proclaimed as a self-evident necessity for all the Muslim peoples. He recalled the proposals made by Ākhūndzāda on his visit in 1863 and other discussions of the matter in the newspaper *Mühbir* two years previously. His own view of the desiderata of a reform was also given: "The intelligent and active men of Islam must do something so that vowel signs be written mixed together with the letters [meaning, presumably, they should be included among the letters of the alphabet and written on the same level as the consonants], and all dots must be removed." As the great obstacle to the implementation of the plan, he presents the opposition of the ulama, and expediently resorting to pseudoreligious argumentation, asks his readers: "But how can this great barrier be removed? Is it possible to prove to the ulama that as long as they persist in their present state of ignorance and absolute rejection of European science and progress, the faith of Islam will weaken day by day and head for destruction?"

40. Ākhūndzāda to Mīrzā Yūsuf Khān, June 8, 1871, in *Alifbā-yi Jadīd va Maktūbāt,* p. 238.

41. This article and Malkum's comments on it have been discussed by Tansel, *op. cit.* (n. 19, above), pp. 227–232; Levend, *op. cit.* (n. 19, above), pp. 171–172; and Lewis, *op. cit.*, p. 422, where he erroneously identifies Malkum as "Persian ambassador to the Sublime Porte."

Then, in his best simplistic style, he proceeds:

> The ignorance of the people of Islam and their separation from present-day progress are caused by the defectiveness of the alphabet. The non-existence of popular rights and freedoms, the lack of security for life, honor, and property, are caused by the defectiveness of the alphabet. The delapidation of highways, the abundance of cruelty and oppression, the scarcity of justice and equity—these, too, are caused by the defectiveness of the alphabet.

After this piece of analysis, Malkum recounts new efforts for alphabet reform undertaken a few months earlier by "a person in Istanbul." These efforts had been frustrated by the opposition of the ulama. Nonetheless, it was necessary to persist, and *Hürriyet* should open its columns to a discussion of various proposals for reform. Among these were Ākhūndzāda's suggestions, those presented in the *Mühbir*, and finally the scheme of separate letters evolved by the "person in Istanbul" (probably Malkum himself).[42]

Malkum's references in this letter to "Islam," "the people of Islam," and "the Muslims" deserve careful attention. Both he and Ākhūndzāda hoped for the adoption of their revised scripts by the three main languages of the Islamic heartlands and regarded the question of alphabet reform as common to both the Ottoman Empire and Iran. Hence they spoke of the "Islamic script" and the "Islamic languages," rather than of the Arabic script and the Arabic, Turkish, and Persian languages.[43] To the words "Islam" and "Islamic," they gave, however, an almost entirely secular content: their concern for the "people of Islam" was directed to the westernization and reform of a geopolitical entity, defined by cultural tradition and able to be regarded as an entity even without specifically religious bonds. This secularization of the word "Islam" (influenced, possibly, by European usage) is best exemplified by the utterances of Jamāl ud-Dīn Afghānī, a later associate of Malkum Khān. In Afghānī's thought, the community, admittedly an important concept in the formulation of Islamic life, is elevated to the highest degree and becomes almost synonymous with "Islam."[44] It is only in the context of such considerations that

42. By presenting this scheme on behalf of an anonymous "person in Istanbul," he may have wished to gauge initial reactions before claiming the honor of the invention for himself. The proposal presented in the *Mühbir* was by Ali Suavi, published in no. 48. He concluded that the only real need was for consistent use of *iʿrāb* and the use of numbers to distinguish various sounds rendered by the letter *vāv*.

43. See, for example, the beginning of Ākhūndzāda's Persian treatise in *Alifbā-yi Jadīd va Maktūbāt*, p. 3.

44. See Nikki R. Keddie, *An Islamic Response to Imperialism: Political and Religious Writings of Sayyid Jamal ad-Din "al-Afghani"* (Berkeley and Los Angeles, 1968).

any sense can be made of Malkum's assertion that without the adoption of European science "the *faith of Islam* will weaken day by day and head for destruction."

Apart from the semantic implications of Malkum's use of the word "Islam," a consciousness of the religious associations of the Arabic script is also present. Repeatedly he informs Ākhūndzāda that alphabet reform is being opposed in Istanbul as contrary to the faith: "They say . . . our script is part of our religion."[45] Suspicions that a revised alphabet was of heretical inspiration could only be strengthened by presenting its use as analogous to the writing of Turkish in the Greek and Armenian alphabets. Such use of these scripts was made, after all, only by Turcophone non-Muslims. In general, however, Malkum and Ākhūndzāda sought diligently to present alphabet reform as not only compatible with religion, but even as favorable to it. While in Istanbul in 1863, Ākhūndzāda claimed that adoption of his revised script, through encouraging literacy, would in turn enable the people to be better aware of their religious duties.[46] He submitted to the Ottoman Scientific Society a treatise of his own composition concerning the religious permissibility of alphabet reform, claiming that the transition from Kufic to Naskh furnished a legitimizing precedent, and he entrusted his friend, Ākhūnd Mullā Aḥmad Ḥusaynzāda, shaykh ul-Islām of the Caucasus, with the task of searching out a relevant *fatvā*.[47] Malkum in his treatise *The Shaykh and the Vizier* (discussed below) also affirmed the religious innocuity of alphabet reform and claimed the replacement of Kufic by Naskh as a precedent that had aroused no religious opposition.[48]

Discussion of the relation between alphabet and religion, particularly in the context of the Near East, need not detain us here. It is relevant, however, to note the connection, in both Malkum Khān and Ākhūndzāda, between their attitudes to religion and to alphabet reform. Ākhūndzāda had set himself the fundamental task of eradicating Islam and devoted himself to literary activity tending to the achievement of that aim. There is no doubt that alphabet reform constituted

45. Malkum to Ākhūndzāda, May 27 (no year), in *Alifbā-yi Jadīd va Maktūbāt*, p. 408.

46. *Ibid.*, p. 10.

47. Ākhūndzāda to Malkum Khān in *ibid.*, pp. 107, 237; and Ākhūndzāda, "Investigation Concerning the Islamic Script," *ibid.*, pp. 55–59.

48. *Kullīyāt-i Malkum Khān*, ed. Hāshim Rabīʿzāda (Tabriz, 1325 lunar/1908), p. 118. In his preface to the *Gulistān* in "reformed" letters (London, 1885), Malkum was later to claim that "many words in the Glorious Qurʾān have been written with separate letters" (p. 10). One can only presume that Malkum meant the letters of disputed meaning that stand at the beginning of several *sūra's*. (e.g., II, III, XII). But even these are more frequently than not written together.

for Ākhūndzāda an integral part of his efforts to uproot the Islamic faith. In a letter to Malkum Khān, he tells of his endeavors to secure the publication and diffusion, in the Muslim countries, of his *Letters of Kamāl ud-Daula,* and links the success of the cause of alphabet reform to the anticipated impact of that antireligious tract:

> Soon my friends will be printing it somewhere, and then distributing it throughout Asia and Africa. Then let us see how the ministers at Istanbul preserve their religion! Then indeed their religion will be lost, and they will be obliged to accept our alphabet. Days of joy and prosperity will become their lot, they will regret their former behavior to us and beg our forgiveness.[49]

Thus Ākhūndzāda expected an immediate and total collapse of religious belief to entail an equally prompt acceptance of his proposal for a radically revised alphabet.

In addition to his hostility to Islam, Ākhūndzāda nurtured a complementary hatred of the Arabs, attested in a letter to Jalāl ud-Dīn Mīrzā, whose Tehran residence, it will be remembered, housed Malkum's farāmūshkhāna, and who was an early proponent of "pure Persian." In his letter, Ākhūndzāda thanks Jalāl ud-Dīn for sending him a copy of his *Nāma-yi Khusruvān* and congratulates him on avoiding the use of Arabic words in its composition. He then goes on to say:

> Your excellency has freed our tongue from the domination of the Arabic language; I am now attempting to free our people from the Arabic script. Would that someone else might join us to free our people from the bondage of the disgusting customs of those Arabs who destroyed our thousand-year-old monarchy of justice and high renown, and utterly destroyed our country which was once a paradise on earth![50]

Here again we see clearly illustrated the radical ideological motives inspiring Ākhūndzāda's demand for alphabet reform and determining its urgent and thoroughgoing nature.

By contrast, Malkum Khān's proposed revision of the alphabet foresaw gradual change, and this corresponds to a similar gradualism in his planned subversion of Islamic beliefs. We have already shown how an "Islamic reformation" was to be used as a cloak for wholesale westernization: the aim was not to destroy Islam from without, but rather to use it for purposes fundamentally alien to its own genius and to effect thereby an almost unseen transition to Western values and ideals. So, too, as Malkum later wrote in the introduction to his

49. Ākhūndzāda to Malkum, June 2, 1871, in *Alifbā-yi Jadīd va Maktūbāt,* pp. 234–235.

50. Ākhūndzāda to Jalāl ud-Dīn Mīrzā, June 15, 1870, in *ibid.,* p. 172.

edition of Saᶜdī's *Gulistān* in the revised alphabet, a modified Arabic script was intended as a preliminary to its total replacement.[51] It is thus comprehensible that Malkum should not have followed Ākhūndzāda in his abandonment of the Arabic script altogether in favor of a mixture of Roman and Cyrillic.[52]

Namık Kemal, in his reply to Malkum's letter printed in number sixty-one of *Hürriyet* on August 23, 1869, restricts discussion of the question to the problems of Turkish. All existing proposals he found unacceptable, involving as they would either the abandonment to oblivion of the old literature or its reprinting, at great cost, in the new script. All he considered necessary was to differentiate the various values of *kāf* (by using two dots beneath the letter when read as *yā*, one above when read as *nūn*, and an extra stroke when read as Persian *gāf*), and to use *iᶜrāb* when instructing children. Reverting to the theme of his previous article, Kemal stresses again the necessity of reform of educational method, rejecting Malkum's claim that the alphabet was the chief cause for the stagnation of the Muslim peoples. He pointed out that England and America sustained an incomparably higher level of education than Spain, despite the defects of English orthography and the greater consistency of Spanish. The Arabic alphabet, moreover, had never presented an obstacle to the cultivation of the sciences in the golden age of Islamic civilization.[53]

Although the discussion continued for some time in the Turkish press, Malkum appears not to have made any further direct intervention, and he took little account of Kemal's arguments in his subsequent writings.[54] It seems that he anticipated the final rejection of his and Ākhūndzāda's proposals in Istanbul, for some time during the year 1870 he composed a treatise in Persian entitled *Shaykh va Vazīr* (The shaykh and the vizier), which was intended to propagate the cause of reform in Iran. Copies of it were sent directly to Iran by Malkum, and others were forwarded from Tiflis by Ākhūndzāda who added his own recommendations.[55]

51. *Gulistān* (London, 1885), p. 6.

52. Specimens in *Alifbā-yi Jadīd va Maktūbāt*, pp. 52–54 and 438–440. Baykara's assertion (*op. cit.* [n. 1, above], p. 154) that Ākhūndzāda, "who knew the fanaticism of the Islamic faith," first prepared a reform of the Arabic alphabet as a preliminary to its replacement, appears unfounded. On the basis of his writings, it seems that he was logically propelled by the extensive nature of his planned reform to a complete replacement of the alphabet.

53. Tansel, *op. cit.* (n. 19, above), pp. 232–233.

54. Details in *ibid.*, p. 233 f., and Levend, *op. cit.* (n. 19, above), pp. 172–173.

55. Ākhūndzāda to Mīrzā Yūsuf Khān, December 17, 1870 in *Alifbā-yi Jadīd va Maktūbāt*, p. 176; Ākhūndzāda to Mīrzā Muṣṭafā Khān, of the Ministry of Foreign Affairs, January 1871 in *ibid.*, p. 190; and Ākhūndzāda to Malkum Khān, June 2, 1871 in *ibid.*, p. 336.

This treatise, first published in 1907 after the Constitutional Revolution, takes the form of a fictitious dialogue in three scenes (*majlis*) between a reactionary shaykh and a progress-loving minister.[56] Although composed in Persian and distributed, as far as can be established, only among Iranians, the dialogue is set in Istanbul and contains many references to the Christian minorities and to the needs of the Turkish language. The device of the dialogue was employed by Malkum elsewhere, in, for example, his treatise *Rafīq va Vazīr* and in some numbers of *Qānūn*. In general, the technique proves effective for the forceful presentation of simple ideas, and in *Shaykh va Vazīr* we see the shaykh ill-equipped to rebut the arguments of the minister and ultimately obliged to concur with them, however reluctantly.

In the first scene, the question of alphabet reform is placed where, for Malkum, it belonged: in the context of a wholesale importation of European inventions and institutions. The shaykh begins by accepting the adoption of the material advances of Europe as legitimate, but rejects unconditional imitation. By contrast, the minister claims that any attempt to distinguish between acceptable and unacceptable aspects of European civilization is meaningless. Just as the telegraph had been developed "after a thousand years of effort," and should be adopted by the Muslims without any attempt at independent invention of the same device, so too the principles of government elaborated in Europe were to be followed en bloc, without reshaping or adaptation. The protection of "Islam" (i.e., the lands traditionally Muslim) would be impossible without this self-effacing subordination to European example. In reply, the shaykh defends the achievements of his ancestors, but is countered with reference to the deficient state of education among the Ottoman Turks. The minister elaborates Namık Kemal's theme of the educational inferiority of the Muslims to the non-Muslim minorities and obtains the shaykh's reluctant agreement. With the ground thus prepared, the defectiveness of the alphabet is introduced as the prime reason for this regrettable state of affairs. The minister claims that it is impossible to learn Turkish in ten years, whereas Italian may be learned in twenty days. In order to read the Arabic script correctly, first the content of what is written must be understood. With other scripts, comprehension follows and results from reading, a more logical and desirable procedure. Indeed, so great are the difficulties of the Arabic script that they have effectively prevented the absorption of the Christian minorities.[57]

In the second scene, the minister attempts to strengthen his case by listing twenty-four deficiencies of the existing alphabet. Many of these

56. *Kullīyāt-i Malkum Khān*, pp. 87–124. 57. *Ibid.*, pp. 87–103.

are familiar from previous discussions of the question, but some are novel: the impossibility of sending telegrams in the Arabic script, the difficulty of writing with a reed pen (!), and the difficult "nongeometric" shape of the Arabic letters, correct formation of which requires years of practice. The practice of joining letters together is, however, the greatest drawback of the alphabet. Joined letters should be used only in handwriting; printed letters should be separate, as in the Roman and Cyrillic alphabets. Worse still, the rules for the joining of letters in the Arabic script are not uniform for the whole alphabet: their mastery requires two whole years.[58]

In the final scene, a few weak objections are raised by the shaykh and receive summary treatment. The minister concedes that scholars are able to cope with the existing alphabet, but insists that its continued use is incompatible with the attainment of universal literacy. When the shaykh points out that a reform would make it necessary to reprint all existing literature, the minister replies that flint rifles and sailing ships had been exchanged, without great difficulty, for more modern weaponry and for steamships; literature too might be reprinted with similar ease. As for the expense, "all the books of Islam can be reprinted for the cost of a steamer." Moreover, no valid religious objection could be raised, for Kufic had once been replaced by Naskh without arousing protest.[59]

These theoretical considerations completed, the minister presents his proposals for reform, the first of which Malkum had first enunciated with his prototype revised alphabet: separation of letters, introduction of vowel letters, and "perfection" *(takmīl)* of the shapes of the letters. The second of these principles Malkum had probably adopted as a result of persuasion by Ākhūndzāda, and the third appears to have been independently evolved. "Perfection" of the shapes meant reducing the component shapes of letters to lines or circles and the abolition of "superfluous" curves at the end of such letters as *ṣād, sīn and ʿayn.*[60]

Despite their differences of approach to the alphabet question, a fundamental sympathy and mutual admiration linked Malkum Khān and Ākhūndzāda for a number of years, as is amply attested by their correspondence. We have seen that Malkum Khān, in his pseudo-autobiographical statement delivered in London and recorded by Blunt, claimed that his followers gave him the title of "Holy Ghost."[61] In reality, it was Ākhūndzāda who bestowed the title upon him, and there is no record of anyone else referring to him by it. In a letter to Jalāl ud-

58. *Ibid.*, pp. 104–114. 59. *Ibid.*, pp. 115–118. 60. *Ibid.*, pp. 119–122.

61. W. S. Blunt, *Secret History of the English Occupation of Egypt* (London, 1908), p. 84.

Dīn Mīrzā, Ākhūndzāda wrote, probably in response to a query: "His excellency the Holy Ghost (*Rūḥ al-Quds*) is Mīrzā Malkum Khān, son of Mīrzā Yaʿqūb Khān. It is I who gave him this title, because of the joy and ecstasy I experienced on reading his treatises."[62] *Rūḥ al-Quds* is a miraculous sign of God vouchsafed to Jesus in confirmation of his prophetic mission (Qurʾān, II: 87, 253; V: 110; XVI: 102), and Ākhūndzāda's bestowal of it on Malkum implies that he performed the same miracle as that for which Jesus is chiefly renowned in Islamic tradition—the resuscitation of the dead. Ākhūndzāda elsewhere indicates similarly high estimates of the value of Malkum's writings. In his letter concerning Rūmī he compares the alleged incoherence of the *Mathnavī* unfavorably with the stylistic perfection of Malkum's treatises. Even if Malkum's works were translated into Chinese, their meaning would still be clear and easily comprehensible.[63] Publication of Malkum's treatises, together with his own *Letters of Kamāl ud-Daula,* would enable Iran, in the space of fifty years, to become "like the well-ordered states of Europe."[64] In a similar vein, Ākhūndzāda advised Malkum to keep copies of all the letters they exchanged in a special album, for it would become "of historical and antiquarian interest [*tārīkh va āntīq*] to coming generations."[65]

Malkum Khān responded with almost equal warmth to the admiration of his friend. In a letter specially composed in his revised script, he wrote to Ākhūndzāda: "You have toiled for long for the improvement of our script. The ignorant have failed to understand your lofty intent, but do not despair, for future generations will laud the extent of your learning and endeavor and will curse those who now oppose you. Let me convey to you the gratitude of centuries yet to come."[66] Even more fancifully, Malkum predicted the time when their graves would become places of pilgrimage.[67]

This exchange of admiration was for the most part mixed with assurances of sympathy and the consoling prediction of posthumous fame with the ultimate triumph of alphabet reform. There came, however, a time when it appeared that alphabet reform, at least in one country, might be in sight within their lifetime. In late 1871, following the visit of Nāṣir ud-Dīn Shāh to Arab Iraq, Mīrzā Ḥusayn Khān was recalled from his post at Istanbul and after a few months appointed prime minister. His protégé Malkum was not forgotten, and he invited him to continue in his function of "special adviser" in Tehran. Thus the way was opened for Malkum to resume an active political career and also, it might be thought, to press more effectively for alphabet reform in Iran.

62. *Alifbā-yi Jadīd va Maktūbāt,* p. 176.
63. *Äsärläri,* II: 209.
64. *Alifbā-yi Jadīd va Maktūbāt,* p. 213.
65. *Ibid.,* p. 246.
66. *Ibid.,* p. 382.
67. *Ibid.,* p. 409.

Ākhūndzāda, however, had his misgivings about Malkum leaving Istanbul, particularly because he was to serve again under Mīrzā Ḥusayn Khān. On March 8, 1872, as Malkum was preparing to depart, he wrote:

> They say you have been invited to Tehran. I don't know if you will be going or not. If you hope to put your alphabet reform into effect, then go. But otherwise, why go? To make a name for yourself, to gather titles and positions? . . . You know your own interests best; I won't interfere. Indeed, if you go, I will be happy, since you will be nearer to me. But if you do, you should keep your Ottoman nationality for a number of reasons until you see how matters turn out. For I can't make out whether Nabī Khān's son [Nabī Khān, a baker, was the father of Mīrzā Ḥusayn Khān] is inviting you with good and sincere intentions, to make use of you, or whether he simply wants to prevent a learned and eloquent person like yourself from being outside the country and beyond his control.[68]

Ākhūndzāda's forebodings that Malkum would busy himself with gathering "titles and positions" and forget the cause of alphabet reform came to be largely justified. The cause was, however, still prominent in Malkum's mind shortly before his departure from Istanbul, for later in March we find Ākhūndzāda commenting on a new draft alphabet received from Malkum.

> What script is this you are sending for my perusal? I don't understand your purpose or aim. It is the very same script, with the same forms that we already have: one of the four forms of those dreadful letters. . . . If you intend, by this device, to establish a phonetic alphabet [this is presumably what is meant by *alifbā-yi alfābītī*], written from left to right, with the same pleasing forms you previously worked out and sent me; and want, through various stratagems, to fasten a phonetic script onto the necks of our people, then I must concur with your intention.[69]

En route from Istanbul to Tehran, Malkum passed through Tiflis, arriving there at the end of March and spending several days as the guest of Ākhūndzāda. Among the matters they discussed were presumably their cherished projects of alphabet reform, but the scope of their conversation ranged wider, too, to include a number of other topics. These were carefully noted down by Ākhūndzāda, who deliberately built up his own archive with a view to posthumous glory. First among them was the necessity of granting patents to inventors, a subject of concern to the two men possibly because of their invention of new alphabets: they may have thought the day at hand when it would be necessary to defend their brainchildren against a host of imitators.[70] Of greater interest are Malkum's statements concerning religion and its

68. *Ibid.*, p. 279. 69. *Ibid.*, pp. 383–384. 70. *Ibid.*, pp. 286–288.

alleged harmful effects on mankind. According to Malkum, veneration for the Prophets and for those who undertake the propagation of the religions they have founded leads mankind inevitably to scorn of reason and the intellect. Thus, religion demands belief in the birth of Jesus from a virgin, while science and reason dismiss the possibility. Those who would follow the dictates of reason are subject to persecution such as that visited upon heretics by the Spanish Inquisition. "Hence, the felicity and triumph of the human race will become possible only when human reason, both in Asia and in Europe, is freed from its eternal bondage to become sole guide and authority in the affairs and thoughts of mankind, displacing religious tradition [*naql*]."[71]

The third section of Ākhūndzāda's notes deals with the proper manner in which this ideal state may be achieved. In Malkum's view, Ākhūndzāda's method of frontal attack on the doctrines of religion, as exemplified in the *Letters of Kamāl ud-Daula,* was unsuitable, for it tended to provoke only hostility and resistance and to confirm the believer in his baseless convictions. Indirect argumentation, emphasizing the assertion that God had allowed false faiths to flourish in the world for thousands of years and thus left mankind without true guidance, would automatically destroy faith in the allegedly revealed religions also. "Was God asleep for so long, and did He suddenly wake up and see that false faiths had polluted His world? Then did He conceive the idea of sending Moses and his friends?"[72] This record of Malkum's opinions on the question of religion, if accurate—and there is no reason to suppose that it is not—is of great interest in revealing his true attitudes. In oral communication with a fellow atheist, he had no reason to hide his true feelings and no advantage to be gained by posing as a Muslim or Christian. This record of Malkum's statements also shows the goal to which many of his efforts were bent—the replacement of religion by science and reason as the sole guides of man. It needs to be added that Malkum lacked the necessary seriousness and consistency of purpose to pursue this abstract goal methodically, and much of his career was dominated by the pursuit of more immediate, personal and concrete objectives.

The ultimate goal of dethronement of religion needed to be pursued with caution. Pronouncements of Malkum demonstrating his intention to use Islam as a cloak for westernization, as a subtle means for introducing that which might otherwise be repugnant, have been quoted in these pages already. There existed a further reason for refraining from an open attack on religious beliefs such as that mounted by Ākhūndzāda: concern for the maintenance of popular morality. This he also expounded to Ākhūndzāda while in Tiflis. According to Mal-

71. *Ibid.*, pp. 288–290.

72. *Ibid.*, pp. 290–291.

kum, every religion consists of three elements: beliefs (*iʿtiqādāt*), rites (*ʿibādāt*), and ethics (*akhlāq*). Now the real purpose of religion is constituted by the third element, beliefs and rites serving only to reinforce and provide sanction for a moral code. Thus hope of reward and fear of punishment in the hereafter are the most effective guarantees of socially desirable behavior in this world, and it is necessary to assume the existence of a supernatural being to dispense such reward and punishment. If, however, morality could be secured by nonreligious means, beliefs and rites would lose their raison d'être and automatically collapse. "The diffusion of the sciences in most countries of Europe and America has enabled people to dispense with beliefs and rites for the purpose of sustaining morality. But in Asia, the sciences are not yet widespread, and it is therefore necessary to maintain these two elements in order to secure the morality which is the fundamental aim of every religion."[73]

Malkum had himself borrowed from freemasonry certain elements of a nonreligious code of morality, and after discussing the link between religion and morality, he set forth to Ākhūndzāda his view of the seven basic ethical duties of man which, he confirmed, formed part of instruction at the farāmūshkhāna.[74] This list concludes Ākhūndzāda's notes on the meeting.

From Tiflis, Malkum proceeded to Tehran where he resumed his function of special adviser to Mīrzā Ḥusayn Khān, who by now had been appointed prime minister. Henceforth Malkum's correspondence with Ākhūndzāda appears to have diminished and indeed to have come to a complete halt some time before the latter's death in 1878. This cessation of correspondence was doubtless accelerated by Malkum's appointment as Iranian plenipotentiary in London in 1873, on the eve of Nāṣir ud-Dīn Shāh's first visit to Europe. We find Ākhūndzāda writing wistfully to Mīrzā Yūsuf Khān in February 1875:

> I have no news of *Rūḥ al-Quds*. What is he doing, and how is he? It is a pity that he has left Tehran. His presence in London has no use, even for himself, other than material benefit. Alas! In Iran a wise writer had made his appearance, but they failed to appreciate him and imprisoned him in London. Is it his real task to be an ambassador? No, his real task is writing down his thoughts and knowledge. If he had remained in Tehran, his efforts would probably have achieved the change of the Islamic alphabet.[75]

Ākhūndzāda assumed in Malkum a sustained consistency of radical purpose that he never possessed. Malkum's concern with alphabet reform appears ultimately to have been little more than a diversion to

73. *Ibid.*, pp. 293–294.
74. *Ibid.*, pp. 294–295; and see above, p. 38.
75. *Ibid.*, p. 334.

occupy his hours in Istanbul before returning to the politics of Tehran, and its active resumption again took place in exile, this time in London. His years in Tehran as adviser to Mīrzā Ḥusayn Khān and his term of service as Iranian minister in London were marked by more concrete and lucrative concerns than the revision of the Arabic alphabet. If earlier he had proclaimed the *sine qua non* of all progress in Iran to be the separation of the legislative from the executive branches of government, and, in Istanbul, denounced the deficiencies of the alphabet as the root cause of all backwardness, now Malkum found a new preoccupation, a new cure for the ills of Iran: the promotion of commercial concessions with a view to an economic regeneration that was hardly less personal than national.

CHAPTER 5

NĀṢIR UD-DĪN SHĀH was, in his own way, a pious monarch, fond of religious ceremony and especially devoted to commemoration of the Twelve Imams. It was in his reign that the birthdays of ʿAlī b. Abī Ṭālib and of the Imam Ḥusayn became official festivals, typically celebrated with fireworks and military parades.[1] In accordance with the precedent established by previous Qajar monarchs, he also bestowed his signs of generosity on the ʿatabāt, and it was only natural that this love of religious display, combined with his passion for travel, should sooner or later induce him to visit Arab Iraq and to perform the pilgrimage to the Shiʿi shrines. His visit to the ʿatabāt in 1871 was not, however, purely religious in its purpose and effects, for in addition to meeting the ulama of Kāẓimayn, Najaf, and Karbalā, Nāṣir ud-Dīn Shāh also spent much time in the company of Mīrzā Ḥusayn Khān, who had come from Istanbul to be in attendance on his master. The ambassador took advantage of Nāṣir ud-Dīn's presence in Baghdad to draw his attention to improvements effected in the condition of the city and the province by Midhat Paşa, who had governed the Baghdad province from February 1869 to May 1871[2] and to suggest the desirability of similar reforms in Iran.

The monarch was evidently impressed by what he saw, and his own dormant interest in governmental reform and reorganization was reawakened. When he arrived back in Tehran on Dhū-l-Ḥijja 1, 1287/

1. Muḥammad Ḥasan Khān Iʿtimād us-Salṭana, *al-Maʾāthir va Āthār* (Tehran, 1306 lunar/1889), p. 96; J.-B. Feuvrier, *Trois Ans à la Cour de Perse* (Paris, 1899), p. 205.

2. His achievements are summarized by Roger Mantran in his article "Bağdād à l'époque ottomane," *Bağdād: Volume Special Publié a l'Occasion du Mille-deux-centième Anniversaire de la Fondation* (Leyden, 1962), p. 322.

February 22, 1871, he was accompanied by Mīrzā Ḥusayn Khān whom, it can be assumed, he had already decided to appoint prime minister.[3] Initially, however, Mīrzā Ḥusayn Khān was entrusted with the Ministries of Pensions and Endowments (*vaẓāʾif va auqāf*) and Justice. The former can have made few demands on his time, for in practice its functions were fulfilled by the Ministry of Finance. It was in his capacity as minister of justice that Mīrzā Ḥusayn Khān was able to begin the task of reform. In Rabīᶜ uth-Thānī 1288/June–July 1871, he took steps to improve the functioning of the *dīvānkhāna* (the name by which the ministry still went, despite the introduction of the term *ᶜadlīya* in 1858) and to centralize the administration of justice throughout the country. Provincial governors were forbidden to pronounce and execute judgment. Their sole function became to arrest the accused, carry out preliminary investigations, and then dispatch the prisoner and evidence to the Ministry of Justice in Tehran for final action. According to Mīrzā Ḥusayn Khān's plan, each major town was ultimately to have its own *dīvānkhāna,* functioning as a branch of the Ministry of Justice, but initially he contented himself with sending to each city where a governor resided an official of the ministry who was to supervise observation of the new regulations limiting the governor's powers. It was further stipulated that soldiers be consistently subject to civil jurisdiction and that cases involving foreigners be referred to the Ministry of Foreign Affairs for settlement.[4]

Later in the year, Mīrzā Ḥusayn Khān received the additional post of minister of war and the title *sipahsālār* (commander). His appointment coincided with the celebration of Nāṣir ud-Dīn Shāh's birthday on Rajab 13, 1288/September 28, 1871, and the occasion was marked by the appearance of the monarch, for the first time, in military uniform. In the course of a speech delivered to those assembled to congratulate him on his birthday, Nāṣir ud-Dīn Shāh remarked on the past neglect of military affairs in Iran and expressed his determination to strengthen the army. He announced that henceforth he would regard himself as the supreme commander of the army, and that urgent measures of reform would be undertaken by Mīrzā Ḥusayn Khān as minister of war. It is probable that the entire speech was written, or at least inspired, by Mīrzā Ḥusayn Khān: the use of the ward *ᶜaskarīya* to denote army instead of the usual *qushūn* seems to be the first occurrence of the term

3. ᶜAbdullah Mustaufī, *Sharḥ-i Zindagānī-yi Man yā Tārīkh-i Ijtimāᶜī va Idārī-yi Daura-yi Qājār* (Tehran, 1341 solar/1962), I: 110.

4. On these measures, see *ibid.*, I: 115; Firīdūn Ādamīyat, *Fikr-i Āzādī va Muqaddima-yi Nihḍat-i Mashrūṭīyat* (Tehran, 1340 solar/1961), pp. 74–75; Maḥmūd Farhād Muᶜtamad, *Mushīr ud-Daula Sipahsālār-i Aᶜẓam* (Tehran, 1326 solar/1947), p. 38; and Muḥammad Ḥasan Khān Iᶜtimād us-Salṭana, *Mirʾāt ul-Buldān-i Nāṣirī* (Tehran, 1294–1297 lunar/1877–1880, III: 6–9.

in Persian and a borrowing from Ottoman Turkish that Mīrzā Ḥusayn Khān had absorbed during his residence in Istanbul.[5]

The entire process of governmental reform in Iran had begun with the military when, under the pressure of Russian attack, the crown prince ᶜAbbās Mīrzā had instituted a corps of soldiers trained and equipped more or less in accordance with contemporary European standards. Here, as was frequently the case, the European model was perceived through the lens of Ottoman example, and for the newly instituted corps the name *Niẓām-i Jadīd* was borrowed from the military reforms of Sultan Selim III.[6] After the death of ᶜAbbās Mīrzā, the process of military reform was not seriously pursued. Although uniform was repeatedly modified, varying tunics and hats were experimented with, and even an amount of modern weaponry was procured, the fundamental weakness and corruption of the army's administration were left untouched, and Iran's defensive capacities remained slight. Mīrzā Ḥusayn Khān, no less than his predecessors, paid attention to matters of dress, but went beyond them to concern himself with reforming the administration of the army. He first separated the military from the civil establishment and forbade interference by the military in civil matters. If in some provincial city disputes over spheres of responsibility were to occur between the governor and the local army commander (*raʾīs-i niẓām*), the matter was to be referred to Tehran for settlement. A special budget was to be set aside for the army, under the exclusive control of the Ministry of War. Salaries were to consist of a fixed amount and to be paid promptly at regular intervals. Most important, appointments in the army were to be made on the basis of competence and suitability, not friendship and ties of family.[7]

Nāṣir ud-Dīn's confidence in Mīrzā Ḥusayn Khān resulted finally in his appointment as prime minister on Shaᶜbān 29, 1288/November 13, 1871.[8] Thus established in the seat of power, Mīrzā Ḥusayn Khān was able, a few months later, to invite Malkum to join him in Tehran as special adviser to the prime minister, and thereby to resume the relationship that had existed between the two men in Istanbul. The appointment was accompanied by the granting of the *Nishān-i Humāyūn* (Imperial Order), first class and of the title Nāẓim ul-Mulk (Orderer of the Realm).[9]

5. Mustaufī, *op. cit.*, I: 115–116.

6. See Hamid Algar, *Religion and State in Iran: the Role of the Ulama in the Qajar Period* (Berkeley and Los Angeles, 1969), pp. 75–78.

7. On these measures, see Mustaufī, *op. cit.*, I: 118; Ādamīyat, *op. cit.*, pp. 84–86; and Iᶜtimad us-Salṭana, *Mirʾāt ul-Buldan-i Nāṣirī*, III: 220–222.

8. Mustaufī, *op. cit.*, I: 116; Ādamīyat, *op. cit.*, p. 58.

9. Khān Malik Sāsānī, *Siyāsatgarān-i Daura-yi Qājār* (Tehran, 1338 solar/1959), I: 131.

It is true that some such title went together with every government post of any importance in the Qajar period, but there is reason to think that this title was chosen by Malkum himself. He always demonstrated extreme concern for the figure he cut in European circles, and we have already seen the extravagant lengths of invention to which he went in order to impress Wilfred Scawen Blunt.[10] In polite society it was clearly an advantage to go by the title of prince, especially if no one was likely to inquire too closely after the dynasty to which one belonged, and Malkum never felt shy to style himself Prince Malcom Khan.[11] Mīrzā, it is true, corresponds approximately to prince, being a corruption of *amīrzāda* (born of an amir), but it bears this meaning only when following a name, as, for example, ʿAbbās Mīrzā. When it precedes a name, as in the case of Mīrzā Malkum Khān, it signifies nothing more elevated than a scribe, a teacher or a government official. To add further allure to his person and to pose as a kind of progressive aristocrat, acceptable equally to conservative and liberal tastes, Malkum frequently referred to himself in European circles as *le Prince Réformateur*.[12] He presumably derived this additional epithet of reformer from the title now bestowed on him of Nāẓim ul-Mulk (later revised to Nāẓim ud-Daula). Malkum was not the first to go by this title, nor did it necessarily imply the quality of reformer. There is, nonetheless, an etymological and semantic connection between it and the terms *naẓm* (order), *tanẓīm* (ordering, reform, in Ottoman and then Persian usage), and *munaẓẓam* (orderly, reformed), all much beloved of Malkum and important items in his vocabulary. It is, then, reasonable to suppose that the title was chosen by Malkum himself as being most suitable to his self-image as savior of the Iranian state.

Malkum had doubtless anticipated the summons of Mīrzā Ḥusayn Khān, and anxious to participate in his protector's good fortune set out from Istanbul in February 1872. After a brief stay in Tiflis with his confidant Ākhūndzāda, he arrived in Tehran in the early spring. It is comprehensible that Mīrzā Ḥusayn Khān should have wished to have at his side in Tehran one whose outlook in matters of reform he shared and who had acquired a wide reputation for knowledge of European political and legal systems, above all by means of his various treatises. Indeed, Mīrzā Ḥusayn Khān's entire program of reform has been attributed to the inspiration and even direction of Malkum,[13] and it is

10. See above, pp. 11–12.

11. See, for example, Malkum's letter to *The Times*, March 16, 1891.

12. Sāsānī, *op. cit.*, I: 131.

13. See H. L. Rabino, "Une tentative de réformes en 1875," *Revue du Monde Musulman*, XXVI (1914): 133.

of some interest to establish the share which he had in its elaboration and execution.

Mīrzā Ḥusayn Khān's judicial and military reforms were for the most part initiated before Malkum's return in Iran in the spring of 1872, even though their implementation continued progressively until his dismissal in September 1873. It is nonetheless possible to assume a certain influence by Malkum on their conception: there is much in them reminiscent of the proposals made in his early treatises. The intention ultimately to establish separate *dīvānkhāna*'s in each provincial city to function as branches of the Ministry of Justice, corresponds to law thirty-five in Malkum's first treatise, the *Kitābcha-yi Ghaybī,*[14] and the necessity of the measure is also set forth in a later treatise, *Ḥarf-i Gharīb* (Strange words), composed, it appears, in about 1877.[15] Similarly, many of Mīrzā Ḥusayn Khān's measures of military reform were the same as those adumbrated in the treatise *Dastgāh-i Dīvān,* written by Malkum in Istanbul: insistence upon suitability and competence in the appointment of officers, separation of the military from the civil establishment, and the regular payment of salaries to all members of the army.[16] It is thus possible that Mīrzā Ḥusayn Khān was influenced in his measures of reform by the contents of Malkum's treatises and that this influence was reinforced by correspondence between the two men before their reunion in Tehran. It is, however, also possible that Mīrzā Ḥusayn Khān was inspired to act by his favorable impressions of the Ottoman Tanzimat or simply enacting certain elementary and urgent measures dictated by his own common sense.

The influence of Malkum is clearer in the case of Mīrzā Ḥusayn Khān's most important and comprehensive measure of governmental reform, one which was initiated soon after Malkum's return to Tehran. On Shaʿbān 12, 1289/October 15, 1872, the sipahsālār presented to Nāṣir ud-Dīn Shāh the text of a decree which would establish two bodies responsible for the administration of affairs. These were to be called the *Darbār-i Aʿẓam* (The Great Court), alternatively known as the *Dār ush-Shūrā-yi Kubrā* (The Supreme House of Consultation), and the *Majlis-i Mashvarat-i Vuzarā* (Consultative Assembly of Ministers), also referred to as *Hayʾat-i Daulat* (Council of State) or simply *Kābīna* (cabinet). The former was to consist of nine ministers in addition to the prime minister and—although this is left ambiguous in the sipahsālār's formulation of the project—a number of more or less arbitrarily selected princes who held no specific administrative responsibility. These latter were pre-

14. *Majmūʿa-yi Āthār,* pp. 39–40.
15. *Kullīyāt-i Malkum,* ed. Hāshim Rabīʿzāda (Tabriz, 1325 lunar/1908), p. 37.
16. *Majmūʿa-yi Āthār,* pp. 89–92.

sumably to act in an advisory capacity, for the ministers presided over by the *ṣadr-i aᶜẓam* constituted, in Mīrzā Ḥusayn Khān's expression, "the heart and soul of the *Darbār-i Aᶜẓam*." The nine ministers were to be individually responsible to the *ṣadr-i aᶜẓam*, who in turn was responsible to the shah; their spheres of responsibility were to be precisely defined, and no minister might interfere in the work of another, being free to express an opinion on matters outside his own competence only at meetings of the assembly of ministers. Within each ministry, the minister would be free to pursue his own policies, except that the fixing of salaries, the creation of new posts, and the dismissal of officials were all to be subject to the approval of the *Darbār-i Aᶜẓam*.[17] After a week's consideration, the shah gave his consent to the proposal, and the *Majlis-i Mashvarat-i Vuzarā* met for the first time on Shavvāl 2/December 4, as a preliminary to the promulgation of the *Darbār-i Aᶜẓam*.[18]

The two bodies established by this measure bore a close resemblance to those suggested by Malkum in his *Kitābcha-yi Ghaybī*. The *Darbar-i Aᶜẓam* corresponded to the *Majlis-i Tanẓīmāt* (Reform Council) he had proposed to create, consisting also of the ministers, headed by the *ṣadr-i aᶜẓam*, together with a number of princes and advisors (*mushīrhā*). He had, however, included the shah among the members of the council and explicitly defined its function as that of the legislative organ of state.[19] The task of the *Darbār-i Aᶜẓam* was by contrast defined by Mīrzā Ḥusayn Khān as "the execution of all royal commands and the administration of all state affairs."[20] The Consultative Council of Ministers established in 1872 can also be compared with Malkum's proposed *Majlis-i Vuzarā* (Council of Ministers), intended by him to act as the executive organ of the state.[21] Its composition differed only slightly from that of the body proposed by Malkum: it was to consist of nine ministers, whereas Malkum had foreseen only eight. To the eight ministries suggested by Malkum was added one somewhat vaguely entitled *Vizārat-i Favāʾid*, which appears to have fulfilled approximately the function of a Ministry of Works.[22] The measure of 1872 corresponded to Malkum's proposal in the *Kitābcha-yi Ghaybī* in its omission of all reference to the superfluous Ministry of Pensions and Endowments, one of the six ministries instituted by Nāṣir ud-Dīn Shāh in 1858.

In addition to these and other specific points of resemblance, there is observable throughout the formulation of Mīrzā Ḥusayn Khān's pro-

17. See Mustaufī, *op. cit.* (n. 3, above), I: 119–121; Ādamīyat, *op. cit.* (n. 4, above), pp. 79–81.

18. Mustaufī, *op. cit.*, I: 122; Ādamīyat, *op. cit.*, p. 82.

19. *Majmūᶜa-yi Āthār*, pp. 24–25, 27.

20. Mustaufī, *op. cit.*, I: 121.

21. *Majmūᶜa-yi Āthār*, p. 25.

22. Mustaufī, *op. cit.* (n. 3, above), I: 121.

posal a similarity with Malkum's customary manner of expression. It may well be that in his capacity of special advisor Malkum in fact undertook to draft the entire measure. ᶜAbdullāh Mustaufī remarks in the course of his memoirs that the wording of the measure strongly suggests a foreign code of law as source of inspiration and that Malkum Khān may have translated and adapted to Iranian requirements some foreign constitutional law.[23] There is no doubt that in a general sense the measure was due to foreign example, but it is unlikely that Malkum —or the sipahsālār—should have based it directly upon the translation of some European law. The stylistic unfamiliarity upon which Mustaufī comments should be taken as reflecting the novelty of the whole subject of constitutional law in nineteenth-century Iran. Unfamiliarity and even awkwardness of expression were the inevitable concomitant of innovation; these are visible equally in the proposed laws set out in the *Kitābcha-yi Ghaybī* and Malkum's other treatises and in the measure of October 1872.

Accompanying the draft proposal was a letter to Nāṣir ud-Dīn Shāh in which Mīrzā Ḥusayn Khān explained its purpose and anticipated advantages. Here too the hand of Malkum is apparent. In precisely the same way as he had once pronounced the prosperity and progress of the state to be dependent on the separation of the legislative from the executive, so too in this letter the implementation of the proposed measures was presented as a sure key to the welfare of the state. "The orderly functioning of all the affairs of state depends on putting into effect these few simple items." Similarly, in a manner typical for Malkum, the experience of Europe is invoked as ultimate authority for the efficacy of the measures proposed: "The fruits of these measures must be observed in the experiences of other states."[24]

It seemed at first that in Iran too their fruits would come to be observed. Particularly the measures limiting the judicial and penal powers of provincial governors appear to have taken immediate effect,[25] and it might have been thought that at last a time had come when a thorough program of reform could be implemented at Malkum's bidding. In 1858, Malkum had been unable to do more than present proposals to Nāṣir ud-Dīn Shāh and had not enjoyed the support of a powerful ally sharing his interest in the cause of reform. Now, by contrast, he had been appointed special advisor to a prime minister who held the full confidence of the shah. The measures initiated in 1872, however, had little permanent effect: Malkum was soon to leave Iran again for Europe and Mīrzā Ḥusayn Khān to be dismissed from his post as prime minister.

23. *Ibid.*, I: 123.
24. *Ibid.*, I: 120; Ādamīyat, *op. cit.* (n. 4, above), p. 80.
25. *Ibid.*, pp. 79–80.

The failure of Malkum and his patron to achieve thorough and lasting governmental reform may in part be attributed to the widespread opposition they encountered, both in certain circles in Tehran and among the provincial governors. Their failure was, however, due equally to their simultaneous pursuit of another objective: the involvement of foreign capital and commercial enterprise in Iran through the hawking of concessions. It may well be argued that the cause of administrative and governmental reform was ultimately inseparable from that of economic development: an efficiently functioning state presupposed an increase in taxation and revenue, which was in turn dependent on greater national prosperity. In the writings of Malkum which set forth the need to attract foreign capital to Iran, there is, however, a noticeable change of emphasis from his earlier treatises: instead of the separation of the legislative from the executive, economic development is proclaimed to be the *sine qua non* of national salvation. It is hard not to connect this change with Malkum's new official position and the opportunities for personal enrichment that flowed from his proximity to the seat of power. Before examining the use he made of these opportunities, it will be convenient to discuss his thoughts on economic matters, written down in the 1870s, a decade of intense concession-mongering by Iranian ministers and envoys. Malkum's writings on economics, it is true, were not exclusively inspired by enlightened and patriotic concern, but they are nonetheless deserving of consideration as the earliest treatment of economic problems in nineteenth-century Iran.

In a treatise entitled *Uṣūl-i Tamaddun* (The principles of civilization) that appears from internal evidence to have been composed in London in about 1875,[26] Malkum proposes the opening of Iran to

26. The treatise appears under this title in *Kullīyāt-i Malkum,* pp. 4–35. Firīdūn Ādamīyat, in his *Fikr-i Āzādī* (p. 154, n. 1), remarks that the text appearing in this edition of Malkum's treatises is inaccurate and incomplete. More recently, he has published a new text, based on a manuscript copied by Mīrzā Muḥammad ᶜAlī Khān Farīd ul-Mulk Hamadānī, under the title "Uṣūl-i Taraqqī" (The principles of progress") in the monthly periodical *Sukhan* (XVI [1345 solar/1966]: 70–73; 131–135; 250–254; 406–414; 481–489; 622–630). The manuscript used by him evidently treats as one continuous work two treatises printed separately, though consecutively, by Hāshim Rabīᶜzāda, the editor of *Kullīyāt-i Malkum,* and entitled by him "Uṣūl-i Tamaddun" and "Ḥarf-i Gharīb." It is true that the copyist of Ādamīyat's manuscript was for many years secretary at the Iranian legation in London while Malkum was envoy, and might thus be thought to have been particularly well acquainted with Malkum's work. It must also be conceded that Malkum's treatises are often weak in structure and full of repetition, and hence confusion might often arise as to the point of separation between one treatise and the next. It is nonetheless unlikely that "Uṣūl-i Tamaddun" and "Ḥarf-i Gharīb" should form a single work. "Ḥarf-i Gharīb" is a shorter treatise than "Uṣūl-i Tamaddun," repeating in summary the contents of the

foreign commercial and financial enterprise. This proposal occurs in the framework of a general exposition of economic principles. The whole of the treatise is inspired by an acute awareness of the intense commercial activity engaged in by European states and a desire to convey something of this awareness to his "Asiatic" readers, who are totally oblivious of the realities of international life. Malkum finds it necessary to stress that the power of Europe is not, in the first place, military, but economic and commercial. War itself in the modern age has been abandoned as a means of enrichment: energies have been transferred to economic competition, and it is the interests of trade which determine war and peace, rather than the simple urge to conquest. "The real war between states in this epoch is in the production of cheap goods."[27]

Iran is clearly in no position to enter this war as one of the chief contestants, but can nonetheless achieve a greater degree of wealth and commercial activity. The first step lies in the realization that prosperity is not a fixed quantity, immutably determined by the extent of natural resources, but depends on the volume of production of goods. "The path of enrichment of a people is none other than this, that they work hard and produce many goods, and trade plenteously."[28] This simple point is repeated frequently throughout the treatise, and Malkum says explicitly: "This fact must be repeated a thousand times, for it is now several thousand years that it has remained uncomprehended by the Asiatic intelligence."[29] It has traditionally been thought that gold itself constitutes wealth, whereas it functions only as a medium of exchange and valuation. Monetary principles are totally unknown in the East, and nobody is aware that the quantity of money in circulation will depend on the volume of commercial exchange.[30]

Once these simple economic facts have been grasped, it is incumbent on Iran to create conditions favoring an expansion of trading relations with the outside world. Above all, communications should be

---

latter as well as proposals earlier made for political and administrative reform. It appears to have been intended primarily for the perusal of Nāṣir ud-Dīn Shāh, while "Uṣūl-i Tamaddun" was directed more to the attention of government ministers. In view of these considerations, reference will here be made to the printing of the treatise in Rabīᶜzāda's edition, despite the numerous typographical errors and eccentric punctuation with which it is marred.

The approximate date, 1875, suggests itself from the statement of Malkum that two years previously the sale of concessions would have been an easy matter, but that at the time of writing Iranian concessions no longer enjoyed any credit on the London market. This would seem to be an allusion to the cancellation of the Reuter concession in 1873 and the loss of credit is entailed.

27. *Kullīyāt-i Malkum*, p. 13.

28. *Ibid.*, p. 6.

29. *Ibid.*

30. *Ibid.*, p. 10.

improved. Traditionally roads have been built only for military purposes or along pilgrim routes, and the needs of commerce have never received serious consideration. The establishment of a network of roads would enable goods to reach their destination with greater speed and at lesser cost, thus bringing down their price and making them available to an increased number of customers. It is only the absence of roads that prevents Iran from exporting fifteen million *tomans'* worth of wool annually and from becoming an exporter of wheat.[31]

Second, internal customs and tolls should be totally abolished. Although apparently productive of revenue, they rob the state of the far greater income that would result from an increased flow of goods.[32]

Third, the value of the coinage should be fixed and tied to a definite standard. The devastating effects of its fluctuation could fairly be said to be worse than those produced by the Mongol invasions.[33]

These elementary requirements having been met, it is necessary to understand that any productive process requires four elements: natural resources, labor, capital, and skill.[34] The first two are already available in Iran, but the second two are lacking. As for capital, its lack may be partially offset by the establishment of investment banks which would place idle and unused wealth at the service of economic enterprise. Malkum proposes that loans be made on interest to encourage the freer circulation of money, and it is worthy of note that despite his general concern for the preservation of an Islamic exterior, he shows no awareness on this occasion of the religious objections to which his proposal was liable. Numerous banks offering loans should be set up for the financing of agriculture and commerce and also a central bank to control the issue of currency.[35]

A further condition of expanded trade and prosperity is the establishment of security for life and property, in such manner that it should no longer be dependent on the moral qualities of the monarch, but guaranteed by a justly constituted system of administration.[36]

This much having been established, Malkum warns that only through such measures of reform and economic improvement can Iran hope to defend its independence against the onslaught of Europe. For imperialism, acting as an agent of universal progress, seeks out backward and impoverished states as its rightful prey.

31. *Ibid.*, pp. 13–14.

32. *Ibid.*, p. 15.

33. *Ibid.*, p. 16.

34. *Ibid.*, p. 17.

35. *Ibid.*, pp. 20–21. In 1872, Malkum participated in inconclusive deliberations on the establishment of a bank, presided over by Mīrzā Ḥuṣayn Khān. See Ṭabāṭabā'ī's introduction to *Majmūʿa-yi Āthār*, p. xi.

36. *Kullīyāt-i Malkum*, pp. 23–24.

> The chief cause for the enmity and hatred of the states and peoples of Europe for the states of Asia is this: they say that the states of Asia, through insecurity of life and property, have submerged a choice region of the globe in the sea of abjection and made it the disgrace of mankind. The states of Europe, by virtue of this very security of life and property [which they enjoy] consider the occupation and possession of all the countries of Asia to be their divine right and certain duty.[37]

The trading states of Europe cannot afford to leave Asia stagnating in its backwardness, for their prosperity is dependent on the material progress of all parts of the world, and for this reason the European powers sincerely desire the prosperity of Iran. "The peoples of Europe have no aim and business in foreign lands other than the expansion of trade and the increase of prosperity."[38] The survival of unprogressive governments is intolerable for Europe, and when a European power occupies an Asiatic state, it is not to enjoy the glories of conquest and plunder, but to further the cause of trade and mutual profit. "Not a single *dīnār* from the revenue of India enters the British treasury."[39] The removal of backward states, then, can be strictly regarded as "the justice of divine destiny."[40]

It is remarkable how Malkum thus fully assimilated the European conviction that encroachment on the countries of Asia represented a species of historical destiny, having as its aim the general improvement of the planet. A contrast between Europe and Asia as two antithetical spheres inhabited by fundamentally divergent human types was implicit in much that Malkum wrote, and it is clear from his manner of expression that he identified himself fully with European values and assumptions. The salvation of all mankind was thought to flow from the blessed touch of European commerce, and Asian states hostile or indifferent to the furtherance of trade were regarded not simply as unreasonable, but as downright wicked.[41] Malkum makes no protest against this view of European activity in Asia, and it is thus fair to conclude that when, several years later in the columns of *Qānūn*, he came to protest against the selling of Iran to foreign interests, his change in attitude corresponded to a change of personal fortune and position. Similarly, in the early 1870s, his advocacy of European economic involvement in Iran tended to serve his own prosperity more than the welfare of the country or even the enrichment of those

37. *Ibid.*, pp. 25–26.
38. *Ibid.*, pp. 27–28.
39. *Ibid.*, p. 29.
40. *Ibid.*, p. 30.
41. On the currency of such attitudes, see Norman Daniel, *Islam, Europe and Empire* (Edinburgh, 1966), especially Chapter Five.

Europeans whose interest had been aroused in the salvation of this piece of benighted Asia.

Against this background of threatened chastisement for the sin of backwardness and neglect, Malkum proposes as an immediate and urgent measure the attraction of foreign companies to operate in Iran. Lack of capital can be partially offset by the mobilization of idle wealth and the institution of banks, but inexperience in matters such as the formation of joint-stock companies is a more serious deficiency.[42] Until it is remedied, "for the sake of the prosperity of Iran, it is necessary to introduce companies from abroad. The wise ones of Iran[43] are still of the opinion that foreign companies would take over Iran: this opinion is the very essence of ignorance." The presence of a foreign company is no more harmful than that of an individual. If Iran desires total isolation, it should close its borders, like Khiva and Bukhara, but even then it should realize that it is not immune from attack, for a thief can break into even the most well-guarded house.[44]

This being the case, "the leaders of the state must, without delay, turn over the construction of railways, the operation of mines, the establishment of a bank, and all public works and structures to foreign companies. . . . The government of Iran must grant as many concessions to foreign companies as possible."[45] The granting of such concessions should not be regarded as an act of generosity; on the contrary, Iran should be grateful to the foreign companies that come to operate on its soil. Such gratitude should determine the spirit of all negotiations. "Whenever anyone asks the government for a concession, the government replies, 'How much will you pay?' This question, in one second, destroys a hundred advantages for Iran."[46] No immediate profit should be expected from a concession, for the prosperity automatically resulting from its implementation would benefit the state immeasurably. In the case of previously untapped mineral resources, the government should demand no share in the profits of exploitation, which would "inevitably" revert to state and people.[47] The only condition for the successful functioning of a concession is that it be granted to a reputable person: previously too many nonentities (*ashkhāṣ-i bī sar-au-pā*) had been appointed concessionaires. So desirable, indeed, is the attraction of reputable financiers and companies that money should be given to a Rothschild to induce him to operate in Iran, rather than demanding payment from him.[48]

42. *Kullīyāt-i Malkum*, p. 30.

43. *ʿUqalā-yi Īrān*: Malkum's sarcastic designation for ministers and government officials.

44. *Kullīyāt-i Malkum*, pp. 31–32.

45. *Ibid.*, p. 33.

46. *Ibid.*

47. *Ibid.*, p. 34.

48. *Ibid.*, p. 35.

Many of the arguments advanced in *Uṣūl-i Tamaddun* are repeated in the shorter treatise, *Ḥarf-i Gharīb* (Strange words), composed about five years later and evidently intended for the perusal of Nāṣir ud-Dīn Shāh.[49] Here, measures for the expansion of trade are linked with the proposals for governmental reform that Malkum had first made in 1858. The security upon which increased productivity depends can be achieved only through the establishment of a *dīvānkhāna* in each province, the regulation of the army, and the institution of a police force separate from the military.[50] Of greater interest in the treatise is the elaboration of the thesis that expanded commercial intercourse constitutes Iran's only defence against European invasion. The possibility of military resistance to Russian attack must realistically be discounted, and therefore the argument that the construction of harbors and roads is an invitation to foreign conquerors is irrelevant. Certain countries may be desired by European powers for strategic reasons, and such countries must look to the cannon for their defence; in others, commercial opportunity will be the extent of European demand.[51] Now the conquest of Iran is not strategically imperative for Russia, and hence it is foolish to object that the extension of harbor facilities at Anzalī would aid a Russian invasion. The expanded trade with Mazandaran and Gilan made possible by the improvement of the port would be far more attractive to the Russians than the burdens of conquest and administration.[52] Indeed, a diversity of foreign commercial interest should be attracted to prevent the preponderance of a single power and to create a general desire among European states for the continued independence of Iran. The security of Japan rests upon her commercial intercourse with a wide variety of nations, and in general friendship in international affairs can be said to depend on the volume of commercial exchange.[53]

The relevance of all these arguments to the granting of the celebrated Reuter concession in 1873 is clear enough. In conjunction with his patron, Mīrzā Ḥusayn Khān Sipahsālār, Malkum Khān strove, in his own words, "without delay [to] turn over the construction of railways, the operation of mines, the establishment of a bank and all public works and structures to foreign companies." The fact that he advocated the granting of such comprehensive concessions after the failure of Reuter's venture, may indicate a sincere and persistent belief in the need for

49. *Ibid.*, pp. 36–56. The fact that the treatise was obliquely addressed to Nāṣir ud-Dīn Shāh may be deduced from its closing paragraphs in which Malkum praises the monarch fulsomely and offers to elaborate his proposals to the shah if able to do so in confidence.

50. *Ibid.*, p. 37.

51. *Ibid.*, pp. 42–43.

52. *Ibid.*, p. 44.

53. *Ibid.*, pp. 45–46.

attracting foreign capital to Iran, and the validity of some of his arguments may be conceded. Nonetheless, the effect of the two treatises discussed is weakened by the tone of contemptuous impatience and dogmatic assertion in which they are written and still more by knowledge of the profits Malkum extracted from the concessions with which he was associated.

In the case of Mīrzā Ḥusayn Khān, a similar duality of pecuniary interest and political consideration may be noted in the advocacy and promotion of the Reuter concession. The sipahsālār had acquired a belief in the salubrity of European influence on Asiatic states during his residence in Istanbul. There, he had noted the pressure exerted by Britain and France on the Ottoman government to bring about reform and reported favorably of it to the Ministry of Foreign Affairs in Tehran, apparently considering it necessary though unpleasant. For Iran, too, Mīrzā Ḥusayn Khān would have welcomed foreign, particularly British, influence as a means of hastening reform, and the acquisition of economic interests would clearly have provided the soundest basis for political influence.[54] The Reuter concession, however, proved less effective in obtaining British support for Iranian reform than in enriching Mīrzā Ḥusayn Khān: he is reputed to have received more than £50,000 in bribes at various stages of the negotiations with Reuter.[55]

The history of Iranian concession-mongering began in 1864, when both Mīrzā Ḥusayn Khān and Malkum's opportunities for patriotic endeavor and personal enrichment were still restricted to the Iranian embassy in Istanbul. A certain M. Savalan, an Austrian subject, came to Tehran in that year, and, although unsuccessful in his bid for a concession to construct railways and exploit mines, he was given the assurance of first option on any such concession that might subsequently be offered.[56]

Two years later, Mīrzā Muḥsin Khān Muᶜīn ul-Mulk, Iranian envoy in London and, like Malkum, an initiate of the Paris lodge Sincère Amitié,[57] disposed to a Prussian financier named Strousberg of a concession for the building of a railway line from Tehran to the shrine at

54. Ādamīyat, *op. cit.* (n. 4, above), p. 61.

55. Accusation made by Muḥammad Ḥasan Khān Iᶜtimād us-Salṭana in his *Khvābnāma.* The charge is put into the mouth of Amīn us-Sulṭān. Relevant section quoted by Sāsānī, *op. cit.* (n. 9, above), II: 173.

56. Firuz Kazemzadeh, *Russia and Britain in Persia, 1864–1914* (New Haven, 1968), p. 101; L.E. Frechtling, "The Reuter Concession in Persia," *Asiatic Review,* XXXIV (1938): 519.

57. Mīrzā Muḥsin Khān was at the time counsellor at the Iranian legation in Paris. Together with other members of the legation, he was initiated on February 28, 1860. See *Bulletin du Grand Orient de France,* XV (5860–1860): 396–397.

Shāh ᶜAbd ul-ᶜAẓīm, nine miles to the south of the capital. The concession proved unworkable, largely because of the uncooperative attitude adopted by officials in Tehran, and Strousberg paid Muḥsin Khān £4,000 to be rid of his obligations. The money was reputedly kept by the minister as a well-earned fee for his services.[58]

Encouraged by this promising beginning, Muḥsin Khān sought to interest various London financiers in the purchase of a similar concession, but initially with little success. Iranian credit on foreign stock exchanges was already low, and investors who might otherwise have been prepared to risk loss for the sake of large-scale profit were dissuaded by official advice. In July 1871, Alison, the British minister in Tehran, wrote in a dispatch that "the projects presented from time to time by Europeans have been entertained principally as a means of profit to the Persian ministers and the agents employed by them" and that transactions with such agents abroad "ought not to be concluded without good advice."[59]

Ultimately, however, Muḥsin Khān found an investor whose greed exceeded his caution. This was Baron Julius de Reuter, founder of the celebrated news agency and a wealthy financier of German Jewish origin who, since 1857, had been a British subject. Although Reuter sought to present his contemplated enterprise in Iran as a service to his adopted homeland, official British support for his activities was at all times minimal, and patriotic motives were as little in evidence in his calculations as they were in those of the Iranian side. The profits he hoped to reap in Iran were immense: the projected concession not only included railways, the subject of earlier agreements, but offered him the possibility of a comprehensive purchase of Iran's economic resources. The magnitude of the prospect, far from causing him to reflect before proceeding, only increased his eagerness to see an agreement concluded so that he might set to work in Iran. In order, as he thought, to guarantee Muḥsin Khān's continued support for his candidacy as concessionaire, he offered him and his brother, Muḥammad Āqā, a secretary in the Iranian legation, shares in the company which was to operate the concession. According to one account, he further gave Muḥsin Khān a straightforward bribe amounting to no less than £20,000.[60] After the ground had been prepared, a preliminary agreement was reached in London, and Reuter dispatched an agent to Tehran to elaborate details of the concession and to conclude a final contract.

The agent, Edouard Cotte, arrived in Tehran early in 1872, shortly

58. Kazemzadeh, *op. cit.*, p. 101.

59. Quoted in Kazemzadeh, *op. cit.*, p. 102, n. 3; and Frechtling, *op. cit.*, p. 519.

60. Ibrāhīm Taymūrī, *ᶜAṣr-i Bīkhabarī ya Tārīkh-i Imtiyāzāt dar Īrān* (Tehran, 1336 solar/1957), p. 107.

before Malkum's return from Istanbul.[61] In the negotiations that then took place between Cotte and the Iranian government, Malkum appears to have played a role of some importance.[62] As special advisor to Mīrzā Ḥusayn Khān and as one, moreover, who made constant profession of expertise in all matters relating to Europe, Malkum was clearly the most suitable person to deal with Cotte, and we find his signature among those affixed to the contract.[63] That the terms of the concession granted to Reuter were at least in part Malkum's work is suggested by his continued support for such comprehensive schemes even after Reuter's failure and the downfall of Mīrzā Ḥusayn Khān.[64]

On July 25, 1872, the concession was finally signed in Tehran by Cotte and members of the Iranian government. In fulfillment of Reuter's hopes, it represented a virtual surrender of the entire economic life of the country to his control and exploitation. The monopoly to be established had the exclusive right to construct a railway line from the Caspian Sea to the Persian Gulf, "with such branch lines as he [Reuter] shall think fit"; to build and operate tramways at its will throughout the country; and to exploit all mineral resources, with the exception of gold and silver. Moreover, it might undertake any irrigation works it pleased, selling the water obtained thereby, and having the right to dispose of all barren lands reclaimed through irrigation. The customs were to be farmed out to the monopoly for twenty years, and it would have first option on any concession that might be granted for the establishment of a bank or such enterprises as "gas, the paving and decorations of the capital, roads, postal and telegraphic arrangements, mills, manufacturies and factories, for which privileges might hereafter be requested."[65]

The concession was to be valid for a period of seventy years, and Reuter thus might have looked forward to a steadily increasing flow of profit from Iran to augment his already considerable fortune. Yet this was not to be. Not only did the comprehensive scope of the con-

61. Kazemzadeh, *op. cit.*, p. 104; Frechtling, *op. cit.*, p. 520.

62. Sir Henry Rawlinson, who, as a member of the Council of State for India, had been consulted by the Foreign Office on the implications of Reuter's project for British interests in the area, couples the name of Malkum with that of Mīrzā Ḥusayn Khān Sipahsālār as jointly responsible for the concession (*England and Russia in the East* [London, 1875], p. 123). See too Ādamīyat, *op. cit.* (n. 4, above), p. 87.

63. See Mīrzā ʿAlī Khān Amīn ud-Daula, *Khāṭirāt-i Siyāsī*, ed. Hāfiz Farmānfarmāʾīān (Tehran, 1341 solar/1962), p. 42.

64. This support is expressed in the treatise "Uṣūl-i Tamaddun" and in numerous dispatches from London. See below, p. 000.

65. Provisions of the concession summarized in Kazemzadeh, *op. cit.*, pp. 105–108; an abstract given in Rawlinson, *op. cit.*, pp. 373–376; complete Persian text in Amin ud-Daula, *op. cit.*, pp. 36–42.

cession arouse immediate opposition, both in Iran and abroad, but the agreement itself contained certain obstacles to its own fulfillment. In the unobtrusive placing of these obstacles, Malkum's oft-proclaimed financial and economic expertise may be thought to have proved itself. One provision of the agreement was to be of crucial value to the Iranian government in its disputes with Reuter and attempts to rescind the concession. Article Eight stipulated that Reuter should deposit the sum of £40,000 as caution money in the Bank of England. If the works provided for in the various articles of the concession were not commenced within fifteen months of ratification, the deposit was liable to forfeiture. The minimum indication of commencement was to be the arrival at Anzali of the requisite quantity of rails for the construction of a line from Rasht to Tehran, verified by the governor of the province of Gilan.[66] By the time that Nāṣir ud-Dīn Shāh had decided to nullify the concession in November 1873, Reuter could point to no more than the completion of one kilometer of earthwork and the laying of ballast and sleepers "throughout a great part of that length."[67] This slight accomplishment was deemed inadequate to prevent forfeiture of the caution money.

Apart from thus helping to incorporate in the text of the concession articles tending to facilitate its annulment under conditions favorable to the Iranian government, Malkum played a more direct role in frustrating its implementation. In so doing, he was able to earn his first considerable profits from the concession business, an aspect of the matter he neglected to mention in his treatises.

After ratification of the concession on July 15, 1872 and the deposit of the caution money in the Bank of England, Reuter naturally expected the immediate delivery of the concession to Cotte and permission to begin operations. At this point, however, Mīrzā Ḥusayn Khān insisted on appending to the agreement an additional article whereby no work could be undertaken in fulfillment of any clause until the details had been agreed to by both parties and set out in a *cahier des charges.* In negotiating these agreements in detail, the representative of the Iranian government was to be Malkum Khān, whose inspired idea the additional article may well have been.[68] It is an interesting comment on the sincerity of Malkum's concern for the economic regeneration of Iran through foreign enterprise that he now played the role of chief frustrator of the same concession he had helped to elaborate and promote. The purpose of the additional article appears to have been twofold: to

66. Kazemzadeh, *op. cit.*, p. 106; Frechtling, *op. cit.*, p. 520; Amīn ud-Daula, *op. cit.*, pp. 37–38.

67. Kazemzadeh, *op. cit.*, p. 129.

68. Frechtling, *op. cit.* (n. 56, above), p. 521.

create further obstacles which Reuter could remove or circumvent only by renewed bribery and, by delaying the start of operations, to bring closer the end of the fifteen-month period when the concession might be annulled and the £40,000 claimed for the royal treasury.

Cotte attempted to begin negotiations with Malkum on a *cahier* for the purchase of railway material and a survey of the route for the projected line. Malkum then politely informed him that since he would shortly be proceeding to Europe, it would be more suitable for him to discuss the matter with the baron in person.[69] Malkum was about to leave Iran and again take up residence abroad: he had been appointed envoy to Britain. Mīrzā Ḥusayn Khān's successor as minister in Istanbul, Ḥasan ʿAlī Khān Garūsī, had resigned from his post, and Mīrzā Muḥsin Khān was sent from London to replace him. His removal to Istanbul robbed him of the chance of further enrichment through Reuter's bribes, and his resentment at Malkum's succession to his lucrative position in London placed a strain on their fraternal relations. In the words of Amīn ud-Daula, who knew both men well: "Ḥājjī Muḥsin Khān saw himself deprived of a part of his benefits, and a dispute arose between two old friends."[70] Evidently the dispute was settled amicably enough, for in later years Muḥsin Khān was still commonly identified as a follower of Malkum and a sympathizer with his ideas.[71]

Malkum set out from Iran early in 1873, less than a year after his return from Istanbul. He was in Iran only three times again, staying no more than a few months on each occasion, and the remainder of his career was spent in critical observation of his homeland from afar. The opportunity to pursue a thorough reform of the Iranian state from a position of influence in Tehran had been lost without a serious attempt at exploiting it. Seeing that Malkum's renewed departure abroad was connected with the business of the Reuter concession and his motives in promoting and pursuing the matter were in large part personal and financial, it is hardly an exaggeration to say that the chance of national reform was sacrificed to the cause of individual profit. It is true that other factors, notably the hostility of certain elements at court and in the capital, might sooner or later have robbed him of the position of special adviser to Mīrzā Ḥusayn Khān.

The business of the Reuter concession was not the only reason for Malkum's appointment to London. Nāṣir ud-Dīn Shāh was about to make the first of his excursions to the West, to observe the curiosities of European civilization and at the same time himself to afford interest and diversion as an oriental curiosity. The journey took place at the suggestion of Mīrzā Ḥusayn Khān, who after introducing his monarch

69. *Ibid.*

70. Amīn ud-Daula, *op. cit.*, p. 41.

71. See below, pp. 202–203 and 233.

to the benefits of westernization in Baghdad, now sought to impress them on him firsthand at the wondrous fountainhead of progress. There was also the hope that Britain might be induced in some way to guarantee Iran's territorial integrity against further Russian encroachment, an eventuality that seemed particularly likely after recent Russian operations in Transcaspia.

Malkum seemed the obvious choice for preparation of the shah's journey and for making the necessary arrangements for his reception in sundry European capitals. His useful role in facilitating the work of Farrukh Khān Amīn ud-Daula's mission to Paris in 1856 was doubtless remembered, and he too must have been gratified to receive his first full-fledged diplomatic post and to be able to shine in European high society as an oriental prince. Duly equipped with credentials appointing him plenipotentiary to a number of European states,[72] Malkum set out for Europe and traveling by way of Istanbul, Vienna, Berlin, Brussels, and Paris arrived in London in March 1873.

Once in London, Malkum called on Lord Granville, the Foreign Secretary, and informed him of Iran's desire for British friendship and investment. As an expression of this desire and "to judge for himself the advanced state of civilization" in England, Nāṣir ud-Dīn Shāh would shortly be arriving on a state visit. Granville expressed his satisfaction and assured Malkum that the shah would be fittingly received.[73]

Malkum's encounter with Reuter proved considerably less agreeable and smooth. Anxious to avoid further loss of time, the baron had traveled to meet Malkum in Vienna and open negotiations on a *cahier*. Malkum refused to give Reuter immediate satisfaction, and although the financier waited on him during his stops in Berlin, Brussels, and Paris, matters were still not settled by the time he arrived in London. Once Malkum had reached his final destination, and the chase was thus at an end, the existence of yet another obstacle to the implementation of the concession was revealed. What appeared to Reuter as one more in a series of difficulties may have been for Malkum the core of the whole project. Not only did Reuter stand to lose £40,000 caution money

72. Copies of letters appointing him minister to Austria, Holland, Italy, Spain, Switzerland, and Greece are contained in one of the volumes of his papers preserved at the Bibliothèque Nationale (Supplément Persan, 1986, ff. 1–4, 6, 9, 10). After his appointment to London, Malkum presumably functioned as nonresident envoy to these countries. In the pseudo-autobiographical statement recorded by W. S. Blunt (*Secret History of the English Occupation of Egypt* [London, 1903], p. 85), Malkum places his appointment as envoy to London immediately after the episode of the farāmūshkhāna, thus excising almost a decade of his life: "I wrote to the Shah, who replied offering me any appointment I would, so I would remain abroad; and I accepted the position of Ambassador-General to all the Courts of Europe."

73. Kazemzadeh, *op. cit.* (n. 56, above), p. 112.

if work had not started within fifteen months after signature of the concession, and not only was this period likely to expire in protracted negotiations on matters of detail, but he was now informed that even his title to the concession itself was not as complete as he had every reason to assume. Malkum claimed that he himself held title to a fourth of the concession, and that he was at liberty to dispose of it as he wished. Since the text of the concession explicitly gave Reuter an exclusive and undivided right to undertake the construction of railways and other works, it can only be concluded that Malkum's claim to one-fourth was a delicate way of requesting a bribe. He was willing to be reasonable and not retain his share or sell it to another party; instead, he offered it to Reuter for a consideration which, in the words of one writer, "came rather high: £20,000 cash and three further annual payments of £10,000."[74] It is evident that on this occasion Malkum transgressed against the principles set forth in *Uṣūl-i Tamaddun* and asked the forbidden question: "How much will you pay?" In the manner of a gambler risking ever greater sums in an effort to escape total loss, Reuter acceded to Malkum's demand and bought his fictitious share for the sum proposed.

When Malkum had received the £20,000, negotiations for a *cahier* finally began. They were concluded on July 5, 1873, almost a year after the signing of the concession in Tehran.[75] Reuter had little more than three months left in which to begin work on the railway line from Rasht in order to avoid forfeiture of his deposit.

A week before this removal of what was apparently the last obstacle in Reuter's path, Nāṣir ud-Dīn Shāh, with a retinue that included the sipahsālār, arrived in England after visiting Russia, Germany, and Belgium. His reception in St. Petersburg had been less than cordial, for the Russian chancellor, Gorchakov, thought Reuter's enterprise in Iran was sponsored, or at least supported, by the British Foreign Office in an effort to displace Russian influence in Iran. Special care was taken to make Mīrzā Ḥusayn Khān aware of Russian displeasure at his dealings with a British subject.[76] The outward splendor of the royal party's reception in London seemed to compensate for the coldness of St. Petersburg. The shah was honored with a luncheon at Guildhall, visited Queen Victoria at Windsor,[77] looked over Madame Tussaud's and the

74. Frechtling, *op. cit.* (n. 56, above), p. 522. In his *Khvābnāma,* Iᶜtimād ud-Daula similarly accuses Malkum of receiving £50,000 in bribes from Reuter. Relevant section quoted in Sāsānī, *op. cit.* (n. 9, above), II: 173.

75. Frechtling, *op. cit.*, p. 522.

76. Kazemzadeh, *op. cit.*, p. 114.

77. The episode of the visit to Windsor has been described in fictitious form in Laurence Housman's comic sketch "A Star from the East," *Palace Scenes* (London, 1937), pp. 111–128. Malkum (referred to only as the ambassador) makes a brief ap-

Crystal Palace, reviewed the fleet at Spithead, and toured the industrial cities of the north. Everywhere he went he was greeted with amicable curiosity, and he for his part received favorable impressions of England, which he recorded in one of his celebrated diaries of travel.[78] While the Reuter concession enjoyed little official support in Britain, the London press was almost unanimous in celebrating it as an imaginative yet wise project, redounding to the credit of both Reuter and the Iranian government. The *Illustrated London News* was particularly lavish in its approbation: in an editorial welcoming the Iranian monarch, it proclaimed the concession to do "infinite credit to the Shah's courage, earnestness, foresight and patriotism." The last of these qualities was already in doubt, and events were soon to show him lacking in the other three.

Behind the outer show of public welcome, little was achieved in advancing the specific aims of Nāṣir ud-Dīn's visit. The Foreign Office showed itself unwilling to offer a firm guarantee of Iranian territorial integrity against Russia: Granville contented himself with a verbose and noncommittal statement advising Iran to "studiously fulfil in all respects her treaty engagements with each power [i.e., Britain and Russia] and so ensure the continuance of the friendship which both Powers, even for their own interest, should desire to maintain with her."[79] Sententious counsel such as this was essentially all that Malkum was able to transmit to Tehran during his term as minister in London, and British distaste for direct involvement in Iran was to continue for many years.

Nor did the confrontation of Reuter with Nāṣir ud-Dīn Shāh solve definitively the ever more complex problem of the concession. For Malkum, the central question had been solved in an eminently satisfactory way, but for others difficulties persisted. Reuter had expected the royal journey to do away with any remaining obstacles to the implementation of his concession, for he imagined himself able to hold the shah to ransom. Before the party left Tehran in May 1873, he had proposed to Nāṣir ud-Dīn Shāh that he meet the traveling expenses of the monarch and his entourage by making £200,000 available in various European capitals. The sum was to be repaid in Tehran and used by him in works undertaken in fulfillment of the concession. His offer was accepted, and an initial £20,000 was made available in St. Petersburg,

---

pearance and it is remarked of his English that he speaks "in a very foreign accent" (p. 121).

78. First published in Tehran in 1874 and then in Bombay in 1880. A recent edition is *Safarnāma-yi Nāṣir ud-Dīn Shāh* (Tehran, 1343 solar/1964). The section descriptive of England is found on pp. 83–128 of this edition. The journal was translated by J. W. Redhouse and entitled, *The Diary of H. M. the Shah of Persia during his Tour through Europe in A.D. 1873* (London, 1874).

79. Kazemzadeh, *op. cit.* (n. 56, above), p. 115–116.

but further payments were withheld in order to force Nāṣir ud-Dīn Shāh to accept certain demands. The demands, however, were rejected and alternative sources of finance sought and found by the royal party.[80]

The ultimate failure of Reuter was due less to the venality and procrastination of Malkum Khān and the sipahsālār and the disinterest of the monarch in seeing the concession implemented, than to the domestic and foreign hostility that the enterprise increasingly encountered. Opposition to the concession and the prime minister under whose aegis it had been negotiated was already apparent on the eve of Nāṣir ud-Dīn Shāh's departure for Europe. The ulama had been requested to instruct the people of the useful nature of the shah's journey, but instead began to denounce the sipahsālār and his policies.[81] Opposition mounted during the royal trip abroad. Two men in particular were active in agitating for Mīrzā Ḥusayn Khān's removal from the prime ministership: Mullā Ṣāliḥ ᶜArab and Mullā ᶜAlī Kanī, the latter the most influential cleric of the capital.[82] Their hostility to Mīrzā Ḥusayn Khān had in part been aroused by his refusal to permit their customary intervention in affairs of state;[83] they may, too, have been aware of his desire ultimately to secularize all jurisdiction and to abolish the courts over which they presided.[84] The protest against the sipahsālār centered, however, on the Reuter concession, which was attacked as a surrender of the economic life of the nation to non-Muslim foreigners. The proposed construction of railways was considered particularly fraught with danger, as tending to open Iran to a horde of unwanted Europeans whose influx would destroy the religious quality of Iranian life. Mullā ᶜAlī Kanī thus wrote to Nāṣir ud-Dīn Shāh: "With the onslaught of the Europeans on Iran by railway, what influential [religious] scholar will remain? And if he remains, will he have life and breath enough to cry even once: Alas for the faith! Alas for the nation!"[85]

Other elements in Tehran whose hostility Mīrzā Ḥusayn Khān had aroused made common cause with the ulama. Among these were Mustaufī ul-Mamālik, who felt his influence weakened by the introduction of the cabinet system,[86] Farhād Mīrzā Muᶜtamad ud-Daula, a prince who had been entrusted with the affairs of the capital during the

80. Frechtling, *op. cit.* (n. 56, above), p. 523.

81. G. N. Curzon, *Persia and the Persian Question* (London, 1892), I: 405.

82. Taymūrī, *op. cit.* (n. 60, above), p. 39. For a brief biography of Mullā ᶜAlī Kanī, see ᶜAbbās Iqbāl, "Sharḥ-i Ḥāl-i Marḥūm Ḥājj Mullā ᶜAlī Kanī," Yādgār, V (1326 solar/1947–1948):72–78.

83. Mīrzā Ḥusayn Khān to Nāsir ud-Dīn Shāh, quoted in Taymūri, *op. cit.* (n. 60, above), pp. 43–44.

84. See Ādamīyat, *op. cit.* (n. 4, above), p. 65.

85. Quoted in Taymūrī, *op. cit.*, pp. 124–126.

86. *Ibid.*, p. 39.

absence of Nāṣir ud-Dīn Shāh,[87] Mīrzā Saʿīd Khān, the russophile minister of foreign affairs, and finally Anīs ud-Daula, the shah's favorite wife, whom the sipahsālār had caused to be sent home from Moscow and thus deprived of the rest of her European trip.[88] While the royal party was on its way back to Iran, these individuals came together in a coalition that was to force the dismissal of Mīrza Ḥusayn Khān and contribute to the cancellation of the Reuter concession.

The domestic opposition to Mīrzā Ḥusayn Khān and the Reuter concession was powerfully reinforced by Russian hostility to the minister and the British influence he was thought to represent and foster. Already in St. Petersburg, the Russians had shown Nāṣir ud-Dīn Shāh their displeasure at the policies of his minister, and Gorchakov managed with surprising ease to extract from Nāṣir ud-Dīn Shāh an informal undertaking to rescind at least part of Reuter's concession and to grant to a Russian subject the right of building railways in Iran.[89] After this early, if minor, victory, the Russians were assured by the Foreign Office that Reuter's venture was a strictly private one and did not represent any change in British policy towards Iran.[90] They were thus doubly encouraged to press on and obtain both the dismissal of Mīrzā Ḥusayn Khān and the cancellation of the Reuter concession. It may be assumed that Russian and domestic plans to bring about these aims were coordinated: the Iranian consulate in Tiflis furnished a convenient point of contact.

As Nāṣir ud-Dīn Shāh arrived back on Iranian soil at Anzalī in September 1873, he was presented with a petition signed by eighty notables of Tehran calling for the dismissal of Mīrzā Ḥusayn Khān. The petition was accompanied by a telegram from Farhād Mīrzā informing him that the signatories had taken refuge in the house of Anīs ud-Daula, refusing to emerge until their demand was met. The shah was clearly alarmed at the prospect of being barred from his own capital by the rebelliousness of its notables, and he yielded to their demand. Changing his mind he then reinstated Mīrzā Ḥusayn Khān, but was obliged to dismiss him anew as the persistence and seriousness of the opposition became apparent.[91]

As for the Reuter concession, its cancellation was not long in coming. Two months after being dismissed from the premiership, Mīrzā Ḥusayn Khān, though now without a government post, was entrusted

87. Muʿtamad, *op. cit.* (n. 4, above), p. 189.
88. Kazemzadeh, *op. cit.* (n. 56, above), pp. 112–113, 116–117.
89. *Ibid.*, p. 114.
90. *Ibid.*, pp. 116–117.
91. *Ibid.*, pp. 118–120; Mustaufī, *op. cit.* (n. 3, above), I: 127–128; Muʿtamad, *op. cit.*, p. 184.

by Nāṣir ud-Dīn Shāh with the business of voiding the concession he had once promoted. Its implementation had never been a matter of serious concern to the shah. Now that he had lost the minister whose project it had been, and was moreover faced with Russian and domestic hostility on its account, there was no reason to prolong the life of Reuter's enterprise. The fifteen-month period for the importing of rails and the commencement of works was anyhow at an end, without the concessionaire being able to point to any substantial achievement, and the £40,000 caution money could be claimed on the strength of Article Eight of the contract. Nor could Reuter look to the Foreign Office for the defence of his concession: British support was limited to belated and half-hearted espousal of his claims when a retired Russian general, von Falkenhagen, sponsored by the Russian legation in Tehran, demanded a concession for a line from Julfā on the Aras to Tabriz. The conditions of the proposed concession were such as to make of Azerbayjan a virtual Russian protectorate, and it became expedient for Britain to insist on the validity of Reuter's "rights" as a means of frustrating its conclusion.[92]

Malkum's involvement in these events, leading to the downfall of his patron and the annulment of an enterprise he had helped in turn to promote and frustrate, was slight. It is likely that Mīrzā Ḥusayn Khān's association with Malkum was a subsidiary cause for the clerical hostility directed against him, inasmuch as the irreligious episode of the farāmūshkhāna had not been forgotten in certain circles in Tehran.[93] It was indeed fortunate for Malkum that he had received a new appointment abroad. If in September 1873 he had still been special adviser to Mīrzā Ḥusayn Khān, he would inevitably have fallen with his patron. As it was, not even his long-time enemy, Mīrzā Saʿīd Khān, wished to displace him from his London post, thinking doubtless that his remoteness from Tehran was all to the good. Nāṣir ud-Dīn Shāh probably credited the warm welcome he had received in England at least in part to Malkum's skillful preparations, and Malkum continued to enjoy royal favor and approbation until the scandal of 1889 made of him, by force of circumstance, an enemy of the regime and an impassioned critic of its corruption.

As envoy in London, Malkum continued to have sporadic contact with Reuter. Imagining the receipt of bribes to have imposed certain obligations on Malkum, the financier sought to obtain his support in fighting the cancellation of the concession, but with little success. For Malkum, as for all concerned except Reuter himself, the issue had finally been settled, and the extent of his intervention on Reuter's behalf

92. Kazemzadeh, *op. cit.*, pp. 130–142; Frechtling, *op. cit.*, pp. 530–532.

93. See Taymūrī, *op. cit.* (n. 60, above), p. 124; Ṭabāṭabāʾī, introduction to *Majmūʿa-yi Āthār*, p. xii.

was to convey to Tehran, in 1888, the information that his claims then enjoyed official British support.[94] Reuter nonetheless saw fit to pay Malkum yet another £20,000 in order to obtain, through his good offices, the charter for foundation of a bank in Iran, with the promise of a further £30,000 on successful conclusion of the affair. This comparatively modest ambition was fulfilled early in 1889, but less through the exertions of Malkum than those of a more sincere friend of Reuter, Sir Henry Drummond Wolff, the new British minister in Tehran. Reuter thus saw no reason to part with the additional £30,000, despite Malkum's outraged protests.[95] The next financial coup of this enlightened patriot was to take place in conjunction with less eminent speculators than the baron.

Meanwhile, Malkum had been one of the few beneficiaries of the entire concession episode. Mīrzā Ḥusayn Khān had lost his premiership on account of the concession, and at one point even feared for his life;[96] Reuter's greed and lack of caution cost him much frustration and financial loss. Malkum, by contrast, pocketed £50,000 in bribes, was appointed, partly on account of the unfinished business of the concession, Iranian minister in London, and kept the post for sixteen years after the downfall of his patron and the discomfiture of Reuter.

He had returned with the royal party to Iran, but clearly found it advisable not to delay before returning to London. He apparently set out from Tehran in early November, shortly after the decision had been taken to annul the concession, for there is record of his passing through Istanbul in December 1873. While there, he paid what was probably a return visit to the Proodos masonic lodge,[97] a lodge affiliated with the Grand Orient of Greece. Meetings were conducted alternately in Greek and Turkish, but patronized also by Iranian diplomats in the Ottoman Empire.[98] The meeting that Malkum attended had been arranged for the initiation of the Iranian consul in Antioch, Mūsā Antippa, and among the guests was not only Malkum, but also Mīrzā Muḥsin Khān and Mīrzā Najaf Qulī Khān, chief dragoman at the Iranian legation.

Mūsā Antippa's responses "hardly appeared to be in conformity with masonic morality," according to the report that appeared in the Paris masonic review, *Le Monde Maçonnique,* and his initiation was

94. Sāsānī, *op. cit.* (n. 9, above), II: 183.

95. Kazemzadeh, *op. cit.* (n.56, above), p. 242.

96. *Ibid.*, p. 120.

97. See above, p. 72.

98. Concerning the Proodos lodge, see the anonymous work *Dünyada ve Türkiyede Masonluk* (Istanbul, 1965), p. 296; and concerning Scalieri and his plot in 1878 to restore Sultan Murad to the throne, see Bernard Lewis, *The Emergence of Modern Turkey* (Oxford, 1961), pp. 172–174.

accordingly postponed. The meeting, however, continued and the master of the lodge, Scalieri, addressed himself to the Iranians present, appealing to them to continue their masonic work in Iran. "Yes, illustrious Brothers, it is up to you to kindle anew in Persia, homeland of the Zoroasters [*sic*], the torch of this philosophy to which we fondly refer the origins of our order."

Malkum Khān in replying affirmed his enthusiastic belief in the principles of freemasonry and promised to do his utmost for their further propagation in Iran. Although his brief stay in Istanbul would not permit him to participate in the work of the Proodos lodge, he promised regular attendance on the part of Mīrzā Muḥsin Khān.

Scalieri again spoke, and made glowing reference to the "masonic devotion" of Malkum Khān, which was "universally known." "In fact, we have not forgotten that it was he who some time ago founded a lodge at Tehran, and that he suffered considerable loss as a result of this noble initiative."[99] It is worthy of note that this acknowledgment of Malkum's services to masonry, implying recognition of the farāmūshkhāna as a regularly constituted lodge, was uttered in Istanbul and not in Paris, probably in ignorance of the truth. Not long before, in July 1873, a reception had been held in Paris by the Sincère Amitié lodge for visiting Iranian masons in the retinue of Nāṣir ud-Dīn Shāh, then passing through Paris on his way home from London. At this gathering (which Malkum failed to attend), no mention was made of the farāmūshkhāna.[100] Similarly, at the meeting of the same lodge in February 1860, convened for the purpose of initiating Mīrzā Muḥsin Khān, the house of oblivion received no mention, and instead the name of Farrukh Khān Ghaffārī Amīn ud-Daula was celebrated as that of the most devoted servant of masonry in Iran.[101]

Early in 1874, Malkum Khān was back at his post in London, and there he remained with brief interruptions for fifteen years, until another controversial concession and its cancellation came to rob him of his appointments and titles transforming him from dilettante reformer to dilettante revolutionary.

99. *Le Monde Maçonnique*, XV (1873): 35–38.

100. Account given in *ibid.*, pp. 174–181.

101. Account given in *Bulletin du Grand Orient de France*, XV (5860=1860): 396–397.

CHAPTER 6

It was Iran's misfortune, in the classical age of imperialism, to lie athwart the path on which two expansionist powers threatened to collide. If earlier her strategic proximity to the Caucasus, Anatolia, Central Asia, and India had made it possible to encroach on areas contiguous to the Iranian plateau and incorporate them within the boundaries of the state, now in the nineteenth century she was shorn of many former provinces and dependencies and confined to that northwestward-pointing triangle which may be thought of as irreducible Iran. The weakness that accompanied this territorial shrinkage was made doubly manifest and painful by the almost unchecked penetration of external forces—political, military and economic—that played havoc with the national life. The very survivial of the entity "Iran" was at the discretion of London and St. Petersburg, and the manner of its survival, whether as buffer state between the powers or sphere of influence divided between them, was constantly at issue. To concentrate on the Western impact as the central phenomenon in the nineteenth-century history of the Muslim lands is often the result of European ethnocentricity; yet it is undeniable that at least the political affairs of Iran were throughout the period seldom free of the imprint of real or imagined European influence. Superimposed on the rivalries and intrigues constituting the Iranian political process was a weightier and greater contest, that between Britain and Russia.

As a member of Mīrzā Farrukh Khān's mission in 1857, Malkum had already had a glimpse of London, the capital of one of the imperial giants whose shadow was cast across Iran. On that occasion his concern had been with practical arrangements and matters of protocol, not the formulation of policy. Now he had returned as envoy, and he was to hold the post for fifteen years, the longest period of uninterrupted official service in his entire career. It was fitting that Malkum, the Armenian intermediary between European civilization and Iran, should now represent Iran abroad, and that from London he should seek to continue the transmission of European precepts and examples. Inspired by his observations in Istanbul, Malkum hoped to enlist the Foreign Office on the side of Iranian reform, and to join the authoritative voice of British "advice" to his own constantly repeated proposals.

His term in London, it is true, both opened and closed with a more or less scandalous involvement in the concession trade, and it was, as Ākhūndzāda had foreseen, chiefly productive of "material benefit" for Malkum. It must also be remarked that the activities of the British minister in Tehran were of greater weight in determining the course of Perso-British relations than those of his Iranian counterpart in London. Malkum nonetheless played a certain role in the elaboration of those relations, and almost alone among Iranian men of state in the nineteenth century, he appears to have had a clear understanding of Iran's position between the powers. His conduct of diplomatic business in London, so far as it was free of direction from Tehran, reflects this understanding, and he sought to impart some of its results to Nāṣir ud-Dīn Shāh and his ministers in the hope of making them the basis of a purposeful foreign policy for Iran.

His most important tenet may be summarized as the pursual of a limited alignment with Britain in order to obtain a foreign sponsor for reform and to prevent a total domination by Russia which would have resulted in the extinction of even the forms of independence. Espousal of such an alignment has earned him membership in the motley throng of Iranian politicians commonly identified as agents of British policy,[1] and it is true enough that many of the proposals for reform that he advanced while envoy in London closely corresponded to the paternal advice periodically bestowed on Iran by the Foreign Office. Nonetheless, such advice was on the whole sparse and given with evident reluctance; it was frequently Malkum's initiative that succeeded in eliciting it. He then presented it to Tehran as something firmer and more mandatory than had been intended. It has been seen that while in Istanbul Mīrzā Ḥusayn Khān had acquired a belief in the salutary effect of British pressure on Muslim states, and Malkum similarly hoped to obtain British support for the cause of reform, or at least to give the appearance of having obtained it. Britain had, however, little interest in promoting an Iranian Tanzimat.

Malkum's advocacy of an alignment with Britain may in part be explained by his personal circumstances in London. Close links with

1. See, for example, Khān Malik Sāsānī, *Siyāsatgarān-i Daura-yi Qājār* (Tehran, 1338 solar/1960), I: 77.

Britain would have brought with them an expansion of British commercial and financial activity in Iran from which Malkum stood to profit handsomely, as Muḥsin Khān had done on a more modest scale before him. At the same time, Malkum may be presumed to have had something of a genuine sympathy for British institutions, which offered the model of a monarchy working through the rule of law instead of the arbitrary whims of a despot. His education and early intellectual background had been French, and the accusation of French-inspired republicanism raised against him during the farāmūshkhāna episode may not have been entirely false. France, however, exerted only a certain cultural influence on Iran, and it had no essential political or strategic interest in the country. The choice of the lesser evil had to be made between Russia and Britain, and Malkum thought the latter more favorably disposed to the cause of Iranian reform. The presumption had proved virtually baseless by the last year of Malkum's life, but the case of the Ottoman Empire, as observed by Mīrzā Ḥusayn Khān and Malkum, made it appear plausible in the 1870s.

Malkum's thoughts on foreign policy are compendiously set forth in a treatise entitled *Pūlitīkhā-yi Daulatī* (International politics), belonging to that group of his writings intended obliquely for the attention of the monarch.[2] The treatise consists of a review of Iranian foreign relations from the time of Fatḥ ʿAlī Shāh onwards, an analysis of the position of the country in the late 1870s, and some hints for the formulation of future policy. As is so often the case in Malkum's writings, here too we observe an irritating mixture of accurate analysis and exposition with charlatanry and egoistic posturing. He finds it impossible to refrain from sarcastic thrusts at "the wise ones of Tehran" who have not, like him, enjoyed the benefits of a European education and are thus ignorant of the world and all therein. Yet he has himself little better to offer by way of solution to Iran's problems than hints at an alignment with Britain and mysterious allusions to a plan of salvation that he would reveal only in confidential dialogue with the shah.

The treatise opens with a depiction of the Iranian ship of state foundering in heavy seas. It is only the captain (the shah) who is at all concerned at its lack of direction, while his ignorant and incompetent officers are totally oblivious of impending wreck. At this critical juncture, Malkum presents himself as the much-needed pilot, equipped with an accurate chart and able to guide the ship out of the stormy waters about to engulf it.[3]

After this exordium, Malkum proceeds without delay to enounce

2. *Kullīyāt-i Malkum*, ed. Hāshim Rabīʿzāda (Tabriz, 1325 lunar/1908) pp. 125–167.

3. *Ibid.*, pp. 125–126.

the basic political fact of the age: the Anglo-Russian rivalry in which Iran has unwillingly become involved and which threatens it with destruction. Iran itself is not the prize in this struggle, but India and its riches; it will serve instead as battleground—military or diplomatic—for the contestants. Its proximity to India was the cause of its introduction to great power rivalry, when early in the century Napoleonic France and Britain both sought ascendancy in Iran, and dispatched ambassadors and gifts to the court of Fatḥ ʿAlī Shāh. The appearance of French representatives in Tehran offered Iran a unique opportunity to participate in the destruction of both Russia and Britain, the two powers that were to plague it for many years. Napoleon's essential aims, the destruction of British power in India and the stemming of Russia's advance in the same direction, corresponded exactly to Iranian interests and their realization should have been ardently pursued. Instead, the opportunity was lost: "The men of state of Iran, without being in the least aware of the aims of the different parties, as soon as they heard the clink of English money, hastily expelled the representative of Napoleon from Iran and thus threw the ship of state back a hundred years, or, better to say, at that very moment they destroyed the Iranian state."[4] Such accusations come ill from Malkum who also acted with hasty greed on hearing the clink of money. In any event he neglects to mention the shifting alignments among European states that led to the Treaty of Tilsit (1807) and the loss of French interest in Iran.

After the downfall of Napoleon, Anglo-French rivalry was replaced by a contest between Britain and Russia. Russian expansionist tendencies were more serious than those of Napoleon, for they were the result not of an individual's ambitious dreams but of a long-standing national policy. Against this Russian wave, Britain sought to erect a series of barriers in the form of buffer states, powerful enough to maintain a semiindependent existence but not strong enough to oppose British dictates and desires. Such entities, in reality "pensioner states" (*duval-i mavājib-khur*), were called "friendly states in English political terminology,"[5] and control of them was generally attained by intervention in dynastic quarrels. The price paid by the successful contestant for support in his struggle for the throne would be supervision of his foreign relations, the stationing of a British garrison on his soil, and British officering of his army. The friendship thus established would soon become indistinguishable from occupation, and examples had been furnished by the fate of Deccan, Gwalior, Sind, and other princely states of India.[6]

The British had begun to execute the same policy in Iran during the reign of Fatḥ ʿAlī Shāh when they paid the monarch a regular

4. *Ibid.*, pp. 139–140. 5. *Ibid.*, p. 142. 6. *Ibid.*, p. 143.

subsidy, sent officers to train his army, and unobtrusively supported pretenders to the throne.[7] Russian victory in the Second Perso-Russian War (1826–1828) prevented, however, the final conclusion of amity with Iran, and Britain was obliged to turn elsewhere, to Afghanistan, in its search to multiply the buffer states standing in the way of Russia. Shah Shujāᶜ was to be imposed on Afghanistan as ruler to guarantee the implementation of the conditions of friendship, but British hopes were checked once more when the Afghans rose and slaughtered the British garrison in Kabul. By way of consolation, the British then proceeded to subjugate Sind and having done so, established Attock as their first line of defence.[8]

The logic of strategy would not, however, permit them to remain content with Sind as a "friendly" state. For it was too close to the heart of British India to provide real security, and interest in Iran and Afghanistan could not be abandoned. Both states, and particularly the former, were weak and vulnerable to Russian advance, so much so, indeed, that the question of Iranian willingness to "consent" to the passage of Russian troops en route to the conquest of India was entirely artificial. Hence, a forward line of defence within Iran itself was necessary. If the Persian Gulf littoral were secure in British hands, a Russian advance might be checked to the north of the Zagros, with a second line of defence standing ready in Sind and the Punjab in case of need. Thus the purpose of the British attack on Iran in 1856 had not been simply to force the evacuation of Herat, but also to demonstrate British supremacy in the Gulf. Hence, too, the British interest in cultivating relations with the Imam of Muscat, in the opening of consulates in ports along the Gulf, and in opposing the appearance of any flag other than the British on its waters. In the future, Sistan would be particularly exposed to British desires, for its occupation would tend "naturally" to follow on the annexation of Sind and Baluchistan. It was true that Britain had not yet attempted permanent occupation of Iranian territory, but her policy had the same continuity of purpose as that displayed by Russia. In the light of that purpose, "the friendship and trust of

7. Malkum cites as an example of such support the case of Ḥusayn ᶜAlī Mīrzā Farmānfarmā who, on the death of Fatḥ ᶜAlī Shāh in 1834, made a bid for the throne in Isfahan. His ambitions, however, were finally defeated by a force containing several British officers (see J. B. Fraser, *Travels in Koordistan, Mesopotamia etc.* [London, 1849], II: 282; and Mīrzā Muḥammad Ḥasan Khān Iᶜtimad us-Salṭana, *Tārīkh-i Muntaẓam-i Nāṣirī* [Tehran, 1330 lunar/1883], III: 162). It is, on the other hand, true that his sons, in exile in Baghdad, enjoyed British protection and later visited England as official guests. See J. B. Fraser, *Narrative of the Residence of the Persian Princes in London in 1835 and 1836, with an Account of their Subsequent Adventures*, 2 vols. (London, 1838).

8. *Kullīyāt-i Malkum*, pp. 145–146.

Britain towards Iran will come into being only when we adopt as our model the circumstances of Hyderabad and the Deccan."[9]

If British policy aimed at the erection of barriers, Russian strategy was devoted to their destruction, and from this difference derived varying attitudes to conquest. Britain, in order to conserve India, its essential and most precious possession, was obliged by the force of events, though without noticeable reluctance, to encroach on the lands to the northwest of India. Russian policy, by contrast, had acquisition as its explicit aim, not maintenance and defence: it was therefore more inclined to outright conquest and occupation.[10]

The aims of Russian policy admitted of no doubt and had not changed after being first formulated in the celebrated testament of Peter the Great.[11] It was true that the rate of Russian expansion into Asia had been decreased by the prolonged preoccupation of Peter's successors with the affairs of Europe. In the nineteenth century, however, this mistaken policy had been reversed, ambitions in Europe had been largely foresworn, and the whole of Russian power was turned on Asia. Russian expansion enjoyed the support of all Europe, save only Britain, for Russia was believed to have a civilizing mission in the East to be fulfilled through trade and conquest. In the face of this Russian threat, "the British danger is as nothing."[12] Iran offered the most suitable route for an invasion of India, preferable by far to Turkistan, and no strategic or logistic considerations stood in the way of a Russian advance into the very heart of Iran. "Today Iran is in the hands of Russia."[13]

In the face of these two permanent and ineluctable dangers, the Iranian men of state displayed their customary childishness and lack of perception. They imagined political questions to be capable of solution through mere trickery and posturing and appeals to right and justice.

> The Russian government has its plans concerning Astarabad [present-day Gurgan, a city near the southeastern corner of the Caspian Sea], but our consul in Astrakhan conducts himself with haughty pride. British policy demands the occupation of the south of Iran, but if we are unkind to one of their officials, doubtless they will change their policy. Our ministers wish to preserve the state with this kind of measure, but let them clearly realize that if they dismiss ten ministers for the sake of the good pleasure of the British

9. *Ibid.*, pp. 147–149.

10. *Ibid.*, p. 151.

11. *Ibid.*, p. 153. On the widespread credence accorded in nineteenth-century Iran to the apocryphal testament of Peter the Great, see Sir Percy Sykes, *A History of Persia*, 3rd ed. (London, 1963), II: 232, 244–246.

12. *Kullīyāt-i Malkum*, p. 155.

13. *Ibid.*, p. 158.

legation; if they kiss the hands and feet of the Graf[14] twenty times a day; if they restrict the foreign ambassadors so much that they are imprisoned in their homes; if our officials are so bold as even to curse and swear in conversations of state; if our battalions become as expert as those of Europe in every science—still the Russian armies will pass over Iran as and when they wish, and still British policy will aim to subjugate Iran like the states of India. The means for changing a nation's policy, the resources for preserving a state are not the absurdities which until today have wasted the time of our men of state. One of their strange ideas consists in this, that they constantly say: "Such-and-such a state is not in the right; Iran is in the right." O dear sir! O fifty-year-old child! What is meant by right? What is justice? What connection do international politics have with justice? Did England occupy India by right? Did Russia inherit a right to Georgia? The right of nations reposes in the demands of strategy and the mouth of the cannon.[15]

After this fine satirical tirade, it might be expected that Malkum would proceed to expose a plan of national salvation. Instead, he merely hints at the desirability of alignment with Britain as the lesser evil confronting Iran. Russian occupation of India would involve the liquidation of Iran, and hence the maintenance of British power in India was to be desired. If Iran were to arouse British enmity, the loss of the Persian Gulf ports and the southeastern provinces of the country might ensue, but the outcome of Russian hostility would be a final loss of independence. Britain, however, could not engage in open alliance with Iran, for such a relationship, no less than a total absence of British interest, would immediately invite a Russian attack.[16]

The position might then appear hopeless, but the Iranian men of state, far from registering signs of despair, persisted in the utmost tranquility and assurance, "as if they were honored guests at a wedding."[17] Worse still, "whatever we say, we will be unable to make the statesmen aware of the dimensions of the danger."[18] Since the statesmen were thus irremediably stupid, any attempt to instruct them would be wasted. Instead, the captain of the ship of state should himself assume responsibility, and all advice should be directed to him.

Were I one of the respected wise men of the state—that is, if I walked around with fifty hungry servants, dragging a few filthy nags in front of me, and if I consumed 20,000 *tomans* of the state's wealth every year;[19] if I were completely innocent of all the sciences that accompany education; if my ancestors had, in turn, one after the other plundered the provinces of Iran in the name of governorship; if I were a personage adorned with all kinds of

14. I.e., Count Ivan Alekseyevich Zinovyev, Russian envoy in Tehran.
15. *Kullīyāt-i Malkum*, pp. 161–162.
16. *Ibid.*, pp. 164–165.
17. *Ibid.*, p. 166.
18. *Ibid.*
19. See, however, n. 106 below.

> difficult accomplishments and considered my skill in deceit a proof of loftiness of mind—then, trusting in such considerations, I would say that Iran has two policies, little and great.[20]

By "little" policy was meant submission to Russia, of the abandonment of all attempts at maintaining independence. The "great" policy could not be frivolously revealed, for it was the product of several years' care and toil; yet, "in my opinion, I have discovered a plan for the salvation of Iran."[21]

This treatise is typical of Malkum's writing on political matters, combining three essential elements: a measure of accurate analysis, scornful mockery of Iranian politicians, and the claim, wreathed in a cloud of egotism, to possess a plan of salvation.

Elsewhere, in somewhat more sober tone, Malkum gave indications of what the "great" policy involved. It appears to have been fundamentally the same alignment with Britain hinted at in *Pūlitīkhā-yi Daulatī*, one stopping short of open alliance, but involving Britain in Iranian affairs to such an extent that an unspoken commitment to defend Iranian territorial integrity could no longer be avoided. Such involvement was to be in part economic and commercial, but also administrative, and in general so comprehensive in scope as to have inevitable political consequences.

In a letter to the Iranian Ministry of Foreign Affairs sent from London on Dhūl Ḥijja 14, 1294/December 20, 1877, Malkum set forth a project for European—primarily British—involvement in Iran, in comparison with which the Reuter concession appears to have been a timid and unsubstantial affair. He implied that the measures of reform expounded in his project were being impatiently awaited in London and that far-reaching expectations had been aroused by the shah's journey to Europe in 1873. The existence of such expectations, at least in official circles, may however be doubted, and for many years thereafter Britain remained averse to the assumption of active and continuous responsibility in Iran. The administrative aspects of Malkum's proposals seem, in fact, to have anticipated the Anglo-Iranian Treaty of 1919, signed by Vuthūq ud-Daula but never ratified, which would have turned Iran into a virtual British protectorate.[22] Malkum advocated the importation of a hundred administrators and advisors to take full responsibility for the running of all the ministries, subject only to the general supervision of an Iranian minister. The crown lands should similarly be entrusted to a foreign administrator, while at least twenty foreign companies should

20. *Ibid.*

21. *Ibid.*, p. 167.

22. See Rouhollah K. Ramazani, *The Foreign Policy of Iran, 1500–1941* (Charlottesville, 1966), pp. 160–161.

be invited to operate in Iran. Their task should be the construction of railways and highways; the expansion of ports and the introduction of commercial navigation on inland waterways; the exploitation of mines; the reformation of the currency and the fiscal system; and the foundation of commercial, agricultural, and estate banks. The importation of foreign administrators and entrepreneurs should be complemented by the dispatch to Europe of one thousand Iranian students to become acquainted with European learning. "Send a thousand students to Europe, not in order for each of them to marry two or three wives as has hitherto been the case, but for them all to be locked up in colleges for ten years on end, so that a third of them die from overwork and the rest make something of themselves."[23]

The letter proposing these measures concludes, like the treatise *Pūlitīkhā-yi Daulatī,* with expressions of helplessness and despair that there is none in Tehran to heed such sound advice and that Malkum stands tragically alone in his patriotic concern. "You will shake your heads regretfully and ask yourselves with a sigh, why this simpleton Malkum is thus ignorant of the state of Iran. Then you will answer me to the effect that 'friend, this is Iran, this is the land of Islam, a hundred breezes have wafted here.' "[24] Malkum's habit of thus pronouncing the recipients of his advice incapable of understanding it seems in itself to have been an obstacle to communication, for Nāṣir ud-Dīn Shāh noted on the back of the letter just discussed: "Open the letter again in Malkum Khān's presence and have him read it. There is no one in Iran who can understand it."[25]

In *Pūlitīkhā-yi Daulatī,* Malkum remarked on the inability of the British to enter into an open alliance with Iran, and throughout his term in London he found the Foreign Office largely unreceptive to his proposals and representations. Soon after returning to his post in 1874, Malkum sought to warn Britain of the consequences of a Russian occupation of Marv and the final extinction of even formal Iranian sovereignty over that city. "On the day when the Russian flag restores order and security in Merv [*sic*], that destined capital will be re-established; and nature itself, aided by Russian administration, will inevitably render it the most active centre of new enterprises and certain success; for we may be sure, when Merv is once in the hands of Russia, all barriers will be broken down and neighbouring states blotted out."[26] Thus

23. Letter quoted in Firīdūn Ādamīyat, *Fikr-i Āzādī va Muqaddima-yi Nihḍat-i Mashrūṭīyat* (Tehran, 1340 solar/1961), p. 152.

24. *Ibid.*

25. *Ibid.*

26. Malkum to Derby, 1874, quoted by Firuz Kazemzadeh, *Russia and Britain in Persia, 1864–1914* (New Haven, 1968), p. 38.

did Malkum seek to profit from the British fear of barriers being swamped by the India-bound Russian wave in order to awaken an active British interest in Iran. Yet Lord Derby, the foreign minister, showed himself no more disposed to a close alignment with Iran than his Liberal predecessor, Granville, had been the year before when Nāṣir ud-Dīn Shāh visited London. Malkum's exaggerated estimate of the decisive strategic role of Marv was not accepted, and no guarantee of Iranian territorial integrity was forthcoming.[27]

Russian expansion in Central Asia, and with it certain encroachments on northeastern Iran, were regarded as inevitable if unpalatable by both Conservative and Liberal administrations. True, the wave had to be stopped short of India, but to the north of a certain line that remained undefined until 1907 only temporary obstacles could be placed in the path of a Russian advance. It was felt that Britain should concentrate its attention upon the southern provinces of Iran, areas that were still free of Russian commercial and economic penetration and capable of constituting, as Malkum correctly observed, a forward line for the defence of India. Such considerations induced Britain to connive at the loss of Marv to Russia, for it pursued a policy of ending Iranian sovereignty over fringe territories in the south similar to that enacted by Russia in the north. Thus, the final detachment of Bahrayn and Kalāt from Iran was completed as early as 1869,[28] and, with the southeastern approaches to Iran thus secure, British interest turned to the southwest, to the province of Khuzistan (then known as Arabistan).

The river Kārūn, virtually Iran's sole navigable inland waterway, which flows up from its junction with the Shaṭṭ al-ᶜArab at Khurramshahr (formerly Muḥammara) to Ahvāz, Shushtar, and beyond, was thought to furnish a sure means of commercial penetration into southwestern and central Iran. Not only would Khuzistan be directly linked with the outside world by steam navigation, but also goods could be transported overland from Ahvāz to Isfahan more swiftly than from Bushire and other ports on the Persian Gulf.[29] It was therefore demanded with increasing insistence that Iran should permit British steamers to navigate the Kārūn much as they already operated on the Shaṭṭ al-ᶜArab and the Tigris. While Britain showed itself reluctant to guarantee Iranian independence, Nāṣir ud-Dīn Shāh was reciprocally unwilling to open the Kārūn to foreign shipping,[30] and the matter dragged on for seventeen years, from 1871 to 1888.

Malkum's role in the negotiation and ultimate settlement of the question was slight and of less importance than the repeated demands of successive British envoys in Tehran, W. T. Thomson and Sir Arthur

27. *Ibid.*
28. *Ibid.*, pp. 150–151.
29. *Ibid.*, p. 149 f.
30. *Ibid.*, p. 160.

Nicolson. Malkum's voice was, however, one of those that proclaimed the benefits of opening the Kārūn, and when in his letter of December 1877 he listed the navigation of inland waterways as one of the tasks to be entrusted to foreign enterprise, doubtless he had in mind primarily, if not exclusively, the Kārūn and British desires to sail its waters. British interest in Khuzistan presumably appeared to Malkum as a desirable step in the direction of a more comprehensive involvement in Iran and a full commitment to the promotion of reform. It may be no coincidence that there is a strong similarity between Malkum's treatises *Uṣūl-i Tamaddun* and *Ḥarf-i Gharīb*, previously discussed,[31] and many of the British communications to Iranian officials designed to elicit the opening of the Kārūn. In both cases, commercial intercourse is stressed as providing the only sound basis for friendship among nations or, more exactly, British interest in preserving Iran from Russian expansion.

In February 1884, the Russians finally captured Marv and three months later occupied Sarakhs, a city that had been somewhat more effectively under Iranian rule. Fearful of still further encroachments on his territory, Nāṣir ud-Dīn Shāh turned to Britain for some guarantee of Iranian integrity and independence. Malkum visited Granville, by then reinstated in the Foreign Office, to present Nāṣir ud-Dīn's request and was told in return simply that Britain would be prepared to use its good offices and convey Iranian representations to St. Petersburg.

Beyond that, he was informed, British support of Iran depended largely upon "the amount of sympathy which is felt by the British nation towards that country." Such a feeling of sympathy was

> undoubtedly checked by the almost entire absence of commercial intercourse between England and Persia, and especially by the obstacles which exist to trade with the southern provinces of Persia which, if these obstacles were removed, would be easily accessible to English and Indian commerce. The repeated efforts of H.M.'s Minister at Tehran, to obtain the opening of the Karoon river to navigation, have hitherto been unsuccessful, and the want of good and safe roads from the interior to the Persian Gulf represents a serious drawback to enterprise.[32]

In a letter to the Iranian minister of foreign affairs, Nicolson used almost identical language, when he wrote that the heart of British public opinion would beat for Iranian independence only if British goods were gracing Iranian markets.[33] Thus it seemed that the British were furnishing proof of Malkum's contention that the only guarantee

31. See above, pp. 108–113.

32. Granville to Malkum, August 16, 1884, quoted by Kazemzadeh, *op. cit.*, p. 91.

33. Letter dated December 23, 1885, quoted by Ādamīyat, *op. cit.*, p. 164.

of independence lay in the encouragement of foreign trade. In Tehran, however, it was felt that vague hints of willingness to intercede in St. Petersburg were not worth the opening of the Kārūn, and an arrangement was reached with Russia, ceding Sarakhs as well as Marv.[34]

Undaunted, the following year Malkum again approached the British government in the hope of encouraging an assertive attitude to Iranian affairs and eliciting authoritative advice he could convey to Tehran. He specifically proposed a clear British guarantee of Iranian independence and territorial integrity and the appointment of British advisers to the Iranian government as a symbol of that guarantee. These proposals Salisbury, the Conservative prime minister, refused to entertain, and he was reluctant even to comply with the request for advice. Finally, however, he expressed the view that

> if England in the future was to be of any use in sustaining Persia against the probable encroachments of and gradual absorption by Russia, two things were necessary. In the first place that such strategic precautions should be taken as should oppose the greatest difficulty to a Russian attack, and give the greatest facility for *possible* [emphasis supplied] English succour; and in the second place that the corruptions which were eating into the kingdom and bringing it to decay should be attacked with a firm hand.

As a strategic precaution, Salisbury had in mind particularly the removal of the capital from Tehran, which was "uncomfortably near to the Russian strongholds on the Caspian and dangerously distant from the more friendly shore of the Indian Ocean," to Isfahan.[35] At last Malkum had laid hold of some British advice, and he duly conveyed it to Tehran, presenting it as more official and authoritative than Salisbury had intended it to be. Yet Salisbury need not have been concerned, for the advice reluctantly offered was ignored by Nāṣir ud-Dīn Shāh.[36]

Malkum continued to believe in the possibility of allying himself with Britain in order to promote Iranian reform, and he supplied the Foreign Office with copies of various proposals that he made to Nāṣir ud-Dīn Shāh and his ministers.[37] Yet on the actual course of Anglo-Iranian relations he had little if any effect. When, in October 1888, the equation of British trade and Iranian independence had been finally accepted in Tehran, and the Kārūn was opened to British shipping, it was due more to the efforts of Sir Henry Drummond Wolff, the new

34. Kazemzadeh, *op. cit.*, p. 92.

35. Salisbury to Thomson, August 6, 1885, quoted in *ibid.*, pp. 98–99, and R. L. Greaves, *Persia and the Defence of India*, 1884–1892 (London, 1959), pp. 87–88.

36. *Ibid.*, p. 89.

37. See, for example, "Papers submitted to Malkum Khan to Nasiruddin Shah and communicated to the Marquess of Salisbury on February 13, 1888," in F. O. 60/497.

British envoy, than to Malkum's recommendations.[38] Malkum informed the Russian ambassador in London, Baron de Staal, that he had had no part in the negotiations leading to the opening of the Kārūn, although he would not deny his approval of the measure.[39] De Staal was reluctant to believe him, suspecting him, not without reason, of constant duplicity because of his professions of russophilia. But on this occasion Malkum may well have been speaking the truth. Wolff's arrival in Tehran marked the beginning of a more active phase of British policy towards Iran, but Malkum was unable to exert any influence upon it, let alone direct it towards the imposition of reform. Instead, not long after the opening of the Kārūn, he brought his term of service in London to an end with a spectacularly successful swindle.

Unable to recruit the Foreign Office as an imperious ally that would, through benevolent advice, impose his program of reform on Iran, Malkum was obliged to continue his efforts at influencing affairs through contacts and correspondence with prominent acquaintances who, in part, shared his outlook and aspirations. Closest at hand were the Iranian envoys accredited to other European capitals.

Mention should first be made of Mīrzā Yūsuf Khān Mustashār ud-Daula, who was chargé d'affaires in Paris from 1866 to 1870 and reputedly visited Malkum in London four times to discuss the situation in Iran and the reforms that seemed necessary.[40] The fruit of these discussions was supposedly Mīrzā Yūsuf Khān's treatise known as *Yak Kalima* (One word), the title alluding to the fact that Iran's needs could be summarized in one word—law. The treatise may be defined as a commentary on French constitutional law in terms of Islamic precepts: its principles are explained and vindicated with reference to Qur'ānic verses and traditions of the Prophet and the Imams. The establishment of a similar equation between Western and Islamic concepts was one of Malkum's concerns. But for simple chronological reasons *Yak Kalima* cannot be accepted as the result of discussions between the two men in London. Malkum's appointment to England did not come until 1873; Mīrzā Yūsuf Khān's term in Paris ended in 1870—the same year in which *Yak Kalima* was written—and he was back in Tehran by August

38. See Kazemzadeh, *op. cit.* (n. 26, above), p. 195.

39. A. Meyendorff, ed., *Correspondence Diplomatique de M. de Staal, 1884–1900* (Paris, 1929), I: 446–448. Compare Amīn ud-Daula to Malkum, Rabīᶜ uth-Thānī 6, 1306/December 11, 1888: "Doubtless the ministry has left you uninformed about the Karun affair and the basis of the matter. But since Salisbury will have learned about it in detail from Sir Henry [Wolff], it is wrong that you should remain in ignorance" (Bibliothèque Nationale, Supplément Persan, 1997, f. 91).

40. See Nāẓim ul-Islām Kirmānī, *Tārīkh-i Bīdārī-yi Īrānīān* (Tehran, n.d.), p. 177.

1871, at the latest.[41] Nonetheless, Malkum's more remote influence on the composition cannot be discounted. The two men had been in contact since the early 1860s, when Malkum was special adviser to Mīrzā Ḥusayn Khān at the Iranian legation in Istanbul and Mīrzā Yūsuf Khān, Iranian consul-general in Tiflis. They had in common a sympathetic friendship with Ākhūndzāda and an interest in alphabet reform, though Mīrzā Yūsuf Khān's interest appears to have been entirely passive.[42] Between Istanbul and Tiflis, they exchanged their writings on political and economic reform and appear largely to have approved of each other's views. Thus Mīrzā Yūsuf Khān informed Ākhūndzāda in July 1866, that he had sent Malkum a composition entitled *Ramz-i Yūsufī* which he had received with enthusiastic praise.[43] It is then possible that *Yak Kalima* should have been the fruit of an exchange of views by letter, if not in person.

In such an exchange, it would be incorrect to assume that Malkum was the more active partner merely because of his greater fame and the relative obscurity of Mīrzā Yūsuf Khān in the history of Qajar Iran. It is possible that certain of Malkum's typical positions were due to Mīrzā Yūsuf's influence or at least clarified and strengthened thereby. Although Malkum claimed to have sought the introduction of material reform under an Islamic guise as early as the farāmūshkhāna episode, it may be that he was attributing to himself in retrospect a clarity of purpose that he did not possess. His explicit statements of intention—such as the lecture on Persian civilization delivered in 1891—are all relatively late, even though elements of the theme of identity of European civilization and Islamic precept can be seen in his earlier treatises. By contrast, as early as 1869 Mīrzā Yūsuf Khān composed a work entitled *Rūḥ ul-Islām* (The spirit of Islam),[44] in which the author, in his own words, "found proofs and evidences from the Glorious Qurʾān and reliable traditions for all the means of progress and civilization, so that none henceforth shall say, 'such-and-such a matter is against the principles of Islam,' or, 'the principles of Islam are an obstacle to progress and

41. See Mīrzā Yūsuf Khān to Ākhūndzāda, August 18, 1871, in *Alifbā-yi Jadīd va Maktūbāt*, eds. Ḥ. Muḥammadzāda and Ḥ. Ārāslī (Baku, 1963), p. 398.

42. See Mīrzā Yūsuf Khān to Ākhūndzāda, November 17, 1867, applauding Malkum's revised script, in *ibid.*, p. 366. It is also relevant to note that Mīrzā Yūsuf Khān was, like Malkum, a mason, having been initiated into the Clémente Amitié lodge in Paris. See Ismāʿīl Rāʾīn, *Fārāmūshkhāna va Frāmāsūnrī dar Īrān* (Tehran, 1348 solar/1969), I: 480.

43. Mīrzā Yūsuf Khān to Ākhūndzāda, November 17, 1867, in *Alifbā-yi Jadīd va Maktūbāt*, pp. 360–361.

44. The identity of the title of this treatise with a more celebrated apologetic, the Indian Amir Ali's *Spirit of Islam*, a work of similar content, is an interesting coincidence.

civilization.' "[45] It may be assumed that in keeping with custom he sent a copy of this treatise to Malkum in Istanbul. At the very least Malkum must have found its contents useful in supplying precise arguments for the thesis he had adopted: his acquaintance with Qur'ān and *ḥadīth* can have been only slight, considering his education.

It is also of relevance to note a certain difference of tone between the views of Mīrzā Yūsuf Khān and those of Malkum. For Malkum the equation between progressive Europe and ideal Islam was purely expedient, but Mīrzā Yūsuf Khān appears to have had some substantial belief in the concept. Indeed, the tendency of *Yak Kalima* is to show that since European political ideals are equivalent to those of Islam, all that need be done to attain a progress and prosperity equal to those of Europe is to make a revitalized *sharīʿa* the law and basis of the state. Ākhūndzāda took Mīrzā Yūsuf Khān to task for this assertion, listing a number of provisions of Islamic law he thought incompatible with justice.[46] Such an exertion would have been unnecessary if he had thought Mīrzā Yūsuf to be expediently concealing his true, progressive disbelief.

After his return to Tehran, Mīrzā Yūsuf Khān occupied a number of government posts which alternated with periods of disfavor earned by his reformist views. One such period came in 1890, when he was imprisoned in Qazvin, and coincided with Malkum's publication in London of the early numbers of *Qānūn*.[47] He was thus identified with Malkum and his outlook, and although no letters from him are to be found in the collection donated by Malkum's widow to the Bibliothèque Nationale, he may be thought to have remained in contact with him during his years in London.

Malkum's contacts with Mīrzā Yūsuf Khān's successor in Paris, Naẓar Āqā, are somewhat better attested. The two men formed with Narīmān Khān, minister in Vienna, and Mīrzā Muḥsin Khān Muʿīn ul-Mulk, minister in Istanbul, an intimate circle of friends in constant communication, who frequently met together to discuss matters of policy on their own initiative, not on instructions from Tehran. Thus in 1887 Muʿīn ul-Mulk came from Istanbul to Carlsbad to take the waters, and there he was joined by Malkum and Narīmān Khān. After a time the trio proceeded to Paris and pursued their deliberations in the

45. *Alifbā-yi Jadīd va Maktūbāt*, p. 372.

46. M. F. Akhundov, *Äsärläri* (Baku, 1961), II: 188–197 (Azeri translation of his letter), 308–316 (Persian original). A Russian translation of his letter, entitled "Kritika Yek Kel'me," is to be found in M. F. Akhundov, *Izbrannoye* (Moscow, 1956), pp. 266–271.

47. For a concise summary of Mīrzā Yūsuf Khān's career and a consideration of his writings, see Ādamīyat, *op. cit.* (n. 23, above), pp. 182–198.

presence of Naẓar Āqā.[48] The group was held together not only by the common profession of diplomacy but also by masonic ties, all of the four having been initiated into the lodge Sincère Amitié of the Grand Orient of France.[49] In the absence of relevant documents, the extent and nature of the contacts between the four envoys can hardly be assessed. It seems, however, probable that Malkum's diplomatic colleagues were commonly regarded as his followers and sympathizers, as was the case with Mīrzā Yūsuf Khān, and Mīrzā Muḥsin Khān ultimately lost his post in Istanbul because of his ties with Malkum.[50]

Beyond Europe, Malkum maintained a copious correspondence with Iran, much of which is preserved in the Bibliothèque Nationale. The collection consists for the most part of the letters that Malkum received, containing hardly any that he wrote, and it is moreover carefully compiled to exclude any discreditable material: thus it contains virtually nothing bearing on the lottery concession of 1889 and its cancellation. It is nonetheless possible to gain from the collection an insight into the nature of Malkum's relations with princes and ministers in Iran and the concerns which agitated him during his fifteen years as minister in London.

Among Malkum's correspondents was Muẓaffar ud-Dīn Mīrzā, governor of Azerbayjan and heir apparent. The shah evidently disliked his son, and his position as heir rested solely on primogeniture (among male offspring by wives of noble birth), not paternal affection. Muẓaffar ud-Dīn was reputed to be of weak character, and this inherent incapacity to rule was strengthened by the conditions of his residence in Tabriz, where he was kept isolated from the conduct of affairs and deprived of financial resources appropriate to his station. Curzon wrote:

> If the prince is, as alleged, of weak character and easily led—although such a lack of individuality is denied by others, it is largely owing to the inexcusable position of subordination in which he, a man of nearly forty years of age, the second personage in the kingdom, and the future sovereign, has been placed by the shortsighted apprehensions of his father. Though nominally Governor-General of a great province, he has hitherto been allowed no more voice in the actual administration than a lacquey at his table; a child in leading-strings has more control over his own movements than this pseudo-ruler has had over his own subjects.[51]

48. Ḥājjī Pīrzāda Nāʾīnī, *Safarnāma*, ed. Ḥāfiẓ Farmānfarmāʾīān (Tehran, 1343 solar/1965), II: 22.

49. Narīmān Khān had been initiated in 1857 together with Malkum (see above, p. 24), and Naẓar Āqā and Mīrzā Muḥsin Khān three years later (*Bulletin du Grand Orient de France*, XV [5860=1860]: 396–397).

50. See below, p. 203.

51. G. N. Curzon, *Persia and the Persian Question* (London, 1892), I: 414.

Muẓaffar ud-Dīn would nonetheless most probably succeed to the throne, and if he was ignorant of affairs and malleable of character, then so much the better: he would be more disposed to learn uninhibitedly from Malkum's instruction. Thus it was that Malkum did not neglect, while in London, to maintain the friendly contact with Muẓaffar ud-Dīn Mīrzā that he had evidently established some time before.

The Bibliothèque Nationale collection contains letters from Muẓaffar ud-Dīn ranging in date from 1874 to 1886. Many of them are little more than brief notes requesting Malkum to purchase and dispatch to Iran such items as hunting rifles, telescopes, seeds, and writing paper.[52] They are all, however, remarkable for the affection which speaks from them and which suggests that Malkum had been able to gain Muẓaffar ud-Dīn's affection as he had once charmed the shah his father in the 1850s. Thus the heir apparent wrote in Shavvāl 1299/May 1882, begging Malkum to write more frequently: "You know the extent of my inward attachment to you, my affection for you; there is no need to write of it." In a postscript to this letter he asked Malkum to supply him with political information and proposals for reform, which he would do his best to implement: "I am extremely fond of you; know that I am completely in accord and agreement with you."[53] Muẓaffar ud-Dīn seems to have appreciated Malkum as one of the few individuals who would communicate with him seriously on political matters.

Malkum sent Muẓaffar ud-Dīn information on current events, together with various of his writings on reform, which were received gratefully but not uncritically. Muẓaffar ud-Dīn displayed a certain reserve towards Malkum's sweeping proposals which belied his affirmation of complete agreement with him. Thus he wrote in Dhūl Qaᶜda 1303/August 1886:

> Indeed your booklet contains all kinds of important point and subtlety. I took especial care to read it over, time and again. The truth of the matter is just as Your Excellency says. The world is greatly changed, and much different from the situation in which we find ourselves. Just as you wrote, I too hope that the measures of His Imperial Majesty—may my soul be his ransom!—will remove all defects in the state. In a short time he has performed feats that were beyond the imagination of us all, and he has greatly assisted in the education of the people of Iran. No other country has so just and compassionate a ruler. You yourself must be aware that matters cannot be accomplished all at once; they must ripen gradually, and nowhere in the world is perfection reached abruptly.[54]

Malkum's correspondence with Muẓaffar ud-Dīn appears to have had no conclusive result beyond maintaining a friendly relationship

52. Supplément Persan, 1989, ff. 3, 4, 8, 11, 12, 13.

53. *Ibid.*, f. 5.

54. *Ibid.*, ff. 6–7.

which assumed some practical importance after Muẓaffar ud-Dīn's succession to the throne in 1897 and Malkum's emergence from disgrace.

More copious and of greater interest is his exchange of letters with Muẓaffar ud-Dīn's half-brother, Masᶜūd Mīrzā Ẓill us-Sulṭān, the governor of Isfahan.[55] Masᶜūd Mīrzā was a man of markedly different character from Muẓaffar ud-Dīn, ambitious and assertive instead of weak and pliable, and it was frequently thought that he would challenge his brother's right to the succession, notwithstanding his mother's lowly birth. While Muẓaffar ud-Dīn was virtually powerless in Azerbayjan, Ẓill us-Sulṭān was able, through his energetic governorship, to extend the sphere of his control from Isfahan to Fars, Yazd, Kurdistan, Luristan, and Khuzistan, and he developed a semiindependent army as outward token of his power.[56] The rise of Ẓill us-Sulṭān's dominance in the south made it inevitable that the British should seek his favor, and in exchange for the Grand Cross of the Star of India he was persuaded to lend his influence to the cause of opening the Kārūn.[57] Precisely this visible alignment with British power led to Ẓill us-Sulṭān's downfall: his concentration of strength, once complete with British support, was too great a threat to be countenanced, and accordingly, early in 1887, he was dismissed from all his posts except the governorship of Isfahan.[58]

In addition to a shared attitude of anglophilia, there was much else that bound Malkum to Ẓill us-Sulṭān. Malkum's father, Mīrzā Yaᶜqūb, had been the prince's tutor in French, and the affection that he gained was inherited by Malkum. Ẓill us-Sulṭān was in general well disposed to the Armenian community of Julfa,[59] and it can be deduced from several of his letters to Malkum that he was in regular contact with a number of his relatives who lived in the Armenian suburb.[60]

Among all the Qajar princes, it was Ẓill us-Sulṭān who proclaimed most frequently the need to westernize,[61] and so far as this was the expression of a genuinely held belief, it may be thought to have strengthened his attachment to Malkum Khān.

55. The content of Ẓill us-Sulṭān's correspondence with Mīrzā Malkum Khān (Bibliothèque Nationale, Supplément Persan, 1990) has been summarized in an article copiously illustrated with facsimiles of the letters: Jahāngīr Qāᶜimmaqāmī, "Ravābiṭ-i Ẓill us-Sulṭān va Mīrzā Malkum Khān," *Barrasīhā-yi Tārīkhī*, III:6 (Bahman-Isfand, 1347/January–February, 1969), 83–120.

56. Curzon, *op. cit.*, I: 416.

57. Kazemzadeh, *op. cit.* (n. 26, above), pp. 163–165, 184.

58. *Ibid.*, p. 184.

59. Jane Dieulafoy, *La Perse, la Chaldée et la Susiane* (Paris, 1887), p. 222.

60. Supplément Persan, 1990, ff. 14–15, 20–21. Qāʾimmaqāmī (*op. cit.*, p. 92) suggests that the person by the name of Takrān Malkum referred to in these letters may have been a brother of Malkum.

61. Curzon, *op. cit.*, I: 419.

Equally important for the sympathetic relationship between the two were a common distaste for religion and a profession of freethinking which did not exclude expedient appeals to Islam. As Curzon put it with obvious approval, Ẓill us-Sulṭān treated the ulama with "refreshing contempt."[62] The French traveler, Jane Dieulafoy, relates that he had a pigsty erected in his palace garden, and that he would force the ulama of Isfahan to pass through the befouled courtyard when they attended his Naurūz reception.[63] He further made a point of shocking religious sentiment by attending services at the Anglican church in Isfahan and letting it be known that he enjoyed the consumption of European literature.[64] It was nonetheless necessary to maintain a certain minimum of external religiosity, and he once explained the manner in which he did so to Colonel R. M. Smith, head of the Iranian section of the Indo-European Telegraph: "The mollahs and many of the people here think me an unbeliever because I read Feringhi [*sic*] newspapers and order my son to learn French. They are afraid to tackle me openly on the subject, but I know their thoughts and satisfy the fools by saying I read Feringhi's writings, not in search for any good, but in order to see their evil and study how to avoid it."[65] In his memoirs, Ẓill us-Sulṭān similarly attempted to dissimulate his unbelief by affirming that he was indeed "a lover of the House of Purity and devoted to the servants of the Twelve Imams," and that he was "an extremely fanatical Shiᶜi." His enmity was directed solely against false, corrupt, and hypocritical ulama who usurped the people's property and delivered unjust judgments.[66] Since he was universally recognized to be at least the equal of corrupt mujtahids such as Āqā Najafī in greed, cruelty, and extortion, such affirmations of concern for true Islam are implausible. It is ironic that Malkum, who is commonly regarded as an ancestor of constitutionalism, should have been the intimate of this ambitious tyrant.

The warm and affectionate tone of Ẓill us-Sulṭān's letters to Malkum is too consistent to be false or the result of mere politeness. A convincing proof of the confidence of Ẓill us-Sulṭān reposed in him, is furnished by the occasion on which he implicitly admitted to him his ambitions for the throne: "Why not address me as heir apparent, just as a joke [*mahḍ-i rīshkhand*]?"[67]

62. *Ibid.*, I: 417.

63. Dieulafoy, *op. cit.*, p. 253.

64. S. G. W. Benjamin, *Persia and the Persians* (London, 1887), p. 359.

65. Smith's report to Nicolson, July 14, 1887, in F.O. 60/487.

66. Masᶜūd Mīrzā Ẓill us-Sulṭān, *Tārīkh-i Sargudhasht-i Masᶜūdī* (Tehran, 1325 lunar/1907), p. 96.

67. Ẓill us-Sulṭān to Malkum, Rajab 25, 1325/September 3, 1907, in Supplément Persan, 1990, f. 35.

Ẓill us-Sulṭān's friendly feelings for Malkum appear to have been finally confirmed by an encounter in Tehran in 1872, a few months before Malkum's departure for Europe to prepare the way for Nāṣir ud-Dīn Shāh's first journey. In a letter dated Jumādī ul-Ukhrā 1, 1289/August 6, 1872, Ẓill us-Sulṭān assures Malkum that he is constantly in his mind: "In truth, you have, as it were, ravished my heart, and I frequently recall your kind conduct towards me."[68]

The following eight years nonetheless went by without further correspondence, for it is not until 1880 that we find Ẓill us-Sulṭān again lamenting his separation from Malkum. He had fallen temporarily into disfavor and been obliged to take up residence at Burūjird in Luristan.

> You may imagine that in a place like this, where no conversation is to be had except with a few illiterate Lurs, what effect would be produced on me by the receipt of a letter from a wise philosopher such as yourself, a letter overflowing from start to finish with wisdom and the truths of civilization. Since the year of the famine [i.e., 1872] when I met Your Excellency in Tehran and listened to your wise utterances, I have had no contact with you, either in speech or writing.

Malkum's unexpected letter had apparently been accompanied by certain proposals for reform to which he might have thought Ẓill us-Sulṭān particularly receptive while in disfavor. Ẓill us-Sulṭān's response was indeed favorable, though somewhat prevaricatory: he professed inability to help Malkum in securing the acceptance of his proposals while in Burūjird. Malkum, however, should persist in his efforts: "Today the situation in Iran is different from what it used to be. Most people are thinking seriously about civilization and have formed certain intentions. . . . They need only a slight incentive to be set in motion. The times are such that the presence in Iran of a wise philosopher such as Your Excellency is an absolute necessity." Malkum should arrange to arrive in Tehran as soon as Ẓill us-Sulṭān was permitted to leave Burūjird.[69]

Similar advice, to return to Tehran and strike a decisive blow for reform, was given to Malkum at about the same time by another of his correspondents, Mīrzā ʿAlī Khān Amīn ud-Daula, minister of private correspondence and a confidant of the shah. Amīn ud-Daula's acquaintance with Malkum was of long standing. Born in 1845, he had been one of the members of Malkum's farāmūshkhāna, and he reestablished contact with him after his return to Iran from Istanbul in 1872. More than either Muẓaffar ud-Dīn Mīrzā or Ẓill us-Sulṭān, Amīn ud-Daula was genuinely devoted to the cause of governmental reform, and this devo-

68. *Ibid.*, f. 1.

69. *Ibid.*, ff. 3–4.

tion formed a solid basis for his continuing friendship with Malkum.[70] Although zeal for reform did not totally exclude pecuniary greed in his case any more than it did with Malkum, we see that his interest in reforming the state was real and constant, and on occasion he vented his irritation at Malkum's lack of seriousness.

Many of the letters written by Amīn ud-Daula to Malkum during his first decade in London relate to the persistent question of railways: by whom and where they should be constructed. Solution of the question was ultimately dependent on Anglo-Russian maneuverings in Iran, and each power was more interested in preventing the building of a railway by the other than in accomplishing the feat itself. Nonetheless, within the bounds of those maneuverings, Iranian politicians had a certain scope of action: various schemes might be forwarded or frustrated. Despite frequent references to the railway question, it is not possible to deduce from Amīn ud-Daula's letters whether Malkum lent his support to any specific scheme or would-be concessionaire. More probably his role was limited to reiteration of the civilizing virtues of the steam engine, a theme first enunciated at the time of the Reuter concession.[71]

In one letter, however, Amīn ud-Daula wrote of his own participation in a commercial venture which he invited Malkum to join. This was a company for the production of alcoholic beverages, the brainchild of Naẓar Āqā and Narīmān Khān, and christened, at the shah's suggestion, Société Internationale de l'Agriculture de la Perse, to avoid probable religious opposition. Amīn ud-Daula had joined the venture unaware of its true purpose, but having learned of the type of agriculture in which it intended to engage, saw no pressing reason to withdraw.[72] Evidently, nothing came of the proposed company, for in 1889 the shah granted a concession for the manufacture of liquor to a Belgian firm.[73]

In addition to discussions of the railway question, Amīn ud-Daula's letters supplied Malkum with summaries of current events in Tehran and commentaries that swung back and forth between the optimistic and pessimistic. When he saw reason to be optimistic, he would advise Malkum to return to Tehran and profit from the favorable situation, and when in a pessimistic mood, to stay clear, for he would find the atmosphere intolerable. On September 2, 1878, Amīn ud-Daula complained to Malkum: "There is nothing we can do. Day by day we become more desperate. . . . We want to become world famous for ex-

70. On the life of Mīrzā ᶜAlī Khān Amīn ud-Daula, see his memoirs, *Khāṭirāt-i Siyāsī*, ed. Ḥāfiẓ Farmānfarmāʾīān (Tehran, 1341 solar/1962).

71. See Amīn ud-Daula's letters in Supplément Persan, 1997, ff. 7, 9, 17.

72. *Ibid.*, ff. 12–13, 14.

73. Kazemzadeh, *op. cit.* (n. 26, above), p. 242.

cellent, outstanding deeds, but we have no plan, no organization, no money. Our state of beggary worsens by the hour, our ruin increases by the minute."[74] By contrast, in March 1879, prospects appeared more hopeful. Amīn ud-Daula had brought certain of Malkum's writings to Nāṣir ud-Dīn Shāh's attention, and some response seemed to have been evoked. "The difficulties and obstacles are formidable, but the confusion of affairs has made His Majesty inclined to recognize the necessity of some really useful change."[75] By April 28, Amīn ud-Daula's mood had reversed itself again: "What do we want with these useless thoughts [of reform]? What profit are we to expect of them? Let's give a thought to our own lives! These fancies and imaginings will make lunatics of us yet."[76] This pessimism persisted until July 1880, when we find him advising Malkum to keep away from Iran because he would find a single day there unbearable.[77] By May of the following year, Amīn ud-Daula was feeling more hopeful: Malkum should come to Tehran, for after the strain caused by his father's recent death in Istanbul he needed something of a change, and in any event the shah wished to confer with him.[78]

Yielding to royal desire and the advice of Ẓill us-Sulṭān and Amīn ud-Daula, Malkum finally arrived in Tehran on a brief return visit on March 9, 1882, staying with Amīn ud-Daula as his guest.[79] For whatever reason Nāṣir ud-Dīn Shāh had wished to summon Malkum, no substantial discussions on any matter of importance took place. Malkum was instructed to confer with various ministers and princes, including Amīn ud-Daula and Ẓill us-Sulṭān, but nothing conclusive emerged from their meetings. The shah himself, in the words of Muḥammad Ḥasan Khān Iᶜtimād us-Salṭana, his minister of publications, would speak only "of fruit, of roses and of nightingales."[80]

The most visible result of Malkum's visit to Tehran was promotion from the title of *Nāẓim ul-Mulk* (Orderer of the Realm) to *Nāẓim ud-Daula* (Orderer of the State), in recognition of his services at the Congress of Berlin.[81] He had been instructed to participate in the congress as Iranian delegate, and partly through ingratiating himself with Bismarck had been able to secure for Iran the restoration from the Ottoman Empire of the border area of Quṭūr.[82] In addition to the elevation of his title, his diplomatic rank also rose, from plenipotentiary (*vazīr-i mukh-*

74. Supplément Persan, 1997, f. 3.
75. *Ibid.*, f. 6.
76. *Ibid.*, f. 7.
77. *Ibid.*, f. 16.
78. *Ibid.*, f. 17.
79. Muḥammad Ḥasan Khān Iᶜtimād us-Salṭana, *Rūznāma-yi Khāṭirāt*, ed. Īraj Afshār (Tehran, 1345 solar/1966), p. 171.
80. *Ibid.*, p. 180.
81. *Ibid.*, p. 192.
82. The restoration was stipulated in article lx of the Treaty of Berlin. See E. Hertslet, *The Map of Europe by Treaty* (London, 1891), IV: 2796.

tār) to ambassador (*safīr-kabīr*).[83] Titles were always a matter of importance to Malkum Khān and he was still visibly elated with pride when Iᶜtimād us-Salṭana went to visit him a week after his promotion. Iᶜtimād us-Salṭana had a certain respect for Malkum who had once taught him the elements of French, but on this occasion his impressions of his former tutor were unpleasant: "My teacher and preceptor has gone slightly mad. He has preferred egotism to patriotism."[84]

The slight lunacy noted by Iᶜtimād us-Salṭana evidently had not left Malkum by the time he reached Tiflis en route back to London. There he met Mīrzā Riḍā Khān Arfaᶜ ud-Daula, a member of the staff of the Iranian consulate-general, who presented him with a treatise of his own composition on the subject of alphabet reform.[85] Malkum responded by bestowing on him the surname Dānish (knowledge), in an absurdly bombastic letter:

> You have accumulated profound acquaintance with most of the subtleties of progress in our age, and you are doubtless fully aware that everyone must have a family name in addition to a personal name. I will not trouble to explain to you the necessity and advantages of having a surname. I will say only this: choose such a name for your family. Considering the various accomplishments which I am delighted to observe you in the possession of, I think it appropriate for you to take the name Dānish.[86]

Arfaᶜ ud-Daula agreed and henceforth used Dānish as his pseudonym in the mediocre poetry he was wont to compose.[87]

With little if anything of value achieved, Malkum arrived back in London, where he resumed the somewhat empty game of sending reports, pamphlets, and recommendations to Tehran. The progress of the game may again be followed through an examination of the letters he received from Ẓill us-Sulṭān and Amīn ud-Daula. While still en route, he had sent Ẓill us-Sulṭān a letter from Qazvin containing proposals for reform and suggesting that he show them to Nāṣir ud-Dīn Shāh. This Ẓill us-Sulṭān duly did, offering to convey any other proposals Malkum might care to submit and to inform him of the monarch's reactions.[88] In

83. Iᶜtimād us-Salṭana, *Rūznāma-yi Khāṭirāt*, p. 192.

84. *Ibid.*, p. 193.

85. Mīrzā Riḍā Khān's treatise was entitled *Alifbā-yi Bihrūzī* and was written in "pure Persian," that is, in a idiom artificially free of Arabic loan words (see E. G. Browne, *The Press and Poetry of Modern Persia* [Cambridge, 1914], p. 163). I have not had access to a copy and cannot therefore determine the nature of Mīrzā Riḍā Khān's proposals, nor the degree to which they correspond to those of Malkum.

86. Arfaᶜ ud-Daula, *Īrān-i Dīrūz* (Tehran, 1345 solar/1966), p. 71.

87. On his poetic production, see Franciszek Machalski, *La Littérature de l'Iran Contemporain* (Warsaw, 1965), I: 29–30.

88. Supplément Persan, 1990, f. 8.

subsequent letters to Malkum, while encouraging him to persist, he began to display the same pessimism that Amīn ud-Daula frequently expressed:

> Useful and good work has no chance of succeeding here; yet for how much longer, on the other hand, are we to work evil and be disgusted with ourselves? You wrote concerning your observations of that Blessed Being [*vujūd-i mubārak*, i.e., the shah]. Indeed he is a sacred personage, who alone in all Iran is not engaged in evil thoughts and who has the progress of the people at heart. But his low inclinations are now blocking the path of his good intentions.[89]

This degree of frankness concerning Nāṣir ud-Din Shāh is a further indication of the confidence Ẓill us-Sulṭān reposed in Malkum.

We next find Malkum receiving a letter from Ẓill us-Sulṭān in March 1885. It appears that Malkum had persisted, in accordance with Ẓill us-Sulṭān's advice, in sending pamphlets and proposals to Tehran and that Ẓill us-Sulṭān had done his best to draw the royal attention to them: "Concerning the numerous treatises and items you wrote for His Majesty, he was pleased, as a sign of favor, to show them to me in order that I might compose a suitable reply. I made humble submission of the few thoughts that occurred to my deficient intellect. Of course, all that accords with the will of God and the inclination of His Imperial Majesty will duly come to pass at its appointed time."[90] It is not possible to deduce with certainty whether this prediction was intended sarcastically or as an indication to Malkum that he should show more patience. The latter is more probable, for in a letter written some six months later Ẓill us-Sulṭān assures Malkum that the shah is genuinely disposed to enact reform, but cannot proceed immediately because he is not omnipotent (*qādir-i muṭlaq nīstand*).[91]

Malkum's relations with Ẓill us-Sulṭān had been strengthened by their reunion in Tehran, but his friendship with Amīn ud-Daula was temporarily clouded by some indiscretion he committed while staying as guest in his house: for this we find Amīn ud-Daula gently reproaching him in a letter he was intended to receive at Tiflis en route back to London.[92] The breach in amicable relations was, however, soon mended, and Amīn ud-Daula, like Ẓill us-Sulṭān, again encouraged Malkum to forward reports and recommendations to Tehran.[93] Even more explicitly than the prince, he promised to cooperate with Malkum and "follow his instructions."[94] Yet the instructions were often slow in coming; for all Malkum's show of despair at the unrelieved stupidity of those in

89. *Ibid.*, ff. 10–11.
90. *Ibid.*, f. 15.
91. *Ibid.*, f. 16.
92. Supplément Persan, 1997, f. 21.
93. *Ibid.*, f. 22.
94. *Ibid.*, f. 23.

charge of the state, it seems he was reluctant to take matters seriously even when enjoying the eager and intelligent support of Amīn ud-Daula. The "instructions" had to be elicited, much as Malkum himself sought to persuade the Foreign Office to utter its authoritative counsel.

> Your Excellency must write concerning the nature of events and the demands of the hour, for now is the time for reform. It will be bad indeed if reform does not come to pass. Write, for example, about [the Congress of] Berlin, your conversations with the Emperor Wilhelm and Prince Bismarck, their benevolent advice, their counsels of reform, to rid the state of the weakness and defects that have accrued to it from the selfishness and dominance of the ulama and certain other individuals. . . . Then write that they [the Emperor and Bismarck] say that if we put our affairs in order, they will help us to progress, guarantee our integrity and protect our rights. . . . You should write something lively and interesting.[95]

Less than a month later, Amīn ud-Daula repeated his suggestion: it should be impressed on Nāṣir ud-Dīn Shāh that German support for Iran would be forthcoming once reform was carried through. The possibility of such support offered Iran an opportunity to escape from the tutelage of Britain and Russia for the first time since the downfall of Napoleon.[96] As early as June 1874, Malkum had paid a call on Count Münster, German minister in London and attempted to impress on him the desirability of establishing a German mission in Tehran as a counterweight to Russian influence. The response Bismarck instructed Münster to convey to Malkum was cautious and reserved: the matter should wait until Iran dispatched a representative to Berlin.[97] German reluctance to antagonize Russia by taking an active interest in Iran persisted for many years, and it seems probable that Amīn ud-Daula was now doing little more than suggesting to Malkum a harmless fabrication that might benefit the cause of reform.[98]

The suggestion was sent to Malkum while he was still traveling back to London, and immediately after his return he put it into effect with a letter to the shah. It produced little visible result, but Amīn ud-Daula recommended to Malkum that he persist and write at least once a week to the Iranian Ministry of Foreign Affairs.[99]

95. Amīn ud-Daula to Malkum, Shavvāl 9, 1299/August 24, 1882, in *ibid.*, ff. 25–26.

96. Amīn ud-Daula to Malkum, Dhū-l-Qaʿda 4, 1299/September 17, 1882, in *ibid.*, f. 27.

97. Bradford G. Martin, *German-Persian Diplomatic Relations, 1873–1912* ('s-Gravenhage, 1959), pp. 26–29.

98. In 1885, Bismarck turned down an Iranian request for military instructors and an administrative adviser. See Martin, *op. cit.*, pp. 33–34.

99. Amīn ud-Daula to Malkum, Dhūl Ḥijja 19, 1299/November 1, 1882, in Supplément Persan, 1997, f. 30.

The extent to which Malkum was unable to influence the Ministry of Foreign Affairs, and was indeed totally ignored by it in all important questions of policy, is apparent from another letter of Amīn ud-Daula in which he reveals the existence of a secret treaty with Russia. The treaty had been concluded early in 1882 on the initiative of Mīrzā ʿAli Aṣghar Amīn us-Sulṭān, a minister whose star was rising at the time and concerning whom more will soon be said. It provided for certain adjustments of the northeastern frontier between Iran and the Russian Empire in favor of the latter, adjustments which would be undertaken apparently unilaterally by Russia and then silently accepted as a *fait accompli* by Iran. Zinovyev, the Russian ambassador, had insisted that none save Amīn us-Sulṭān and the shah himself should know of the existence of the treaty, and he threatened a complete rupture of relations if Britain should learn of the secret agreement. Before signing the document, the shah nonetheless consulted both Amīn ud-Daula and Nāṣir ul-Mulk, an anglophile statesman acquainted with Malkum. Amīn ud-Daula thought it best to inform Malkum of the whole affair so that he might explain matters to the British if the need arose.

> If the British do not abandon us because of this sin, if they have pity on our wretchedness and pay us some attention in the future, not only will we not have to abandon to Russia the path to India, and become instead their obedient servants, but they can also reform and administer our affairs as they will. . . . If you explain all this to them, you will have saved us: Russia will have been prevented from swallowing us, and our affairs will have been set in order through British dominance. Reforms will then be enacted without a doubt. Let us see what miracle, what magic you can work! [100]

In fact, Malkum was able to work no magic at the Foreign Office; Russian encroachment on northeastern Iran was more or less acceptable, and the prospect of reforming and administering Iranian affairs tempted no one. The information conveyed to Malkum by Amīn ud-Daula nonetheless proved useful in his dealings with Baron de Staal, appointed two years later Russian minister in London. De Staal assumed that Malkum's knowledge of Perso-Russian relations was restricted to what the Iranian Ministry of Foreign Affairs thought good for him, and he took superfluous care to "observe a certain reserve in discussions with him, above all concerning our secret arrangements with Persia." [101]

The obvious lack of trust in Malkum displayed by Amīn us-Sulṭān and the Ministry of Foreign Affairs contrasts strangely with Amīn ud-Daula's assurances that the shah read Malkum's reports with eager in-

100. Amīn ud-Daula to Malkum, Muḥarram 30, 1300/December 11, 1882, in *ibid.*, ff. 33–34.

101. Meyendorff, ed., *op. cit.* (n. 39, above), I: 50.

terest. These reports tended to be increasingly sporadic, like the "instructions" Amīn ud-Daula proclaimed himself always ready to follow. A number of letters complaining of Malkum's apathy were necessary to elicit a new *kitābcha,* a new booklet for the royal perusal,[102] which reached Tehran early in 1884. It drew the shah's attention to recent Russian advances in Transcaspia and to the resultant dangers for Iran, which could be offset only by an implementation of those same measures of reform first proposed in the 1850s. It was particularly urgent to strengthen the army and increase the revenue of the state. Nāṣir ud-Dīn read the booklet with care and expressed unqualified approbation of its contents.

> We have seen many such booklets from the pen of both Nāẓim ud-Daula himself and the late sipahsālār [Mīrzā Ḥusayn Khān had died in 1881], yet never have we read one whose contents were so fresh, true, and profound as this. I have given deep thought and consideration to all it says, and I see it to be entirely true and written out of a genuine concern for the welfare of the state.[103]

The booklet was passed on to the council of ministers for their consideration, in order that they might express their views and then assist Mīrzā Saʿīd Khān, the minister of foreign affairs, in drafting an answer to Malkum. It was further considered in an enlarged meeting in which not only ministers but also a number of princes including Ẓill us-Sulṭān participated.[104] At this second meeting, all the participants, predictably enough, echoed the monarch's praise of Malkum and approved the booklet's contents and clearly would have been glad to let the matter rest at that. When pressed by Amīn ud-Daula to say something more specific, one of those present objected to Malkum's assertion that the revenue of the state could be increased to 35 million *tomans,* and another hesitantly observed that the most important task facing Iran was to establish security for life and property.

Matters had not progressed beyond this stage when the princes and ministers were summoned into the presence of the shah to give an account of their deliberations. Amīn ud-Daula improvised, as the consensus of the meeting, a vague statement on the necessity for accumulating capital and creating conditions of security, and the whole affair was postponed for further discussion, which never took place.[105]

The silence of the ministers at the meeting convened on the shah's

102. See Amīn ud-Daula, *op. cit.* (n. 70, above), pp. 104–105.

103. *Ibid.*

104. Amīn ud-Daula to Malkum, Rabīʿ ul-Avval 11, 1301/January 10, 1884, in Supplément Persan, 1997, f. 14.

105. Amīn ud-Daula, *op. cit.* (n. 70, above), pp. 105–106.

orders, beyond a formal concurrence in his praise of Malkum, is interesting. Malkum no doubt would have attributed it to the ignorance and stupidity of those concerned, but at least one among them felt a reciprocal contempt for Malkum and his writings. Iᶜtimād us-Salṭāna confided this sentiment to his diary: "Amīn ud-Daula has been summoned by the shah on account of the writings Malkum has sent from London. They remained closeted with Amīn us-Sulṭān for two hours and read through the absurdities of that son of a burnt father, that traitor to the state and people who gets 20,000 *tomans* out of Iran every year!"[106]

This farcical episode understandably induced in Amīn ud-Daula another period of prolonged pessimism, attested by several letters to Malkum. On Dhūl Qaᶜda 16, 1302/August 27, 1885, he wrote: "It has to be stated quite openly. It is true that Your Excellency's pen clarifies matters as well as could be desired, but be certain that all of your explanations cannot make them in the least aware of the essence of the problem. In fact, by taking pleasure in your eloquence, we are simply sinking deeper into our sleep of neglect."[107]

Throughout the rest of 1885, Amīn ud-Daula advised Malkum to refrain from further visits to Tehran, for he considered the cause of reform to be lost. Early in 1886, he reversed his opinion and suggested that Malkum's presence in Tehran would be useful in a discussion of the perennial railway question.[108] It has been seen that frequent allusions to the problem occur in Amīn ud-Daula's earlier letters and that Malkum appears not to have espoused any particular project or supported any aspirant to a concession. It is true that in 1880 he had expressed an interest in himself obtaining a concession for a railway from the capital to Shāh ᶜAbd ul-ᶜAẓīm and that Amīn ud-Daula promised to discuss terms in Tehran on his behalf.[109] Nothing came of it, and the concession was in the end granted to a Belgian concern two years later.[110] Malkum's recommendations on the subject of railways appear to have been entirely general and theoretical, and we find Amīn ud-Daula irritatedly complaining after receiving one such letter in praise of steam:

106. Entry for Ramaḍān 7, 1301/July 2, 1884, in Iᶜtimād us-Salṭana, *Rūznāma-yi Khāṭirāt*, p. 343. Malkum's annual salary was, to be precise, 19,640 *tomans*. See Qavām ud-Daula to Malkum, Ṣafar 26, 1304/November 24, 1886, in Supplément Persan, 1995, f. 13.

107. Supplément Persan, 1997, f. 53.

108. *Ibid.*, f. 61.

109. Amīn ud-Daula to Malkum, Jumādī ul-Ūlā 23, 1297/May 4, 1880, in *ibid.*, f. 55.

110. See Amīn ud-Daula to Malkum, Rabīᶜ ul-Avval 6, 1300/January 15, 1883, in *ibid.*, f. 125; and Curzon, *op. cit.* (n. 51, above), I: 617.

Now tell us exactly what it is you want. People here have no sense left in them; they can't understand open, straightforward statements, so how do you expect them to grasp your hints and allusions? Now as for what you wrote, it is quite true that the country will benefit from railways, not the company [operating them]. I further agree that if the country is benefited it will in all respects be to the advantage of the government also. But you do not say what we must do to fulfill this high intention. It is as if you were trying to put us through an examination. What kind of joke is this? We have taken many examinations at your hands and passed them every time. Now, what needs to be done? I want to know your plan and project so that I can then try to solve the question.[111]

The plea for more specific instructions is repeated two weeks later in another letter in which Amīn ud-Daula mentions various railway projects under consideration in Tehran, one submitted by Winston, an American entrepreneur, and another supported by Sir Arthur Nicolson.[112] The shah was delaying his decision until Malkum arrived in Tehran, and therefore Malkum should prepare his project carefully for presentation on arrival.[113]

It is doubtful whether Malkum ever had any exact project in mind or even held a sincere belief in the possibility of constructing railways. Shortly before setting out for Tehran, in accordance with Amīn ud-Daula's request, Malkum went to inform de Staal of his forthcoming departure and the reason for his return visit to Iran. In a dispatch to St. Petersburg, de Staal recorded that Malkum was convinced that any railway built would be "only a plaything, not an important enterprise." With his customary and unconvincing display of russophilia, Malkum nonetheless assured the envoy that he would do his best to have the railway built northward from the capital rather than southward, thus favoring Russian instead of British commerce.[114]

Malkum arrived in Tehran on September 30, 1886, on what was to be his last visit to the land of his birth. Three days later, he had an interview with the shah, who appeared to repose the greatest confidence in him and still regard him with the same awe that he had first inspired

111. Amīn ud-Daula to Malkum, Ramaḍān 4, 1303/June 6, 1886, in Supplément Persan, 1997, f. 61.

112. Amīn ud-Daula to Malkum, Ramaḍān 19, 1303/June 21, 1886, in *ibid.*, f. 61. On these projects and others submitted during the period 1875–1890, see Kazemzadeh, *op. cit.* (n. 26, above) Chapter Three. Nicolson at one point had aspirations of gaining a concession for himself and appears to have enjoyed Malkum's support. See Martin, *op. cit.* (n. 97, above), p. 42.

113. Amīn ud-Daula to Malkum, Shavvāl 26, 1303/July 28, 1886, in Supplément Persan, 1997, f. 64.

114. Meyendorff, ed., *op. cit.* (n. 39, above), I: 303.

in him thirty years earlier, as a paragon of learning and intelligence.[115] No urgency was felt, however, with respect to the supposed reason for his presence in Tehran, and it was not until two weeks later, on October 18, that a meeting was finally convened to discuss the railway question. The gathering took place at the house of Kāmrān Mīrzā Nā'ib us-Salṭana, the shah's third son and governor of Tehran, with the participation of Malkum, Amīn us-Sulṭān, Amīn ud-Daula, and Qavām ud-Daula, then foreign minister.[116] The content of the discussions that ensued is unknown, but it cannot have been anything conclusive, for Nāṣir ud-Dīn's indecision on the railway question continued unresolved, and British and Russian pressure and counterpressure were to leave Iran without railways for many decades to come. The remainder of Malkum's visit to Tehran appears to have been spent in pleasant sociability, and on October 22 he had the honor of making the acquaintance of Malījak, a Kurdish youth for whom the shah had conceived an eccentric affection.[117] From Tehran he proceeded to Isfahan where he renewed his acquaintance with Ẓill us-Sulṭān[118] and, presumably, paid a last visit to relatives in Julfā. On December 29 he set out from Tehran for London again, leaving benighted Asia behind him for the last time.[119]

With Malkum back in London, correspondence with Ẓill us-Sulṭān and Amīn ud-Daula resumed, and again Malkum dispatched his magisterial advice into the void. The game, however, was wearing thin. Ẓill us-Sulṭān, endangered by royal jealousy and suspicion, intimated to Malkum that he could not afford the possibility of risking additional danger by pressing for reform.[120] When Malkum refused to accept his withdrawal of support, Ẓill us-Sulṭān found it advisable to be more blunt:

> Since it is not my habit to waste the time of respectable people with meaningless answers, and since the courier is about to leave, I wish to give you a frank and unadorned reply. It is true that for a time, out of feelings of honor and patriotism, I used to engage in certain discussions, and that I was not averse to hearing and saying certain things. But since I have suffered personal loss, all my reformist zeal is now devoted to my own affairs. I have totally renounced my previous discussions, and I wish to inform Your Excellency that I am henceforth not to be counted on. I do not consider it my duty to

115. Iᶜtimād us-Salṭana, *Rūznāma-yi Khāṭirāt*, p. 520.

116. *Ibid.*, p. 523.

117. *Ibid.*

118. See Ẓill us-Sulṭān to Malkum, Shaᶜbān, 1304/April–May 1887, in Supplément Persan, 1990, f. 17.

119. Iᶜtimād us-Salṭana, *Rūznāma-yi Khāṭirāt*, p. 529.

120. Ẓill us-Sulṭān to Malkum. Shaᶜbān 17, 1304/May 11, 1887, in Supplément Persan, 1990, f. 19.

> lay your submissions in the blessed dust of His Imperial Majesty's feet, may our souls be a ransom for him . . . I have completely renounced such matters and am, in short, disgusted with the world and with myself.[121]

For Amīn ud-Daula, such expressions of pessimism, more elegantly phrased, were already customary, and after the fiasco of Malkum's second return visit to Iran, they set the tone of his correspondence.[122] In the extremity of his pessimism, Amīn ud-Daula also found occasion to express himself with bluntness, and in a letter he asked Malkum to burn after reading he wrote:

> The trouble with our master is that he knows everyone and knows too what their thoughts and opinions are. However much we strain ourselves and tell him, "Bravo, what an intelligence," "What skill and competence are yours," "What profound experience you have amassed," you know quite well that we are contradicting our own inmost beliefs. He permits himself to do things that are quite incapable of rational interpretation. . . . Now if you applaud his present deeds, it is certain not only that you do not believe yourself, but also that you are mocking him in your heart of hearts. . . . You know quite well what skill he has in concealing his thoughts and deceiving people, in addition, of course, to deceiving himself.[123]

From this warning of Amīn ud-Daula it may be deduced that Malkum was persisting in that fulsome flattery of the shah which had accompanied most of his recommendations of reform since the 1850s and which continued uninterrupted until the lottery scandal and his dismissal from the embassy in 1889.

The results of Malkum's continuing agitation for reform while ambassador in London were slight indeed. The Foreign Office was uninterested in lending its authority to his advice, and the support of Ẓill us-Sulṭān and Amīn ud-Daula in Iran was largely ineffective. It might then be asked why Malkum persisted for fifteen years in the sending of generalized proposals which he must have known would fall on deaf ears and why he maintained a correspondence with Ẓill us-Sulṭān and Amīn ud-Daula that was not purely personal in content. It seems fair to point initially to his love of posing as a lonely champion of enlightenment and reform and, so far as this love inspired his communications with Iran, their practical effect could have been of only secondary concern. On the other hand, any expectation that Malkum's writings, even

121. Ẓill us-Sulṭān to Malkum, Jumādī ul-Ukhrā, 1304/February–March 1887, in *ibid.*, ff. 23–24.

122. Supplément Persan, 1997, ff. 67, 81, 83.

123. Amīn ud-Daula to Malkum, Rabīᶜ uth-Thānī 6, 1306/December 31, 1888, in *ibid.*, f. 91.

if totally serious in tone and inspired by the purest motives, could have achieved significant effect, would be misplaced. Unqualified acceptance of his views by the shah, as in 1884, meant nothing in practical terms, and, as Amīn ud-Daula wrote, no amount of eloquence could have saved Iran.

Finally, it may be noted that Malkum's correspondence with Ẓill us-Sulṭān and Amīn ud-Daula served at least one practical purpose: to obtain the payment of his salary. The Ministry of Foreign Affairs was evidently as remiss in paying him as it was reluctant to send him information on affairs of state, and both correspondents helped to ensure that Malkum not be left penniless. Ẓill us-Sulṭān, for example, came to an arrangement with the chief of the tradesmen's guild of Bushire, who sent Malkum regular sums with the revenue of Fars as surety.[124]

Malkum's term in London ended with his finances well assured; but before considering the enterprise which both enriched him and turned him to thoughts of revolution, it will be convenient to examine his resumption, while envoy in London, of an earlier and less venal interest—alphabet reform.

After his departure from Istanbul and loss of contact with Ākhūndzāda, Malkum's concern with the alphabet question lay dormant for a number of years. It is not until 1879 that we find proof of his continuing interest in the matter. At the time, he was evidently experimenting with the shapes to be used in his revised alphabet, based upon the same principle as his very first essay—separation of letters. Amīn ud-Daula wrote to him on July 2, 1879:

> Your draft alphabet is improving, although it is to be feared that because of unfamiliarity the reader's eyes will tire easily. As I have previously said, it is possible to differentiate most of the letters without the use of dots. For example, *sīn* and *shīn* may be written سـ and س respectively. . . . Also, put vowel signs on a level with the consonants, so that they may gradually come to be regarded as letters.[125]

It is interesting to find Amīn ud-Daula raising independently two of the criticisms made ten years earlier by Ākhūndzāda.

Amīn ud-Daula appears to have been the most enthusiastic supporter of alphabet reform recruited in Iran by Malkum. In September 1879, he informed Malkum of his intention to set up a printing press in Tehran for printing in the revised alphabet and asked him to inquire in Europe about the purchase of the necessary equipment.[126] There is

124. Ẓill us-Sulṭān to Malkum, Jumādī ul-Ukhrā 4, 1302/March 21, 1885, in Supplément Persan, 1990, f. 14.

125. Supplément Persan, 1997, f. 8.

126. *Ibid.*, f. 11.

no evidence that this project was ever realized, although at some point Amīn ud-Daula was able to show Nāṣir ud-Dīn Shāh a printed sample of the script.[127] The monarch expressed polite interest, but Amīn ud-Daula built no hopes on his support. Like Münif Paşa and Ākhūndzāda before him, he concluded that to teach the revised script at elementary schools constituted the best basis for its future currency.[128]

The year 1885 marked the climax of Malkum's active interest in alphabet reform. In the space of a year, he had printed in his separate letters of "perfected" shape, the *Gulistān* of Saᶜdī, a selection from the *Nahj al-Balāgha* (*Aqwāl ᶜAlī*) and a collection of Turkish proverbs, *Dürub-u Emsâl-i Müntehabe,* attempting thus to demonstrate the applicability of his invention to the three chief languages of Islam. The transcription was undertaken by Farīd ul-Mulk, scribe of the Iranian embassy in London and the printing done privately near Malkum's residence at Notting Hill Gate.[129]

Malkum's edition of the *Gulistān* contains a lengthy preface on the subject of alphabet reform. Here we find little not previously stated elsewhere; it is interesting to note, however, that the preface starts with a rejection of the charge that the Islamic religion is hostile to progress. The root cause of Muslim backwardness lies in the defectiveness of the alphabet, which prevents the easy acquisition of literacy and therefore of useful knowledge. The Arabic script is "at least forty times more difficult" than the Roman.[130]

With his usual penchant for simplicity at the cost of literal truth, he continues:

> Every beginner in two or three days, nay, two or three hours, can read correctly French, Italian, or Russian in any kind of book, whereas there is no philosopher who after forty years of study can read our books faultlessly. Since each line in our script can be read in a hundred different ways, unless one is completely acquainted with the principles of our languages and can perceive the intention of the author from the context, he cannot make out a simple concept with certainty.[131]

He then refers to thirty shortcomings of the Arabic alphabet, and although conceding that other scripts are by no means perfect (remembering, perhaps, the arguments of Namık Kemal), he claims that it is

127. *Ibid.*, f. 54.

128. *Ibid.*

129. See introduction by Firidūn Ādamīyat to Malkum's "Uṣūl-i Taraqqī," *Sukhan*, XVI (1345 solar/1966): 69; and E. G. Browne, *The Persian Revolution* (Cambridge, 1914), p. 38.

130. Introduction to *Gulistān*, printed at "Taraqqi Press" (London, 1302 lunar/1885), pp. 2–3.

131. *Ibid.*, p. 3.

only the Arabic alphabet which combines so many defects. Before setting forth the remedy, he feels it necessary to establish his own seriousness and competence. His success in so doing may be doubted:

> It must not be imagined that some ill-informed beginner has collected these ideas from his immature thoughts and set them down here. The writer of these words, from his earliest youth, in the course of his occupation with weighty affairs of state, both in the lands of Islam and the regions of Europe, has had experience in every field of investigation and examination of the principles of the world's progress. In all his strivings and observations, at every step he has found a new proof that the revival of the Muslim peoples will not be possible unless they adapt their alphabet—the prime instrument for the acquisition of knowledge—in accordance with the principles of the age.[132]

This much established, Malkum considers the merits of complete replacement of the existing script. "In order to attain this purpose, it was first proposed to establish a new script. Such a task presents no difficulty. From the two hundred alphabets existing in the world, it is possible in the space of an hour to put together some such script, one more complete in every respect [than the Arabic alphabet]. The question is, securing its currency." The only immediately practical course is a revision of the alphabet in order to eliminate as many of its defects as possible. Years of effort had been spent on this purpose. "Fifty different kinds of letters were cut and set up in my presence and under my constant supervision. After all kinds of tests, the result is the specimen which you will find at the end of these pages."[133]

This specimen was characterized, like Malkum's prototype of 1868, by disjointed letters. Separation of the letters would permit the incorporation of vowel signs into the alphabet. By way of preparation, *fatḥa* and *kasra* were to be written vertically, not diagonally, and initial short vowels *"a"* and *"i"* were to be distinguished through prolonging the *alif* respectively above and below the level of the rest of the letters. Initial *"u"* was represented by a *vāv* with closed "eye"; *vāv* with open "eye" stood for the long vowel *"ū"* and the consonant *"v."*[134]

The step of using the modified *ḥarakāt* as letters was not taken with the *Gulistān*. In his selection of Turkish proverbs, however, after first giving examples printed with separate letters but the *ḥarakāt* in their accustomed place, Malkum takes this step also, and the result is what must be regarded as his definitive revised version of the Arabic alphabet. The special needs of Turkish receive inadequate attention, and only for the vowel sound *"ü"* is a letter invented—*vāv* with a dot underneath.[135]

132. *Ibid.*, p. 5.
133. *Ibid.*, pp. 7–8.
134. *Ibid.*, pp. 12–16.
135. *Dürûb-u Emsâl*, p. 14 *passim*.

In accordance with desiderata established by the minister in his dialogue with the shaykh, the forms of the letters in the *Gulistān* and the collection of Turkish proverbs have been "perfected." This means in effect that their height or width has been increased or decreased to fit a uniform standard: thus a *tā* is the same height as a *dāl*, as is the shrunken version of an isolated *nūn*. It is odd that in his efforts to rationalize the alphabet, Malkum should have used two forms of the letter *tā* (ﺗ and ت) and two of the letter *bā* (ﺑ and ب) without any apparent purpose.

One is forced to conclude that this script, the fruit of Malkum's concern with alphabet reform, is highly unsatisfactory. It fails to establish a fully phonetic alphabet, and the "perfected" forms of its letters are ugly and misshapen. Malkum failed to realize what Ākhūndzāda, with his greater thoroughness, came to perceive: if the alphabet stood so badly in need of reform that its reformed version bore only incidental resemblance to the original, then total abandonment and replacement of the existing script could be the only effective solution.

These products of Malkum's labors received certain dissemination in Iran and elsewhere. In Tehran, Amīn ud-Daula distributed copies of the *Gulistān* in Malkum's revised alphabet, but thought the *Gulistān* an inappropriate work to use for propagating alphabet reform. An entirely new work, particularly a translation, would be preferable, since those interested in reading it would have to learn the revised script. Moreover, its capacity for the accurate rendering of foreign proper names would be fully demonstrated.[136] Some years later, another correspondent of Malkum, Mīrzā Āqā Khān Kirmānī, was to set up a bookstore near the Galata bridge in Istanbul to sell books in the revised script, together with copies of *Qānūn*.[137]

Little reaction, however, was aroused by Malkum's revised alphabet. Evidently some attempt was made to associate its use with the *Jāmiʿ-i Ādamīyat* (The League of Humanity), the secret society established as a successor to the farāmūshkhāna. Membership cards were printed in disjointed letters, and a pamphlet setting out the revised script, published in London in 1885, was entitled *Namūna-yi Khaṭṭ-i Ādamīyat* (Specimen of the script of humanity).[138]

Such was the scope of application decreed to Malkum's alphabet. Ākhūndzāda, with his final project of a mixed Roman and Cyrillic alphabet, anticipated the measures taken in the present century in both

136. Amīn ud-Daula to Malkum, dated November 30, 1885, in Supplément Persan, 1997, f. 56.

137. Mīrzā Āqā Khān Kirmānī to Malkum (n.d.), in Supplément Persan, 1996, ff. 90–91.

138. Ādamīyat, *op. cit.* (n. 23, above), p. 179.

Turkey and his native Caucasus; these measures have been accompanied, perhaps, by the realization, in different degrees, of the ideological aims he associated with alphabet change. Malkum's projects, less serious in their conception and less careful in their execution, remained virtually without echo. His fame in Iranian history rests not so much upon his efforts at disturbing writing habits as upon a more successful piece of innovation—the newspaper *Qānūn*.

CHAPTER 7

In the early summer of 1889, Nāṣir ud-Dīn Shāh undertook a third journey to Europe, and, as in 1873, the climax and most enjoyable part of the trip was furnished by his stay in Britain. Again the British imagination was excited by the exotic sight of the shah and his entourage; official and popular reception of the royal party was enthusiastic and friendly; the artists of the *Illustrated London News* etched busily away as they followed the shah; and Nāṣir ud-Dīn recorded his happy impressions in another travel diary.[1] His first visit, some sixteen years before, had been at the urging of Mīrzā Ḥusayn Khān and had been ostensibly for the purpose of enabling the monarch to "judge for himself the advanced state of civilization in England."[2] This time, Sir Henry Drummond Wolff, the British ambassador in Tehran, had decided that he should gain "a more extensive knowledge of Britain" than had been possible on his first venture abroad.[3] The journey, however, had a narrower purpose than mere contemplation of the wonders of the Victorian age and, as the first journey had been in large part associated with the unfinished business of the Reuter concession, so too was the third journey productive of several concessions and transactions. With one of these, Malkum was closely associated.

Sir Henry Drummond Wolff, the son of an itinerant preacher of German Jewish origin whose wanderings had taken him as far as Bukhara, the celebrated Joseph Wolff, had been appointed minister in Tehran in the spring of 1888. His official objective in Iran has been

1. Nāṣir ud-Dīn Shāh, *Safarnāma-yi Farang* (Tehran, 1308 lunar/1891). The section describing his stay in Britain is found on pp. 171–264.

2. See above, p. 119.

3. Sir H. D. Wolff, *Rambling Recollections* (London, 1908), II: 351.

summarized as "revitalisation of the buffer policy,"[4] that is, to be no longer content with the gaining of a foothold in the south, but also to combat Russian influence and hegemony in the capital itself. Wolff was a strong believer in the desirability of an Anglo-Russian entente and it might have been thought that he was scarcely the best choice for the implementation of such a policy. Yet the means for a new entrenchment of British influence in Iran were to be above all commercial and economic, with political paramountcy as the aim at least as much as profit. For the employment of these means, Wolff was well qualified: he had extensive and friendly ties with numerous financiers in the City, with the Rothschilds, the Sassoons, and, not least, Baron Julius de Reuter. Although he may have had reservations about engaging in rivalry with Russia, to promote the interests of his financier friends in the country to which he was accredited must have been a source of greater joy. Wolff's arrival in Tehran was immediately followed by an influx of investors and concession seekers, including George Reuter, the Baron's son.[5]

Wolff's Russian counterpart, Dolgorukov, intended to pursue an equally energetic policy. From the beginning of his appointment in Tehran, he had lent vigorous support to various Russian projects for railway construction and with equal dedication sought to prevent the opening of the Kārūn to British shipping. The vigor of his conduct, which bordered on the arrogant and offensive, tended to prevent the realization of his aims. It became obvious that Russia was demanding not simply commercial advantage and opportunity in Iran, but outright political domination. The shah and his chief minister, Amīn us-Sulṭān, reacted to Russian intimidation by seeking British protection, and Wolff was thus fortunate enough to find them willing collaborators in his policy.[6]

Amīn us-Sulṭān had in common with Malkum Khān a Caucasian and Christian ancestry. He was the grandson of one of the Georgian captives brought to Iran by Āghā Muḥammad Khān after the sack of Tiflis in 1795.[7] The captive was presented to a Qajar prince, Qāsim Khān, embraced Islam and married an Isfahani woman. The four sons born from this union entered the service of Nāṣir ud-Dīn when he was still heir apparent and governor-general of Azerbayjan, and the third among them, Ibrāhīm, was particularly successful in gaining the favor

4. R. L. Greaves, *Persia and the Defence of India, 1884–1892* (London, 1959), p. 157.

5. Firuz Kazemzadeh, *Russia and Britain in Persia, 1864–1914* (New Haven, 1968), pp. 184–187, 209.

6. *Ibid.*, p. 192 f.

7. During the agitation against Amīn us-Sulṭān in 1902, it was asserted, mistakenly, that he was of Armenian origin. See Aḥmad Kasravī, *Tārīkh-i Mashrūṭa-yi Īrān*, 5th ed. (Tehran, 1340 solar/1961), p. 26.

of the prince. Holding initially the lowly post of *ābdārbāshī* (chief water carrier), Ibrāhīm swiftly advanced to more exalted status and received the title of Amīn us-Sulṭān (the trusted one of the king). Upon the death of Ibrāhīm in 1883, his eldest son, Mīrzā ʿAlī Aṣghar, succeeded to both his title and his position of trust, and within a few years he had become the most powerful figure in Iran after the shah himself.[8]

It has been noted that Mīrzā ʿAlī Aṣghar was, in 1882, intimately concerned with the negotiation of a secret agreement with Russia. He was nonetheless trusted by the British legation in Tehran and remained closely identified with British policy until the aftermath of the Tobacco Concession and its repeal in 1892 made realignment with Russia advisable. In 1884, he was already collaborating with the British envoy, Nicolson, against Russian policy in Iran, and the association was strengthened with the arrival of Wolff in Tehran. The two men appear to have reposed great trust in each other. Wolff respected the innate qualities which had assisted Amīn us-Sulṭān in his rise to power and thought him a cool-headed and capable man. Amīn us-Sulṭān in return gave every support to Wolff's policies, communicated to him the content of various negotiations in which he engaged with Russia and made a general profession of anglophilia.[9] The first fruit of the cooperation between Wolff and Amīn us-Sulṭān was the opening of the Kārūn in 1888.[10] Early in 1889, a few months before the shah's departure for Europe, this was followed by the granting of a concession to Reuter for the foundation of a state bank to be known as the Imperial Bank of Persia.[11]

The evolution of Anglo-Iranian relations that these events signified might have been both agreeable and beneficial to Malkum. British policy in Iran was at last becoming more ambitious, and the concession business was reviving after more than a decade of largely inconclusive negotiations. Yet Malkum was unable to profit directly from these developments. The two chief architects of the Anglo-Iranian alignment, Wolff and Amīn us-Sulṭān, appear both to have mistrusted him and to have worked for his discomfiture and dismissal from the post in London. In his memoirs, written in the year of Malkum's death, Wolff is reticent concerning him, but it can be assumed that his friend Reuter had told him something of Malkum's duplicity in the negotiations of 1873 and that the unfavorable impression left by this information was supplemented by a degree of acquaintance with Malkum. Amīn us-Sulṭān's

8. On the ancestry and career of Amīn us-Sulṭān, see Kazemzadeh, *op. cit.*, pp. 192–193; G. Curzon, *Persia and the Persian Question* (London, 1892), I, 426–428; and Ibrāhīm Ṣafāʾī, *Rahbarān-i Mashrūṭa: Atābak* (Tehran, 1345 solar/1966), *passim.*

9. Kazemzadeh, *op. cit.*, p. 216.

10. *Ibid.*, p. 195.

11. *Ibid.*, pp. 210–212.

dislike for Malkum may be held in part to be a consequence of his general enmity towards all possible rivals and their associates and protégés. His hostility embraced Nā'ib us-Sulṭana, Ẓill us-Sulṭān, Yaḥyā Khān Mushīr ud-Daula, first minister of justice and after—at least formally—of foreign affairs, and Mīrzā ᶜAlī Khān Amīn ud-Daula.[12] With all except the first of these, Malkum enjoyed varying degrees of cordiality, and the hostility of Amīn us-Sulṭān was therefore inevitable. If Malkum was left without adequate intelligence and regular salary by the Ministry of Foreign Affairs, it was primarily because of this enmity, for Amīn us-Sulṭān exercised, in all but name, the functions of foreign minister.[13]

Despite this ascendancy of Amīn us-Sulṭān in Tehran and his alliance with Wolff in enmity to Malkum, it still appeared to one of Malkum's associates that some benefit might accrue to him from the shah's forthcoming journey to Europe. Ẓill us-Sulṭān continued to be in contact with Malkum, despite his renunciation of active support for his projects, and, in an undated letter probably written in the spring of 1889, he predicted that the journey would be productive of results favorable to Malkum's position.[14] On the eve of the shah's departure, he wrote again in similarly optimistic vein: "God willing, the exertions made by Your Excellency over the past forty years, and all the analyses you have written, will reach a successful conclusion in the course of this auspicious journey, and be a source of joy, happiness and tranquillity to His Imperial Majesty."[15]

Amīn ud-Daula expressed himself more reservedly. Some "good" —for Malkum and the cause of reform—might emerge from the journey, but it was unlikely. He accompanied the royal party, which included his enemy, Amīn us-Sulṭān, as far as Berlin, and by the time of his arrival there his doubts had turned into certainty that the journey would fail to be beneficial. From Berlin he proceeded alone to Paris, and before rejoining the royal party in London he wrote to Malkum advising him not to speak to the shah of "improving matters" and to content himself instead with demonstrating the influential position he had succeeded in establishing for the Iranian embassy in London society.[16]

Malkum had little intention of mentioning tedious subjects of reform to Nāṣir ud-Dīn Shāh while in England; he was to concentrate instead on more immediate and alluring prospects of reward. To realize these prospects, however, it was necessary to placate the hostility of Amīn us-Sulṭān, and we find Malkum writing, on April 7, 1889, in ex-

12. *Ibid.*, p. 193.
13. Curzon, *op. cit.*, I: 426.
14. Supplément Persan, 1990, ff. 27–28.
15. Ẓill us-Sulṭān to Malkum, Shaᶜbān 1306/April, 1889, in *ibid.*, ff. 29–30.
16. Supplément Persan, 1997, f. 92.

tremely fulsome terms to the same minister he would execrate a few months later in the columns of *Qānūn* as the son of a water carrier:

> God has bestowed on the Iranian realm a great and extraordinary monarch, but with a thousand regrets we have to say that we have all, for the past forty years, been wasting our lives looking for a great minister, without attaining our desire. Now, in my old age, I have been forced to awaken from the sleep of despair and to say to myself, Why should this minister for whom we have been looking for forty years be any other than Amīn us-Sulṭān?

Malkum went on to express his anticipation of pleasurable and useful talks with Amīn us-Sulṭān in London during the shah's visit, and assured him of his full support, confidence, and admiration.[17]

Amīn us-Sulṭān was not thus easily to be placated, and his relations with Malkum during the royal party's stay in London were strained. After a somewhat unpleasant visit to St. Petersburg, Nāṣir ud-Dīn Shāh had proceeded through Germany to Belgium, and on June 22 he arrived in Antwerp, thence to embark for England.[18] Malkum came to Antwerp the following day in order to greet the monarch and accompany him to London, and Arfaᶜ ud-Daula, a member of the royal retinue, was already able to perceive a certain tension between him and Amīn us-Sulṭān.[19]

Matters did not improve after the passage to England. Malkum everywhere escorted the shah as interpreter and guide,[20] and Amīn us-Sulṭān was obliged to suffer his company. During a tour of the British Museum, however, underlying tensions finally broke forth, and Amīn us-Sulṭān and his followers abruptly separated themselves from the rest of the party and walked out.[21]

If Wolff intended the shah's journey to benefit his friends in the City—the Reuters, the Rothschilds, and the other aristocrats of profit and speculation—Malkum wished to make a similar use of Nāṣir ud-Dīn's presence in England on his own account. In between visits to Buckingham Palace, Windsor, the zoo, and Ten Downing Street, Malkum found the opportunity to introduce various would-be investors and concessionaires to the shah.[22] From London, the royal party, accompanied by Malkum, proceeded northward to Scotland, visiting a succession of ducal homes and factories en route. The shah's enjoyment of the trip was interrupted by the sight of kilts at a ball in Balmoral,

17. Ibrāhīm Ṣafāʾī, ed., *Asnād-i Siyāsī-yi Daurān-i Qājārīya* (Tehran, 1346 solar/1967), pp. 305–307.

18. Muḥammad Ḥasan Khān Iᶜtimād us-Salṭana, *Rūznāma-yi Khāṭirāt*, ed. Īraj Afshār (Tehran, 1345 solar/1966), p. 742.

19. Mīrzā Riḍā Arfaᶜ ud-Daula, *Īrān-i Dirūz* (Tehran, 1346 solar/1966), p. 238.

20. See Nāṣir ud-Dīn Shāh, *Safarnāma-yi Farang*, pp. 177–210.

21. Arfaᶜ ud-Daula, *op. cit.*, p. 245.

22. *Ibid.*, p. 246.

causing his sudden and disgusted exit.[23] His good humor was restored by the more dignified spectacle of the newly completed bridge across the Firth of Forth, of which he drew a sketch that the *Illustrated London News* was pleased to reproduce.[24] It was in Scotland too that Malkum's endeavors to elicit a concession were successful: the infamous lottery concession was granted to a certain Buzie de Cardoël, and thereby was set in motion the chain of events that led to Malkum's dismissal and disgrace.

The text of the concession was brief but explicit:

> The exclusive right to all lottery operations, viz., the drawing of lots, the raising of public loans by lottery, the formation of lottery companies, the sale of lottery tickets, and all public gaming including roulette, is hereby assigned for a period of seventy-five years beginning with the year 1306 [1889], under the following conditions:
>
> that of the net profit accruing from all these operations, after the deduction of expenses and the payment of five percent interest on invested capital, twenty percent be annually paid into the Iranian treasury;
>
> and that Iran shall have the right to designate an official to investigate the annual net profit of the concessionaire.
>
> Dated Dhūl Qaᶜda 22, 1306/July 20, 1889, Scotland.[25]

De Cardoël, a French subject, was a clerk at the Iranian embassy in London, and in obtaining the concession he was acting at Malkum's behest and on his behalf.[26] Malkum can have had little intention of securing the implementation of the concession. From his experience with the Reuter concession, he must have been well aware of the difficulties facing any concessionaire in Iran who wished to exploit the document he had bought. It might also be wondered how a Muslim country such as Iran could be hoped to furnish a large-scale clientèle for gambling operations. The conclusion is inescapable that the lottery concession was intended simply as a means for profitable operations on the London money market.

In these operations, Malkum wished to remain as inconspicuous as possible. After he had hidden behind de Cardoël in obtaining the concession, the next step was to institute companies and corporations which might give the whole enterprise a respectable and substantial aspect, and act as channels for the money that was to be gathered in. In the late summer of 1889, a number of Malkum's associates from the

23. *Ibid.*, p. 256.

24. See Nāṣir ud-Dīn Shāh, *op. cit.*, p. 244, and Ḥusām Muᶜizzī Najafqulī, *Tārīkh-i Ravābiṭ-i Īrān bā Dunyā* (Tehran, 1325 solar/1946), p. 110.

25. Quoted in Khān Malik Sāsānī, *Siyāsatgarān-i Daura-yi Qājār* (Tehran, 1338 solar/1960), I: 133–134.

26. Kazemzadeh, *op. cit.* (n. 5, above), p. 242.

London financial underworld formed the Persian Investment Corporation. Among its directors were Sir Charles Lewis, W. W. Cargill, also a director of two other organizations—the New Oriental Bank Corporation and the Anglo-Asiatic Syndicate—and Malkum's second brother, Mikāʾīl Khān, whom he saw no harm in appointing secretary at the embassy despite his frequent condemnations of nepotism and corruption in others. The prospectus of the corporation happily announced that "His Highness Prince Malcom Khan has authorised the constitution of the company" and described its general purpose as "the acquisition of any concessions, rights or privileges for any objects or purposes whatsoever granted by His Majesty the Shah of Persia."[27]

Behind the Persian Investment Corporation stood the Anglo-Asiatic Syndicate, and behind it in turn stood Malkum. The syndicate appeared to be respectable enough and had as its directors Lord Charles Kerr, the Hon. A. C. Cadogan, and Colonel Laurence Cloete, who happened also to be Iranian consul-general in London.[28] Cloete, a South African, had been Malkum's nominee for the post, and according to Sir Henry Drummond Wolff who had inquiries made about him, his antecedents were "not of the first lustre."[29] Kerr, Cadogan, and Cloete were at the same time directors of the Persian Investment Corporation, and they transmitted to it shares in the syndicate that had been bought for £100 each and then swiftly appreciated, merely, as Wolff put it, "on the mysterious hopes held out by anonymous projectors."[30]

On October 3, de Cardoël, still acting as Malkum's nominee, concluded an agreement with the Anglo-Asiatic Syndicate for the sale of the lottery concession for a total price of £120,000: £20,000 was to be paid on execution of the deed of transfer and the delivery of the concession to the syndicate, £40,000 in November 1889, and the balance thirty days after the issue of any bonds or at the expiration of six months from the date of the agreement.[31] Nine days later, de Cardoël received a check for £20,000 on delivering the concession, and the next day the check was paid into Malkum's account at the Burlington Gardens Branch of the Bank of England. Still keeping Malkum, the ultimate

27. Quoted in *ibid.*, pp. 242–243.

28. See report of extraordinary general meeting of shareholders of the Anglo-Asiatic Syndicate in *The Times*, October 4, 1890.

29. Kazemzadeh, *op. cit.* (n. 5, above), p. 243. Cloete was also involved in the business of the tobacco concession and eventually landed in jail as the result of a particularly daring transaction. See Nikki R. Keddie, *Religion and Rebellion in Iran: The Tobacco Protest of 1891–1892* (London, 1966), p. 61.

30. Quoted in Kazemzadeh, *op. cit.*, p. 243.

31. See statements of plaintiff in "Persian Investment Corporation Ltd. and Sir Charles Lewis and others versus Prince Malcom Khan," High Court of Justice (Chancery Division), reported in *The Times*, May 6, 1892.

beneficiary of all these maneuvers, loyally and discreetly in the background, de Cardoël stipulated that the remaining £100,000 be paid to Mikāʾīl at the times agreed. Then, on November 15, the Persian Investment Corporation concluded an agreement with the Anglo-Asiatic Syndicate for the purchase of the concession, which was thus to change hands again, even before its previous sale was complete.[32] Mikāʾīl had been designated as payee by de Cardoël, and similarly the money that the corporation would pay to the syndicate was to pass through his hands.

It appears to have been only Mikāʾīl (and possibly Cloete) who were fully aware of Malkum's plans. In order to quell any doubts that might have arisen in the minds of other members of the corporation about the value of the concession, on November 18 Malkum addressed a formal letter to its directors, "expressing distinctly the approbation of his master the Shah to the concession, and promising that a commissioner should be appointed for the purpose of protecting the interests of the concession."[33] This assurance was taken at its face value, and no one appeared to regret the payment made three days earlier.

Matters thus seemed to be going well; an unworkable concession was circulating on the London money market and gathering money as it went. Yet difficulties arose for which Malkum had not fully provided in his plan, and these were to reduce his profits from the whole affair and make them costlier than he had anticipated. Official objections to the lottery concession and the shadowy corporations that passed it back and forth arose in both London and Tehran.

Wolff in particular expressed strong disapproval of the scheme. He was probably motivated not only by dislike for Malkum, but also by concern for the maintenance of a favorable atmosphere in which concessions he himself wished to promote might flourish and succeed. Back in Tehran, he urged the shah to revoke the concession and at the same time persuaded the Foreign Office to investigate the possibilities of prosecuting the Persian Investment Corporation under British law. It appeared that members of the corporation might be guilty of contravening the Lottery Act of 1826. The Law Officers of the Crown ultimately advised the Foreign Office as follows:

> We . . . think that the undertaking is within mischief contemplated by the Laws relating to Lotteries and Gaming, and that persons receiving money for the purposes of this Company are in fact keeping a lottery within the meaning of these Statutes.

32. *Ibid.*

33. Statement of Sir Charles Lewis at extraordinary general meeting of Persian Investment Corporation on August 29, 1890, reported in *The Times* the following day.

We advise that the Public Prosecutor should be instructed to write to the secretary of the Company, saying that Her Majesty's Government are advised that the enterprise is unlawful, and that, if continued, the Directors and the Secretary and other persons engaged therein will render themselves liable to proceedings.[34]

Accordingly, on December 17, the directors of the corporation received a letter from the treasury solicitors warning them that their enterprise could expose them to prosecution. After a legal wrangle, the directors vindicated themselves in terms of British law, and the issue was settled in their favor on April 18, 1890: to found a company for the purpose of instituting gambling operations abroad was held not to infringe the Lottery Act. The case, however, made the directors of the corporation realize that their project was regarded with disfavor by the Foreign Office, and aware of the additional obstacle to implementing the concession that lack of official support would pose, they began efforts to dispose of it to yet another buyer, this time on the continent.[35]

Meanwhile the shah himself was having second thoughts. The Russian chargé d'affaires had joined his representations to those of Wolff, and Amīn us-Sulṭān was only too pleased to support their demands for cancellation of the concession. Malkum's predicament offered an ideal opportunity to encompass his downfall. According to the account of ʿAbbās Mīrzā Mulkārā, a brother of Nāṣir ud-Dīn Shāh, Amīn us-Sulṭān had been unaware of the granting of the concession, and it was not until the royal party was back in Iran that he learned of its existence. In his anger at being ignored and circumvented, he proceeded to work for its cancellation.[36]

Amīn ud-Daula, who had rejoined the royal party in London and accompanied it to Scotland, writes in his memoirs that Amīn us-Sulṭān was, on the contrary, aware of the granting of the concession and indeed delighted at this supposed coup of Malkum and the opportunity it afforded him to disgrace Malkum in the eyes of the shah. Amīn us-Sulṭān went, it is said, to the monarch and informed him that the concession he had given for nothing to de Cardoël at Malkum's urging, had shortly afterwards changed hands for 100,000 *tomans*. Malkum had thus committed the mortal crime of depriving the shah of money.[37] Although

34. Quoted in Kazemzadeh, *op. cit.* (n. 5, above), p. 244.

35. Report of statutory general meeting of Persian Investment Corporation, March 24, 1890, in *The Times*, March 25, 1890; and of extraordinary general meeting of the corporation held on August 29, 1890, in *The Times*, August 30, 1890.

36. ʿAbbās Mīrzā Mulkārā, *Sharḥ-i Ḥāl*, ed. ʿAbd ul-Ḥusayn Navāʾī (Tehran, 1325 solar/1946), p. 109.

37. Mīrzā ʿAlī Khān Amīn ud-Daula, *Khāṭirāt-i Siyāsī*, ed. Ḥāfiẓ Farmānfarmāʾīān (Tehran, 1341 solar/1962), p. 146.

Amīn ud-Daula, as we have seen, stood close to Malkum and might therefore be regarded as a reliable witness of what transpired, his account appears unlikely. It is improbable that Nāṣir ud-Dīn Shāh should have parted with a concession merely in the hope of future profit; his interest in all his financial dealings was the prospect of ready cash. Malkum, in a letter to Qavām ud-Daula, claimed to have laid 30,000 *tomans* at his master's feet in exchange for the concession,[38] and the payment of some such consideration would have been in conformity with previous practice.

A third and more likely account suggests that Malkum had promised Amīn us-Sulṭān a share of the profits he anticipated from hawking the concession, but then failed to keep his word. Amīn us-Sulṭān thereupon made public the terms of the concession and without difficulty obtained a *fatvā* condemning the whole undertaking as contrary to Islamic law.[39]

Given the opposition of the British and Russian envoys and Amīn us-Sulṭān, there was no pressing reason for Nāṣir ud-Dīn Shāh to refuse their request and uphold the validity of the concession. Malkum had already paid him 30,000 tomans, and there seemed to be little likelihood

38. Telegram dated December 10, 1889, quoted in Kazemzadeh, *op. cit.* (n. 5, above), p. 245. There are certain minor inaccuracies in Amīn ud-Daula's account of the affair which make its reliability suspect. The French employee of the embassy who was the nominal recipient of the concession is mistakenly called de la Rue, instead of de Cardoël (*Khāṭirāt-i Siyāsī*, p. 146) and Malkum is stated to have sold £50,000 shares in the Persian Investment Corporation before the cancellation (*ibid.*, p. 147). The second inaccuracy may reflect misinformation by Malkum, who wished to present his profits to his friend as legitimate and innocent.

39. Ibrāhīm Taymūrī, *ᶜAṣr-i Bīkhabarī yā Tārīkh-i Imtiyāzāt dar Īrān* (Tehran, 1332 solar/1953), p. 315. Curzon remarks in a curiously reticent paragraph on the lottery affair that the concession was cancelled "in consequence of the inclusion of other and less desirable items in its terms" (*Persia and the Persian Question*, I: 484). We have seen, however, that the terms of the concession were restricted to the single vice of gambling. He continues: "In apparent ignorance of these facts, the concession was disposed of to a syndicate, and again passed on to a Company (the Persian Investment Corporation), whose final collapse agitated the London market in 1890; the result of the entire series of transactions, the moral blame of which I do not pretend to distribute, being that a great shock was given to Persian credit and that capital was scared away from Persian investment" (*ibid.*). Curzon's reluctance to state the facts of the case, let alone distribute moral blame, is remarkable. His work was completed in 1892, and it is inconceivable, in view of his general eagerness to accumulate knowledge of contemporary Iran, that he should have failed to see the accounts of the lottery affair published in *The Times* (of which he was for a time the correspondent in Iran) in 1890 and 1891. It may be that, aware of the fluidity of political fortune in Iran and also of Malkum's professed anglophilia, Curzon had no desire to antagonize in print a figure who might attain prominence in Iran and be of value to British policy. E. G. Browne's pretense at ignorance of the lottery affair, one totally unacceptable, will be discussed below (see p. 219).

of the concession ever beginning to operate and yielding 20 percent of its annual profit to the treasury. Therefore, on December 5, 1889, he sent a telegram to Malkum announcing its cancellation: "As the matter of a lottery in Iran is contrary to the *sharīʿat*, and a cause of mischief and corruption, it has been suspended by order of the government, and the agreement for its privilege is void and invalid. Notice will be given officially, also to the British legation resident in Tehran."[40]

The cancellation clearly endangered the £20,000 Malkum had already pocketed and, worse still, threatened to deprive him of the additional £100,000 provided for in the agreement between de Cardoël and the Anglo-Asiatic Syndicate. Suppressing any vestigial scruples he may have had, Malkum therefore decided to keep the cancellation secret as long as possible, and in the meantime to gather in as much of the outstanding sum as appeared feasible. One of the directors of the Persian Investment Corporation, Sir Charles Lewis, was feeling anxious about the concession's future, and early in December, shortly after Malkum's receipt of the shah's telegram, he came to the Iranian embassy seeking comfort and reassurance. These Malkum did not hesitate to provide; he affirmed that the concession was still in existence and "unimpeachable."[41]

On December 10, Qavām ud-Daula, titular minister of foreign affairs, officially informed Wolff that the concession had been repealed, for after it had been granted, "it appeared that he [Malkum] had put in other games which are contrary to the noble laws of the Mussulman faith and the establishment of which in Persia might give rise to endless troubles, therefore by obligation the above-mentioned concession was annulled and cancelled."[42] This explanation for the repeal of the concession was not only a fabrication, but a foolish one. There was no evidence that Malkum had sought to insert other "games" in the text of the concession, and in any event it was repugnant to Islamic law as it stood, for any form of gambling is forbidden in Islam (see Qurʾān, 5:90–91). If religious considerations had been of importance, the concession would never have been granted in the first place. Amīn us-Sulṭān was seeking to draw a veil of pious concern over the sordid maneuverings that constituted Iranian politics.

A copy of this communication was sent to Malkum in London, but only three days later without a qualm he pocketed a further £20,000. The check for this amount, made out to Mikāʾīl Khān, represented the

40. Quoted in Kazemzadeh, *op. cit.* (n. 5, above), p. 245, Taymūrī, *op. cit.*, p. 216.

41. Report of "Persian Investment Corporation versus Prince Malcom Khan," *The Times*, May 6, 1892.

42. Quoted in Kazemzadeh, *op. cit.*, p. 245.

first payment of the Persian Investment Corporation to the Anglo-Asiatic Syndicate for the worthless and canceled concession. The syndicate had not yet completed its purchase of the concession from de Cardoël, and Mikāʾīl Khān arranged on behalf of the syndicate to turn the money over to him as a second installment of the £120,000.[43] These were, however, formalities. Whether by way of the syndicate or the corporation, of de Cardoël or Mikāʾīl, all roads led ultimately to Malkum's bank account.

Having netted this second £20,000, Malkum was unwilling to renounce the other £80,000 he stood to gain under the original agreement between de Cardoël and the syndicate. He therefore cabled Qavām ud-Daula in an attempt to force the restoration of the concession. He protested energetically that the terms of the concession were in full accord with the *sharīʿat*, that the corporation, the latest proud possessor of the concession, was a respectable and legally constituted body, and complained that he had already suffered an outlay of 30,000 *tomans*, presented to the shah in Scotland in exchange for the concession given to de Cardoël.[44]

Simultaneously, other pressures were exerted on the shah and his ministers. The Foreign Office was advised by the Law Officers of the Crown to press the Iranian government for the return of the £40,000 disbursed by the syndicate and the corporation for a concession now generally known to be worthless, despite Malkum's reticence.[45] Nāṣir ud-Dīn Shāh was unwilling to accede to the demand, which would have caused him considerable financial loss. Faced with the persistent refusal of Malkum to acquiesce in the cancellation, he decided to take the drastic but less costly step of dismissing him from the post of ambassador and stripping him of all official titles.

On December 18, a brief notice appeared in *The Times*, announcing Malkum's dismissal and the appointment in his place of Mīrzā Muḥammad ʿAlī Khān ʿAlā us-Salṭana, formerly consul-general in Tiflis. The events that had led to his dismissal remained unknown in England for several months, and the notice concluded noncommittally: "It is said that the change is the result of differences between the Prince and the Grand Vizier, and that the Shah has admitted the Grand Vizier's complaints to be justified."

Anxious to preserve his respectability in British eyes, the next day Malkum had the following paragraph inserted in *The Times*: "We are requested to state that Prince Malcom Khan, who has lately had some

43. *Ibid.* and report of "Persian Investment Corporation versus Prince Malcom Khan," *The Times*, May 6, 1892.

44. Kazemzadeh, *op. cit.* (n. 5, above), p. 245.

45. *Ibid.*, p. 246.

personal disagreements with the Grand Vizier, and who has resigned his post [!], intends going to Persia for a short time. His permanent home will, however, be in England, where he has lived for so many years, and his residence will continue to be at Holland Park." Malkum's resourcefulness, even in the hour of defeat, is well exemplified by this attempt to disguise dismissal as resignation.

His efforts are further attested by a report of the Russian ambassador in London, de Staal, to his superiors in St. Petersburg. Malkum evidently went to visit his Russian colleague and informed him of his "resignation," claiming that "he had been brought to the decision by the intrigues of the Grand Vizier, together with those of Sir H. Wolff." It was of course true that both Amīn us-Sulṭān and Wolff had been instrumental in the cancellation of the concession, but Malkum was being considerably less than honest. De Staal commented in his report: "I do not think Malkum Khān's account is complete; but I found it best not to pursue a matter which he appeared to find painful."[46]

Malkum's efforts to conceal the cancellation of the concession enjoyed only limited and temporary success. It appears that the Foreign Office was guilty at least of collusion, for it made no firm public announcement of the cancellation for several months, hoping presumably that Malkum and the Iranian government would compose their differences and avoid a scandal. Wolff had been officially advised of the cancellation on December 10, only five days after the shah's telegram to Malkum, and the news was transmitted to the Foreign Office. Yet it was not until August 1890, when the Persian Investment Corporation was engaged in efforts to dispose of the concession to a foreign buyer, that its directors were officially informed by the Foreign Office of its cancellation. The letter they received included the first mention of Wolff's dispatch of the previous December, in which he had conveyed the contents of Qavām ud-Daula's communication. In the same letter, the directors were advised to cease all attempts at selling the concession.[47]

This they duly did, and the uninitiated among them began to realize the magnitude of the fraud Malkum had perpetrated. When the cancellation finally became public knowledge in August 1890—thanks to the belated letter of the Foreign Office—the enraged shareholders of the Persian Investment Corporation summoned an extraordinary general meeting. It was presided over by Sir Charles Lewis, who had difficulty in making himself heard above the indignant shouts of some of

46. De Staal to Giers, December 4, 1889, in A. Meyendorff, ed., *Correspondance Diplomatique de M. de Staal* (Paris, 1929), II: 60.

47. Report of extraordinary general meeting of the Persian Investment Corporation, August 29, 1890, in *The Times*, August 30, 1890.

those attending. He reviewed the various transactions that had taken place, but was evidently still unaware of the crucial role that had been played by Malkum in concealing the cancellation in December 1889. He promised that no further payments would be made to the syndicate, which had passed all money on to the original and titular holder of the concession, de Cardoël. It appears that Malkum succeeded in temporarily diverting Lewis' attention from his guilt by suggesting that the money received by de Cardoël had as its final destination the shah and his entourage in Tehran. "In answer to a question, he [Lewis] said that he could not go so far as to accuse the Shah of having had the money, but it had gone pretty high up, and that was the secret of it, for because the high-up people did not share and share alike the concession was attempted to be withdrawn [*sic*]."[48]

Recognizing Malkum to be the source of this insinuation, ᶜAlā us-Salṭana struck a counterblow on the instructions of Amīn us-Sulṭān. On September 13, 1890, the following appeared in *The Times*:

> We have been requested by the Persian Minister to announce that the statements recently made in the City reflecting on the credit and loyalty of the Persian government are engaging the serious attention of his Majesty the Shah and that steps are in contemplation which will remove all matters of misconception to ground altogether distinct from that which they now occupy. The lotteries concession alone has been cancelled, for reasons as well known in London as in Teheran, and under circumstances the justice and sufficiency of which will be universally recognised. In order that no one should be injured, these reasons were announced to all concerned at the time of the withdrawal. The Persian Legation therefore protest energetically against the malicious insinuations that have been so recklessly made.

Amīn us-Sulṭān was also being less than honest. The reasons for the cancellation were by no means "as well known in London as in Teheran," nor was it true that "these reasons were announced to all concerned at the time of the withdrawal." It was precisely the failure to inform anyone of the cancellation except Malkum and Wolff that had enabled the former to pocket his second £20,000 on December 13, 1889.

On September 19, 1890, a further meeting of the Persian Investment Corporation was held, this time in order to discuss the advisability of voluntarily winding up and thereby avoiding the necessity of further payments to the Anglo-Asiatic Syndicate. Despite Malkum's continued efforts of dissimulation, the truth was beginning to emerge. Lewis told the assembled shareholders that "on the part of some person or persons there had been a very grave withholding of information during a period

48. *Ibid.*

of some days in which the first payment of the purchase money was made by the company, in perfect good faith, and without the slightest inkling of the withdrawal, or the attempted withdrawal of the concession, having happened or being about to happen." It was also emerging that Mikāʾīl Khān had acted as agent for Malkum. One shareholder inquired "whether it was not a fact that one of the directors of the corporation was a brother of the Persian minister to London. The chairman replied that the gentleman referred to had not been a director for some little time, but he was a director at the time. Mr. Beard– 'He was also secretary of the Persian Embassy here.' The chairman–'I am not aware of that. I do not think so.' " Most serious of all, it was becoming clear that Malkum was the manipulator and ultimate beneficiary of the whole affair, and Lewis announced that he had in his possession a canceled check, "the company's cheque, for £20,000, which they paid as part of the purchase-money, which went into Prince Malcom Khan's bank account." Malkum was represented at the meeting by a Mr. Campbell, who on hearing this disquieting announcement tried to revive the rumor that the money had somehow reached the pocket of the shah. The suggestion did not seem as plausible as it had the month before.[49]

Despite his outward bravado, Malkum was clearly afraid of the possible consequences of the affair. Even while publishing *Qānūn* and attacking Amīn us-Sulṭān in bitter terms–as will be seen–he was writing him a series of letters, most of which went unanswered, begging for forgiveness and reinstatement in favor. Thus, on November 27, 1890, he wrote as follows:

> It cannot be denied that Your Excellency has considered it permissible to be exceedingly ungracious towards me, but I swear, with deep shame, that as long as I am alive I shall be sorry and repentant for the wrong I have committed. Custom and breeding alike, as well as the dictates of power, should have caused me to respond to Your Excellency's unkindness with the utmost submission and goodwill, and in this respect I have committed a grave error. Now, in order to compensate for this unworthy error, I give you my full assurance that however much henceforth–may God forbid!–you may be ungracious to me, you shall see no shortcoming from me.

Malkum concluded by asking Amīn us-Sulṭān to intervene with the shah and obtain a new appointment for him abroad.[50]

It appears that Amīn us-Sulṭān was at least initially disposed to take pity on Malkum and save him from final and complete disgrace. He offered him the post of Iranian envoy in Rome, on condition that

49. Report in *The Times*, September 20, 1890.
50. Ṣafāʾī, ed., *op. cit.*, pp. 301–302.

Malkum accept the cancellation of the concession as final and come to some agreement with the Persian Investment Corporation.[51] To disgorge the £40,000 and be relegated to this relatively minor diplomatic post in Italy was too much for Malkum to accept, and he continued to hold out for a reconciliation with Tehran on more favorable terms. Amīn us-Sulṭān, fully supported by the shah, who was no longer enchanted by Malkum's dazzling talents, remained adamant, and by early 1891 Malkum was near despair. He asked his successor as envoy, ʿAlā us-Salṭana, to intercede on his behalf, and from his telegram to Amīn us-Sulṭān dated Jumādī ul-Ūlā 6, 1305/January 17, 1891, it may be deduced that Malkum had regretted his abrupt rejections of Amīn us-Sulṭān's terms. He was now, according to ʿAlā us-Salṭana, "ready for any kind of compliance and obedience" and was waiting for instructions. In reply, Amīn us-Sulṭān demanded that Malkum should settle the affair of the lottery, "and then I will be ready to do anything."[52] He was doubtless aware, however, that affairs in London were reaching a point where a settlement with the corporation was no longer possible, and hence his promise was little more than a subtle means for increasing Malkum's agony. To the shah, Amīn us-Sulṭān expressed himself quite openly, and the monarch wrote in reply to a note he had addressed to him: "As for Malkum Khān, the whole affair has become clear. What you wrote about Malkum is quite right. He is finished, and is like a drowning man clutching at every straw. There is no reason to pay him any attention."[53]

Malkum was, however, despite his own apprehensions, by no means finished, and thanks to the careful planning that had gone into the concession transactions he was able to escape legal consequences. Prosecution was first directed against Mikāʾīl Khān, when the Persian Investment Corporation had a writ served on him for the restitution of £20,000. Shortly before the writ could be served, Mikāʾīl took the precaution of leaving England for an unknown address in Nice and instructed his lawyers to have the writ set aside on grounds of diplomatic immunity. Malkum obligingly testified that Mikāʾīl (to whom he referred as "General Mickayl") was indeed in the employ of the Iranian embassy as counsellor. The court, however, took notice of the fact that Malkum was no longer envoy and preferred to inquire of his successor whether or not Mikāʾīl might deserve diplomatic immunity.[54] ʿAlā us-Salṭana announced in reply that Mikāʾīl had been dismissed from the

51. See Amīn ud-Daula's letter to Malkum dated Dhū-l-Ḥijja 16, 1308/July 23, 1891, in Supplément Persan, 1997, f. 120.

52. Safāʾī, ed., *op. cit.* (n. 8, above), pp. 291–292.

53. *Ibid.*, p. 294.

54. Report in *The Times*, February 7, 1891.

service of the embassy at the same time as Malkum.[55] The case against Mikāʾīl was not pressed, and instead the lawyers of the corporation began to prepare for the prosecution of the chief culprit, Malkum.

Malkum was engaged meanwhile in further efforts to preserve a respectable public image and to obfuscate the reasons for his dismissal. While still ambassador, he had made the acquaintance of the publicist and poet, Wilfred Scawen Blunt and with a fanciful if highly inaccurate description of his career, had left him "more convinced than ever of the superior intelligence of the Eastern mind."[56] It was probably through Blunt that Malkum gained access to liberal circles in London in which he successfully posed as the "reforming prince," the enlightened aristocrat from darkest Asia.[57] Having been dismissed from the embassy, it was only natural to pretend to be the victim of reactionary and corrupt forces in Iran.

As evidence of his self-effacing concern for reform, in February 1891, he delivered a lecture in Chelsea at the house of a Rev. H. R. Haweis which was later published in the *Contemporary Review* under the title, "Persian Civilisation."[58] At the beginning of the lecture he posed the question: "Why is it that European people have made such wonderful progress, while the Asiatic races, who were the first promoters of civilisation, have lagged so far behind?" In answer, he rejected the possibility of racial inferiority, and also the responsibility of Islam for "Asiatic" backwardness. The Qurʾān was only "a sort of revised Bible," containing nothing "directly opposed to Christian principles." Islam itself was not merely a religion, but "the accumulated wisdom of the East," "an ocean where you can find everything which is good to be known," offering "all kinds of facilities for the progress of the people." This being so, the resistance of the Muslims to "civilising" endeavors could be explained only in terms of fear and misunderstanding. The adoption of European civilization was thought to involve the substitution of Christianity for Islam and was therefore strenuously opposed. The only way to remove the obstacle was by presenting the "principles of civilisation" as deriving from Islam.

> I can assure you that the little progress which we see in Persia and Turkey, especially in Persia, is due to this fact, that some people have taken your

55. Report in *The Times*, April 9, 1891.

56. W. S. Blunt, *Secret History of the English Occupation of Egypt* (London, 1907), p. 85. See also above, pp. 11–12.

57. On similar European fantasies concerning Jamāl ud-Dīn Asadābādī, see Homa Pakdaman, *Djamal-ed-Din Assad Abadi dit Afghani* (Paris, 1969), p. 80.

58. Malkum Khān, "Persian Civilisation," *Contemporary Review*, LIX (1891): 238–244.

> European principles, and instead of saying that they came from England, France or Germany, have said, "We have nothing to do with Europeans; these are the true principles of our own religion (and indeed that is quite true) which have been *taken by Europeans*!" That has had a marvellous effect at once.

Malkum concluded by recommending that European politicians should thenceforth "present European civilisation independent of Christian dogma." The lecture is interesting as a frank statement of the policy of expedient appeal to Islam that he was pursuing in the pages of *Qānūn* at the time.

Malkum's fair repute in London suffered something of a blow when, on March 16, 1891, *The Times* published the translation of an article in the official gazette *Īrān*, condemning Malkum and setting forth something of his role in the lottery affair.[59] With remarkable audacity and resourcefulness, Malkum responded with the following letter to the editor:

> I see in one of your telegrams that some of our ministers at Teheran imagine they are able to take, even in England, our personal titles and our legitimate rights in the same manner as they take the heads of our unfortunate people in Persia. In my private case, there is no need of any explanation for my countrymen. They have acquired under our present Ministers ample experiences of all kinds of childish caprices associated with the classical abominations of Asia, and they know particularly well that our greatest ministers, who had the best reasons to believe till the last moment that they had the perfect confidence of their sovereign, perished suddenly under the most horrid treatment. As for my European friends, I have only to say that during my long career not only have I never received from my Government a single word of disapprobation, but by an extraordinary chance that no merit on my part can justify, there is in our language no expression of esteem, flattery, gratitude and veneration, which has not till this day been addressed constantly and most emphatically by my Sovereign and by his Ministers to my humble person. When I will publish my long correspondence with His Majesty the Shah and His Government, even my enemies will recognise that my only fault with our ministers has been that, educated in Europe, I have tried perhaps with too much courage, to modify a peculiar regime which has, unfortunately, too often darkened the history of our present administration.
>
> Your obedient servant,
> Prince Malcom Khan.

With typical shamelessness, Malkum thus presented himself as the enlightened victim of Asiatic "abominations" and, striking a particular-

59. The article was written by Mīrzā Ḥasan Khān Iʿtimād us-Salṭana on royal command. See his diary entry for Rajab 23, 1308/March 4, 1891, in *Rūznāma-yi Khāṭirāt*, p. 843.

ly heroic pose, tried implicitly to identify himself with Iran's "greatest ministers," such as Mīrzā Abūl Qāsim Qāʾim Maqām (d. 1836) and Mīrzā Taqī Khān Amīr Kabīr (d. 1851), who had indeed "perished suddenly under the most horrible treatment." The abomination of the lottery swindle he carefully suppressed, and while claiming, with some justification, that he had always been the object of limitless veneration, he omitted all mention of the flattery that he had repeatedly lavished on both the shah and Amīn us-Sulṭān.

An even more remarkable document is the following letter from Malkum to Khālid Bey, the Ottoman ambassador in Tehran,[60] in which Malkum seeks to present his dismissal as a welcome turn in his career, finally freeing him from the affairs of state and enabling him to devote himself wholeheartedly to his inmost desire, the cause of reform. In reality, he bitterly resented his dismissal, and it was the desire for personal revenge and satisfaction that turned him to abuse and denunciation of the regime:

> You are an enlightened friend of Persia, and I am an ardent partisan of her progress. We can therefore speak to each other freely. The clearest point of the situation is that Persia, if not already lost, is certainly in great danger. She is already divided in principle, and our Government is doing all it can to make that division a reality. Struck with the situation and inspired with some exceptional knowledge, I have entertained from youth upwards the presumption to form a plan for the regeneration of my country. This plan has been studied, discussed, corrected and recorrected for forty years. Every innovation which has been attempted during the reign of the present Shah has been merely a feeble reflection of certain details belonging to my programme. Its fundamental ideas have remained barren, stifled by the pressure of my official position. In my ardent wish to give a liberal impetus to these ideas I have often cast about for some way of getting rid of my official responsibilities; with each renewed effort the infinite kindness of the Shah has kept me like a slave at my post. Whilst I was struggling in silence between the exigencies of my official position in London and the irresistible desire to enter freely upon a campaign in favour of serious reforms in Persia, the inconceivable frivolity and recklessness of the young Ministry surrounding the person of the Shah came to my assistance. The opportunity for an open rupture presented itself. I seized it eagerly, with open arms, as a piece of good fortune. Your Excellency is doubtless aware that at Tehran every conceivable thing has been done to heal this rupture. His Majesty the Shah in his extreme goodness offered me personally every possible satisfaction. I met everything with pointblank refusal; with regret, no doubt, but also with this conviction—that I had a more sacred duty than what belonged to my own

60. Khālid Bey subscribed to *Qānūn*, strangely enough through Wolff. See Amīn ud-Daula to Malkum, Muḥarram 9, 1309/August 25, 1891, in Supplément Persan, 1997, f. 110.

> safety or advantage to fulfill towards my sovereign and my country. I saw that this was perhaps the last occasion on which I could publicly bring forward the programme of reform which had been my life-work and which in my eyes sums up the last chances of Persian regeneration.[61]

Despite this resourceful publicity campaign, Malkum's public disgrace in England was drawing ever closer. By the spring of 1892, the Persian Investment Corporation had completed preparing its case against him, and proceedings opened on May 5 in the Chancery Division of the High Court of Justice. The plaintiff began by rehearsing the history of the concession affair: its original purchase by de Cardoël from the shah, the subsequent agreements for its sale first to the Anglo-Asiatic Syndicate and then to the Persian Investment Corporation, the payments that had taken place, and the gradual discovery of its cancellation in December 1889. The corporation sought an order compelling Malkum to refund the £20,000 paid to Mikāʾīl on December 13, 1889, together with 5 percent interest on the sum.

Malkum in reply denied that Mikāʾīl had at any point been acting as his agent or that he was in any way personally interested in the transactions surrounding the concession. The first payment of £20,000, made by the syndicate to de Cardoël on October 13, had not been paid into his personal bank account, but rather that of the Iranian embassy, which admittedly bore his name.

> So far as regarded the payment of the cheque for £20,000 to the banking account of the Persian Embassy kept in his name, and the application of the same, and the communications received by him from his Government, he acted under the direct commands of his Sovereign, the Shah of Persia, and he could not state particulars or give information or discovery without communicating and making public facts and matters in which the Persian Government was interested, and which, having regard to his position as ambassador, he was not bound to disclose; and he submitted that he ought not be required to disclose information as to such matters and facts.

61. The letter was published in the *Madras Times* for July 5, 1891. Malkum was also able to have the following inserted in the *Bombay Gazette* for July 17, 1891: "Malcolm Khan is an old hand at constitutional reform. He is said in his student days in France to have made a special study of constitutional law, and when he went back to high office in Persia, he did his best to persuade the Shah to introduce reforms of various kinds. Nothing came of his reforming energies—not even his own banishment and disgrace; and the deposition from his government of the Zil-e-Sultan [*sic*]—the most distinguished representative of liberal ideas in Persia—showed clearly enough that the day for reform had not come." Malkum's purpose in having these items published in the Indian press was presumably to create a favorable impression on the Iranian mercantile community in India, particularly in Bombay and Calcutta.

The plaintiff responded by demanding that Malkum produce a statement of his personal account from October 1, 1889 onwards and also "a copy of the telegram alleged to have been addressed to the defendant by the Government of Persia dated the 8th. of December 1889, and a copy of a telegram to the Government of Persia from the defendant, dated the 22d. of December, 1889." As for Malkum's claim that the check for £20,000 had been paid into the account of the embassy: "We are to inform you that Lord Salisbury has reason to believe that this assertion is incorrect, and that the present Persian Minister at this court would, if communicated with, probably be found ready to furnish evidence to this effect." The solicitors of the embassy had written to the plaintiff that "the Persian Government has never had a bank at the London embassy" and that none of the £40,000 Malkum had received ever found its way to Iran. Finally, the plaintiff himself was able to produce a copy of the telegram dated Rabīᶜ uth-Thānī 11, 1307/December 5, 1889, which had informed Malkum of the cancellation, a full week before the corporation disbursed £20,000 to Mikāʾīl.

Malkum replied rather feebly by repeating his assertion that the account which had been enriched by £20,000 belonged to the embassy, not his person. The passbook could not be produced because of the general nature of its contents "touching other matters relating to the affairs of the embassy." In any event, the money received by Mikāʾīl—all £20,000—had been used "to repay the expenses and for the services of the promoters in Persia." As for the telegram, he had ignored it at the time of receipt, imagining it to be a forgery put out by his enemies in Tehran.[62]

The case dragged on for a number of months, and it was not until March 15, 1893, that judgment was finally delivered. The action against Malkum was dismissed, for, Justice Chitty pointed out, the money claimed by the corporation had been paid to the syndicate and with it Malkum had no proven and demonstrable connection, despite the fact that he was the ultimate recipient of the money. Malkum's precautions—his involvement of Cardoël and Mikāʾīl, the setting up of the syndicate and the corporation—thus richly paid him off. He had obtained £40,000 for a worthless and unworkable concession, and the swindle was legally foolproof. Malkum, however, did not escape verbal chastisement from the presiding judge, and for once in his life he was obliged to hear his probity publicly impugned:

> It was . . . very plain that a person with a high sense of honour would not feel comfortable at having received a large sum of money and pocketed it

62. Report in *The Times*, May 6, 1892.

> for nothing. The defendant had got £20,000 from the syndicate and £20,000 from the plaintiffs, and being a man apparently of prudence he had carried the money out of the jurisdiction of this court, and neither the syndicate nor the plaintiff had got any concession. So he had made a very good thing out of it.[63]

Thereafter Malkum laid low in England. He appears to have made no further attempts to arouse sympathy and support as a wronged and enlightened man struggling nobly against the barbarities of Asia. Meanwhile, however, he embarked on a project whose success totally obscured his scandalous dealings from the eyes of his countrymen, earned him an honorable place among the fathers of Iranian constitutionalism, and proved to be the highpoint of his career. This most remarkable fruit of his talent for transmuting disgrace into fame and honor was the celebrated newspaper, *Qānūn*.

63. Report in *The Times*, March 15, 1893.

CHAPTER 8

ESSAYS IN THE FOUNDATION of a press were among the earliest symptoms of westernization throughout the Middle East. The innovation was first seen in Egypt during the reign of Muḥammad ʿAlī Pāshā, and the earliest newspaper to appear in any of the languages of the Muslim heartlands was *al-Waqāʾiʿ al-Miṣrīyya,* first published in 1828.[1] It was followed three years later by the Turkish *Takvîm-i Vakâyi,* closely modeled on its example.[2] Eight more years were to pass before Iran saw its first newspaper, the *Akhbār-i Vaqāyiʿ*, edited by Mīrzā Ṣāliḥ Shīrāzī, a member of the first group of young Iranians sent to study in Europe. Little is known of the duration of this enterprise, but it appears to have been simply an irregular news sheet consisting of two pages of court intelligence.[3]

A more regular and substantial publication of similar type was instituted in 1851 by Mīrzā Taqī Khān Amīr Kabīr, founder of the Dār ul-Funūn where Malkum's public career had begun. The *Rūznāma-yi Vaqāyiʿ-i Ittifāqīya* appeared at regular weekly intervals, and although consisting, like its predecessor, primarily of official announcements, it made a modest start in the inclusion of items concerning the outside world. With this journal the modernizing role of the Persian press may be said to have begun. Among the items reported by the newspaper during its first year of publication were the struggles of Mazzini against the Habsburg Empire, the drawing up of the Suez Canal project, and assorted scraps of geographical and scientific information. To the function of the newspaper as court gazette, Amīr Kabīr added social and

1. See article "Matbuat:Araplar," *İslam Ansiklopedisi,* VII: 362–363.

2. "Matbuat: Türkler," *İslam Ansiklopedisi,* VII: 367; and Bernard Lewis, *The Emergence of Modern Turkey* (Oxford, 1961), p. 73.

3. Jan Rypka, *Iranische Literaturgeschichte* (Leipzig, 1959), p. 324.

educational purpose. This he set forth in the seventh issue, tactfully attributing his initiative to Nāṣir ud-Dīn Shāh:

> Since His Imperial Majesty's endeavors are directed to the education of the people of his country, nobles and commonalty, traders and artisans alike, he has commanded that a newspaper be printed and published in the well-protected realm [of Iran] in order for their insight and knowledge to be increased, and for them to be aware of events at home and abroad. It is greatly hoped that by means of this newspaper the state of information, awareness and perspicacity of the people shall be increased.[4]

Still, however, the style of the paper was awkward and artificial, the same that was still current in the chancelleries of the age, and its contents bore no real relation to current political happenings. It is significant that in the titles of all these early newspapers—the Egyptian, the Turkish, and the Iranian—the word *waqāʾiᶜ/vakâyi/vaqāyiᶜ* (happenings, events) occurs; their style and purpose are essentially those of the traditional chroniclers (*vakᶜanüvisler/vaqāyiᶜnagārān*), who continued to exercise their profession into the second half of the nineteenth century. These first essays in journalism might, in fact, be thought of as periodic supplements to the chronicles composed at the order and for the benefit of the court. It was more than twenty years after the downfall of Amīr Kabīr that a Persian newspaper genuinely reflecting the political affairs of the day began to appear, taking the development of Persian journalism one stage further.

This was *Akhtar* (The Star), published in Istanbul and doubtless inspired chiefly by the Turkish press which had greatly expanded in the preceding decade. The first number appeared on Dhūl Ḥijja 1, 1292/January 13, 1876, under the editorship of Muḥammad Ṭāhir Tabrīzī, a member of the numerous Azerbayjani community in Istanbul who had lived in the Ottoman capital since his twenty-fourth year. Through much of its career, *Akhtar* had the active support of the Iranian minister in Istanbul, Ḥājjī Muḥsin Khān Muᶜīn ul-Mulk, an associate and brother mason of Malkum. The newspaper was further connected with the embassy in the person of Najaf Qulī Khān, the consul-general, who extended to Muḥammad Ṭāhir some editorial assistance. After sixty numbers, publication was suspended because of financial difficulties, but was soon resumed on Muḥarram 28, 1894/February 12, 1877, with the dual patronage of Sultan ᶜAbd ul-Ḥamīd and Nāṣir ud-Dīn Shāh. Najaf Qulī Khān now left the service of the embassy to devote himself to the newspaper. The acceptability of *Akhtar* in Iran came temporarily

4. Quoted in Firīdūn Ādamīyat, *Fikr-i Āzādī va Muqaddima-yi Nihḍat-i Mashrūṭīyat* (Tehran, 1340 solar/1961), pp. 45–46.

to an end with an indiscreet article on Russo-Iranian relations, and the journal came increasingly under Ottoman influence, serving as an organ of Pan-Islamist propaganda. In 1892 when Muʿīn ul-Mulk, who had continued his patronage of the paper despite opposition in Tehran, was dismissed from the embassy, *Akhtar* lost much of its strength. Although a change in editorial policy was able to bring about a more favorable attitude in Tehran, the newspaper's fortunes declined and before long publication ceased.[5]

Akhtar's achievement lay in its reporting of current political events in a comprehensible and lively manner, and it was for this reason much appreciated in Iran. The celebrated Cambridge Orientalist, E. G. Browne writes that during his visit to Iran in 1888, *Akhtar* furnished the only intelligence to be had of happenings both within the country and abroad.[6] Despite its temporary prohibition in Iran and its later Pan-Islamist stance, *Akhtar* did not function as the organ of a distinct political attitude. If it is the task of a press not only to inform but also to direct opinion and agitate for action, this next step in the development of Persian journalism was taken by Malkum with his *Qānūn*.

Malkum had doubtless been aware of the importance of the newspaper as a medium of communication long before he began to issue *Qānūn* in 1890. He was familiar not only with the Iranian press, rudimentary as it was, but also with the more prolific and highly developed products of Turkish journalism.[7] During the years he spent at the Iranian embassy in Istanbul, from 1861 to 1872, several newspapers of importance had made their appearance: Şinasi's *Tasvir-i Efkâr*; the *Tercüman-ı Ahval* to which his father's friend, Ahmet Vefik Paşa, contributed; Ali Suavi's *Mühbir*; and the *Mecmua-i Funun*, edited by his own friend, Mehmed Münif Paşa. That Malkum followed the Turkish press is evident from his participation in the alphabet controversy and above all from his article on the subject in *Hürriyet*.[8] It was probably *Hürriyet* more than any other Turkish newspaper that exercised a

5. On the career of *Akhtar*, see Khān Malik Sāsānī, *Yādbūdhā-yi Sifārat-i Istānbul* (Tehran, 1345 solar/1966), pp. 205–206; E. G. Browne, *The Press and Poetry of Modern Persia* (Cambridge, 1914), pp. 17, 36–37; Muḥammad Ṣadr Hāshimī, *Tārīkh-i Jarāʾid va Majallāt-i Īrān* (Isfahan, 1327–1328 solar/1948–1950), I: 63–64; and Firīdūn Ādamīyat, *Andīshahā-yi Mirzā Āqā Khān Kirmānī* (Tehran, 1346 solar/1967), pp. 10–11.

6. Browne, *op. cit.*, p. 17.

7. On the further development of Turkish journalism, see "Matbuat: Türkler," pp. 367–369; and Lewis, *op. cit.*, p. 151 f. Malkum also, of course, became well-acquainted with the French and British presses during his residences in Paris and London, but developments in Turkey, in this respect as in others, were more immediately relevant to Iran than the example of the West.

8. See above, pp. 89–90.

formative influence upon *Qānūn*. *Hürriyet* was explicitly an organ of opposition in exile, published first from London and then Geneva, attacking Âlî and Fuad Paşas, and filling its pages less with news than with long critical analyses of the state of Ottoman society and politics. To a large extent, *Qānūn* followed the same pattern: its publication was an avowedly political act; it unwearyingly, almost obsessively, attacked Amīn us-Sulṭān in the most bitter terms; and items of news were infrequent in its columns. Malkum's paper might almost be called a periodic propaganda sheet.

It has been suggested by a recent investigator that Malkum had been considering the publication of a newspaper since the mid-1880s.[9] This is possible but unlikely. Possessed of a fluent pen and aware of the influence a newspaper could exert, he might have contemplated founding one. Such an initiative, however, would hardly have been compatible with his position as ambassador in London, a position he valued and did not anticipate losing. So far as he was attempting to promote the cause of governmental reform, he had recourse instead to the composition and circulation of treatises and to correspondence with prominent men in Tehran. It is inconceivable that *Qānūn* should ever have appeared had it not been for the cancellation of the lottery concession and Malkum's dismissal from the embassy.

On this point he expressed himself clearly enough in a letter written in 1890 to the Ministry of Foreign Affairs demanding that he be assigned to a new and acceptable post. Asserting that if need be he could resort to trickery (*ḥuqqabāzī*), establish another farāmūshkhāna and thereby secure an annual income of twenty to thirty thousand tomans, he proceeds with another threat: "If I write a newspaper, I can bring anyone I like to his knees, as the old expression goes. So how do you expect me to bury myself alive?"[10] This was precisely the purpose of *Qānūn*: to bring Amīn us-Sulṭān to his knees and possibly to destroy the whole regime in the process.

In a less frank, because public, statement, composed one and a half years after the first issue of *Qānūn*, Malkum stated his aims in quite different terms:

> The body of doctrine which I seek to explain gradually through the instrumentality of a popular journal diffused throughout Persia, whilst it embraces the essential conditions of civilisation, is strictly founded on the

9. H. Hatämi, *Mühajir Iran Gazetlärinin Müstämläkäjilik vä Imperializm Aleyhinä Mübarizäsi* (Baku, 1964), pp. 57, 83–84. The account of *Qānūn* contained in this work is vitiated by the implicit trust placed by the author in Malkum's words, as well as by a constricting and irrelevant ideological framework.

10. Quoted by Jahāngīr Qāʾimmaqāmī, "Chand Sanad Marbūṭ ba Tārīkh-i Farāmūshkhāna dar Īrān," *Yaghmā*, XVI (1342 solar/1963): 405.

great principles of Islam, and largely answers to the wants and aspirations of the Persian people. Not a word which is not perfectly in agreement with the best science and the purest morality; not a premature idea; no pretension to an advanced western liberalism—nothing but elementary principles universally recognised as just, inoffensive and indispensable. All this I have wrapt up in formulas calculated to strike the imagination and penetrate the heart of the people. As to my immediate object, my ambition goes no further than asking humbly of our government to give us a law. And what law? The very same which the Shah himself is willing to approve—a law which will give us at the very least security for our life and for our possessions; a law, in fact, which might have a tendency to save us from the atrocious disorders, and from that organised system of brigandage, which the complete absence of any law whatever has created throughout this unfortunate country . . . And I hasten to add that when I speak of the vices of our administration, I am not to be understood as casting the slightest reproach on anyone in particular. These vices come from systems, not persons.[11]

The contrast between this carefully phrased declaration, intended for public attention, and Malkum's indiscreet outburst in his letter to the Foreign Ministry needs no emphasizing. His concern with putting an end to "organised brigandage" appears somewhat improbable in the light of his recently completed lottery swindle, and the tone and content of numerous issues of *Qānūn* belie his profession of freedom from bitterness against the persons of Amīn us-Sulṭān and others. It would be wrong, however, wholly to discount the motives here so nobly declared. The entirety of Malkum's career demonstrates an intertwining of extreme personal ambition with a concern for reform which was at least sporadically genuine. Considering himself uniquely fitted by his European education to conduct the westernization of Iran, he came to see the cause of reform and his own advancement and enrichment as linked and interdependent, despite the moral and logical inconsistencies frequently involved. To charge him with hypocrisy would be justified, but it is important, too, to examine the mechanics of his hypocrisy.

His career had begun with a devious bid for political prominence, if not supreme power, through the medium of the farāmūshkhāna and a simultaneous advocacy of reform in a number of treatises, especially the *Kitābcha-yi Ghaybī*. This duality of concern was maintained throughout his career. Both in establishing his pseudomasonic lodge and in circulating his writings on reform, Malkum was addressing himself primarily to the governing elite, the courtiers and politicians. This he continued to do through his years of residence in Istanbul and London, until his dismissal from the embassy. If his early writings reached

11. Open letter from Malkum Khān to Khālid Bey, Ottoman ambassador in Tehran, published in *Madras Times*, July 5, 1891, with the title "Crisis in Persia."

a wider audience, it can only have been in a haphazard and fortuitous manner. Now, deprived of the power derived from official appointment, Malkum was obliged to seek a new source of influence by functioning as the remote but fluent spokesman of popular discontent. The time had come to turn to a broader public for attention, and now the message of reform was directed to all who should have access to a copy of *Qānūn*. It is in this sense that the following statement should be interpreted: "I saw that this was perhaps the last occasion on which I could publicly bring forward the programme of reform which had been my lifework and which in my eyes sums up the last chances of Persian regeneration."[12] Throughout the publication of *Qānūn*, Malkum remained, however, at least as conscious of the effect his newspaper would produce at court and on the ministers in Tehran as he was of its wider influence. That he abandoned its publication immediately after receiving a new appointment is in itself proof enough that his resort to journalism was dictated by his dismissal and disfavor.

The necessity of law had been a favorite theme of Malkum long before the publication of *Qānūn*. Probably the earliest occurrence in Persian of the word *qānūn* in its sense of law came in his *Kitābcha-yi Ghaybī*, composed in about 1858. The need for law as the basis of state and society was repeated in sundry later writings, and, as if to show the way, Malkum himself, in the absence of a legislative assembly, tried his hand at the drawing up of laws based on European codes. One set, consisting of twenty-three separate items and included in the *Kitābcha-yi Ghaybī*, sought to define the essential functions of the state and to regulate the relations of its component organs.[13]

Another, more detailed set, providing the elements of a new penal code, was composed in 1301/1883–1884 under the title of *Daftar-i Qānūn*.[14] Although as usual sent to certain men of prominence in Iran,[15] it received no serious attention until much later, when the first Majlis was considering the institution of a penal code. The *Daftar-i Qānūn* contained the customary preamble, lamenting the ignorance of most of the ministers (with the exceptions left tactfully unspecified) and praising the enlightened and progressive tendencies of the shah. The specific provisions of Malkum's proposed legislation are of little interest; more worthy of attention is his declaration of intent with respect to its proposal. We have already seen that in his first treatise, *Kitābcha-yi Ghaybī*, Malkum suggested the collection of *shar*ᶜ ordinances and their incorporation into the laws of the state "by subjecting them to the conditions

12. *Ibid.*
13. See above, pp. 30–32.
14. Printed in *Majmū*ᶜ*a-yi Āthār* (Tehran, 1327 solar/1948), pp. 119–166.
15. *Ibid.*, p. xii.

of legality [*qānūnīyat*]."[16] In *Daftar-i Qānūn* he expressed himself more clearly on the relation between his proposed laws and the *sharīʿa*:

> It must not be deduced from what I have set forth that my intention is to change the *sharīʿa* of Islam. God forbid! All necessary provisions for personal security have been laid down in perfect form in the immaculate *sharīʿa*. The task that now confronts us is to collect and arrange these ordinances, which are now scattered throughout the *ḥadīth*, and make them the law of the state in the same way that the states of Europe have codified their laws and drawn up a Qurʾān for themselves.[17]

The movement for codification of Islamic law was often a result of the European, colonial impact. The French in North Africa, the British in India, and the Russians in Central Asia all attempted to reduce to a cohesive code of law in the European sense those parts of the *sharīʿa* that were still permitted to operate.[18] Such endeavors sprang from the need of the colonizers to have at their disposal a convenient source of reference for the supervision and control of *sharīʿa* courts. Malkum's purpose in proposing codification appears to have been the concealment of the true nature of his proposals. In the same *Daftar-i Qānūn* he repeated his familiar theme of the inseparable unity of European civilization and the need to adopt it as a whole: just as the Iranians had accepted the camera without independently attempting to invent the same device, so too in the sphere of law and institutions, the product of three millennia of European development and experimentation should be gladly and unquestioningly welcomed. "Let them [the ministers] act precisely as Europe, the teacher, tells them to."[19] The instructions of the teacher were not, however, identical with those of the Qurʾān. There was on Malkum's part a deliberate refusal to confront the substantive differences between European and Islamic law and an attempt to conceal them behind the pretence that *qānūn* meant nothing more than a codified *sharīʿa* and was therefore innocuous from a religious point of view.[20]

16. *Ibid.*, p. 30.

17. *Ibid.*, p. 141. Sporadic attempts were made at codifying the ordinances of the *sharīʿa* current in Iran, first in 1885 by Mīrzā Yaḥyā Khān Mushīr ud-Daula (see Amīn ud-Daula to Malkum, Dhūl Ḥijja 4, 1302/September 14, 1885, in Bibliothèque Nationale, Supplément Persan, 1997, f. 51) and then in 1890, under the direction of ʿAbbās Mīrzā Mulkārā and Amīn ud-Daula successively (see ʿAbbās Mīrzā Mulkārā, *Sharḥ-i Ḥāl*, ed. ʿAbd ul-Ḥusayn Navāʾī [Tehran, 1325 solar/1946], pp. 108–109).

18. On the so-called Anglo-Muhammadan Law evolved in British India, see A.A.A. Fyzee, *Outlines of Muhammadan Law* (Oxford, 1955); and on Russian endeavors to codify Ḥanafī law on matters of personal status and agrarian affairs, K.K. Pahlen, *Mission to Turkestan* (New York and Toronto, 1964), pp. 81–82.

19. *Majmūʿa-yi Āthār*, p. 127.

20. *Qānūn* was often taken in Ottoman usage to refer to natural law, which could more plausibly be equated with the *sharīʿa* than could European law. For

Because Malkum's entire ambition—apart from personal power and wealth—was directed to a "material reformation . . . in the garb of religion," it was entirely appropriate to choose the word *qānūn*, bearing this implication within it, as the title for his newspaper.

The first number of *Qānūn* appeared on Rajab 1, 1307/February 21, 1890, bearing the slogan "union, justice, progress" beneath the title.[21] The address of the newspaper was given as the Oriental Printing Company (*Kumpānī-yi Inṭibāʿāt-i Sharqī*) at 38 Lombard Lane, London, and the annual subscription set at one English pound. The masthead of the paper remained substantially the same throughout its publication: the word *Qānūn* printed in bold type with the three-part slogan immediately beneath. From number ten onward, there was, however, no mention of the Oriental Printing Company, and the subscription was changed from £1 to "adequate intelligence." Ten issues later the subscription was changed again, to "the condition of Humanity" (*sharṭ-i Ādamīyat*), an allusion to the League of Humanity (*Majmaʿ-i Ādamīyat*) that had come into being as a successor to the farāmūshkhāna. In number twenty-three the price reverted to "adequate intelligence," but only two issues later a monetary subscription was demanded, one toman. By number thirty-four, Malkum evidently felt the need for change again, and he required of his readers only "an atom of awareness" (*yek dharra shuʿūr*). This new formula was maintained only for two issues before being replaced by "the trouble of passing it on to another Man [*i.e.*, a member of the League of Humanity]." It is probable that *Qānūn* was throughout distributed free of charge, for Malkum was only too anxious for its contents to be as widely read as possible.[22] He took care to send unbidden at least the early issues to some of his highly-placed acquaintances in Tehran, many of whom proved reluctant recipients. His boast that some issues were selling for ten tomans may nonetheless be justified:[23] in view of the extraordinary popularity that *Qānūn* enjoyed, it is conceivable that scarce back numbers should have fetched high prices.

Qānūn began as a monthly publication and seems to have maintained this frequency of appearance until the spring of 1892, when the movement against the notorious tobacco concession granted by Nāṣir

---

examples of its use in this sense, see verses of Şinasi, Tevfik Fikret, Abdülhakk Hâmit, and others quoted in Hüseyin Kâzım Kadri, *Büyük Türk Lugatı* (Istanbul, 1943), III: 755.

21. Numbers two to nine also carried the title transcribed as "Kanoun" and translated as "The Law" on the top of the back page.

22. Browne, *op. cit.* (n. 5, above), p. 13.

23. *Qānūn*, no. 26, p. 1.

ud-Dīn Shāh came to a successful end. The journal thereafter became increasingly sporadic, and it seems that as much as two or three months elapsed between issues on occasions. In the six years between 1892 and 1898, not more than twenty-two issues appeared, the last number of *Qānūn* appearing late in 1898. Only the first six numbers of the journal were dated, the last of them bearing the date of Dhūl Ḥijja 1, 1307/ July 18, 1890. Malkum at this point doubtless realized the pointlessness of dating the issues of *Qānūn*. His journal was, we have suggested, more of a periodical propaganda sheet than a newspaper in the narrower sense. Topical references were few, and as long as the persons and system of government under attack remained in power, each issue retained its freshness and relevance. It is thus comprehensible that a repeated demand arose for back numbers which had to be met by a reprinting of early issues.[24] Censorship, moreover, made it necessary to resort to devious means of distribution, and months might pass before a new issue arrived in the readers' hands. Malkum was conscious of this, and he wrote, with his usual skill at turning necessity into virtue:

> The wise ones of Tehran seem to think they are extirpating the very names of *Qānūn* and Humanity from Iran, and they still imagine that *Qānūn* is a newspaper the contents of which become useless and outdated if it fails to arrive by post. They have not yet realised that if *Qānūn* comes by post or muleteer, today or next year, its contents will always be fresh.[25]

In order to stress its orthodox nature, Malkum opened the first issue of *Qānūn* with the *basmala* and a prayer in Arabic asking that God make of the paper a means for guiding the believers on the straight path of justice and righteousness. After this pious preamble, Malkum produced the first of the many fabrications that were to fill the pages of *Qānūn*:

> For several reasons, a large number of Iranians have left their customary homeland and become scattered abroad. Among these emigrants, those enlightened persons who have compared the progress of foreign countries with the state of Iran have for many years been wondering how they might render some assistance to their luckless compatriots. After much thought and investigation they have agreed that there is no better means for the salvation and advancement of the people of Iran than a free newspaper. These few patriots, who are aware of the significance and the potentialities of a newspaper, have been traveling all over the world these past four or five years and have collected, by earnest requests and begging, substantial funds from all the friends of Iranian progress. With the help of God, they have recently established a respectable company with the blessed purpose of publishing news-

24. *Qānūn*, no. 13, p. 3; no. 17, p. 4.
25. *Qānūn*, no. 14, p. 2. See too Hatāmi, *op. cit.* (n. 9, above), p. 82.

papers and useful pamphlets and sending them to every corner of Iran. One of their publications is this newspaper, *Qānūn*.[26]

In order to strengthen the pretence that *Qānūn* was a collective enterprise, Malkum advertised in early issues for reporters and correspondents who would receive a salary for their troubles.[27] Whether there was any response to this plea, apart from that of Mīrzā Āqā Khān Kirmānī,[28] is unknown, but it is certain that virtually every word of *Qānūn* was the work of Malkum, and the request for collaborators cannot have been seriously intended. Few of the suggestions made by Mīrzā Āqā Khān Kirmānī were ever adopted by Malkum.

The publishing company allegedly established by Iranian émigrés existed only in Malkum's imagination. *Qānūn* was throughout an individual venture undertaken exclusively by Malkum, and each number, in style, content, and technique, bears his unmistakable stamp and closely resembles his various treatises. His reasons for concealing himself behind a fictitious company are not far to seek. Many in Iran had doubtless heard of the lottery affair and would have been unlikely to take seriously his continued professions of concern for reformed and honest government. The fiction of a publishing company, and the omission of all mention of his own name, enabled him to hide his desire for revenge on Amīn us-Sulṭān behind a show of patriotic endeavor. Malkum also hoped to present *Qānūn* as the mouthpiece of the Iranian mercantile communities abroad and thereby to gain a wider and more attentive hearing than might have been accorded an individual.

The newspaper was published from London where Malkum was known to be, and it was therefore inevitable that he should at least be suspected of some connection with it. He thus deemed it expedient to announce in number ten of *Qānūn* that the London office of the newspaper had been closed down and that henceforth all correspondence should be directed to the representatives of *Qānūn* in Baghdad, Bombay, and Ashkhabad.[29] In reality, of course, the newspaper continued to be published from London, and it is unlikely that *Qānūn* had any regular correspondent in these cities. Evidently this stratagem did not suffice to allay all doubts, for Malkum sought to evade the whole question of authorship by claiming for *Qānūn* the status of a kind of popular oracle: it was quite unimportant to know where and by whom *Qānūn* was published.[30] In number sixteen he wrote with typical glibness:

> Some superficial persons really imagine that someone abroad writes these pages. . . . The name of the writer of these matters is the people of Iran. The

26. *Qānūn*, no. 1, pp. 1–2.
27. *Qānūn*, no. 1, pp. 5, 8; no. 3, p. 4; no. 6, p. 4.
28. See below, p. 216.
29. *Qānūn*, no. 10, p. 3.
30. *Qānūn*, no. 11, p. 2.

> spark of these words proceeds from the burning heart of all classes in Iran. In every corner of Iran, from whatever grave you unearth, you will hear that same cry which the spirit of Humanity broadcasts through these pages of *Qānūn*.[31]

It was not until number twenty-eight, published probably in 1896, that Malkum saw fit to mention his own name in *Qānūn*, and when he did so it was in obscure and deliberately misleading terms.[32]

Having given an account of the fictitious company responsible for *Qānūn*, Malkum proceeded, in the first issue, to explain the title chosen for the newspaper, with an exposition of the evils of lawlessness and tyranny. The insecurity resulting from the absence of law threatens even persons of exalted rank such as ulama and princes, and even the just and noble disposition of the monarch cannot offset the evil.[33] This theme is familiar from Malkum's treatises, as are most of his comments on the state of Iran and the remedies that need to be applied. It would then be tedious to pursue them from issue to issue of his propaganda sheet.

Of greater novelty and possibly, too, effectiveness, was his technique of printing totally fictitious correspondence in *Qānūn*. Already employed in the first issue, it was used extensively throughout the lifetime of *Qānūn*, and sometimes varied with accounts of imaginary meetings between unnamed persons of prominent rank. Use of this technique had many advantages. It implied that *Qānūn* was functioning as a conventional newspaper, receiving and publishing readers' letters, even if their names were withheld for obvious reasons. Malkum was also able to place his comments on the Iranian situation into the mouths of a wide variety of anonymous princes, government officials, and army commanders, thus implying that the views expressed in *Qānūn* had widespread support among these important classes. To a degree, this was true, but Malkum hoped in addition to create panic and confusion in Tehran with the suggestion that a large number of highly placed men secretly supported him. He may well have expected also that the "letters" appearing in *Qānūn* would be taken at their face value and attempts made to discover their authors. Malkum had been well schooled in the intrigue and suspicion of Iranian political life, and his anticipations were at least partially met by the series of arrests ordered by Nāṣir ud-Dīn Shāh of real and imagined supporters of *Qānūn*.[34]

There were several classes of fictitious correspondent whose letters appeared with particular regularity. Supposed communications from mullas furnished one means of proving the religiosity of *Qānūn*.[35] An-

31. *Qānūn*, no. 16, p. 2.
32. See below, p. 233.
33. *Qānūn*, no. 1, pp. 2–3.
34. See below, pp. 203–205.
35. *Qānūn*, no. 4, p. 3; no. 8, pp. 1, 4; no. 19, p. 1; no. 22, p. 3; no. 23, p. 3; no. 37, p. 3.

other group was formed by army officers and commanders, who complained at the sale of positions to totally worthless individuals and at the nonpayment of their salaries. It was hinted that patience was fast being exhausted and that guns might soon be turned against the state.[36] Princes lamented their abject and unworthy condition, which derived from the general insecurity and more particularly from the policies of Amīn us-Sulṭān.[37] Government clerks, ministers, and officials denounced the impecunity and corruption of the administration[38] and merchants the extortionate taxation to which they were subject.[39] Finally, the authority of unnamed foreign ambassadors and travelers was invoked in fictitious reports and communications.[40]

In addition to letters from anonymous members of these classes, Malkum included in *Qānūn* explicit and laudatory reference to various enemies of Amīn us-Sulṭān. Thus, Kāmrān Mīrzā Nā'ib us-Salṭana received favorable mention in early issues, although ironically enough he was later responsible for the arrest of those in Tehran thought to be associated with *Qānūn*.[41] Ẓill us-Sulṭān was praised for his devotion to the throne and competence and his fall from power lamented and ascribed to the hostility of Amīn us-Sulṭān.[42]

Malkum preferred, however, direct and even abusive attack on Amīn us-Sulṭān as a more satisfactory means of revenge. The man who before the lottery affair had been that ideal minister of whom Malkum had dreamt for forty years was now commonly referred to as the "water-carrier-in-chief [*ābdārbāshī*]," and thus painfully reminded of his family's lowly origin. He was held to have transformed the seat of the premiership into an *ābdārkhāna*.[43] Alternatively, he was designated as the "son of a muleteer."[44]

It seems that Malkum was hoping by these insults to obtain some concession from Amīn us-Sulṭān, possibly reinstatement in the London embassy or restoration of the lottery concession. In a letter addressed to Amīn us-Sulṭān in 1892, Malkum theatened him with the publication of unspecified libelous material in *Qānūn* unless certain demands were carried out.[45] The threat was repeated in the columns of *Qānūn*,[46] but

36. *Qānūn*, no. 1, p. 5; no. 14, p. 1; no. 15, p. 3; no. 20, pp. 3–4; no. 37, pp. 3–4.

37. *Qānūn*, no. 10, p. 2; no. 14, pp. 1–2; no. 37, p. 3.

38. *Qānūn*, no. 4, p. 3; no. 10, p. 1; no. 14, p. 2; no. 20, p. 4; no. 22, pp. 1–2; no. 37, p. 2.

39. *Qānūn*, no. 4, p. 3; no. 14, p. 3.

40. *Qānūn*, no. 1, p. 7; no. 5, p. 3.

41. *Qānūn*, no. 1, p. 6.

42. *Qānūn*, no. 2, p. 1.

43. *Qānūn*, no. 10, p. 1; no. 14, pp. 2–4. See too pp. 301–303 below.

44. *Qānūn*, no. 8, p. 3.

45. Malkum to Amīn us-Sulṭān, September 20, 1892, quoted by Ibrāhīm Ṣafā'ī, *Asnād-i Siyāsī-yi Daurān-i Qajārīya* (Tehran, 1346 solar/ 1967), p. 309. Somewhat incongruously, Malkum signed the letter as "your well-wisher." The threats evidently

never fulfilled, probably because Malkum would have inevitably incriminated himself with any revelations made concerning Amīn us-Sulṭān. Open abuse of the minister gradually disappeared from the pages of *Qānūn*, possibly at the urging of Mīrzā Āqā Khān Kirmānī.[47]

Malkum indulged himself more freely in violent abuse of Amīn us-Sulṭān in a piece entitled *Uṣūl-i Madhhab-i Dīvānīān* (Principles of religion for government officials), not published in *Qānūn* but probably composed some time in 1892.[48] A few passages from the opening section of the piece deserve quotation as a specimen of Malkum's satirical talent at its most unrestrained:

> For what purpose has the Lord of the world created the land and people of Iran? So that a few irreligious scoundrels might enjoy themselves. What is the blessed name of these scoundrels? The trustees of the exalted Iranian state. By virtue of what accomplishment have these noble trustees gained such a privilege? By virtue of the fact that they have made Iran poorer, more wretched and desolate than any other place in the world. What virtues must they possess to proceed with their sacred mission?
>
> First, they must not be ashamed of any disgraceful matter. Second, they must sincerely and faithfully be the enemies of learning and the promoters of the utmost vileness [literally, cuckoldry]. Third, they must attain a point of disinterestedness where they can equitably choose as the first among them that villain who by virtue of his innate despicability and lunacy is to be preferred to the rest of them [i.e., Amīn us-Sulṭān]. What is to be the task of that blessed personage?
>
> All honorable and enlightened persons in the kingdom he must vilify and humiliate and persecute with every kind of atrocity. He must put to work around the throne all his brothers, relatives and hangers-on, in particular the least worthy among them, and gather into his own hands all the necessities of the life of the king, in such manner that that auspicious person cannot take a step or even breathe without his permission.[49]

By contrast with this tirade against Amīn us-Sulṭān, Malkum strove persistently to avoid direct criticism of Nāṣir ud-Dīn Shāh. This was doubtless in part because he hoped for a reconciliation and return to favor and in part too because he realized that public opinion in Iran

---

had been continuing for some time; see the dispatch of Kennedy, British minister in Tehran, to Lord Salisbury, dated April 3, 1891, in F.O. 60/120.

46. *Qānūn*, no. 14, p. 2. See too p. 304 below.

47. See his letter to Malkum dated Rabīᶜ uth-Thānī 12, 1307/December 21, 1890, in Supplément Persan, 1989, ff. 61–62. See too Muḥammad Ḥasan Khān Iᶜtimād us-Salṭana, *Rūznāma-yi Khāṭirāt*, ed. Īraj Afshār (Tehran, 1345 solar/1967), p. 1028, where he remarks favorably on the disappearance of abuse from the columns of *Qānūn*.

48. *Kullīyāt-i Malkum*, pp. 253–260.

49. *Ibid.*, pp. 253–254.

was not yet prepared for an attack on the monarch. The publication of *Qānūn* was presented, somewhat implausibly, as an endeavor to realize his desires, and Malkum even offered to stop publication of the journal if it should fail to meet with the shah's approval.[50] This offer was purely formal, for when Nāṣir ud-Dīn Shāh's unmistakable disapproval became apparent, publication went on uninterrupted. The monarch was depicted throughout as innocent of all blame for the evils that beset the country, and he was still credited, as in Malkum's first treatises more than thirty years before, with a just disposition and a sincere desire for progress and reform.[51] Speeches and declarations on the necessity of law and governmental reorganization were attributed to him which in all probability he never uttered.[52] It was exclusively ministers and courtiers, above all Amīn us-Sulṭān, who were responsible for the frustration of the shah's intentions.[53]

Yet in general Malkum's references to Nāṣir ud-Dīn Shāh in the pages of *Qānūn* had a far from flattering effect. He depicted him as powerless and humiliated, totally subject to the dictates of Amīn us-Sulṭān, and ruler in name alone. Thus, in number fourteen of *Qānūn*, Malkum wrote that the shah "trembles night and day in fear, is surrounded by executioners, and has more difficulty in supporting his family than his humblest servant." In the same issue, a "high-minded prince" declared that "our monarch is tired and imprisoned in his *ābdārkhāna*. It is as if he has abdicated and handed Iran over to these vicious rogues."[54] Malkum presumably hoped by this means to arouse Nāṣir ud-Dīn Shāh's anger and resentment to the point of dismissing Amīn us-Sulṭān and thereby avenging him. He miscalculated, however. The shah was gravely insulted and more enraged with Malkum than ever. The insults that were directed against Amīn us-Sulṭān he took to be meant for himself, and the references to his love of justice and progress were incapable of assuaging his anger.[55]

In the first number of *Qānūn*, Malkum happily predicted the impact of his journal on Iran in a fictitious letter, allegedly received from Tehran.

50. *Qānūn*, no. 4, p. 2; Mulkārā, *op. cit.* (n. 17, above), p. 110.

51. *Qānūn*, no. 1, p. 2.

52. *Qānūn*, no. 1, pp. 3–4; no. 3, p. 1.

53. *Qānūn*, no. 10, p. 1; no. 17, p. 1; no. 22, p. 4.

54. *Qānūn*, no. 14, pp. 2–3.

55. See Mīrzā ʿAlī Khān Amīn ud-Daula, *Khāṭirāt-i Siyāsī*, ed. Ḥāfiẓ Farmānfarmāʾīān (Tehran, 1341 solar/1962), p. 147. Nāṣir ud-Dīn Shāh, it seems, was particularly offended by Malkum's references to the princes and thought that he was attempting to turn his family against him. See undated letter of Mīrzā Āqā Khān Kirmānī to Malkum in Supplément Persan, 1996, ff. 78–79.

> An intelligent youth who is informed of the plans of this newspaper writes from Tehran: "As soon as the chief minister sees *Qānūn*, he will jump up half a yard in the air, throw his hat to the ground, tear his collar and after fuming and fretting like a woman he will run up to the foreign ambassadors, kiss their hands and feet, and pawn with their excellencies any remaining rights of the Iranian people so that the newspaper *Qānūn* may be proscribed."

To this Malkum replied: "So much the better. In Iran a newspaper that is not proscribed is meaningless. The greater severity they display, the greater will be the importance of the journal's contents, and the more eager will the Iranian people be to acquire this prescription for salvation."[56]

Despite his miscalculation of the shah's reaction, Malkum's forecast of the disruption that would be caused in Tehran by *Qānūn* proved otherwise accurate. The inevitable proscription came and with it popularity. The first issues of the newspaper appear to have reached Tehran in May 1890. Copies were sent by Malkum to various ministers, presumably in order to render them suspect to Amīn us-Sulṭān and thus narrow the basis of his support.[57] Among these reluctant recipients of *Qānūn* was Iᶜtimād us-Salṭana, the minister of publications. On the arrival of the first number of *Qānūn*, he went to see Amīn ud-Daula, whom he knew to be a confidant of Malkum, and asked him for information on Malkum's intentions. Amīn ud-Daula professed ignorance to his visitor and advised him not to mention the matter to the shah.[58]

Amīn ud-Daula's first reaction to *Qānūn* was negative. He thought that Nāṣir ud-Dīn Shāh was about to dismiss Amīn us-Sulṭān and that the appearance of *Qānūn* would cause him to hesitate for fear of apparently bowing to Malkum's wishes. It would be far better to communicate discreetly with the shah himself, apologizing for the lottery affair, and assuring him that he was constantly grateful for the favors he had received. It had been a mistake to hold Amīn us-Sulṭān responsible for his dismissal from the embassy, for this implied that the shah's power was not absolute and therefore offended him.[59]

Commonly known to be among the closest associates of Malkum, Amīn ud-Daula was placed in a position of extreme difficulty by the appearance of *Qānūn*. He was henceforth obliged to conceal his sym-

56. *Qānūn*, no. 1, p. 3.

57. Mulkārā, *op. cit.* (n. 17, above), p. 110. See too Malkum's statement in *Qānūn*, no. 1, p. 8, no. 2, p. 4.

58. See Amīn ud-Daula to Malkum, August 11, 1890, in Supplément Persan, 1997, f. 109.

59. *Ibid.*

pathies for Malkum (which had evidently survived the lottery episode) in order to keep some influence and even to remain alive, but the claims of friendship could not permit him to break off correspondence with Malkum. Already with the circulation of the first issue of *Qānūn,* he thought it best to assure the shah that he did not agree with Malkum's attribution of supreme power to Amīn us-Sulṭān,[60] and such dissimulation became increasingly necessary. In these circumstances Amīn ud-Daula begged Malkum for some guidance and above all for a clear statement of his aims: "I beg you, write in your own hand and tell me what I am to do in future. If you wish again to hide your real aim and intention, and do not tell me what I am to do, I shall be disgraced in front of God and man."[61] Malkum's answer was evidently satisfactory, for in subsequent letters Amīn ud-Daula no longer criticized the publication of *Qānūn* and instead informed Malkum of the useful influence it had exerted on various individuals.[62]

The ambiguity of Amīn ud-Daula's position is apparent from a letter to Malkum dated Dhūl Ḥijja 6, 1307/July 24, 1890, in which he relates the contents of a communication to the shah. His difficulties arose not only from a conflict between public and private loyalties, but also from the fact that he was minister of posts and therefore responsible for enforcing the ban on *Qānūn*'s entry into Iran. On receiving instructions to make sure that no copy of *Qānūn* arrived by post, Amīn ud-Daula therefore promised to write to all border posts and require that all incoming newspapers be sent to him unless the destined recipient had special permission. He could not guarantee, however, that copies of *Qānūn* would not pass through undetected if enclosed in ordinary letters. The only effective means for suppressing *Qānūn* would, he suggested, be the silencing of its author. All this he passed on to Malkum, together with a promise to inform him of any new measures taken to prevent the entry of *Qānūn* into Iran.[63]

It is thus comprehensible that *Qānūn* continued to circulate with increasing popularity.[64] Not until almost a year after the first issue had appeared did Nāṣir ud-Dīn Shāh begin to show extreme anxiety. This increase in concern derived largely from the critical situation that was developing within Iran. Discontent at the oppressiveness and corruption of Qajar rule and in particular resentment at the flow of economic concessions to foreigners were creating the beginnings of the movement that culminated in the Constitutional Revolution, with its combination of

60. *Ibid.*
61. *Ibid.*
62. Amīn ud-Daula to Malkum (n.d.), Supplément Persan, 1997, f. 120.
63. *Ibid.*, f. 127.
64. Mulkārā, *op. cit.* (n. 17, above), p. 111.

democratic and nationalist motivation. In 1890, as the early numbers of *Qānūn* were appearing in London, the forces of discontent had been powerfully quickened by the visit to Tehran of that turbulent and enigmatic figure, Sayyid Jamāl ud-Dīn Asadābādī, commonly known as Afghānī.

The life and ideas of Jamāl ud-Dīn have only recently been subjected to careful analysis,[65] and it now seems certain that he was of Iranian, not Afghan, birth, despite his proclamations to the contrary. After wanderings in Afghanistan, India, Turkey, Egypt, and Europe, he paid a return visit to the land of his birth in 1886. While in Bushire he received an invitation to the capital from Nāṣir ud-Dīn Shāh, ostensibly to produce a newspaper under his patronage. Soon, however, he was transformed from welcome guest to suspect agitator. In his first audience with Nāṣir ud-Dīn Shāh he spoke openly of the need for reform and offered his own services for the purpose: "I am like a sharp sword in your hands, do not leave me idle. Put me to any great task, or to work against any government. I am sharper than a sword."[66] Taken aback at such violence of expression, Nāṣir ud-Dīn Shāh declined to receive the Sayyid again and instructed his host in Tehran, Ḥājj Muḥammad Iṣfahānī Amīn-i Ḍarb, to restrict his movements in the capital as much as possible. Ultimately, early in 1887, he was persuaded to leave Iran for Russia.[67]

Nearly three years later the Sayyid was back in Iran, having met Nāṣir ud-Dīn Shāh in Munich during his third European trip and apparently effected a reconciliation. Again, however, he was regarded with disfavor, both by the shah and Amīn us-Sulṭān, and his host's residence became a center of attraction for various discontented and oppositional elements. Among those who established contact with him were men who had been associated with Malkum and his farāmūshkhāna, such as Sayyid Ṣādiq Ṭabāṭabāʾī,[68] Shaykh Hādī Najmābādī,[69] and Amīn ud-Daula,[70] as well as numerous others. Disturbed at the agitation Jamāl

65. See Elie Kedourie, *Afghani and ʿAbduh: An Essay on Religious Unbelief and Political Activism in Modern Islam* (London, 1966); and N. R. Keddie, *An Islamic Response to Imperialism: Political and Religious Writings of Sayyid Jamal ad-Din "al-Afghani"* (Berkeley and Los Angeles, 1968). Although some of the points raised in these two works are not perhaps as conclusive as they are presented to be, the general thesis of Afghani's unbelief seems firmly established.

66. Mulkārā, *op. cit.*, p. 112.

67. Amīn ud-Daula, *Khāṭirāt-i Siyāsī*, ed. Ḥāfiẓ Farmānfarmāyān (Tehran, 1341 solar/1962), p. 129.

68. Nāẓim ul-Islām Kirmānī, *Tārīkh-i Bīdārī-yi Īrānīān* (Tehran, n.d.), p. 49.

69. Murtaḍā Mudarris Chahārdihī, *Zindagānī va Falsafa-yi Sayyid Jamāl ud-Dīn-i Afghānī* (Tehran, 1334 solar/1955), p. 65.

70. For Amīn ud-Daula's estimate of Jamāl ud-Dīn, see his *Khāṭirāt-i Siyāsī*, p. 130.

ud-Dīn was conducting, Nāṣir ud-Dīn Shāh ordered preparations to be made to seize him at Amīn-i Ḍarb's house and then to expel him from Iran. The Sayyid was alerted in time and took refuge at the shrine of Shāh ᶜAbd ulᶜAẓīm to the south of Tehran. Yet even there he was not safe: the sanctity of the shrine was disregarded, and Jamāl ud-Dīn was abruptly and humiliatingly transported to Kirmānshāh.[71] Early in February 1891, he was put over the frontier into Arab Iraq, much as Malkum had been thirty years earlier.

With the threat of Jamāl ud-Dīn apparently banished from the scene, Nāṣir ud-Dīn Shāh turned to the problem of *Qānūn*. As Amīn ud-Daula had suggested, the most effective measure would clearly be the suppression of the newspaper in London, and this Nāṣir ud-Dīn Shāh requested from Kennedy, the British minister. He reported to his superiors in London:

> The Shah, who has been thrown by Malkom [*sic*] Khan into one of those paroxysms of irritation and alarm to which His Majesty is liable when he makes any discoveries which seem to threaten, either externally or internally, his sovereign power and authority, specifically asked that Her Majesty's Government would take steps to expel Malkom Khan from London and to suppress his newspaper.[72]

His request was not fulfilled, and he had therefore to content himself with attempts at stopping the circulation of the paper within Iran.

On March 4, 1891, he summoned a meeting consisting of Amīn us-Sulṭān, Amīn ud-Daula, Iᶜtimād us-Salṭana, and his other ministers. Iᶜtimād us-Salṭana had just received the seventh issue of *Qānūn* and dutifully passed it on to the shah. He inquired of the collected notables how it was still possible for *Qānūn* to reach Iran, despite its prohibition. Amīn us-Sulṭān and his supporters took this inquiry as a suitable occasion for attacking Amīn ud-Daula and accusing him of negligence in enforcing the ban, a charge that was probably justified. Only Iᶜtimād us-Salṭana spoke up in his defence, pointing out that even the despotic government of Russia had been unable to prevent nihilist journals from entering the country. A more stringent effort to suppress *Qānūn* was demanded; the shah denounced Malkum and all who might correspond with him as traitors; and the meeting was closed.[73]

Amīn ud-Daula, although facing a long period of fear and insecurity, had survived his most difficult test, but another associate of

71. *Ibid.*, p. 144.

72. Dispatch of Kennedy to Salisbury dated March 10, 1891, in F.O. 60/522. See also R. L. Greaves, *Persia and the Defence of India* (London, 1959), p. 186.

73. Iᶜtimād us-Salṭana, *op. cit.* (n. 47, above), p. 843, entry for Rajab 23, 1308/March 4, 1891, and Kennedy's dispatch of March 10.

Malkum lost his post on the day of this meeting. This was Ḥājjī Muḥsin Khān Muᶜīn ul-Mulk, ambassador in Istanbul.[74] His recall occasioned a minor diplomatic crisis, for Muᶜīn ul-Mulk had established good relations with Sultan ᶜAbd ul-Ḥamīd who now sought to intercede with the shah on his behalf. This foreign intervention made Nāṣir ud-Dīn Shāh only more adamant and Muᶜīn ul-Mulk was obliged to leave Istanbul.[75]

Now that the shah's fear had been aroused, Amīn us-Sulṭān decided to avail himself of the opportunity in an attempt to make a clean sweep of his enemies.[76] It was here that Malkum's miscalculation became evident: *Qānūn* was proving of greater benefit than harm to his adversary. Toward the end of April 1891, threatening letters written from the provinces began to arrive in the capital, denouncing Amīn us-Sulṭān and by implication the shah as well. Some of these letters were found even in the royal palace, and a meeting was summoned to discuss them. Amīn us-Sulṭān declared that Malkum and his followers were responsible for the offensive letters, and despite discreet attempts at contradiction by Amīn ud-Daula, the shah accepted his claims as true. He demanded that a list of Malkum's followers in Tehran be drawn up, and a series of arrests began.[77]

Among the first to be arrested was Mīrzā Muḥammad ᶜAlī Khān Farīd ul-Mulk, formerly secretary to Malkum at the embassy in London. An article was found among his papers which, it was claimed, was intended for publication in *Qānūn*. Mīrzā Muḥammad ᶜAlī denied authorship of the piece, which he said had been transcribed by one Sayyid Valī from an original composed by Mīrzā Dhakā ul-Mulk Furūghī, a former member of the farāmūshkhāna. He was nonetheless imprisoned in the house of Nāʾib us-Salṭana, while Furūghī took to flight.[78]

A dozen other persons identified as supporters of Malkum were also arrested, among them Ḥājj Sayyāḥ Maḥallātī, an acquaintance of Jamāl ud-Dīn,[79] Mīrzā Naṣrullāh Khān, later minister of foreign affairs,[80] and a certain Dāvīd Khān, accused of distributing *Qānūn* in Tehran.[81] After

74. Iᶜtimād us-Salṭana, *op. cit.*, p. 843; Amīn ud-Daula, *op. cit.*, p. 148; *Qānūn*, no. 16, p. 1.

75. See Mīrzā Āqā Khān Kirmānī to Malkum (n.d.), in Supplément Persan, 1996, ff. 81–82.

76. *Ibid.*

77. Iᶜtimād us-Salṭana, *op. cit.*, pp. 854–855, entry for Ramaḍān 13, 1308/April 22, 1891.

78. *Ibid.*; Amīn ud-Daula, *op. cit.*, p. 154. On Furūghī's relations with Malkum, see the note of Mīrzā Muḥammad Qazvīnī in E. G. Browne, *The Persian Revolution of 1905–1909* (Cambridge, 1910), p. 405.

79. Mulkārā, *op. cit.* (n. 17, above), p. 111.

80. See Mīrzā Āqā Khān Kirmānī to Malkum (n.d.), in Supplément Persan, 1996, ff. 125–126.

81. Hāshimī, *op. cit.* (n. 5, above), IV; 99.

a period of incarceration in the residence of Nā'ib us-Salṭana, they were transferred under armed escort to Qazvin where they were detained for a further six months.

In Qazvin they were joined by the most prominent victim of the wave of arrests, Mīrzā Yūsuf Khān Mustashār ud-Daula, the author of *Yak Kalima.* His reformist views and in particular his espousal of the necessity of law made it almost inevitable that he should be seized as an accomplice and supporter of Malkum. At the time of his arrest he was living in Tabriz, whence he was taken to Qazvin in a brutal fashion that weakened his already unsteady health.[82]

One of Malkum's brothers, Iskandar Khān, was in Iran in 1891 (there is no trace of Mikā'īl at this time), but he had the good fortune to be exiled to Russia instead of facing the rigors of imprisonment. Nonetheless, like Mīrzā Yūsuf Khān, he was seriously ill at the time of his banishment, and it was some time before he recovered from the violent treatment he received en route to the frontier.[83]

Amīn ud-Daula was by now in constant fear, for as a correspondent of Malkum he was, according to the shah's definition, a traitor. Amīn us-Sulṭān was, it seems, trying to obtain his banishment to Khorasan, and in this he enjoyed the support of the British minister. As a precaution against his letters from Malkum being opened, Amīn ud-Daula asked that he should henceforth write in code.[84]

Although most of those arrested had some connection with Malkum and *Qānūn,* it is nonetheless clear that Nāṣir ud-Dīn Shāh, encouraged by Amīn us-Sulṭān, was prone to see supporters of Malkum wherever the slightest hint of opposition or reformist tendency could be detected. Mere possession of a copy of *Qānūn* became a crime; and thus the harmless eccentric, Mīrzā Muḥammad Bavānātī, was hauled off to jail as a revolutionary.[85] A certain Muḥammad Khān, former governor of the town of Turshīz in Khorasan, was arrested and accused of being a friend of Malkum's because some foreign books were found in his house.[86] When by chance a consignment of grenades sent from England to a Russian subject by the name of Ḥaydar Khān was discovered in the post, Amīn us-Sulṭān and Nāṣir ud-Din Shāh immediately decided that

82. Mulkārā, *op. cit.,* p. 111; Iᶜtimād us-Salṭana, *op. cit.* (n. 47, above), p. 871 (entry for Dhūl Ḥijja 21, 1308/ July 28, 1891); Ādamīyat, *Fikr-i Āzādī,* pp. 183, 197.

83. Mulkārā, *op. cit.,* p. 111. See also Amīn ud-Daula to Malkum, Jumādī ul-Ukhrā 27, 1315/ November 23, 1897, in Supplément Persan, 1997, f. 133.

84. Amīn ud-Daula to Malkum, Ramaḍān 29 (1308?) in *ibid.,* ff. 106–107. See too ff. 118–119.

85. Browne, *op. cit.* (n. 5, above), p. 36.

86. Iᶜtimād us-Salṭana, *op. cit.* (n. 47, above), p. 1128 (entry for Jumādī ul-Ukhrā 5, 1312/December 4, 1894).

they could have come from none other than Malkum.[87] In this atmosphere of panic and suspicion, it is comprehensible that Iᶜtimād us-Salṭana who had formerly had some dealings with Malkum should have feared arrest and temporarily hidden himself from public view.[88]

This prevalence of suspicion was in part the result of Malkum's technique in the writing of *Qānūn*. Through the inclusion of fictitious correspondence from a wide variety of persons, he created the impression of a vast following in Iran. It might have been suspected that many, if not all, of the letters were forged, yet the widespread popularity of *Qānūn* at the time prevented any firm conclusion. Malkum did moreover have an organized following in Iran, the League of Humanity, the size and strength of which he was constantly proclaiming in the pages of *Qānūn*, in vague and suggestive terms intended to create fear and suspicion in Tehran. Finally, as the arrests were taking place in Iran, Malkum was known to have joined forces in London with the other hated agitator, Sayyid Jamāl ud-Dīn, and the worst was to be expected from their collaboration.

87. *Ibid.*, p. 959 (entry for Rabīᶜ uth-Thānī 11, 1310/November 2, 1892).
88. *Ibid.*, pp. 854–858 (entries for Ramaḍān 13–17, 1308/April 22–26, 1891).

CHAPTER 9

THE ASSOCIATION of Malkum and Jamāl ud-Dīn was only to be expected. Not only had their anger and resentment at the Iranian government been aroused at almost the same time, but there was much in their attitudes, characters, and personal circumstances that drew them together. Both were inordinately ambitious men whose acquisition of power was hindered by impatience and lack of restraint at crucial moments. Both had coupled their ambition to a less than totally sincere desire for reform and regeneration, and both were experienced in dissimulation: Malkum, of his true attitude toward religion, and Jamāl ud-Dīn, of his Iranian birth and origin. Both had been initiated into freemasonry, and both established pseudomasonic organizations of their own.[1] They had, too, certain acquaintances in common: in Istanbul, Münif Paşa;[2] in Iran, Amīn ud-Daula and Ẓill us-Sulṭān;[3] and in London, Wilfred Scawen Blunt.[4]

1. On Jamāl ud-Dīn's masonic activities in Egypt and France, see *Majmūᶜa-yi Asnād va Madārik-i Chāp Nashuda dar bāra-yi Sayyid Jamāl ud-Dīn-i Mashhūr ba Afghānī*, eds. A. Mahdavī and Īraj Afshār (Tehran, 1342 solar/ 1963), pp. 172–173; Ismāᶜīl Rāᵓīn, *Farāmūshkhāna va Frāmāsūnrī dar Īrān* (Tehran, 1347 solar/ 1968), I: 358 f.; and the forthcoming article by Sami Hanna to appear in the *Middle East Journal*. On the secret society founded by Jamāl ud-Dīn and his disciple Muḥammad ᶜAbduh, see Rashīd Riḍā, *Tārīkh al-Ustādh al-Imān ash-Shaykh Muḥammad ᶜAbduh* (Cairo, 1349 lunar/ 1930–1931), I: 284.

2. Niyazi Berkes, *The Development of Secularism in Turkey* (Montreal, 1964), p. 182.

3. Jamāl ud-Dīn had met Ẓill us-Sulṭān in Isfahan in 1886. The prince wanted him to gain Russian support for his claims to the succession. See Shaykh Luṭfullāh Khān, *Sharḥ-i Ḥāl va Āthār-i Sayyid Jamāl ud-Dīn-i Asadābādī Maᶜrūf ba Afghānī* (Tabriz, 1327 solar/1948), p. 98.

4. On Blunt's relations with Jamāl ud-Dīn, see numerous references in his *Diaries* (London, 1932).

Of particular importance for their collaboration were a certain utilitarian attitude toward religion, conceived of primarily, if not exclusively, as a social and political institution, and a willingness to make expedient appeal to religion for political purposes in the absence of personal belief. It has been noted that Malkum was pursuing a "material reformation" in Islamic guise and that he had to this end instituted the farāmūshkhāna and proclaimed the identity of Islamic and European legal concepts. Similar tactics were employed in the production of *Qānūn,* and much effort was spent on giving the journal an Islamic air. Thus in number five, he put forward the familiar equation of *qānūn* (law inspired by European models) and *sharīᶜa;*[5] and in another the "storehouse of the law" was proclaimed to be the "breasts of the ulama."[6] Islam was the source of all progress, Malkum declared, and the "Islam" he had in mind was a secularized one, emptied of all transcendental content and spiritual concern. He regarded Islam—and religion in general—as a question of social regulation, and the message of all the Prophets as bearing essentially on the problems of this world: "All that the Prophets proclaimed was for the sake of the strengthening and execution of law."[7]

> The mission of all the Prophets was propagation of this matter [law and just government]. In the Sacred Books there is not a single point which does not touch upon it. All the Immaculate Imams, the guides on the mystic path, the rightly guided philosophers, at all times and in all places, inwardly and outwardly have propagated the principles of just government.[8]

Malkum's purpose in declarations such as these was to mobilize religious sentiment behind his program of reform and, more specifically, to present himself as an heir of the Prophets and Imams in his strivings for the sake of law.

The attitudes of Sayyid Jamāl ud-Dīn, traditionally regarded as a hero of nineteenth-century Islam and the instigator of an Islamic renaissance, were by no means dissimilar. His concern with Islam was exclusively with the community, which he appears to have regarded as coterminous with the faith. Like Malkum, he saw religion as a social institution. While on his first visit to Istanbul in 1869, he proclaimed in a lecture—of which Malkum, being in Istanbul at the time, may have heard—that prophecy was a craft (*ṣanᶜat*) and that its aim, the intelligent regulation of human affairs, the same as that of philosophy.[9] The virtues

5. *Qānūn,* no. 5, p. 2.
6. *Qānūn,* no. 1, p. 2.
7. *Qānūn,* no. 2, p. 2.
8. "Taufīq-i Amānat," *Kullīyāt-i Malkum,* ed. Hāshim Rabīᶜzāda (Tabriz, 1325 lunar/1908), p. 219.
9. See Berkes, *op. cit.,* pp. 182–187.

ascribed to religion in Jamāl ud-Dīn's lengthiest and best-known work, *The Refutation of the Materialists*, are entirely social and utilitarian: religious belief is productive of social cohesion and vitality, whereas materialism (or various sects and movements identified as materialist) tend to subvert the virtues required for the prosperity of society.[10] As Malkum equated Islamic and Western concepts of law and government, so too did Jamāl ud-Dīn advise Shaykh Hādī Najmābādī to teach the principle of freedom by means of Qurʾānic exegesis, a proposal implying similarly deliberate confusion.[11]

Not only did both Malkum and Jamāl ud-Dīn deem it expedient to cloak aims fundamentally alien to Islam in Islamic guise, but they also found it essential to gain the support of the ulama in securing their attainment. In nineteenth-century Iran, the religious scholars enjoyed a power and influence that was probably unique in the contemporary Muslim world. Many reasons might be adduced, in particular the failure of the Qajars, unlike the Ottomans, to create a strong centralized state and the intermittent anarchy that largely destroyed secular authority in certain provinces. Probably of greater importance, however, was the function of the ulama as defined by Shiʿi *fiqh*: to be exemplary models of guidance in all matters of religious practice. In the absence of the Imam, they could lay no claim to ultimate authority, but still less could the monarch, who was in theory obliged to submit to their guidance and directives. His failure to do so rendered his government doubly illegitimate. Thus, throughout the Qajar period, state and ulama were in constant conflict, and an irreconcilable contradiction underlay the various episodes in which they confronted each other. The fact that much of ulama leadership was situated in the ʿatabāt, outside the frontiers of Iran, and was thus impervious to government control, further enhanced the political role of the ulama.[12] All these facts had to be taken into account by men such as Malkum and Jamāl ud-Dīn who sought to unsettle the regime in Iran.[13]

10. For a recent translation of the "Refutation of the Materialists" see N. R. Keddie, *An Islamic Response to Imperialism: Political and Religious Writings of Sayyid Jamāl ad-Dīn "al-Afghānī"* (Berkeley and Los Angeles, 1968), pp. 130–174.

11. Murtaḍā Mudarris Chahārdihī, *Zindagānī va Falsafa-yi Sayyid Jamāl ud-Dīn-i Afghānī* (Tehran, 1334 solar/1955), p. 65.

12. On the conflict between ulama and state in nineteenth-century Iran, see Hamid Algar, *Religion and State in Iran 1785–1906: The Role of the Ulama in the Qajar Period* (Berkeley and Los Angeles, 1969).

13. In *Qānūn* no. 26, p. 2, there is a brief passage which clearly demonstrates Malkum's appreciation of the importance of the clash between ulama and state: "According to the Shiʿi faith, the present regime in Iran is contrary to the principles of Islam and the shah is a usurper. In view of this religious tenet, Iran today has two governments: one legitimate, pertaining to the scholars of religion; and the other usurpatory, consisting of a band of oppressors."

Malkum's concern for a tactical alliance with the ulama had made itself apparent as early as the farāmūshkhāna episode and was now resumed with the publication of *Qānūn.* When a preacher by the name of Sayyid Fāḍil Darbandī was expelled from Tehran for denouncing the government, Malkum deplored the fact in *Qānūn* and called upon his supporters to assist Sayyid Fāḍil in any way they could.[14] In the following number, he made an appeal to all the ulama to speak out more openly against the corruption and tyranny of the government and to make use of the political potential he perceived in them:

> While the old women of the unbelievers bitterly lament the catastrophes of our fate, you who are the leaders of the people of God, the manifestation of divine beneficence, who are torches on the path of humanity and the best hope of the people of the world—how can you sit unconcerned in the midst of the storm of calamity which has encompassed the whole nation?[15]

Sayyid Jamāl ud-Dīn, while in Tehran, had also addressed himself to the ulama, attempting to arouse them against Nāṣir ud-Dīn Shāh and to intensify their opposition to the foreign interests that were encroaching on Iran's economic life. On his arrival in London, he was thus well prepared for cooperation with Malkum, both ideologically and tactically.

Already in number thirteen of *Qānūn,* Malkum had alluded to the expulsion of Sayyid Jamāl ud-Dīn as an example of lawlessness and tyranny.[16] Four issues later, he announced the Sayyid's arrival in London, in the summer of 1891:

> Why have the ministers of Tehran banished his excellency Sayyid Jamāl ud-Dīn from Iran in such a disgraceful manner that would not occur even to the vilest wretch?
>
> Because that profoundly learned one was inviting men to progress and propagating Humanity with a fervor that should be the model for the ulama of Iran.
>
> Where is he now?
>
> According to trustworthy reports, he has recently reached London in safety and there, having renewed his contacts with the great ones of the age, is sincerely occupied with service to Islam and with kindling the fire of Humanity in Iran.[17]

It is difficult to establish the precise manner and extent of Jamāl ud-Dīn's collaboration with Malkum, to discover exactly how he "was kindling the fire of Humanity."[18] By the "great ones of the age," Mal-

14. *Qānūn,* no. 8, pp. 3–4.
15. *Qānūn,* no. 9, p. 4.
16. *Qānūn,* no. 13, p. 2.
17. *Qānūn,* no. 17, p. 4.
18. Naẓar Āqā, Iranian minister in Vienna, in a dispatch to Tehran expressed

kum doubtless intended primarily himself, but the Sayyid did meet others while in London, including E. G. Browne.[19] Certain public lectures were also arranged.[20] Jamāl ud-Dīn, however, seems to have been occupied chiefly with producing printed propaganda for dispatch to Iran. This propaganda centered on the notorious tobacco concession.

Late in the spring of 1891, the tranquility of Nāṣir ud-Dīn Shāh and Amīn us-Sulṭān was gravely disturbed again. The Sayyid had been expelled and Malkum's followers arrested or dispersed. Yet now a far graver movement of popular protest arose, supported and directed by the ulama. On his third trip to Europe, Nāṣir ud-Dīn Shah had not only given Malkum the lottery concession but also sold to an English company a monopoly for the production and marketing of all Iranian tobacco. Preliminary negotiations were completed before the royal party left London, and agents of the monopoly began arriving in Iran in the spring of 1891. Opposition to their activities was almost immediate. Unlike previous concessions, the tobacco monopoly touched upon an article of almost universal daily use, and thus made the danger of foreign economic domination seem immediate and real. Disturbances began in May 1891 and were marked throughout by close cooperation between those most closely affected, the merchants, and the ulama.

Much of the effectiveness of the campaign against the tobacco concession derived from the pronouncements of a single mujtahid, Mīrzā Ḥasan Shīrāzī, resident in Samarra, who since the early 1870s had established himself as sole *marjaᶜ-i taqlīd,* that is, source of exemplary guidance in matters of practice. He had been preceded in this rank by Shaykh Murtaḍā Anṣārī (d. 1865), a man who had shunned all political involvement and who evidently was disinclined to make use of the political power inherent in his position.[21] Mīrzā Ḥasan Shīrāzī initially displayed a similar reluctance, but in the course of the agitation against the tobacco concession came to deliver a *fatvā* declaring the use of tobacco forbidden by religious law. His ruling was almost universally fol-

---

the opinion that the articles appearing in the Paris *L'Intransigeant* with Jamāl ud-Dīn's signature were in fact the work of Malkum. See Humā Nāṭiq, "Naẓar Āqā va Nāmahāʾī az Ū," *Rāhnamā-yi Kitāb,* XIII (1349 solar/1970): 58–59. Malkum's successor as Iranian envoy in London, ᶜAlā us-Salṭana, thought that Malkum and Jamāl ud-Dīn considered each other as rivals. "They do not like each other and mostly discuss the difference of their opinions. Still, as they know their objects to be of the same nature and are in a position and place that they require each other's approval they are mostly together." (Translation of his dispatch contained in F. O. 248/531).

19. E. G. Browne, *The Persian Revolution of 1905–1909* (Cambridge, 1910), p. 11.

20. See *The Queen,* November 28, 1891; *Pall Mall Gazette,* December 30, 1892; and Jamāl ud-Dīn Afghānī, "The Reign of Terror in Persia," *Contemporary Review,* LXI (1892): 238–248.

21. Concerning Anṣārī, see Algar, *op. cit.,* pp. 162–164.

lowed and resulted in a nationwide boycott of tobacco. Eventually, after a series of clashes in Tehran and numerous provincial cities, the concession was annulled early in 1892, and Mīrzā Ḥasan Shīrāzī lifted his prohibition.[22]

This type of political action by the ulama was much to the liking of both Malkum and Sayyid Jamāl ud-Dīn, and the latter, indeed, may have played some role in bringing Mīrzā Ḥasan Shīrāzī to abandon his political quietism. After his expulsion from Iran, the Sayyid wrote a letter from Basra to Mīrzā Ḥasan in Samarra, condemning Nāṣir ud-Dīn Shāh and Amīn us-Sulṭān for their impiety and the concessions granted to foreigners and urging him to use his authority to preserve the national interests of Iran. Before leaving Basra for Europe, he entrusted the letter to Sayyid ᶜAlī Akbar Fālasīrī, one of the ulama of Shiraz banished for his opposition to the tobacco monopoly and asked him to convey it to Mīrzā Ḥasan in Samarra.[23] Before leaving Basra he addressed another letter of similar content to the ulama of Iran.[24]

Upon reaching London, Jamāl ud-Dīn had numerous copies of these letters printed and forwarded to Iran, with the help of Malkum Khān.[25] Probably the same network of distribution that had been established for *Qānūn* was now entrusted with disseminating Jamāl ud-Dīn's exhortations.[26] At the same time the granting of the tobacco concession was denounced in *Qānūn*, somewhat incongruously: Amīn us-Sulṭān was accused of having sold the country to "some foreign Jews."[27] Malkum evidently had forgotten not only the lottery concession but also his role in promoting the Reuter Concession twenty years earlier. Before, the unlimited granting of privileges to foreign concessionaires had been presented as the first step in national development; now it was repugnant to both Islam and the national honor.

For Malkum and Jamāl ud-Dīn, the success of the tobacco boycott—a success in which they participated only marginally—represented a beginning that should have been followed by more comprehensive and

22. On the campaign against the tobacco concession, see Ibrāhīm Taymūrī, *Taḥrīm-ī Tanbākū ya Avvalīn Muqāvamat-i Manfī dar Īrān* (Tehran, 1328 solar/1949); N. R. Keddie, *Religion and Rebellion in Iran: The Tobacco Protest of 1891–1892* (London, 1966); and A.K.S. Lambton, "The Tobacco Régie: Prelude to Revolution," *Studia Islamica*, XXII (1965): 119–157.

23. Taymūrī, *op cit.*, pp. 53–57.

24. Mīrzā ᶜAlī Khān Amīn ud-Daula, *Khāṭirāt-i Siyāsī*, ed. Ḥāfiẓ Farmānfarmāyān (Tehran, 1341 solar/1962), p. 151.

25. See Amīn us-Sulṭān to Mīrzā Ḥasan Shīrāzī, Rajab 1309/February 1892, quoted by Ibrāhīm Ṣafāʾī, *Asnād-i Siyāsī-yi Daurān-i Qājārīya* (Tehran, 1346 solar/1967), p. 318.

26. Keddie, *Religion and Rebellion*, p. 52.

27. *Qānūn*, no. 23, p. 2. Presumably an allusion to Ornstein, director in Iran of the tobacco monopoly's operations.

ambitious exercise of Mīrzā Ḥasan's authority for political purposes. Their view was shared by Mīrzā Āqā Khān Kirmānī, another of Malkum's collaborators shortly to be discussed, who appears to have furnished some details of the policy applied in *Qānūn*. In a letter to Malkum he wrote the following:

> With well-chosen and clear expressions, either in the form of a proposal from someone or in more straightforward manner, pose this question: why should not one such as Ḥājjī Mīrzā Muḥammad Ḥasan Shīrāzī, whom today fifty million Shiʿis around the world regard as the vicar of the Imam, not be like the Pope of Italy [*sic*] and have ambassadors sent to him from all the governments of the world? Why should he be so obscure and unknown that even the governor of Samarra takes no account of him?[28]

This theme of Mīrzā Ḥasan Shīrāzī as a potential Shiʿi pope was taken up in *Qānūn* in words that betray Mīrzā Āqā Khān's influence: "Why should the spiritual leader of sixty million Shiʿis sit trembling and hidden in the corner of some outlandish village [i.e., Samarra]? Why should not the legitimate head of the community of God be superior to all worldly princes?"[29]

Similarly, number twenty of *Qānūn* contained what purported to be an appeal to the mujtahid from Iranians resident in the Ottoman Empire, urging him to turn the full weight of his authority against the regime in Tehran. The recent movement against the tobacco monopoly had demonstrated the latent power of Islam, but the target of the agitation had been a minor and secondary item. More important was the whole structure of tyranny and corruption which made possible the sale of the nation's rights to foreigners. It was the duty of the ulama and above all of Mīrzā Ḥasan Shīrāzī as sole *marjaʿ-i taqlīd* to proclaim that obedience to a tyrannical state was not a religious duty, contrary to the pretensions of the government. "Should the respected ulama declare tomorrow in the mosques of Iran that the execution of tyrannical commands is contrary to the spirit of Islam, destructive of universal order and deserving of the wrath of God, is there any oppressor who would not awaken in panic from his slumber of drunken pride?"[30]

This petition bears the usual imprint of Malkum's style and probably did not emanate from Iranian émigrés in the Ottoman Empire. It is

28. Mīrzā Āqā Khān to Malkum, ʿĪd ul-Fiṭr (no year), Bibliothèque Nationale, Supplément Persan, 1996, ff. 110–111. Mīrzā Ḥasan Shīrāzī was in fact the object of foreign political attention. After the cancellation of the tobacco concession he received a friendly letter from the tsar (Taymūrī, *op. cit.*, p. 204).

29. *Qānūn*, no. 29, p. 3. It is worth noting that Jamāl ud-Dīn also referred to Mīrzā Ḥasan Shīrāzī as "practically a Persian pope" ("The Reign of Terror in Persia," p. 246).

30. *Qānūn*, no. 20, pp. 1–2.

worth noting, however, that there were those in Istanbul who had drawn from the affair of the tobacco monopoly a conclusion similar to that reached by Malkum and Jamāl ud-Dīn: that Mīrzā Ḥasan's authority should be exploited for more radical purposes. Mīrzā Āqā Khān reported to Malkum from Istanbul:

> Some people here have had the idea of requesting from Mīrzā Ḥasan Shīrāzī a *fatvā* on some matter or other, and then transferring his seal photographically to another piece of paper, which shall say that the payment of taxes to these oppressive tyrants is forbidden and a great sin.[31]

Mīrzā Āqā Khān found the idea unacceptable, but its currency is interesting as an extreme example of the manner in which the political manipulation of religious authority was contemplated. That Malkum was attracted by the idea of a *fatvā* prohibiting the payment of taxes is attested by a passage in number twenty-nine of *Qānūn*.[32]

Worried by the overtures of Malkum and Jamāl ud-Dīn, direct and indirect, to Mīrzā Ḥasan Shīrāzī, Amīn us-Sulṭān wrote the mujtahid a warning letter, denouncing them both as dangerous and irreligious agitators. He condemned Malkum as an apostate and heretic (*zindīq*) and proceeded to give a fairly accurate summary of his career, with special emphasis on the farāmūshkhāna as an irreligious institution which had propagated sexual licence and proclaimed legal all that the *sharīʿa* forbade. As for Jamāl ud-Dīn who had now joined Malkum in London, his show of concern for Islam and the dignity of the ulama was totally false. He had "printed and published very dangerous newspapers condemning Shiʿism" and propagated Babism while in Afghanistan. These particular allegations were probably false and derived from Amīn us-Sulṭān's desire to depict the Sayyid in the blackest of heretical colors. The petition from Iranians living in the Ottoman Empire printed in *Qānūn* was, he continued, a forgery concocted by Malkum and Jamāl ud-Dīn. He concluded his letter by declaring that it was Mīrzā Ḥasan's duty to denounce the two so that they should no longer deceive both people and ulama.[33]

Mīrzā Ḥasan thus was being instructed of his "duty" from two quarters, London and Tehran. He responded, however, neither to the appeals of Malkum and Jamāl ud-Dīn nor to those of Amīn us-Sulṭān.

31. Mīrzā Āqā Khān to Malkum, ʿĪd ul-Fiṭr (no year), Supplément Persan, 1996, f. 111.

32. "If today a ruling were to be issued from that seat of sanctity [*i.e.*, the residence of Mīrzā Ḥasan Shīrāzī] to the effect that this oppressive regime must not be obeyed and that taxes must not be paid, no Muslim anywhere in Iran would disobey the order" (*Qānūn*, no. 29, p. 3).

33. Letter dated Rajab 1309/February 1892, quoted by Ṣafāʾī, *op. cit.*, pp. 314–318.

He was evidently unwilling to do the pleasure of the Tehran regime by denouncing those who at least circumstantially and temporarily were his allies, and he was equally reluctant to be impelled by Malkum and Jamāl ud-Dīn to more extreme action than he thought justified.[34] He did not proceed to initiate a campaign for the overthrow of the Qajar dynasty, and, although the campaign against the tobacco monopoly was in many ways the forerunner of the Constitutional Revolution, several years were still to pass before the ulama fulfilled the expectations of Malkum and Jamāl ud-Dīn.

Late in 1892, Jamāl ud-Dīn was invited by Sultan ᶜAbd ul-Ḥamīd to Istanbul to lend his energies to the Pan-Islamist cause. He appears to have doubted the wisdom of accepting the invitation, perhaps anticipating the restrictions to which he would be subject in Istanbul. Malkum is reputed to have encouraged him to go,[35] and Jamāl ud-Dīn, in optimistic mood during the first weeks of his residence in Istanbul, reciprocated by attempting to have Malkum appointed Ottoman minister of finance.[36] Soon, however, Jamāl ud-Dīn's activities were curtailed by ᶜAbd ul-Ḥamīd, his hopeful mood declined, and his contacts with Malkum appear to have diminished, if not ceased. Only their mutual friend, Mīrzā Āqā Khān Kirmānī, conveyed news of them to each other.[37] After the assassination of Nāṣir ud-Dīn Shāh in 1896 and the consequent extradition and execution of Mīrzā Āqā Khān Kirmānī in Tabriz, this channel of communication was removed, and it is likely that Malkum had no further contact with Jamāl ud-Dīn until the Sayyid's death in March 1897.

The paucity of relevant documents makes it difficult to estimate the exact nature and importance of Malkum's relationship with Jamāl ud-Dīn. As has been shown, they had much in common, in character and outlook. The circumstances of 1891 and 1892 brought them together in the pursuit of similar objectives and the employment of similar tactics. When their efforts to direct Mīrzā Ḥasan Shīrāzī to a radical political goal of their own choosing failed, they parted company again. More volatile than Malkum and with wider horizons of concern that embraced not only Iran but the entire Islamic Near East, Jamāl ud-Dīn

34. It is significant that after his arrival in Istanbul in 1892, Jamāl ud-Dīn published a pamphlet reproaching Mīrzā Ḥasan Shīrāzī for not using his authority to bring about the overthrow of Nāṣir ud-Dīn Shāh. See Yaḥyā Daulatābādī, *Tārīkh-i Muᶜāṣir yā Ḥayāt-i Yaḥyā* (Tehran, n.d.), I: 131.

35. Browne, *op. cit.* (n. 19, above), p. 82; Firīdūn Ādamīyat, *Andīshahā-yi Mīrzā Āqā Khān Kirmānī* (Tehran, 1346 solar/1967), p. 24.

36. Khān Malik Sāsānī, *Siyāsatgarān-i Daura-yi Qājār* (Tehran, 1338 solar/1959), I: 216. This may indicate that Malkum was still retaining Ottoman nationality.

37. See Mīrzā Āqā Khān's letters to Malkum in Supplément Persan, 1996, ff. 66–67, 69, 73, 74–75, 98, 111, 113.

left for new ventures in Istanbul, while Malkum continued to publish *Qānūn* from London and to hope for better times. Their association probably resulted in little exchange of ideas or influence and was of less significance for both than other encounters previously made: that, for example, of Jamāl ud-Dīn with ᶜAbduh and that of Malkum with Ākhūndzāda.

Relations between Malkum and another collaborator in the years that *Qānūn* was published, Mīrzā Āqā Khān Kirmānī, may be more satisfactorily assessed. The Bibliothèque Nationale collection of correspondence addressed to Malkum contains forty-two letters from Mīrzā Āqā Khān, ranging in date from September 1890 to early 1896. These are among the most interesting documents in the collection and throw much light on numerous aspects of the history of the period. Although Malkum and Mīrzā Āqā Khān never met, they appear to have established by correspondence a considerable intimacy and mutual trust, and it can be deduced from the latter's half of the exchange that they confided in each other their frank judgments of persons and events.

ᶜAbd ul-Ḥusayn Kirmānī, commonly known as Mīrzā Āqā Khān, was born in 1270/1853–1854 in the little town of Mashīz near Kirman. He was descended on his father's side from a Zoroastrian convert to Islam and on that of his mother from a follower of Mushtāq ᶜAlī Shāh, the celebrated Niᶜmatullāhī dervish who was put to death in 1790. It may be that this background of religious diversity, supplemented by contact in early youth with a Zoroastrian priest and a mulla with Shaykhī tendencies, predisposed Mīrzā Āqā Khān to his later experiment with Babism and final abandonment of all belief.[38]

He passed the first thirty years of his life in Kirman, fleeing to Isfahan in 1883 as the result of a dispute with the governor of Kirman over fiscal matters. In Isfahan he made the acquaintance of Ẓill us-Sulṭān and joined the staff of the prince, but was soon dismissed at the urging of the governor of Kirman. After wanderings that took him to Tehran, Mashhad, and Rasht, he left Iran and arrived in Istanbul in the summer of 1886. Shortly after, together with his fellow exile from Kirman, Shaykh Aḥmad Rūḥī, he embraced the Azalī branch of the Babi faith and traveled to Cyprus to meet the leader of the sect, Ṣubḥ-i Azal. The impression Mīrzā Āqā Khān made upon him was so favorable that when he returned to Istanbul it was with one of his daughters as wife.[39]

His further intellectual development in Istanbul, however, was to take him away from Azalism to an absence of formal religious belief.

38. Ādamīyat, *op. cit.*, pp. 1–6.
39. *Ibid.*, p. 7.

This appears to have accompanied a growing acquaintance with Western languages and civilization. He had already learned some English from a Zoroastrian priest in Kirman and had begun at the same time to teach himself some French. During his brief stay in Isfahan he pursued his study of French with some Jesuit fathers and in Istanbul was able to advance his knowledge still further. To his traditional learning and familiarity with the classics of Arabic and Persian literature—well attested by the stylistic excellence of his writings—an acquaintance with European ideas and culture was added now. He lost his belief in Azalism, although never totally repudiating some formal connection with it,[40] and turned instead to a species of rationalism.[41] He also fell prey to an exaggerated nationalism, displaying enthusiastic interest in the pre-Islamic past of Iran and a complementary hatred of the Arabs and other Semitic peoples. Unable or unwilling to synthesize his attitudes into a harmonious whole, Mīrzā Āqā Khān never became a systematic thinker, and his chief interest is as an exemplar of various currents in the intellectual history of nineteenth-century Iran. With Malkum he had in common a belief in the primacy of Western civilization and a willingness to make expedient appeal to Islam.[42]

Mīrzā Āqā Khān first wrote to Malkum in the autumn of 1890, in response to the advertisement in *Qānūn* for reporters and correspondents.[43] He seems to have believed that the publishing company mentioned in the first issue actually existed, and it was to it that he directed his early letters. Malkum saw fit to confide the truth in him, for soon his letters were addressed specifically to Malkum, and no further mention is made of the company. For a time he persisted however in his ambition to be a correspondent of *Qānūn* or better still to join Malkum in London and collaborate with him there. He pointed out that he had periodically contributed to *Akhtar* and offered to send specimens of his Arabic and Persian composition. If need be, he could supplement his salary by teaching Oriental languages in London.[44] Malkum's replies were evidently discouraging, for Mīrzā Āqā Khān ultimately announced

40. In an undated letter to Malkum (Supplément Persan, 1996, ff. 117–118), Mīrzā Āqā Khān proposes that Jamāl ud-Dīn be encouraged to write a definitive refutation of Babism, but paradoxically enough refers to himself in the same letter as a member of the sect.

41. His experience in this respect may be compared to that of another confidant and correspondent of Malkum, Ākhūndzāda, in whom irreligion and enthusiasm for Western learning also went together.

42. A full analysis of Mīrzā Āqā Khān's ideas is given in Ādamīyat, *op. cit., passim.*

43. Supplément Persan, 1996, ff. 60, 63–64.

44. Letters in *ibid.*, ff. 76–77, 92–93, 122.

that he was content to stay in Istanbul and serve the cause of *Qānūn* from there.[45]

This he did in a number of ways. He made certain suggestions for improving the style and contents of *Qānūn*. In an early letter, written after the receipt of the first three numbers of the journal, he proposed that violent expressions of abuse such as muleteer (*qāṭirchī*) and water-carrier (*ābdār*) henceforth should be omitted. This suggestion was evidently accepted. Other proposals, by contrast, received no attention. *Qānūn* should, Mīrzā Āqā Khān thought, resemble the contemporary press more than it did: items of scientific interest and descriptions of recent inventions should be included. The printing of foreign news, not necessarily touching upon Iran, would also be of educational value.[46] *Qānūn*, however, continued to be more of a periodic propaganda sheet than a newspaper. In one important respect, that of appealing to the ulama and to Mīrzā Ḥasan Shīrāzī in particular, Mīrzā Āqā Khān's advice was heeded, as has been seen.[47]

In almost every letter, Mīrzā Āqā Khān reported to Malkum at greater or lesser length items of news from Istanbul and Tehran. He did this in the hope that they might prove useful in the composition of *Qānūn*, and he often phrased them in such manner that they could, without adaptation, be printed in the newspaper, with a fictitious heading such as: "an enthusiast writes from Tehran."[48] A slight amount of this material was used by Malkum Khān, but only after receiving the imprint of his own distinctive style.

Probably the most useful service rendered by Mīrzā Āqā Khān was in the distribution of *Qānūn*. In one of his earliest letters to Malkum, dated Rabīᶜ uth-Thānī 12, 1308/November 25, 1890, he asked for further copies of the first three numbers to be sent to him and for a subscription to be entered for Najaf Qulī Khān, then consul-general in Egypt.[49] He undertook the distribution of the newspaper in Istanbul itself, giving copies to the many Iranian merchants who did business in the Valide Han.[50] In order to gain the goodwill of the Ottoman authorities, copies of number sixteen of *Qānūn* were sent to the palace, and ᶜAbd ul-Ḥamīd was reported to be favorably impressed. "I have even heard," Mīrzā Āqā Khān reported, "from one of the sultan's translators that the editor of the newspaper will probably receive some mark of

45. Undated letter in *ibid.*, ff. 94–95.
46. Undated letters in *ibid.*, ff. 90–91, 99–100.
47. See above, p. 212, and also undated letter in *ibid.*, ff. 117–118.
48. Undated letter in *ibid.*, ff. 101–102.
49. Undated letter in *ibid.*, ff. 61–62.
50. Undated letter in *ibid.*, ff. 78–79.

favor." He therefore advised Malkum to send a complete set to the sultan with a covering note in the hope of positive response. Other copies should be sent to Malkum's old friend, Münif Paşa, Rıza Paşa, the minister of justice, and Zühdü Paşa, the minister of education.[51] Mīrzā Āqā Khān also sent some issues to addresses in Iran and at the ʿatabāt,[52] suggested to Malkum various persons who should receive the newspaper,[53] and proposed the names of several others as agents for *Qānūn* in the chief centers of the Iranian commercial community abroad.[54] Finally, when his stocks were exhausted or when special occasion demanded, such as the passage of Iranian pilgrims to Mecca through Istanbul, he would write to Malkum asking for extra supplies.[55]

It appears that many issues of *Qānūn* reached Mīrzā Āqā Khān by means of the Cambridge orientalist, E. G. Browne. The letter in which his name is mentioned unfortunately is silent on his precise function in mailing the copies of *Qānūn*,[56] and in other letters there is only a passing reference to "the same Englishman" (*hamīn shakhṣ-i inglīsī*).[57] Mīrzā Āqā Khān's acknowledgment that he received copies of *Qānūn* via the British post,[58] suggests perhaps that Browne persuaded some friend in the Foreign Office to send *Qānūn* to Istanbul in the diplomatic pouch. The circumstance is, in any event, interesting for the light it sheds on the relations which may have existed between Malkum and the British orientalist. Browne was extraordinarily eclectic in his search for saviors of Iran, and it may be that he saw in Malkum a bright hope for a better Iran. A search in the E. G. Browne Papers in the Cambridge University Library has failed to locate any correspondence with Malkum; yet it is fairly certain that he had sympathetic relations with him.[59] The clearest fragment of evidence is provided by Browne's remarkably disingenuous account of the lottery affair in his *Persian Revolution*; he claimed to be

51. Undated letters in *ibid.*, ff. 78–79, 83–84. It was probably in response to this advice of Mīrzā Āqā Khān Kirmānī that Malkum took care to praise ʿAbd ul-Ḥamīd in several numbers of *Qānūn* (*e.g.*, no. 16, p. 2, where he is described as "the justice nurturing Caliph and the Islam-succouring Shahanshah," no. 20, p. 2, and no. 28, p. 3).

52. Mīrzā Āqā Khān to Malkum, Dhūl Ḥijja 11, 1311/June 15, 1894 in Supplément Persan, 1996, ff. 76–77, and undated letter in ibid., f. 80.

53. Undated letter in *ibid.*, ff. 94–95.

54. Undated letter in *ibid.*, f. 103.

55. Letter dated ʿĪd ul-Fiṭr (no year) in *ibid.*, ff. 110–111; undated letters in *ibid.*, ff. 85–86, 117–118.

56. Undated letter in *ibid.*, ff. 92a-93.

57. Letters in *ibid.*, ff. 83–84, 87–88, 94–95, 127–128.

58. Undated letter in *ibid.*, ff. 123–124.

59. I am informed by Professor Ḥasan Javādī that among the collection of E. G. Browne's correspondence in the keeping of his grandson are several letters from Malkum's son, Firīdūn.

ignorant of the identity of the Iranian subject to whom Nāṣir ud-Dīn Shāh had granted the concession and wrote: "The circumstances surrounding the lottery concession are obscure to me, but one effect of this last, which had several important consequences, was a quarrel between the Shah and Prince Malkom Khan."[60] This profession of ignorance is unacceptable, for the affair was fully reported in *The Times*, and Browne, who always took the keenest interest in Iranian politics, must have been aware of the precise connection between the cancellation of the lottery concession and Malkum's disgrace. We may finally note that it was in Malkum's house that he made the acquaintance of Sayyid Jamāl ud-Dīn[61] and that he was in contact with Malkum's widow in 1924.[62]

It was not only *Qānūn* that Mīrzā Āqā Khān set about enthusiastically distributing in and from Istanbul. He was also one of the few persons to accord a positive reception to Malkum's project of alphabet reform. He appreciated the copy Malkum sent him of his printing of the *Gulistān* in the "perfected script"[63] and forwarded other copies to acquaintances in Iran.[64] At one point he even set up a small bookstore near the Galata bridge to sell copies of books printed in Malkum's revised alphabet together with *Qānūn*.[65]

The extreme degree of Mīrzā Āqā Khān's devotion to Malkum becomes apparent, however, only from an examination of the remarkable praise and lavish epithets he bestowed upon him, with an abandon that went far beyond the polite exaggeration customary at the time. The vocabulary Mīrzā Āqā Khān used in adoration of Malkum had a peculiar pseudoreligious tone, and he variously implied that Malkum enjoyed the favor of the Hidden Imam, was himself Jesus reincarnate or some species of messianic figure, or, strangest of all, the author of a new creation. Ākhūndzāda, we have seen, addressed Malkum as Rūḥ ul-Quds, "Holy Spirit," meaning that he performed through his writings miracles of regeneration akin to those of Jesus. For him, however, it was doubtless no more than a turn of speech. With Mīrzā Āqā Khān, it is difficult to be sure that his strange manner of addressing Malkum was not meant more literally.

The most moderate and orthodox of his attributions to Malkum of religious stature is contained in a letter written in 1891, as Jamāl

60. Browne, *op. cit.* (n. 19, above), pp. 31–32.

61. *Ibid.*, p. 11.

62. *Ibid.*, p. 35 n. 1.

63. Letter dated Dhūl Ḥijja 2, 1311/June 6, 1894 in Supplément Persan, 1996, ff. 74–75.

64. Undated letters in *ibid.*, ff. 80, 81–82, 111.

65. Undated letter in *ibid.*, ff. 90 91.

ud-Dīn was en route to London. In a dream the night before, Mīrzā Āqā Khān related that he had seen the Hidden Imam who had handed him a green letter to be conveyed to Malkum as a guarantee of success. Mīrzā Āqā Khān interpreted this letter as symbolic of Jamāl ud-Dīn, who claimed to be a descendant of the Prophet, and green is the color generally associated with the Prophet's family.[66]

Visions of the Hidden Imam in a dream are acceptable in Twelver Shiᶜism as a source of guidance on religious matters,[67] even though it may seem strange that he should have manifested himself to an ex-Babi rationalist. In contrast, the following bizarre words, replete with Qurʾānic references, addressed to Malkum when describing the spread of his ideas in Istanbul, are eccentric: "Your excellency has kneaded the clay[68] like earthenware,[69] and infused the soul;[70] apart from Iblis and his legions,[71] all prostrate themselves in obedience."[72] The Qurʾānic verses alluded to in these words all touch upon God's creation of man, and Mīrzā Āqā Khān's implication that Malkum, through his propagandistic activities, has duplicated the divine creative act and produced a new humanity, would be repugnant and blasphemous to any believing Muslim. The fact that Mīrzā Āqā Khān had no qualms in addressing these words to Malkum is one more indication of the falsity of the latter's profession of Islam.

Only slightly less offensive to orthodox taste is the following, taken from another letter of Mīrzā Āqā Khān to Malkum: "Soon, innumerable hosts from the unseen will bring you succor,[73] and your life-giving breath will infuse the spirit of humanity into withered frames."[74]

It is implied here that Malkum is performing that miracle of restoring life to the dead for which Jesus is renowned in Islamic tradition and that he, like Jesus and other Prophets, is supported by invisible heavenly hosts.

Even though this peculiar mode of address is repugnant to Islamic orthodoxy—Sunni and Shiᶜi alike—it is not without its precedents in the

66. Undated letter in *ibid.*, ff. 81–82.

67. See D. M. Donaldson, *The Shiᶜite Religion* (London, 1933), p. 235.

68. *Ṭīnat-i ṣalṣālī*, an allusion to Qurʾān, 15:26, 28, 33.

69. *Kʾal-fakhkhār*, quoted from Qurʾān, 55:14.

70. *Nafkha-yi rūh*, an allusion to Qurʾān, 32:9 (*wa nafakha fīhi min rūḥihi*).

71. *Iblīs va junūd-i ān*, an allusion to Qurʾān, 26:95.

72. A reference to the refusal of Iblīs to prostrate himself before Adam, a theme mentioned in numerous Qurʾānic verses. The letter containing this remarkable sentence, dated Rabīᶜ ul-Avval 1, 1309/October 5, 1891, is in Supplément Persan, 1996, f. 65.

73. An allusion to Qurʾān, 9:26, 9:40, 33:9.

74. Undated letter in Supplément Persan, 1996, ff. 87–88.

Islamic world and in fact can be regarded as a minor, latter-day manifestation of ancient heterodox themes. The confused attribution to Malkum of support from the Hidden Imam, of messianic and even divine status, is reminiscent of the ecstatic mixture of extreme Shiʿi and Sufi themes that inspired the claims of Shah Ismāʿīl the Safavid, who variously declared that he was a representative of the Hidden Imam, the Hidden Imam returned, or even a manifestation of the godhead.[75] A more immediate and relevant precedent was furnished by Babism, a faith from which Mīrzā Āqā Khān never entirely cut loose. The Bāb claimed initially to be only the "gate" to the Hidden Imam, that is, a means of communication with him, and then advanced to more ambitious claims. Too much emphasis should not be placed, perhaps, on the bizarre terms in which Mīrzā Āqā Khān proclaimed his adoration of Malkum: in years of religious experimentation, he had doubtless acquired the habit of manipulating religious themes without concern for their precise content and significance.

Although for Mīrzā Āqā Khān Kirmānī pseudoreligious adoration of Malkum may then, after all, have been no more than an eccentric turn of speech, influenced by his Azalī antecedents, it seems that Malkum was regarded with real veneration by certain Babis. Mīrzā Āqā Khān once told Malkum of his meeting in Istanbul with an Azalī leader, descended from one of the associates of the Bāb, who spontaneously began praising Malkum.

> He said that a clear indication has been derived from the exalted principles [*mabādī-yi ʿālīya,* a phrase of unclear intention] that your person is a reincarnation [*rujʿat*][76] of Jesus and will render great assistance to the vicar of the family of Muḥammad [*qāʾim-i āl-i Muḥammad*]. Some time ago, he even said with reference to your alphabet that it was a sign of the day of "we shall separate the books" [*nufaṣṣil al-kutub*], when all the heavenly books shall enter the world of separation. The outward sign of this separation shall be the separation of the letters from each other.[77]

In the 1860s Malkum's proposals for alphabet reform had been attacked in Istanbul as contrary to Islam; now, by way of compensation, he was informed that he unwittingly had fulfilled a Babi prophecy.

That Malkum was thought by some Azalī Babis to be a reincarnation of Jesus is confirmed by another letter in which Mīrzā Āqā Khān reports:

75. See *Il Canzoniere di Šāh Ismāʿīl Haṭāʾī*, ed. Tourkhan Gandjei (Naples, 1959).

76. On early Babi concepts of reincarnation, see Arthur de Gobineau, *Les Religions et les Philosophies dans l'Asie Centrale* (Paris, 1865), p. 186.

77. Undated letter in Supplément Persan, 1996, ff. 117–118.

> It has become a matter of common talk among some of their excellencies the Babis[78] that one of the signs of the manifestation of the Hidden One shall be the descent of Jesus from the heavens and his propagation of true religion. They firmly believe that Malkum Khān is this Jesus who brings back to life the souls of the dead and cures the palsied and the leprous. Soon, through his Jesus-like exhalations [*nafaḥāt-i ᶜīsavī*], the faith of the Imam will prevail. It seems that their leader has issued a clear declaration to this effect. . . . In short, they regard your excellency as sacred.[79]

One wonders whether Ṣubḥ-i Azal, the leader of the Azalī Babis, had in fact declared Malkum to be Jesus reincarnate or whether Mīrzā Āqā Khān was merely relating rumors current among Azalīs in Istanbul, possibly made more definite to flatter Malkum. Married to the daughter of Ṣubḥ-i Azal, Mīrzā Āqā Khān was presumably in a position to know what pronouncements were emanating from the leader of the sect.

The weird attribution to Malkum of messianic status is in any event one more in a series of fragmentary indications that point to at least the possibility of some relation between him and the Babis. He had been impressed, it seems, by the fortitude displayed by the victims of the persecution of 1852, of which he spoke favorably in his pseudo-autobiographical statement recorded by Blunt. It is also possible that the initial success of Babism in inciting an insurrectionary movement in Iran suggested to Malkum the potentialities that could be released by religious or pseudoreligious appeal and hence his own determination to invent a "religion." The episode of the farāmūshkhāna came only a few years after the suppression of Babism, and it is significant that accusations of Babi affiliations were raised against it. Malkum's statement that he "got together 30,000 followers" who forced on him "the character of saint and prophet," while not literally true, is nonetheless interesting as an indication of what he would have liked to achieve, possibly on the model of the Bāb.[80] Finally, when Malkum arrived in

78. *Haḍarāt-i Bābī*: the respectfulness of the phrase is clearly sarcastic and illustrates again the ambivalence of Mīrzā Āqā Khān's feelings to the Babis.

79. Undated letter in *ibid.*, ff. 123–124.

80. Malkum shared Jamāl ud-Dīn's fascination with messianic movements, and much as his friend spoke enthusiastically to Europeans of the Sudanese Mahdi, so too did Malkum celebrate the revolutionary virtues of the Bāb: "At this time of day, owing to a curious concurrence of many circumstances, the Messianic, or Mahdist, belief is so deeply rooted in all Mussulman nations—especially the Schiytes (Persian)—that it has become their life and soul. . . . The root of all these sects, Babis, Shaykhis and others, is a passionate desire for change, reform, innovation, an abiding disgust with the order or disorder of things as they are. It is a constant protest against the narrow orthodoxy of Islam combined with a revolt of the human conscience against the excesses of a barbarous despotism, an irresistible but uncertain and unorganised

Baghdad in 1861, a number of Babi leaders, including the future Ṣubḥ-i Azal, were there, having been expelled from Iran some years before. The possibility of a meeting between them and Malkum is not to be excluded.

None of these considerations is, of course, conclusive: they suggest only that Malkum derived from Babism certain tactics and expedients, not that a working relationship was ever established between him and the sect. Mīrzā Āqā Khān however did propose to Malkum cooperation with the Azalīs in the following cryptic terms:

> A number of means for the improvement of affairs have occurred to me. Maybe you yourself have thought of them—at least this is what I have deduced from [your use of] *Allāhu akbar*. So if you pursue this method and if we seek help from these people in the advancement of Humanity, we will probably reach our goal more swiftly. No vital strength or force remains in any of the Iranian people except this sect that is at least half-alive [*tāʾifa-yi nīm-zinda*]. Of course, they have certain stupid beliefs so that we cannot join hands with them unconditionally. We can co-operate with them only from afar. "A hint sufficeth for the intelligent" [*al-ʿāqil yakfīhi al-ishāra*].[81]

It is interesting that Mīrzā Āqā Khān thought he could detect in Malkum some willingness to cooperate with the Azalīs. The use of *Allāhu akbar* to which he refers is as a password by members of the League of Humanity and as a codeword, without any apparent contextual sense, in various numbers of *Qānūn*.[82] Even before his cryptic proposal of a limited alliance with the Azalīs, Mīrzā Āqā Khān reported to Malkum that rumors had arisen in Tehran of an alliance between his followers and the Azalīs,[83] and it may well be that these rumors were fed by the appearance of *Allāhu akbar* as a codeword in *Qānūn*. For although the phrase is, of course, quintessentially Islamic when used in different contexts, it appears to have been used among Azalīs as a formula of greeting. Of this, Malkum can hardly have been unaware. In one number of *Qānūn* he disingenuously denies the Azalī implications of his use of the formula, and this may be taken as indirect proof that his arousal of suspicion was calculated and intentional.[84]

---

aspiration for a national deliverance." (H.R. Haweis, "Talk with a Persian Statesman," *Contemporary Review*, LXX [1896]: 75). Malkum clearly hoped to profit from these messianic aspirations.

81. Undated letter in *ibid.*, ff. 127–128.

82. *Qānūn*, no. 14, p. 3; no. 17, p. 4.

83. Undated letter, Supplément Persan, 1996, ff. 92–93.

84. *Qānūn*, no. 11, p. 2. If his use of *Allāhu akbar* is proof that he is a Babi (Azalī), Malkum argued, then all Muslims must be Babis, for they daily utter the words in the course of prayer.

Mīrzā Āqā Khān, for one, was not impressed by this denial, and he took it to be Malkum's intention to invite Azalī support and cooperation. He had never wholeheartedly approved of collaboration with the ulama, even while recognizing it as a necessary if temporary expedient, and he once confided to Malkum that "inwardly we must stop hoping for anything . . . from these few idiotic mullas [*in chand nafar mullā-yi aḥmaq-i bī-shuᶜūr*] and do something ourselves."[85] Evidently he regarded the Azalīs as preferable allies, despite his reservations about "certain stupid beliefs" they held. He himself cooperated with a number of Azalīs in Istanbul, under the direction of Jamāl ud-Dīn, in propaganda among Shiᶜi divines in the ᶜatabāt and elsewhere for the political union of Islam under the Ottoman Sultan-Caliph.[86] His suggestion to Malkum may have been an attempt to draw him into immediate contact with this peculiar Azalī Pan-Islamist circle. It is further possible that the alleged designation of Malkum as Jesus reincarnate by Ṣubḥ-i Azal constituted an oblique response to Malkum's hint, through the use of *Allāhu akbar*, of willingness to cooperate.

Until more documents come to light, it is clearly impossible to establish whether Malkum ever established a working relationship with the Azalīs. In the Bibliothèque Nationale collection there is an anonymous letter which, according to Blochet's catalogue, was written by a leader of the Bahāᵓīs, the other sect that emerged from the Babi movement.[87] It begins with acknowledgment of a letter from Malkum and proceeds to an analysis of the state of Iran, referred to as the "country of *kāf*" (*mamlakat-i kāf*), listing the various classes whose hostility to the regime might be transformed into revolutionary activity. The anonymous writer then praises Malkum's journal, but interestingly enough suggests that its title be changed from *Qānūn* to *ᶜAdālat* (Justice), for most people do not understand the word *qānūn* and the ulama imagine it to be some new *sharīᶜa*.[88] Beyond the use of *mamlakat-i kāf*,

85. Mīrzā Āqā Khān to Malkum, Rabīᶜ ul-Avval 12 (no year) in Supplément Persan, 1996, ff. 112–113.

86. See his introduction to *Hasht Bihisht* (n.p., n.d.) and N. R. Keddie, "Religion and Irreligion in Early Iranian Nationalism," *Comparative Studies in Society and History*, IV (1962): 290 f.

87. E. Blochet, *Bibliothèque Nationale: Catalogue des Manuscrits Persans* (Paris, 1934), IV: 291. One wonders if in fact Blochet intended the Bahāᵓīs. Of the two sects that evolved out of the original Babi movement, the Bahāᵓīs were the more numerous and well known, particularly in the West, and it may be that Blochet mistakenly assumed the letter to have been written by a Bahāᵓī instead of an Azalī. The Bahāᵓīs repeatedly sought an accommodation with the monarchy, offering themselves as allies against the ulama and other oppositional elements. The Azalīs persisted in enmity to the Qajars. See H. Roehmer, *Die Babi-Behai* (Potsdam, 1912).

88. Undated letter in Supplément Persan, 1996, ff. 133–134. The letter was prob-

a Babi term, there is nothing in the letter that betrays Bahāʾī ideology and nothing that speaks of effective coordination of action with Malkum. It can be taken only as a marginal indication that Malkum and heterodox movements exerted something of a mutual attraction.

More fragmentary and inconclusive evidence for a relation between Malkum and the Babis is provided by a number of letters in the Bibliothèque Nationale collection from Abūl Ḥasan Mīrzā, known as Shaykh ur-Raʾīs, a Qajar prince of unconventional way of life and views who has been suspected of heterodox connections.[89] It is probable that their contacts were limited to correspondence and began through the medium of Mīrzā Āqā Khān Kirmānī.[90] Mīrzā Āqā Khān had first made the acquaintance of Shaykh ur-Raʾīs in Mashhad in 1886[91] and met him again when he came to Istanbul in 1892. The Ottomans refused him political refuge,[92] and so he went to India where he lived as the guest of the Ismāʿīlī leader, the Agha Khan, first in Bombay and then in Poona.[93]

It was from India that his correspondence with Malkum apparently began. His first letter dated Dhūl Ḥijja 23, 1311/June 27, 1894 was brief and formal, but concluded, significantly, with the formula *Allāhu akbar.*[94] Two months later he wrote again, this time in the same effusive style used by Mīrzā Āqā Khān: "Your excellency Adam! It has been said: 'He taught Adam the names.'[95] There are hundreds of thousands of souls in each vein.[96] The sacred sheets of '*Qāf*: by the Glorious

---

ably written in the summer of 1890, for its author mentions that he has just seen number five of *Qānūn*, which appeared on Dhūl Qaʿda 1, 1307/June 18, 1890.

89. See Ibrāhīm Ṣafāʾī, *Abūl Ḥasan Mīrzā Shaykh ur-Raʾīs*, Rahbarān-i Mashrūṭa, vol. XVIII (Tehran, 1344 solar/1965).

90. The two, however, may have been in contact earlier, or at least sympathetically aware of each other's activities on a masonic basis. Shaykh ud-Raʾīs was an initiate of an Istanbul lodge (see Asad Khān Nāẓim ud-Daula to Nāṣir ud-Dīn Shāh, reproduced in Rāʾīn, *op. cit.*, III: 39), and in one of the letters he addressed to Malkum he urged him to write an exposition of freemasonry (Supplément Persan, 1991, f. 90).

91. Ādamīyat, *op. cit.* (n. 35, above), p. 6.

92. See Mīrzā Āqā Khān to Malkum, Dhūl Ḥijja, 11, 1311/June 15, 1894 in Supplément Persan, 1996, ff. 76–77.

93. See letters dated Dhūl Ḥijja 2, 1311/June 6, 1894 (*ibid.*, ff. 76–77) and Dhūl Ḥijja 27, 1311 (*ibid.*, ff. 115–116). Before leaving for India, Shaykh ur-Raʾīs made a trip to the ʿatabāt where he distributed copies of *Qānūn* among the ulama. See Mīrzā Āqā Khān's undated letter in *ibid.*, f. 98.

94. Supplément Persan, 1991, f. 89. Another letter of Shaykh ur-Raʾīs (*ibid.*, ff. 91–92) similarly concludes with *Allāhu akbar*.

95. Quoted from Qurʾān, 2:31.

96. Meaning, presumably, that just as Adam, the progenitor of humanity, contained within him the souls of thousands yet to come, so too Malkum was to father a new race of men.

Qurʾān'[97] and '*Nūn*: by the pen and what they write'[98] have arrived. Truly they are the summit of eloquence and beauty."[99]

The sense of addressing Malkum as Adam is twofold. First, the word *ādam* (in Persian and other Muslim languages) is not only the proper name Adam but also the substantive "human being." To the organization that succeeded his farāmūshkhāna Malkum gave the title of League of Humanity (*Majmaᶜ-i Ādamīyat*), and its members were known as *ādam*. By addressing Malkum as *ādam*, Shaykh ur-Raʾīs was implying that as head of the organization he was a "human being" par excellence. Second, if the word is taken as a proper noun, Malkum is addressed as a "new Adam," the progenitor of a new type of humanity. For Ākhūndzāda, Mīrzā Āqā Khān, and the Azalīs, Malkum was Jesus reincarnate, infusing life into an expiring humanity; other associates allowed their fancy to roam in other, if equally extravagant, directions.

The reference of Shaykh ur-Raʾīs to the Qurʾānic verses beginning with the letters *qāf* and *nūn* must be intended to imply that *Qānūn* (composed of *qā[f]* plus *nūn*) is a revealed and sacred book, its numbers corresponding to the verses and chapters of the Qurʾān. A grotesque and blasphemous suggestion, but one which Shaykh ur-Raʾīs evidently had reason to think welcome or at least acceptable to Malkum. There are indications from the early part of his career that he presented his writings as somehow inspired and possessed of miraculous qualities.[100] It is also significant that he often referred to the pages of *Qānūn* as "tablets" (*alvāḥ*), an allusion to the tablets of Moses (Qurʾān, 7:150) or possibly to the "preserved tablet" (*lawḥ mahfūẓ*, Qurʾān, 85:22) on which the heavenly archetype of the Qurʾān is inscribed.[101]

Some reciprocation of Shaykh ur-Raʾīs's sympathy for Malkum and his activities is suggested by a strangely worded paragraph in number twenty-eight of *Qānūn* where Malkum writes, referring to his brief residence in Istanbul: "Now Shaykh ur-Raʾīs has joined him [Sayyid Jamāl ud-Dīn], and it is said that he is attempting, with the support of the Sultan, to become the supreme manifestation [*maẓhar-i aᶜẓam*]."[102]

97. Quoted from Qurʾān, 50:1.
98. Quoted from Qurʾān, 68:1.
99. Letter dated Ṣafar 20, 1312/August 23, 1894 in Supplément Persan, 1991, f. 90.
100. See above, p. 33.
101. Certain of the writings of "Bahāʾullāh" were also entitled *Alvāḥ*.
102. *Qānūn*, no. 28, p. 3. The sense of *maẓhar-i aᶜẓam* is obscure, and no definite explanation occurs to the present writer. It may have some significance in Babi terminology. Despite his failure to find refuge in the Ottoman Empire, Shaykh ur-Raʾīs espoused the theme of Pan-Islam, like Jamāl ud-Dīn and his Azalī collaborators in Istanbul. He wrote a tract on the subject entitled *Ittiḥād ul-Islām* and had it published in 1312 lunar/1894 at Bombay.

In sum, Malkum's correspondence with Mīrzā Āqā Khān Kirmānī and Shaykh ur-Raʾīs, the probability that cooperation with revolutionary Azalīs was contemplated and the possibility that it came about, all throw a strange yet revealing light on Malkum's true beliefs during the period that he was proclaiming his fidelity to Islam from the pages of *Qānūn*. Together with other and earlier indications of irreligion in Malkum's career, they take us one step farther into that obscure world where skepticism, heterodoxy, and opportunism all coexisted and increased in mutual fructification behind a show of concern for Islam and the prosperity of the Muslims. It is a world still largely untouched by research, and until more exploratory work has been done, we must be content to say, with Mīrzā Āqā Khān Kirmānī, that "a hint sufficeth the intelligent."

CHAPTER 10

THE YEARS in which *Qānūn* appeared were also those of the League of Humanity, and there was a close relationship between the journal and the organization: frequent, if often cryptic, reference was made to the League in *Qānūn*, and the chief raison d'être of the League appears to have been distribution of the paper.

The League of Humanity was Malkum's second pseudomasonic foundation in Iran. After the dissolution of the farāmūshkhāna it appears that Malkum sought to preserve some form of organization under his leadership, and it was this that finally precipitated his expulsion from Iran. It is possible that some vestigial secret grouping survived his departure, composed of members of the farāmūshkhāna and later of those initiated in European lodges. Malkum also may have attempted to resurrect the farāmūshkhāna on his brief visits to Iran in 1882 and 1886.[1] There is no clear sign, however, of any widespread organization coming into being until his disgrace in 1890 and the publication of *Qānūn*.

The name of the new organization, Majmaʿ-i Ādamīyat, was derived from a variety of considerations. Evidence has already been presented of Malkum's indifference to the forms and teachings of religions: Islam was for him "a revised Christianity," and the doctrines of the Bāb were "identical with those of Jesus Christ." From the equation of religions it was but a step to the formulation of a pseudoreligion which claimed to incorporate all that was essential in different religions, while in fact denying the genius of each.[2] Thus there emerged a so-called "re-

1. Ismāʿīl Rāʾīn, *Farāmūshkhāna va Frāmāsūnrī dar Īrān* (Tehran, 1347/1968), I: 574–576.

2. For a similar development in two Egyptian associates of Jamāl ud-Dīn, Muḥammad ʿAbduh and the Jew, James Sanua, see E. Kedourie, *Afghani and ʿAbduh:*

ligion of Humanity," which in Iran expediently assumed an Islamic form.[3]

The word *ādam,* moreover, has the sense of man not simply as member of the human race, but rather as a being descended from Adam, the first man and the first prophet, ennobled by God and endowed with spiritual qualities which are a dim and microcosmic reflection of divine attributes. *Ādam* denotes a higher state than *insān,* which refers to man only as member of a species.[4] The idiom *ādam shudan* thus has the sense of becoming a true human being or, understood mystically, of realizing one's inborn dignity as a theomorphic creature. We have seen that in the farāmūshkhāna episode Malkum sought to invoke certain Sufi themes and to present the lodge as a place of spiritual striving and advancement, and now, with the successor organization, similar attempts were implicit in the very title of the body. What could be more attractive than to invite men to the realization of their true nature and what, apparently, more innocuous?

In the treatise *Uṣūl-i Ādamīyat* (The Principles of Humanity), Malkum defines the essence of Humanity as progress, and the primary duty of the members of the League as "striving towards spheres peculiar to the human race."[5] In keeping with his determination to clothe a "material reformation" in "the garb of religion," it was necessary to conceal the alien and European nature of this progress-worship behind assertions that the ideology of the league was derived from the teachings of the Prophets and mystics. Humanity, he declared, was a combination of religion and reason.[6] Its establishment upon earth had been the highest goal of all the Prophets.[7] If this complete correspondence between Humanity and the message of the Prophets was not immediately apparent, it was because of the esoteric nature of the doctrine that had been transmitted. Humanity was held to originate either with Adam or with ᶜAlī, who formed the fountainheads of esoteric tradition:

> From that time onward it has always been entrusted to the saints and trustees of God [*auliyā va auṣiyā*]. The secrets have sometimes been mani-

---

An Essay on Religious Unbelief and Political Activism in Modern Islam (London, 1966), pp. 15–16, 19.

3. Malkum stipulated, however, that members of all religions should be admitted to the League of Humanity (*Qānūn,* no. 11, p. 4).

4. In *Qānūn,* no. 13, p. 1, Malkum describes *ādamīyat* as higher than *insānīyat.* In his pseudo-autobiographical statement, however, he reverses the senses of *ādam* and *insān* (W. S. Blunt, *Secret History of the English Occupation of Egypt* [London, 1907], p. 83). This may simply reflect the confusion of Blunt, who knew neither Persian nor Arabic.

5. *Kullīyāt-i Malkum* ed., Hāshim Rabīᶜzāda (Tabriz, 1325 lunar/1908), p. 233.

6. *Qānūn,* no. 13, p. 1.

7. *Ibid.*; no. 16, p. 3; no. 21, p. 1; no. 25, p. 1–5.

fested in the succession of the gnostics and the retreats of the holy. All derived from this same effulgent treasury of Humanity. Some even think that all the arcane teachings of the farāmūshkhāna are that same beam which the ancient sages fragmentarily perceived from the lights of the most sacred throne.[8]

This pseudomystic phrasemongering is a recurrent feature of descriptions of the League of Humanity in *Qānūn*. The founders of the league, readers of *Qānūn* were told, had mastered not only "the common sciences" (*ᶜulūm-i ᶜāmma*), but also "those secrets of knowledge which until today have been hidden from the commonalty."[9] Several numbers of *Qānūn* conclude with cryptically worded appeals to members of the league to arise and establish their dignity as Men:

Awaken, o Man [*ādam*] whose true place is near the throne! Tear apart the veil of oblivion and give ear to the voice from the world of the unseen that says: there is no goal higher than knowledge of the truth, and life cannot be lived except in the ocean of divine unity. There is no god other than Him [*la ilāha illā hū*]![10]

The occurrence of such verbiage in a journal devoted to political propaganda is at first sight remarkable. It is difficult to extract precise meaning from passages such as these, which contradict Malkum's general reputation for exemplarily clear self-expression and are reminiscent of his own parodies of bombastic literary style. They served, nonetheless, several purposes. First, they gratified his ineradicable love of posturing and mystification. Second, they created confusion and uncertainty about the real political aims of his organization. Third, and most important, they were intended to draw into the League of Humanity persons accustomed to Sufi modes of expression and organization, under the misapprehension that it was a new and unprecedentedly powerful *ṭarīqat*.

Akin to these attempts to win the interest of the mystically inclined were certain references to "the signs of the manifestation of the just government [*daulat-i ḥaqqa*]."[11] "Heaven and earth alike give good tidings that the appearance of the just government is coming nearer, minute by minute. One of the clear signs of the approach of this auspicious sun is the wondrous national unity recently established in our land by the finger of divine grace."[12] In Shiᶜi Iran, the establishment of a just government had been traditionally associated with the return of

8. *Qānūn*, no. 25, p. 4.
9. *Qānūn*, no. 19, p. 2.
10. *Qānūn*, no. 11, p. 4. See too no. 14, p. 4 and p. 308 below.
11. *Qānūn*, no. 26, p. 2.
12. *Qānūn*, no. 23, p. 3.

the Hidden Imam to the visible plane, not with secular political activity. It was therefore expedient for Malkum to present the unity allegedly achieved by the League of Humanity as a sign of the propinquity of the Imam's emergence from occultation, and thereby to conceal the break with tradition implied in his activities.

In addition to these Sufi and Shiʿi references, it was necessary, in a narrower and more specific manner, to affirm the total compatibility of the League of Humanity with Islam. This was done on several occasions. In number five of *Qānūn* we read that "the principles of Humanity are so much in accord with Islam and so pertinent to the present woes of Iran that every intelligent Muslim, as soon as he hears of the truths of Humanity, rushes instinctively to enroll."[13] Indeed, anyone who failed to do so was "the enemy of Islam and the denier of God, the blindest creature in the world."[14] Any member of the league who showed himself hostile to Islam was, Malkum asserted, immediately expelled,[15] and if the ulama could perceive anything in the league contrary to Islam, they should inform those responsible so that it might immediately be corrected.[16] Finally, as outward profession of orthodoxy, Malkum sometimes designated his organization as "the party of God" (*ḥizb ʾullāh*: cf., Qurʾān, 5:56, 58:22).[17]

Members of the organization had seven general duties to perform,[18] and four specific: the distribution of *Qānūn*, the recruitment of further members, the propagation of Humanity among their womenfolk, and the extension of aid to their fellow members.[19] Membership could be acquired in two ways: simply by reading *Qānūn* and agreeing with its contents,[20] or more formally by being recruited to a branch of the organization in a certain town or district.[21] The ceremony of initiation for the latter type of recruit was considerably simpler and less imaginative than that practiced in the farāmūshkhāna. The initiate had to swear obedience to the *amīn*, the "trustee" or director of his branch, confess his belief in Humanity, and then take an oath to further the aims of the organization.[22]

Each branch (*jāmiʿ*) of the league contained a minimum of twelve and a maximum of two hundred and forty members.[23] The jāmiʿ should have a monthly general meeting, with additional weekly meetings for

13. *Qānūn*, no. 5, p. 4.
14. *Kullīyāt-i Malkum*, p. 216.
15. *Qānūn*, no. 13, p. 3.
16. *Qānūn*, no. 14, p. 2.
17. *Qānūn*, no. 21, p. 4; no. 23, p. 4; no. 29, p. 2; and *Kullīyāt-i Malkum*, p. 214.
18. *Qānūn*, no. 9, p. 3; *Kullīyāt-i Malkum*, pp. 234–240. These seven duties were the same that Malkum told Ākhūndzāda were the functions of the farāmūshkhāna. See above, p. 38.
19. *Qānūn*, no. 10, p. 4.
20. *Qānūn*, no. 7, p. 2; no. 8, p. 2; no. 13, p. 1.
21. *Kullīyāt-i Malkum*, p. 246.
22. *Ibid.*, pp. 240–243.
23. *Ibid.*, p. 246; *Qānūn*, no. 5, p. 3; no. 7, p. 2; no. 25, p. 3.

more active members,[24] and all gatherings were, if possible, to take place in a mosque.[25]

The jāmi^c was presided over by an *amīn*, an official elected by the members subject to the approval of the central directorate.[26] In places where no jāmiᶜ existed, any individual could regard himself as an amīn and begin gathering around him the requisite minimum of members.[27] Each member was pledged to absolute obedience to his amīn and obliged to keep his identity secret.[28] He was further required to pay a regular sum to the amīn, under pain of expulsion from the league.[29] Each amīn was supplied with a tablet (*lauḥ*) as emblem of office, bearing a number he might use instead of his signature in correspondence with the central directorate.[30] If possible, the amīn was to be a person of religious standing in the community, a mulla, a sayyid, a preacher, or, best of all, a mujtahid.[31]

To his own person as remote and anonymous director of the organization Malkum refers, modestly enough, as "the noble city" (*madīna-yi sharīfa*).[32] This is clearly an allusion to the *ḥadīth* "I am the city of knowledge and ᶜAli is its gate" and has the same motive that impelled him to make the allusion in the ceremonies of the farāmūshkhāna.[33] Concerning the "noble city" Malkum declared: "The sun of knowledge is in the noble city, the point of junction of all the effulgences of the truth. The limit of advancement in Humanity is arrival at the noble city. . . . None can perceive the sun of the city of knowledge unless he be a Man [*ādam*]."[34] More to the point than these peculiar assertions was the fact that "the sums for strengthening the league must all be sent, by

24. *Kullīyāt-i Malkum*, p. 247.

25. *Qānūn*, no. 5, p. 3; no. 13, p. 4.

26. *Kullīyāt-i Malkum*, p. 214. The term amīn was commonly used to denote the head of a trade guild (see Claude Cahen, "Amīn," *Encyclopaedia of Islam*, new ed., I: 437). Malkum's use of it is another indication of the resemblance he deliberately created between his pseudomasonic foundations and traditional forms of social organization.

27. *Qānūn*, no. 7, p. 2.

28. *Qānūn*, no. 21, p. 2.

29. *Qānūn*, no. 5, p. 3; *Kullīyāt-i Malkum*, p. 244.

30. *Ibid.*, p. 228. Shaykh ur-Raʾīs terminates one of his letters to Malkum (Bibliothèque Nationale, Supplément Persan, 1991, f. 90) with the number 132 instead of a signature. This may indicate that he was *amīn* of the Bombay branch of the league referred to by Malkum.

31. *Kullīyāt-i Malkum*, p. 226.

32. *Ibid.*, p. 239 f.

33. See above, p. 45.

34. *Kullīyāt-i Malkum*, p. 234. There may be here a further echo of the *ḥadīth*, namely that part of it which states that none shall enter the city of knowledge except by its gate (ᶜAlī).

means of the amīn, to the noble city."[35] Once again, patriotism and profit coincided.

Malkum was at pains to conceal the fact that he was the "noble city," doubtless thinking that many might suspect his motives in founding the League of Humanity and hence refrain from joining it. In order to increase the appeal of the organization and to give it the appearance of indubitable orthodoxy, he committed the grossest falsehood of his entire career and claimed that the league was directed by none other than the powerful and respected mujtahid, Mīrzā Ḥasan Shīrāzī.

Concerning himself and the league, Malkum wrote in number twenty-eight of *Qānūn*:

> Among the founders of this organization the person whose wretched name has become quite forgotten is that impious Malkum Khān. Nobody knows where he is and what he is doing. Some of the hajjis who saw him in Mecca said that he refuses to speak any more; and others say that he was killed some time ago in India. But a merchant from Yazd who had just returned from Mashhad said that he had recently been seen in Khorasan; while a certain sayyid swears that he is in Tehran at this very minute.[36]

Needless to say, Malkum had never visited either Mecca or India and was neither in Khorasan nor Tehran but London. Having thus attempted to dissociate himself in the public eye from the League of Humanity, Malkum proceeded in the following issue to appropriate Mīrzā Ḥasan Shīrāzī as the leader of the organization: "The head of our league is that same lofty personage whose effulgent guidance has filled the hearts of the people of Iran with hope and whose blessed name is Mīrzā Ḥasan Shīrāzī."[37]

It is beyond doubt that Mīrzā Ḥasan Shīrāzī had not the slightest connection with Malkum, his journal or his organization. By contrast, other individuals are named in the columns of *Qānūn* as members of the League of Humanity who are for the most part known to have been associates of Malkum. Among these are Mīrzā Yaḥyā Khān Mushīr ud-Daula, brother of Mīrzā Ḥusayn Khān Sipahsālār,[38] Muḥsin Khān Muʿīn ul-Mulk,[39] Nāṣir ul-Mulk, Amīn ud-Daula, Mukhbir ud-Daula, Ḥusām ul-Mulk, Shaykh Hādī Najmābādī, and others.[40] It is uncertain whether any of these participated in the activities of the League of Humanity: in the letters that Amīn ud-Daula wrote to Malkum at this period there is no mention of the organization. The individuals named probably formed a loose circle of persons sympathetic to Malkum, but

35. *Ibid.*, p. 244.
36. *Qānūn*, no. 28, p. 3.
37. *Qānūn*, no. 29, p. 3.
38. *Qānūn*, no. 7, p. 3.
39. *Qānūn*, no. 16, p. 1.
40. *Qānūn*, no. 28, pp. 2–3.

not an organization working for definite political aims under unified direction.

It is in general doubtful that the organization ever existed on the scale depicted in *Qānūn*. According to Malkum, it numbered among its members ulama, princes, army commanders, merchants, and even women in the royal household.[41] He claimed that it had branches not only in various districts of Tehran, but also in Isfahan, Mazandaran, Qazvin, Mashhad, Shiraz, and Kirmanshah, as well as among Iranian émigrés in Bombay, Istanbul, Ashkhabad, Herat, Egypt, and the ʿatabāt.[42]

There is little independent confirmation of these claims, and Browne went so far as to doubt whether the League of Humanity ever existed outside the columns of *Qānūn*.[43] It is certain that Malkum in his suggestive descriptions of the organization was seeking to intimidate the government in Tehran, and in the process he was guilty of at least one flagrant lie as well as, probably, much exaggeration. It was one of the advantages of instituting a secret society that the government could never estimate its actual strength and extent and was obliged constantly to be watchful and suspicious. Something of this is suggested by Malkum himself: "It is a cause for amazement that, although in Iran all capable, honorable, and learned men have today come together in this national union, the great men of the state are completely unaware of the affair. Evidently the cause is that they do not admit to their circle unqualified persons."[44]

Yet it would be wrong to conclude that the league had no existence whatsoever. It is generally agreed that *Qānūn* enjoyed extremely wide circulation, and such circulation must have required some organization. Given the loose definition of membership furnished by Malkum, it is justifiable to regard groups distributing *Qānūn* as branches of the League of Humanity. It is certain at least that a branch was established in Istanbul by Mīrzā Āqā Khān Kirmānī for this purpose[45] and that another existed in Kirmanshah. Information about the latter is supplied by the Communist poet, Abūl Qāsim Lāhūtī, who died in the Soviet Union in 1958. His father switched his loyalties from a local Sufi order to the Kirmanshah branch of the League of Humanity and as a member regularly received *Qānūn*. "All the numbers of *Qānūn*," Lāhūtī relates, "used to arrive secretly for my father. I would sit up late at night read-

41. *Qānūn*, no. 5, p. 3; no. 6, p. 2; no. 7, p. 3; no. 9, p. 1; no. 10, p. 4; no. 15, p. 3; no. 17, p. 3; no. 25, pp. 2–3; no. 26, p. 4.

42. *Qānūn*, no. 6, p. 3; no. 7, p. 4; no. 8, p. 3; no. 9, p. 3; no. 15, p. 2; no. 16, p. 3; no. 17, p. 3; no. 22, p. 2; no. 27, p. 3; no. 28, pp. 2–3.

43. E. G. Browne, *The Persian Revolution of 1905–1909* (Cambridge, 1910), p. 42.

44. *Qānūn*, no. 5, p. 3.

45. Letters of Mīrzā Āqā Khān Kirmānī to Malkum in Supplément Persan, 1996, ff. 87–88, 90–91.

ing each number as it arrived. After a while someone would secretly come and take it away. I still do not know who used to bring and fetch the paper."[46] Lāhūtī was sent to study in Tehran at the expense of the league,[47] a fact which suggests that not all the money went to the upkeep of the noble city.

It can be concluded only that the League of Humanity probably had a widespread existence as a network of distribution for *Qānūn*, but was not the close-knit conspiratorial organization depicted by Malkum. Probably its chief importance was as a model of clandestine political organization. Either through working in the league or through reading about it in *Qānūn*, many Iranians learned lessons that were applied in forming the secret societies of the Constitutional Revolution.[48]

If Malkum's motives in publishing *Qānūn* were, at best, of doubtful purity; if the political ideas it proclaimed were, for the most part, banal and repetitive; if the pseudoreligious aspect of the journal strikes a false and repugnant note; if the League of Humanity constantly referred to in *Qānūn* was a mere shadow of the vast revolutionary organization it was portrayed to be—wherein, it may be asked, did the appeal of the journal lie?

The wide circulation and popular impact of *Qānūn* are attested by several contemporary accounts,[49] and Malkum's boast that "the saddlebags of travelers and the pockets of pilgrims are stuffed to overflowing with copies of *Qānūn*" appears to have been justified.[50] Although the claim that the people of Iran were the real authors of *Qānūn* was a stratagem for concealing his authorship of the paper, it was true in the sense that popular grievances were reflected in the columns of *Qānūn*. Malkum's attack on the lawlessness and tyranny of the government and his demand for the establishment of security for life and property, though tedious and of suspect motivation, must have appeared powerful and original in late nineteenth-century Iran. Open denunciation of the

46. Abulqosim Lohuti, *Kulliyot* (Dushanbe, 1963), VI: 99.

47. See *Adiboni Tojikiston*, ed. A. Qodiri (Dushanbe, 1966), p. 14; and E. G. Osmanova and M. Sh. Shukurova, *Ocherk Istorii Sovetskoi Tadzhikskoi Literatury* (Moscow, 1961), p. 275.

48. See A.K.S. Lambton, "Secret Societies and the Persian Revolution of 1905–1906," *St. Anthony's Papers*, IV (1958): 43–60.

49. Mīrzā ᶜAlī Khān Amīn ud-Daula, *Khāṭirāt-i Siyāsī*, ed. Ḥāfiẓ Farmānfarmāyān (Tehran, 1431 solar/1962), pp. 147–148; ᶜAbbās Mīrzā Mulkārā, *Sharḥ-i Ḥāl*, ed. ᶜAbd ul-Ḥusayn Navāʾī (Tehran, 1325 solar/1946), p. 62; and Muḥammad Ḥasan Khān Iᶜtimād us-Salṭana, *Rūznāma-yi Khāṭirāt*, ed. Īraj Afshār (Tehran, 1345 solar/1967), p. 1028.

50. *Qānūn* was eagerly sought after as far afield as Bukhara, where its strictures on tyranny evidently were felt to be as revelant as in Iran. See Baymirza Hayit, *Turkestan im zwanzigsten Jahrhundert* (Darmstadt, 1956), p. 115.

government in frank and forthright language—often reinforced with colloquialisms not commonly used in written Persian—at a time of widespread discontent when opposition to oppressive rule and foreign hegemony was beginning to form, was bound to meet with an enthusiastic and positive response. It may be, too, that Malkum's pseudomystical verbiage was well chosen for the gaining of adherents and possessed an attraction to which latter-day readers are impervious.

Qānūn, moreover, did not merely draw attention to existing evils and remain content with expressing popular dissatisfaction. It pointed the way to future action and radical change, and it is in this that its chief importance lies, despite all the ambiguities of its birth. If Malkum is commonly regarded as an intellectual precursor of the Constitutional Revolution, it is primarily because the demand for a popularly elected legislative assembly was first publicly put forward in *Qānūn*, a decade before the beginning of the constitutional movement.

The demand became ever clearer and more closely defined through the lifetime of *Qānūn*. At first, a more active role was proposed for the existing *darbār-i aᶜẓam*, a body consisting of the ministers and sundry princes which had fulfilled little purpose since its establishment, partly at Malkum's instigation, in 1872.[51] Malkum now proposed that it be given greater powers, including the passage of laws subject to royal consent and the control of taxation and state expenditure. Its membership should also be supplemented with a number of mujtahids and other suitable persons.[52] Malkum later suggested that this extended *darbār-i aᶜẓam* should be renamed *majlis-i shaurā-yi millī* (National Consultative Assembly), the same title ultimately given to the lower house of the Iranian parliament.[53] In the last numbers of *Qānūn*, Malkum proposed as one means of extending the *darbār-i aᶜẓam* that the members of the League of Humanity should join the body en masse.[54]

At the same time Malkum proposed that an assembly of ulama should be convened for the purpose of drawing up laws and supervising their enforcement:

> Today the prosperity of Iran depends on the coming together of those lights of guidance and those effusions of wisdom which have remained scattered and concealed in the persons of the learned ones of Islam. The great ones among them . . . must by means of a popular measure gather together in a Great Assembly [*majlis-i aᶜẓam*] and, in accordance with divine ordinances—the principles of Islam—determine, by means of clear laws, the limits of royal power, the rights of subjects, the conditions of justice, the means of progress and the necessities of public well-being. Thereafter they should establish and perpetuate the execution of these sacred laws under the protection of the

51. See above, pp. 105–106.
52. *Qānūn*, no. 2, pp. 3–4.
53. *Qānūn*, no. 6, p. 2; no. 17, p. 3.
54. *Qānūn*, no. 35, p. 3; no. 37, p. 1.

> monarch and the guarantee of responsible ministers, with the assistance of special assemblies.[55]

Malkum failed to clarify the "popular measure" which should result in the convening of an assembly of ulama—it was possibly a euphemism for election—and also the relationship, if any, of this assembly with the extended *darbār-i aʿẓam* for which he called. It is probable that the proposal was not seriously meant and was intended only to gain the support of the ulama for the concept of constitutional rule.

Malkum's most explicit demand for a constitutional regime came in number thirty-five of *Qānūn,* when he suggested the institution of a regular parliamentary regime, with lower and upper houses:

> The drafting of laws and their passage must take place through consultation and with the approval of two separate assemblies [*majlis*]: one, the assembly of representatives of the people [*majlis-i vukalā-yi millat*], elected by the people themselves, and the other, the assembly of notables [*majlis-i aqṭāb*], consisting of the accomplished and learned ones of the realm.[56]

The two assemblies when meeting in joint session were to be known as the Sublime Gathering (*malaʾ-i aʿlā*).

This call for parliamentary government was a new element in Malkum's political pronouncements. Earlier, in his treatises, he had proposed only the establishment of law and had even defined Iran, in a kind of draft constitution, as "an absolute monarchy operating through law."[57] But his disgrace and dismissal, coming at a time of growing discontent and rebelliousness in Iran, caused him to address himself to a wider audience with more radical proposals. Through his revolutionary stance, he was able to obscure his own role in promoting the corruption he now denounced. Yet again patriotism and personal advantage had been made to coincide, and defeat was somehow transformed into new fame and glory.

Soon, however, the usefulness of *Qānūn* came to an end. In May 1896, Nāṣir ud-Dīn Shāh was assassinated by one Mīrzā Riḍā Kirmānī, incited to the deed by Sayyid Jamāl ud-Dīn in what was possibly his only successful piece of political intrigue. Muẓaffar ud-Dīn emerged from his seclusion in Tabriz to succeed his murdered father, and the new reign brought a partial restoration of Malkum's official fortunes. Although the reforms demanded in *Qānūn* remained as unfulfilled as ever, Malkum quietly abandoned his agitation and settled again into the familiar pattern of exhortation by treatise and private letter. *Qānūn,* for all its significance and the response it aroused, had only been an interlude.

55. *Qānūn,* no. 9, pp. 1–2. See too no. 15, p. 2 and no. 29, p. 4.

56. *Qānūn,* no. 25, p. 3.

57. See above, p. 30.

CHAPTER 11

THE LAST TWELVE YEARS of Malkum's life—from 1896 to 1908—saw the rise, initial triumph, and first defeat of the constitutional movement in Iran. It might be thought that this episode proved a fitting climax to his career of advocating reform and the rule of law, the more so since *Qānūn* had so recently been calling for a parliament. We see, however, that Malkum's role in the Constitutional Revolution was slight and peripheral, restricted to comment and occasional exhortation, and the workings of a secret society inspired by his example yet functioning independently of his immediate direction. This lack of involvement was due in part to his advanced age: he was over seventy when the revolution began in 1905. As we shall see, he had consciously withdrawn from purposive participation in Iranian affairs and decided to spend his declining years in Europe, while still striking a reformist pose. It is fair, also, to remark, once again that Malkum's advocacy of reform had always been linked to a concern for personal eminence and enrichment, and when in the new reign he received the post of ambassador to Rome, the propagation of the rule of law can no longer have seemed so urgent. Hence the disappearance of *Qānūn* and abstention from active support of the constitutionalist cause.

After the death of Nāṣir ud-Dīn Shāh, *Qānūn* continued to appear for about two years; its last issue, the forty-second, appeared in the autumn of 1898. In these remaining numbers, Malkum continued to insist on the need for an expanded *darbār-i aʿẓam*,[1] but this theme was joined by flattering references to the new monarch, and all revolutionary hints at universal discontent and the coming victory of justice vanished from the journal.

Even during the early years of *Qānūn*, Malkum had not forgotten

1. *Qānūn*, no. 36, p. 2; no. 37, p. 1; no. 39, p. 1.

Muẓaffar ud-Dīn, and he made sympathetic if occasional mention of him in its columns. If Nāṣir ud-Dīn Shāh had been angered and offended beyond hope of reconciliation, there remained the possibility of a happier relation with the heir apparent. Before his disgrace, Malkum corresponded from London with Muẓaffar ud-Dīn, sending him political information and advice and running minor errands for him. This correspondence presumably ceased with Malkum's dismissal, yet some kind of indirect communication was assured by the heir apparent's regular receipt of *Qānūn*.[2] There he was able to read that he was enamored of progress and reform, but that more than this could not be said, "for now in Iran one must not speak of the heir apparent and the important princes."[3] Similarly designed to arouse Muẓaffar ud-Dīn's hostility to Amīn us-Sulṭān, but considerably less flattering in effect, was the following description of his miserable lot in Tabriz:

> What should I say concerning the sufferings endured by that noble being who has had the misfortune to see himself designated heir to the throne in this day and age? You must surely be aware that there is not a peasant in the whole of Iran who is at such a loss to secure his daily bread as this high-born prince! Where can one openly declare that in this same province of Azerbayjan, where the appointees of the *ābdārkhāna*[4] waste the salaries of twenty brigades in frivolous amusement, the future king of Iran does not even have a decent room in which to sit?[5]

It seems unlikely that the lugubrious and apathetic Muẓaffar ud-Dīn would have been stung to indignation by these words or have rejoiced at discovering a partisan in Malkum.

Once Nāṣir ud-Dīn Shāh was dead, Malkum thought the time had come to address himself to Muẓaffar ud-Dīn more directly. It was first necessary to dispel all suspicions of hostility to the throne and its new occupant. This Malkum attempted to do by means of a circular entitled *Ishtihārnāma-yi Auliyā-yi Ādamīyat*, sent to all branches of the League of Humanity on the occasion of Muẓaffar ud-Dīn's coronation. The presence of "a just and concerned king" on the throne, Malkum declared, was necessary for the maintenance of Iranian independence, and the description fitted Muẓaffar ud-Dīn.

> This king of goodly disposition had no part in the ruinous events of the recent past . . . and up to the present his auspicious person has not in any way acted contrary to the norms of Humanity. . . . Emphatic instructions are

2. E. G. Browne, *The Persian Revolution of 1905–1909* (Cambridge, 1910), p. 416.

3. *Qānūn*, no. 5, p. 2.

4. *Ābdārkhāna*: the room or outhouse in which a servant prepares coffee, tea, sherbet, or water pipe for his master and his guests.

5. *Qānūn*, no. 14, p. 2.

therefore issued to all branches of the League of Humanity that all our brothers, headed by their trustees, should consider it their duty as members of the human race to obey and venerate that blessed being. Woe to those ignorant and misguided ones who shall commit the slightest treachery to this sinless monarch upon whom depend all the hopes of Iran![6]

This abrupt change from the insurrectional tone of *Qānūn* back to the familiar forms of flattery was partially concealed by the groundless assertion that the new shah would enact every desirable reform that could be conceived and appoint only the most qualified men to government posts. In the new reign the members of the League of Humanity, then, would be pursuing the same aims as they had under Nāṣir ud-Dīn Shāh, although now cooperating with the state instead of opposing it. Further and more detailed instructions on how to support the shah's reformist intentions, Malkum promised, would soon be forthcoming.[7] There is no evidence that any such instructions were ever issued, and it seems probable that this circular signified the dissolution of the league.

In July 1896, shortly after the coronation, Malkum wrote a long, verbose, and flattering letter to Muẓaffar ud-Dīn Shāh, intending to confirm the friendly sentiments expressed in the circular and to pave the way for a recovery of favor and influence. It was, Malkum loyally proclaimed, the duty of every son of Iran "to serve the monarchy and to worship the auspicious person of His Majesty—may my soul be a ransom for him." In the past, he had constantly attempted to serve the throne, but the nature of his services was

much different from prevailing taste in Iran. Some of our present ministers are well aware how, for forty years on end, I persistently sacrificed my personal interests to the task of explaining our situation. His martyred majesty was one of the great intellects of the world, and he was exceedingly disposed to listen to my submissions and to read my treatises. In recent years he used to tell me regretfully, "all you used to say was true and in my best interest, but I was young and I failed to understand. Now they have made me tired, and no time is left." Permit me to say, with the utmost sorrow, that he was right: the conrol of affairs had slipped from his hands.

It was, however, possible for Muẓaffar ud-Dīn to make up for his father's negligence, and the whole world was waiting to see what wise measures he would institute. The most pressing problem facing Iran was that of poverty and the emptiness of the treasury, and it could be

6. *Majmūʿa-yi Āthār*, ed. Muḥīṭ Ṭabāṭabāʾī (Tehran, 1327 solar/1948), pp. 182–183.

7. *Ibid.*, p. 185.

remedied only by study and application of the modern science of economics. Reverting to the style of his earlier treatises, Malkum lamented the failure of the Asiatic intellect to comprehend and to adopt "the remarkable means for the increase of wealth" which, although evolved in Europe, were of universal applicability, like the telegraph and the steam engine.

After this praise of economics, he proceeded to declare that he had no personal interest in the proposals he put forward. In an unusual access of partial honesty, he wrote:

> Today your servant has no kind of personal interest left in this affair. My life has reached its end . . . and I have no desire other than that I should observe from afar my forty years of worthless toil, together with the efforts of other patriots for the advancement and glory of the sublime monarchy, produce those beneficial results the appearance of which all classes in Iran and progress-loving people throughout the world are eagerly anticipating.[8]

The oblique admission that in the past he had pursued personal advantage together with reform was doubtless intended to gain the confidence of the new shah by a show of honesty. But the complementary assertion that he no longer had any personal advantage to seek was untrue, and the whole purpose of the letter, apart from the familiar excursus on economics, was to beg for a new post abroad, whence he might, in comfort, observe developments in Iran.

Muẓaffar ud-Dīn's reply was warm and sympathetic. He wrote that for a long time he had been convinced of Malkum's patriotism and the soundness of his views and that he should return to Tehran to exert his beneficial influence while there was yet time.[9] Whether the invitation was seriously intended is difficult to surmise, but Malkum was in any event quite unwilling to return to Iran. His attitude toward Iran had always been ambivalent, and, despite all professions of concern for the land of his birth, he clearly regarded the Asia of which it formed a part as a dark and degenerate region of the globe, and Europe, by contrast, as the bright summit of human development. Now, like many another Armenian entrepreneur, he had chosen Europe as his home, and he desired of Iran only a new diplomatic post to confer on his old age a modest measure of prosperity and prominence.

In November 1896, his antagonist, Amīn us-Sulṭān, fell from power, and Malkum chronicled the event in *Qānūn* with quiet joy, although charitably proclaiming that he would if necessary defend the rights of the fallen minister against his enemies. In the same number of *Qānūn*, Malkum stressed his determination not to return to Iran:

8. Bibliothèque Nationale, Supplément Persan, 1989, ff. 16–17.
9. *Ibid.*, f. 17.

> It is said that Mīrzā Malkum Khān Nāẓim ud-Daula has been asked, together with some of our ambassadors abroad, to come to Tehran and put his intelligence to work. Of course, among our officials abroad, competent persons must have made their appearance, but it is certain as far as Malkum Khān is concerned that he will not come. He has written to one of his friends saying that he has finished his work in Iran, and that it is now the turn of the people of Iran to set to work themselves. What he says is true, and we must pray that he does not come.
>
> Why? Because we have as a nation been afflicted with the illness of asking in unison: why do *they* not understand? why do *they* not do something? Then this perspicacious man came and in a variety of ways made us understand that instead of this useless question, why others do not work for us, we should ask rather, why we are unwilling to work ourselves.
>
> If he should come to Iran—which God forbid—they would immediately throw a robe of honor over his shoulders and put a muzzle of gold over his mouth, thus transforming him into one of those luckless parasites who in our present state of chaos do nothing but increase the public misery.[10]

Malkum's statement that his work in Iran is finished and that "it is now the turn of the people of Iran to set to work themselves" is an interesting demonstration of his fundamental alienation from Iran, accentuated by the determination to live out his old age in Europe. Yet the request for a new post abroad the shah might have deduced from this complacent piece was not to be fulfilled for two more years.

Amīn us-Sulṭān's immediate successor was ᶜAbd ul-Ḥusayn Mīrzā Farmānfarmā, who was in turn replaced in the middle of 1897 by Malkum's old friend and confidant, Mīrzā ᶜAlī Khān Amīn ud-Daula. A few months after taking office, Amīn ud-Daula wrote to Malkum assuring him that Muẓaffar ud-Dīn wished him to have a new appointment: he had only to suggest the place and the conditions that would be acceptable.[11] But by the time Amīn ud-Daula resigned from the premiership in June 1898, Malkum was still without a post. Some of the reasons for this can be deduced from another letter, written by Amīn ud-Daula in his penultimate month of office. On learning that Malkum was about to receive a new diplomatic post, some petty spirits among the victims of the lottery swindle, it seems, had begun to voice objections, and the British minister conveyed them to Muẓaffar ud-Dīn.[12] "The embassy's

10. *Qānūn*, no. 38, pp. 2–3.

11. Amīn ud-Daula to Malkum, Jumādī ul-Ukhrā 27, 1315/November 23, 1897, in Supplément Persan, 1997, f. 133.

12. It is worth noting that in 1899 the British ambassador in Paris shunned a diplomatic reception at Malkum's Paris residence, citing as reason the lottery affair. See Ḥasan ᶜAlī Khān Navvāb to Amīn us-Sulṭān, Dhūl Qaᶜda 8, 1316/March 20, 1899, quoted in Ismāᶜīl Rāᵓīn, *Ḥuqūbigīrān-i Inglīs dar Īrān* (Tehran, 1347 solar/1968),

tricks have delayed matters somewhat, but I have placed the blame where it belongs, and His Majesty will make up for the past."[13] One wonders precisely where Amīn ud-Daula placed the blame in order to absolve Malkum, but evidently his explanation appeared plausible to Muẓaffar ud-Dīn. As a first installment of Malkum's compensation, his son, Firīdūn, was appointed special adjutant at the Iranian embassy in Paris.[14]

With the resignation of Amīn ud-Daula, Amīn us-Sulṭān soon resumed the premiership, but he did not impede the return to diplomatic service of the man who had denounced him as a muleteer. This was in part because of the presence at the Ministry of Foreign Affairs of Malkum's old associate and brother mason, Mīrzā Naṣrullāh Khān Mushīr ud-Daula.[15] Equally important was the consideration that a minor diplomatic post, carrying with it a respectable salary, was the most effective means of silencing Malkum or, at least, of restricting his subversive activity. That such was Amīn us-Sulṭān's intention is evident from a letter written to Nāṣir ud-Dīn Shah nine years earlier, at the time of Malkum's dismissal from the embassy in London. In a conversation with Sir Henry Drummond Wolff, Amīn us-Sulṭān had suggested that Malkum should first be threatened and then given the post of ambassador to Italy. The British envoy agreed, Amīn us-Sulṭān reported to the shah, remarking that Malkum was "a slave to money" and could be sent

---

p. 242. When the action brought against Malkum by the Persian Investment Corporation had been dismissed in March 1893, Wolff, then British minister in Tehran, had tried to find a lawyer to fight Malkum's acquittal. See Amīn ud-Daula to Malkum, Dhūl Qaᶜda 5, 1310/June 23, 1893, in Supplément Persan, 1997, f. 108.

13. Amīn ud-Daula to Malkum, Dhūl Ḥijja 3, 1315/April 25, 1898, in *ibid.*, f. 134.

14. *Ibid.* Little is known of the life of Firīdūn. He was educated at Eton and St. Cyr (Firīdūn Ādamīyat, *Fikr-i Āzādī va Muqaddima-yi Nihḍat-i Mashrūṭīyat-i Īrān* [Tehran, 1340 solar/1961], p. 112). He is reputed to have incurred the anger of his father by refusing to enter a lucrative marriage with a millionairess widow of avowedly promiscuous habits (Khān Malik Sāsānī, *Siyāsatgarān-i Daura-yi Qājār* [Tehran, 1338 solar/1959], I: 144–145). He translated into Persian a history of constitutional government in England under the title *Tārīkh-i Guzīda* and had the work published in Tehran in 1909 (E. G. Browne, *The Press and Poetry of Modern Persia* [Cambridge, 1914], p. 162). At approximately the same time in Paris he founded a society for the support of the constitution, the *Anjuman-i Īrān-i Javān* (Young Iran Society). His political activity attracted the attention of Jean Jaurès, and he contributed on Iranian affairs to *L'Humanité*. See Ismāᶜīl Rāʾīn, *Farāmūshkhāna va Frāmāsūnrī dar Īrān* (Tehran, 1347 solar/1968), II: 256.

15. Mīrzā Naṣrullāh Khān had been a member of the farāmūshkhāna and was expelled from Iran together with Malkum at the time of its dissolution. See Iᶜtimād us-Salṭana, *Rūznāma-yi Khāṭirāt*, ed. Īraj Afshār (Tehran, 1345 solar/1967), p. 317.

anywhere, "even to America."[16] In 1890, Malkum had refused the post in Rome, to the initial disapproval of Amīn ud-Daula,[17] but now, after all his vigorous denunciation of Amīn us-Sulṭān and agitation against the regime, he quietly accepted the same comfortable sinecure he had earlier rejected. In the spring of 1899, he proceeded to Rome, and the career of *Qānūn* was at an end. The "muzzle of gold" had been fitted without his returning to Iran.

This happy solution of Malkum's predicament was in part the work of Naẓar Āqā, envoy in Vienna, who had been acquainted with him since the days when they both worked as interpreters at the newly founded Dār ul-Funūn. Unlike other diplomatic colleagues of Malkum, Naẓar Āqā had been able to keep his post and to maintain good relations with Amīn us-Sulṭān, with whom he now interceded on Malkum's behalf. In a letter dated Shavvāl 28, 1316/March 11, 1899, he thanked Amīn us-Sulṭān for the forgiveness he had extended to Malkum and recommended that his credentials be sent to him in Rome as soon as the agreed gift (*tankhwāh*) should be received. He had pointed out Malkum's mistakes to him, and if in the future any cause for complaint were to arise, Amīn us-Sulṭān should inform him so that he might immediately bring Malkum back to the right path. "As your excellency is aware, he is by nature somewhat ill-tempered and petty-minded."[18]

As proof of these characteristics and as a token of his desire to cooperate with Amīn us-Sulṭān, Naẓar Āqā enclosed with his letter the copy of a communication he had received from Malkum at the end of January. In the firman appointing him to Rome, there was, Malkum complained, no mention of the titles of "prince" and "altesse" by which he had become commonly known in Europe, nor of anything more exalted than the customary *janāb-i jalālatmaʾāb* (approximately, dignified excellency). How then was he to justify his former claims to princely status?[19]

We do not know how this crucial matter was settled, but Naẓar Āqā soon had cause to be concerned about his protégé and to communicate this concern to Amīn us-Sulṭān. He reported that Malkum had caused false information about the state of health of Muẓaffar ud-Dīn Shah to be published in the European press.

> Since he cannot sit quietly, he now wishes to send these reports to the Persian-language newspapers appearing in Egypt and have them printed there, so that his aim—the ruin of Iran—may be achieved. But I will not permit his

16. Rāʾīn, *op. cit.*, I: 626–627.
17. See above, p. 177.
18. Ibrāhīm Ṣafāʾī, *Asnād-i Siyāsī-yi Daurān-i Qājārīya* (Tehran, 1346 solar/1967), pp. 322–324.
19. Malkum to Naẓar Āqā, January 27, 1899, quoted in *ibid.*, p. 322 n. 1.

articles to be published in Egypt. I do not understand how this man came to be appointed again; it must have been the doing of [Mīrzā Naṣrullāh Khān] Mushīr ud-Daula.[20]

In the same letter Naẓar Āqā had occasion to report another instance of unseemly and suspicious behavior on the part of Malkum. Mīrzā Muḥsin Khān Muᶜīn ul-Mulk had come to Europe early in 1899, and while in Paris he fell sick and died. Malkum left his new post in Rome to join him in Paris and remained constantly at his side until his death, ostentatiously excluding all others from the presence of the dying man. He assisted him, according to Naẓar Āqā, in drawing up his testament, which dealt with political as well as personal matters, and refused to divulge its contents.[21]

Despite minor manifestations of Malkum's old unquiet spirit, his ambitions, political and personal, had been tempered by old age and the possession of a sinecure. After his appointment to the embassy in Rome, he appears to have composed only two treatises calling for reform. The second, a brief memorandum composed in 1907, urging against the contraction of foreign loans, is interesting only as a reversal of his earlier recommendations on the subject.[22] The first, *Nidā-yi ᶜAdālat* (A call to justice), was presented to Muẓaffar ud-Dīn Shāh on the occasion of his third journey to Europe in the summer of 1905. Applying the same technique that he had used in his very first treatise, Malkum cast some of his observations in the form of an imaginary speech delivered by the shah to his ministers. By means of this stratagem, Malkum presumably hoped to flatter Muẓaffar ud-Dīn by presenting him as concerned, enlightened, and progressive, and to give to his own suggestions the appearance of royal sanction.

In the imaginary speech to the Iranian ministers and ambassadors gathered in Paris, Muẓaffar ud-Dīn propounds several of Malkum's favorite themes, previously set forth in other treatises. Iran's persistence in backwardness and neglect invites, even justifies, foreign intervention, and reform is therefore necessary for national survival. Mere advice and exhortation cannot secure reform, or otherwise the words of philosophers and religious teachers would long ago have taken effect. Only the institution of law as the basis of rule can help Iran to escape the troubles threatening to engulf it, and there is no valid reason to reject the remedy since it is fully in accord with religion and, indeed, con-

20. Naẓar Āqā to Amīn us-Sulṭān, Rabīᶜ uth-Thānī 14, 1317/August 22, 1899, quoted in *ibid.*, p. 327.

21. *Ibid.*

22. The memorandum is dated Rabīᶜ uth-Thānī 5, 1325/May 18, 1907. It was addressed to the Ministry of Foreign Affairs and later printed in the newspaper *Ṣūr-i Isrāfīl*. The text is contained in *Majmūᶜa-yi Āthār*, pp. 188–191.

stitutes the core of the message of the Prophets. The monarch concludes that his hearers should submit plans for the salvation of Iran in accordance with these principles; these in turn might be forwarded to a council of mujtahids for their consideration.[23]

After this prologue Malkum obligingly submitted his own plan which, despite his condemnation of mere advice as useless, consisted more of exhortation than detailed proposal. The first necessity for Iran was, he stated, security of life and property to act as incentive to productive labor. The establishment of such security was attainable only through law, not through reliance on the ethical properties of the ruler. In order to institute the rule of law it was necessary to establish a legislative council (*majlis-i qavānīn*) consisting of ulama who would interpret and provide for the application of the general principles of law contained in religion. The implementation of the laws thus laid down should be the task of a revised cabinet, one in which the tasks of ministers should be clearly delineated and the principle of collective responsibility introduced. To provide some guarantee for the efficient and honest functioning of the cabinet, liberty of expression and criticism should be permitted. Such freedom was not to be interpreted in an anarchic sense, but rather as deriving from the Qurʾānic principle of "enjoining the good and prohibiting the evil."[24]

A number of obstacles had hitherto prevented the implementation of this program of salvation. European principles of government had been wrongly equated with Christianity, even though they had been established in the face of bitter opposition from the Christian church and in fact owed their origin to the influence of Islam. Then, too, the ministers of Iran had always thought their innate intelligence, unadorned by modern learning, adequate for the task of government; and the more unprincipled among them had sought to persuade the shah that the institution of law as the basis of rule would destroy his dignity and prerogatives. Finally, men had been unaware of their God-given rights or content to beg for them from those in power. All these obstacles were disappearing increasingly as the ulama came to recognize the political realities of the age and to assume their function of popular leadership.[25]

This treatise, presented to Muẓaffar ud-Dīn Shāh only a few months before the beginning of the sequence of events that were to culminate in the granting of a constitution, is remarkable above all for its loyalist and moderate tone. If Malkum is to be regarded as one of the intellec-

23. *Ibid.*, pp. 194–198. This section of *Nidā-yi ʿAdālat* was printed and distributed in Iran as a ten-page pamphlet. A copy is bound into the volume containing the Cambridge University Library collection of *Qānūn*.

24. *Ibid.*, pp. 199–206.

25. *Ibid.*, pp. 210–216.

tual fathers of Iranian constitutionalism, we might expect to find in this treatise some explicit call for a representative form of government. In fact, however, he appears to have openly demanded a bicameral legislature, with the lower house elected by popular suffrage, only once, in number thirty-five of *Qānūn*, when his lack of official position permitted him to suggest so radical a measure. In *Nidā-yi ᶜAdālat* there is only the same proposal for the institution of separate legislative and executive bodies which he had made some fifty years earlier, supplemented by a reference to popular rights. Only the assertion that the ulama increasingly were coming to assume their function of popular leadership was of direct topical relevance.

The events of the period from December 1905 to July 1906, ending with the decree calling for the establishment of a majlis, are related in detail in a number of works, and there is no need to enumerate them here.[26] Suffice it to say that a widespread urban movement, largely conducted by the ulama and expressing its demands in religious terms, succeeded in obtaining the grant of a constitutional form of government. Malkum's estimate of the capacity of the ulama to instigate and lead popular revolt and of the expediency of presenting westernizing reform in Islamic terms, thus proved well founded. There is, however, no evidence that either he or his prominent associates in Iran played any role in translating this estimate into a serious plan of political action. The most that can be discerned is a certain remote and indirect influence upon various groups active in the constitutional movement. Some of the secret societies formed to promote and defend the constitution saw cooperation with the ulama as a temporary expedient to be abandoned after the firm establishment of the Majlis; the example of Malkum may have influenced their strategy.[27] That his ideas were popular and found to be relevant to the constitutionalist struggle is attested by the fact that several individuals undertook the reprinting of *Qānūn* and the publication, for the first time, of his treatises.[28] Various articles from his pen were unearthed and published in newspapers such as *Tamaddun*, *Ḥabl ul-Matīn*, and *Ṣūr-i Isrāfīl*.[29] The last of these, one of the best written and most influential papers of the period, explicitly modeled itself on *Qānūn*, praising its author in these lavish terms:

26. See Aḥmad Kasravī, *Tārīkh-i Mashrūṭa-yi Īrān*, 5th imp. (Tehran, 1340 solar/1961); Mahdī Malikzāda, *Tārīkh-i Inqilāb-i Mashrūṭīyat-i Īrān* (Tehran, 1327 solar/1948); E. G. Browne, *Persian Revolution*; and M. S. Ivanov, *Iranskaya Revolyutsiya 1905–1911 Godov* (Moscow, 1957).

27. Yaḥyā Daulatābādī, *Tārīkh-i Muᶜāṣir yā Ḥayāt-i Yaḥyā* (Tehran, n.d.), II: 47.

28. See introduction to *Majmūᶜa-yi Āthār*, p. xlii.

29. See Ẓill us-Sulṭān to Malkum, Ramaḍān 25 (no year), in Supplément Persan, 1990, f. 40.

"Whoever has read *Qānūn* knows well that from the beginning of the Islamic era to the present, none has put pen to paper in the Persian language with the same fluency and eloquence."[30]

In the Caucasus, too, Malkum had his admirers and imitators, and numerous articles from *Qānūn* as well as other of his writings were reproduced in the celebrated Azerbayjani satirical periodical *Molla Näsräddin*, published in Tiflis from 1906 onward.[31]

Although Malkum's ideas thus enjoyed a certain vogue among the supporters of the constitution, there is unfortunately little record of his attitude toward the movement. According to Kasravī's history of the revolution, Malkum sent messages of encouragement to the first session of the Majlis which were gratefully received,[32] but the precise content of these is unknown. It seems however that his interest in the constitutional movement as a vehicle for fundamental change and the regeneration of Iran was strictly limited. The final stage of his career consisted less of open advocacy of the movement he had done something to generate than of obscure and ambiguous maneuvers proceeding from his still lively sense of egoism. This will become apparent from an examination of the Society of Humanity.

The League of Humanity apparently was dissolved at Malkum's direction in 1896, but there came into being some years later yet another pseudomasonic organization, closely modeled of its example. This was the Society of Humanity (*Jāmiᶜ-i Ādamīyat*), established and directed throughout its life by one ᶜAbbās Qulī Khān Qazvīnī, who took to himself the principle of the Society—*Ādamīyat*—as surname. Although the new organization had the approval of Malkum and was intermittently subject to his general supervision from Rome, its foundation was the result of ᶜAbbās Qulī Khān's initiative, and its policies were elaborated by him in Tehran.

Born in Qazvin in 1861, he lost his father in early childhood and was brought up my his brother-in-law, Mīrzā Muḥammad Khān Qazvīnī Munshībāshī, a member of the staff of Nāʾib us-Salṭana. On the recommendation of Mīrzā Muḥammad Khān, he joined the staff of Mīrzā Yaḥyā Khān Mushīr ud-Daula, and in 1881 began working under him in the Ministry of Justice. It was through Mīrzā Yaḥyā Khān that ᶜAbbās Qulī Khān became acquainted with Malkum when he paid his brief visit to Iran in 1886. In the course of his four months in Tehran, Malkum appears to have made a considerable impression on ᶜAbbās

30. *Ṣūr-i Isrāfīl*, no. 5, quoted in Muḥammad Ṣadr Hāshimī, *Tārīkh-i Jarāʾid va Majallāt-i Īrān* (Isfahan, 1327–1329 solar/1948–1950), IV: 96.

31. See Nazim Akhundov, *Azärbayjan Satira Zhurnalları* (Baku, 1968), p. 240 f.

32. Kasravī, *op. cit.*, p. 352.

Qulī Khān, for after his departure we find the young man diligently applying himself to the copying and distributing of Malkum's treatises, as well as enlisting others to performing these tasks. When after Malkum's dismissal from the embassy *Qānūn* began to appear and the League of Humanity was established, we may presume that ʿAbbās Qulī Khān was among those who distributed *Qānūn* and joined the branches of the league.[33]

It was not until the early years of the twentieth century that ʿAbbās Qulī Khān emerged as a figure of some importance. In 1904, he established the Society of Humanity as a successor to the league and began to enroll members in the capital and elsewhere. More than three hundred persons joined the society in its four years of life, the majority of them court and government officials, together with a few prominent traders and ulama.[34] Its composition thus resembled that of the farāmūshkhāna more than that of the League of Humanity, which drew more widely on various classes for its membership. In aim, too, this third pseudomasonic foundation was more akin to the first than to the second: it was an élite, reformist group rather than a protorevolutionary organization.

The Society of Humanity had four separate branches in Tehran, one presided over by ʿAbbās Qulī Khān himself, another by a certain Ḥājjī Mīrzā Ghulām Riḍā, and the remaining two by persons unknown.[35] Provincial branches existed in Mazandaran, Gilan, Malāyir, Kirmanshah, and possibly elsewhere.[36] The activities of all branches were coordinated by a twelve-man council in Tehran, including the leaders of the four Tehran branches, and under the direction of ʿAbbās Qulī Khān. The members of this council were given the title of trustee (amīn), the same designation by which the leaders of the various branches of the League of Humanity had been known.[37] All authority appears to have been vested in these twelve trustees, and although Malkum was periodically consulted by ʿAbbās Qulī Khān and corresponded with other trustees, he exercised no direct or continuous supervision.

The ceremony of initiation into the society was less complex than that Malkum had evolved for the farāmūshkhāna. The new member was required to swear an oath of allegiance to the "Principles of Humanity" and to sign a written declaration of loyalty to which were affixed the seals and signatures of two sponsors. He then paid a fee of ten *tomans* and in exchange received a membership card inscribed with the cele-

33. Ādamīyat, *op. cit.* (n. 14, above), pp. 206–208.
34. *Ibid.*, p. 241 f.; Rāʾīn, *op. cit.* (n. 14, above), I: 637.
35. Ādamīyat, *op. cit.*, p. 219; Rāʾīn, *op. cit.*, I: 638.
36. Ādamīyat, *op. cit.*, p. 223; Rāʾīn, *op. cit.*, I: 645.
37. Ādamīyat, *op. cit.*, p. 218; Rāʾīn, *op. cit.*, I: 638.

brated distich of Sacdī: "The sons of Adam are members of each other" printed in Malkum's reformed alphabet.[38]

The society does not appear to have been greatly active in the early stages of the constitutional movement. It is known only that in May 1906, cAbbās Qulī Khān, together with other members of the society, attempted to dissuade government troops from firing on demonstrators in Tehran,[39] and that when the firman for the summoning of a Majlis was issued, the society sent Muẓaffar ud-Dīn Shāh a memorandum on the necessity of capable persons being elected to the assembly.[40] Not until the death of Muẓaffar ud-Dīn Shāh in January 1907 and the start of the struggle between his autocratic successor, Muḥammad cAlī Shāh, and the Majlis, did the society begin to play a distinct political role of some importance.

The first Majlis contained fifteen members of the Society of Humanity including several prominent figures,[41] among them Mīrzā Maḥmūd Khān Iḥtishām us-Salṭana, an associate of Amīn ud-Daula, who in August 1907 became the second chairman of the Majlis,[42] and Mīrzā Javād Khān Sacd ud-Daula, a man whose career spanned both the constitutionalist and reactionary camps. Sacd ud-Daula's official career started with his appointment to the post of chargé d'affaires in Brussels. On his return to Iran he became minister of trade, but in the incidents of December 1905 that began the chain of events leading to the grant of a constitution, he espoused the cause of the merchants of Tehran against the governor of the city and lost his post. This earned him the goodwill of the constitutionalists, and he was elected to the first Majlis where he played an active role, particularly in drafting the supplementary constitutional law (*mutammim-i qānūn-i asāsī*). Because he was of ambitious nature, and moreover unable to establish his complete dominance over the Majlis, he gradually abandoned his constitutionalist loyalties and joined the reactionary camp.[43]

The career of Sacd ud-Daula is typical of the ambiguities that came to surround the political activities of the Society of Humanity. Ostensibly one of the societies founded for promoting the constitutionalist cause, it contained many reactionary courtiers and even, as we shall see, counted the shah among its members. This was in part the result of cAbbās Qulī Khān's ambitiousness, of his desire to enroll as many powerful men as possible in the society he directed. It was, too, the result of a deliberate policy, for the Society of Humanity sought for a

38. Ādamīyat, *op. cit.*, pp. 220–222; Rā'īn, *op. cit.*, I: 639, 665.

39. Nāẓim ul-Islām Kirmānī, *Tārīkh-i Bīdārī-yi Īrānīān* (Tehran, 1332 solar/1953), p. 408.

40. Ādamīyat, *op. cit.*, p. 251.

41. *Ibid.*, p. 241.

42. *Ibid.*, pp. 236–237.

43. *Ibid.*, pp. 232–235.

reconciliation between shah and Majlis, by bringing together reactionaries and constitutionalists under its wing and directing the energies of both to support of the constitution. This tactic doubtless was inspired by Malkum's essentially reformist outlook and by the example of the farāmūshkhāna which had similarly attempted to create a union of courtiers and politicians dedicated to moderate reform. The moderation of the society was also evident in the policies it pursued within the Majlis, opposing both the extremist revolutionaries, the representatives of Azerbayjan, and the clerical members of the assembly who wished to make the *sharīᶜa* the basis and source of legislation.[44]

The remarkable case of Amīn us-Sulṭān (retitled Atābak in 1903) suggested that reconciliation of reformists with erstwhile reactionaries, and their cooperation for the sake of the constitution, was indeed possible. Already something of an unspoken reconciliation between Amīn us-Sulṭān and Malkum—or at least a lessening of overt enmity—had taken place when Malkum was appointed to the embassy in Rome in 1899. Events soon led to a more genuine rapprochement between the two men.

After being dismissed from office for the second time in September 1903, Amīn us-Sulṭān sought permission to travel abroad and make the pilgrimage to Mecca. He followed a circuitous route to Arabia, traveling via Russia, China, Japan, the United States, and Egypt.[45] Japan in particular appears to have left a great impression on him. During the twenty-two days he spent in Tokyo and Yokohama, he saw evidence of the swift economic and social progress that Japan had achieved in the Meiji period, and he concluded therefrom, as did many of his contemporaries in the Muslim world, the desirability of industrialism and parliamentary rule. This lesson of Japan became particularly relevant to Iran when constitutionally governed Japan defeated absolutist Russia in 1905. Amīn us-Sulṭān set out from Japan, he relates, "in a state of inner turmoil: I saw that I was no longer the ᶜAlī Aṣghar of ten years before."[46]

After performing the hajj, Amīn us-Sulṭān proceeded to Europe by way of Syria, North Africa, and France, and went on to Carlsbad, on a species of lesser pilgrimage, to meet his old adversary, Malkum.[47] Carlsbad was a meeting place much favored by the Iranian ambassadors in

44. *Ibid.*, pp. 254–255.

45. Amīn us-Sulṭān was accompanied on this journey by Mahdī Qulī Khān Hidāyat Mukhbir us-Salṭana who wrote a colorful account of their travels, entitled *Safarnāma-yi Tasharruf ba Makka-yi Muᶜaẓẓama az Ṭarīq-i Chīn va Zhāpun va Amrīkā* (Tehran, n.d.).

46. Statement to ᶜAun ul-Mamālik, quoted in Ādamīyat, *op. cit.* (n. 14, above), p. 261.

47. Mukhbir us-Salṭana, *op. cit.*, p. 186.

Europe, and Malkum was in the habit of making an annual excursion there from Rome. Amīn us-Sulṭān related his experiences in Carlsbad in the following allusive terms:

> At the instructions of the first intellect of Iran, Prince Malkum Khān, I went to Carlsbad. Outstanding men from all parts of the world who throughout the year are occupied with the service of humanity in India and Europe, Asia, America, and Africa, who plan the destinies of mankind, gather at that place once a year for rest and recreation. One of those great ones present in Carlsbad at the time of my visit was Prince Malkum Khān. Several other persons who were there I had seen and become acquainted with on my previous travels, but not in the same way that I now saw them. Some I had known as ministers in such-and-such a government, others as judges and scholars. But now on this journey they revealed to me certain matters which had never crossed my mind nor, indeed, that of any Iranian. How remote we are from the understanding of human affairs! We Iranians think to ourselves that today will soon pass, and as for tomorrow, God is great; or that if we can pass through flood and fire, to hell with our brothers and fathers. I traversed a whole new world which cannot be described in words—a world of the spirit yet tangible and visible for those acquainted with the art [*ᶜulamā-yi fann,* an obscure phrase]. In short, they melted me there in the furnace and fashioned me anew, or in a phrase, they made a human being of me and said to me: "Man may reach a station where he beholds naught but God."[48]

This ecstatic description of his experiences in Carlsbad suggests that Amīn us-Sulṭān was there initiated, under Malkum's sponsorship, into freemasonry. The phrase "they made a human being of me" (*ādamam kardand*) would seem in particular to admit of no other interpretation. The "outstanding men" from all parts of the world whom Amīn us-Sulṭān had previously known only in their official capacities but who now revealed to him unimaginable mysteries doubtless constituted an international masonic gathering in which Malkum held a respected place. It is unfortunate that Amīn us-Sulṭān's description of the occasion is not more explicit and that his motives in seeking initiation, as well as those of his initiators, have remained unknown. Freemasonry exercised in general a widespread attraction on prominent Iranians in the nineteenth century, and Amīn us-Sulṭān might simply, at this point in his career, have succumbed to the fascination. It is obvious, however, that he must have been in correspondence with Malkum on the subject before his arrival in Carlsbad, and political considerations are not to be excluded from his initiation. He was contemplating a return to political life in Iran and the unseen but powerful support foreign masonic connections could secure may have seemed to him a useful accessory for the furtherance of his career. It is also possible that, after a genuine

48. Quoted in Ādamīyat, *op. cit.*, pp. 261–262.

conversion to the cause of reform, Amīn us-Sulṭān found masonry attractive as an ideology preaching secular progress.

Shortly after succeeding to the throne, Muḥammad ʿAlī Shāh had entered into correspondence with Amīn us-Sulṭān in order to persuade him to return to Iran, thinking that he would find in him a powerful supporter to pit against the Majlis. When the masonic neophyte decided to return, it was however with the approval of the wise men of Carlsbad and with their instructions to establish the rule of law and justice in Iran.[49] Malkum, fully satisfied with the change that had been wrought in him, wrote to the Society of Humanity and instructed them to cooperate with him to the full upon his return. He wrote:

> I am certain that the Atābak who is unrivalled in quickness of mind and resourcefulness stands in great need of the cooperation of capable men. Now reason and religion alike, as well as a hundred other considerations, decree that all the great and all enlightened individuals in Iran should cast aside petty self-interest and with their entire beings strive for the independence of Iran and be ready to sacrifice themslves on the imperial threshold.[50]

Amīn us-Sulṭān arrived back in Iran in the spring of 1907 and was appointed prime minister by Muḥammad ʿAlī Shāh at the beginning of May. Three months later, Mīrzā Ibrāhīm Khān ʿAun ul-Mamālik went to see him on behalf of the Society of Humanity to gauge his intentions and to offer the support of the society. Amīn us-Sulṭān related to him in some detail his experiences abroad and the change in his outlook they had brought about. Upon his return, he declared, he had attempted to persuade Muḥammad ʿAlī Shāh and his courtiers to abandon their opposition to the constitution, but in vain: he had been able to obtain only their temporary and pretended support. He was persisting in his attempts to preserve the Majlis from Muḥammad ʿAlī Shāh's enmity and would welcome the cooperation of the Society of Humanity.[51]

ʿAun ul-Mamālik reported favorably on his meeting, and it was decided to institute a formal link between him and the society. On Rajab 15, 1325/August 14, 1907, ʿAbbās Qulī Khān administered to Amīn us-Sulṭān a series of oaths for the protection of the constitution, in the presence of the entire council of trustees of the society. He swore on the Qurʾān to continue opposing the tyrannical tendencies of the shah and to consult the society in formulating his policies.[52] These oaths do not

49. *Ibid.*, p. 262.

50. Undated letter reproduced in facsimile in Rāʾīn, *op. cit.* (n. 14, above), II: 269.

51. Ādamīyat, *op. cit.*, pp. 260–265.

52. *Ibid.*, pp. 266–268.

appear to have constituted his formal acceptance into the society, even though shortly afterwards two of his relatives were enrolled.[53]

There was little left of Amīn us-Sulṭān's career, too little for the oaths to be put into effect. One week after they had been sworn, he was shot dead on emerging from the Majlis. His assailant, ᶜAbbās Āqā, was a member of the terrorist committee (*hay'at-i mudhisha*) presided over by one Ḥaydar ᶜAmūoghlī and affiliated both to the Caucasian Social Democratic Party and the extremist revolutionary society (*anjuman*) of Azerbayjan.[54] Amīn us-Sulṭān was an object of suspicion and dislike not only to the extreme constitutionalists—because they doubted the sincerity of his reformist sympathies—but also to his royal master—because he thought them genuine. Various theories, more or less fanciful, have been put forward on the ultimate responsibility for the assassination. The possibility of Muḥammad ᶜAlī Shāh's collusion with his extremist opponents cannot entirely be excluded. At the time of the assassination such was the confusion surrounding the event that ᶜAbbās Qulī Khān was a suspect because, it appears, of the hostility to him of Ṣanīᶜ ud-Daula, chairman of the Majlis, and the allegations of one of his own sons, Ṣādiq Khān, who had become estranged from him for reasons personal rather than political. After four days, ᶜAbbās Qulī Khān was released, and no further charges were raised against him.[55]

With the assassination of Amīn us-Sulṭān, the Society of Humanity was robbed of a powerful collaborator. Yet its most influential period was still to come, when none other than the autocratic shah himself sought admission to its ranks. This extraordinary phenomenon was the result of several factors. When ᶜAbbās Qulī Khān was arrested, the papers of his organization had been seized by the police and came under the scrutiny of the shah and his ministers. They were returned one month later, and soon after the society began to receive an influx of members from the court.[56] It appears that despite the untimely death of Amīn us-Sulṭān, liberal elements at the court had begun to gain ascendancy and to persuade Muḥammad ᶜAlī Shāh that a *modus vivendi* with the Majlis could be elaborated. The Society of Humanity seemed to have similar aims and thus to be a suitable body through which to operate. Muḥammad ᶜAlī Shāh for his part was genuinely fearful of the extremists inside and outside the Majlis and probably thought it wise to align himself explicitly with the moderate constitutionalist sentiment represented by the Society of Humanity.

In September 1907, Muḥammad ᶜAlī Shāh first indicated his desire to join the society. ᶜAbbās Qulī Khān replied that two conditions first needed to be fulfilled: the shah would have to appear before the Majlis

53. Rā'īn, *op. cit.*, II: 278–279.
54. Ādamīyat, *op. cit.*, p. 269.
55. *Ibid.*, p. 271; Rā'īn, *op. cit.*, I: 649–650.
56. Ādamīyat, *op. cit.*, p. 276.

and unmistakably declare his loyalty to the constitutional principle and then sign a written declaration to the same effect. Both conditions were accepted and fulfilled: Muḥammad ʿAlī Shāh swore before the Majlis his loyalty to the constitution and several days later put his signature to a declaration drafted by ʿAbbās Qulī Khān that was printed and distributed throughout the capital.[57] Preparations were then made for a worthy ceremony of initiation, and the occasion was set for the last day of Ramaḍān (November 6, 1907) so that the morrow of the day might be doubly joyous.

In the company of the entire council of trustees, ʿAbbās Qulī Khān set out for the royal palace at half past two in the afternoon of the appointed day. Upon arrival, he administered to the shah the following oath, the text of which he had already approved:

> By the resplendent truths of the Glorious Qurʾān I swear, with true faith and pure intent, from the date inscribed below to the end of my life, never to act contrary to the sacred instructions of Humanity, and always to consider the precise implementation of every point contained in the "Principles of Humanity" incumbent on my royal person. Should I be guilty of any shortcoming in the execution of my undertakings—may God forbid!—let me be, in this world and the hereafter, entirely deprived of the refuge of God, the Almighty and Vengeful.[58]

After the shah had sworn this oath upon the Qurʾān, Ḥājjī Nadīmbāshī, one of the trustees, read aloud the entire "Principles of Humanity," a treatise first composed by Malkum for the League of Humanity and subsequently adopted by the society. When this procedure was over, the shah wrote a few words on the last page of the treatise, affirming that it had been read to him and that he had taken cognizance of its contents. Instead of the customary ten *tomans,* Muḥammad ʿAlī Shāh then paid an admission fee of a thousand *ashrafīs,* and the ceremony was at an end. The same evening he wrote in his own hand a further affirmation of his loyalty to the "Principles of Humanity" and forwarded it to the society.[59] ʿAbbās Qulī Khān in return instructed his followers to afford the shah their closest support.[60]

With the entry of Muḥammad ʿAlī Shāh to the Society of Humanity, it seemed as if one of Malkum's long-standing ambitions had at last been realized: to obtain from the ruling monarch a firm commitment to the cause of governmental reform and an undertaking to submit to his lofty guidance. Nāṣir ud-Dīn Shāh had been early attracted to Mal-

57. *Ibid.,* pp. 278–280.
58. *Ibid.,* pp. 281–282; Rāʾīn, *op. cit.,* I: 668–669.
59. Ādamīyat, *op. cit.,* pp. 282–283; Rāʾīn, *op. cit.,* I: 660–670.
60. Rāʾīn, *op. cit.,* I: 673.

kum and seemed receptive to his exhortations, but the episodes of the farāmūshkhāna and the lottery concession successively alienated him. As for Muẓaffar ud-Dīn Shāh, he had been a weak-willed ruler whose reign was brief. Now, however, Muḥammad ʿAlī Shāh had sworn allegiance to Malkum's "Principles of Humanity" and joined the organization which he supervised from afar in Rome.

At this important juncture in the career of the Society of Humanity, ʿAbbās Qulī Khān decided to visit Malkum in Italy to discuss future policy. The shah entrusted him with a letter for Malkum, full of obsequious flattery and assurances of devotion. He began by lauding the eternal "Principles of Humanity" and repeating his unshakable loyalty to them. Then he thanked God that:

> Your excellency, by virtue of heavenly decree, innate nobility and the lesson of uninterrupted experience, has throughout his life been fully immersed in all the great affairs of the world and devoted his entire life, in public and in private, to the progress of the sacred fatherland and the preservation of Iranian independence. We, in our royal person, give thanks for the blessing of your excellency's existence and acknowledge gratefully your great services and the extent of your knowledge and learning. It may well be imagined that we deeply regret the failure of our predecessors to perceive your love for knowledge, your lofty ideas and enlightened thoughts.

The letter concluded, however, that Muḥammad ʿAlī Shāh would fully compensate for this failure by obeying all of Malkum's instructions.[61]

The reading of this letter must have afforded Malkum great pleasure, and he could hardly have worded it more pleasingly himself. Indeed the fact that it was written so much to Malkum's taste leads one to doubt that Muḥammad ʿAlī Shāh was its author, even though his signature appears at the end of the letter. In 1897, it is true, Muḥammad ʿAlī, then crown prince, had of his own accord written a friendly note to Malkum inviting him to return to Iran and enter government service again,[62] but as far as is known no close or sympathetic relationship ever existed between the two men. Muḥammad ʿAlī, moreover, was aware that Malkum enjoyed a continuing friendship with Ẓill us-Sulṭān, to whom he correctly attributed a persistent ambition for the throne[63] and who had met Malkum in Europe as recently as the summer of 1907.[64] It is therefore unlikely that he should have been willing to place

61. Muḥammad ʿAlī Shāh to Malkum, Shavvāl 28, 1325/December 4, 1907, quoted in Ādamīyat, *op. cit.*, p. 285, and Rāʾīn, *op. cit.*, I: 655–656.

62. Muḥammad ʿAlī to Malkum, Rabīʿ ul-Avval 27, 1315/September 25, 1897, in Supplément Persan, 1989, f. 18.

63. See Rāʾīn, *op. cit.* (n. 14, above), I: 659–660, and Ẓill us-Sulṭān to Malkum, Rajab 25, 1325/September 4, 1907, in Supplément Persan, 1990, ff. 34–35.

64. See his letters to Malkum in *ibid.*, ff. 33, 44–45, 46–47.

complete trust in Malkum as mentor and adviser. The most plausible explanation is that the letter was written by ʿAbbās Qulī Khān and then, like the declaration of loyalty to the constitution, handed to Muḥammad ʿAlī Shāh for his signature. This probability is strengthened by the fact that the letter contains generous praise of ʿAbbās Qulī Khān in terms only slightly less lavish than those accorded to Malkum.

The fact that Muḥammad ʿAlī Shāh could be persuaded to sign such a letter was a clear measure of the ascendancy of the Society of Humanity. Yet it was not to last. Not only did Muḥammad ʿAlī Shāh soon turn away from the verbose undertakings he had given, but the support of ʿAbbās Qulī Khān among lesser individuals also began to erode. He left Tehran on his long journey to Rome on Dhūl Qaʿda 2, 1325/January 6, 1908, in the company of Ḥājjī Nadīmbāshī, but he was destined to get no farther than Rasht, which he reached three weeks later after a prolonged stop in Qazvin. In Rasht he heard disturbing rumors that the extremists of Azerbayjan had instructed their agents in the Caucasus to murder him on his way through Russia. Worse still, news arrived that one of the four branches of the society in Tehran had denounced him as a swindler and seceded to form a new society, the Anjuman-i Ḥuqūq (The rights society). Faced with this sudden crisis, ʿAbbās Qulī Khān returned to Tehran, and Ḥājjī Nadīmbāshī proceeded alone to Rome to convey his regrets to Malkum.[65]

The leader of the Anjuman-i Ḥuqūq, Mīrzā ʿAlī Khān Intiẓām ul-Ḥukamā, had begun to show signs of disagreement with ʿAbbās Qulī Khān before his departure from Tehran, but evidently the dispute was not thought serious. On Dhūl Qaʿda 22, 1325/January 26, 1908, the secession of the Anjuman-i Ḥuqūq was announced in the *Ḥabl ul-Matīn*, and rumors began to circulate that ʿAbbās Qulī Khān had joined the reactionary camp and was intending to spend the treasury of the society for his personal pleasure in Europe.[66] These and other charges were contained in an anonymous pamphlet entitled *Taqallub: Ṭarḥ-i Jadīd* (A new design for trickery).[67] The accusation that ʿAbbās Qulī Khān had betrayed the constitutionalist cause doubtless sprang from the initiation of Muḥammad ʿAlī Shāh, and was probably unjustified; if the charge of financial trickery was true, it would have been in accord with his general imitation of Malkum's example.

Upon his return to Tehran, ʿAbbās Qulī Khān hastily summoned the remaining trustees of the society and set about mending the breaches.[68] Soon, however, another blow was struck at its repute. In the spring of 1908, the first "regular" Iranian masonic lodge, affiliated with

65. Ādamīyat, *op. cit.*, p. 303 f.; Rāʾīn, *op. cit.*, I: 657.
66. Ādamīyat, *op. cit.*, pp. 310–311.
67. Rāʾīn, *op. cit.*, I: 642–643.
68. *Ibid.*, I: 658.

the French Grand Orient, the Bīdārī-yi Īrān (The awakening of Iran) had been founded in Tehran.[69] Its establishment was accompanied by the revelation that Malkum's farāmūshkhāna had not been a genuine masonic lodge, authorized by any of the European obediences.[70] It is not clear whether ᶜAbbās Qulī Khān ever sought to present the Society of Humanity as a masonic organization; but the realization that Malkum's first secret society had been partly based on fraud was bound to hurt it, for his association with it and its leader, though remote, was well known.

More important than any of these unexpected blows, Muḥammad ᶜAlī Shāh was tending steadily to a more hostile attitude towards the Majlis. The curious episode of his enrollment in the Society of Humanity and his submission to ᶜAbbās Qulī Khān's directives had clearly been only a temporary expedient, resorted to in the hope of establishing some workable relationship with the Majlis. ᶜAbbās Qulī Khān now reminded the monarch of his undertakings, but to little purpose.[71] On Muḥarram 25, 1326/February 28, 1908, an unsuccessful attempt had been made on his life, and now that he was convinced of the impossibility of coexistence with the Majlis, it was only a matter of time before he undertook the forcible suppression of the constitution. This came in June: the Majlis was bombarded, several of its members were arrested and put to death, and political life in the capital ceased. The Society of Humanity which had sought rapprochement between monarch and Majlis had neither the possibility to remain in existence, nor any purpose in doing so. It was more militant elements that one year later were to bring about a temporary resurrection of the constitution.

On July 13, 1908, about a month after the bombardment of the Majlis, Malkum died while on a visit to Switzerland, at the age of seventy-four.[72] One wonders if the last weeks of his life were made especially painful by the news from Iran, or if he had finally abandoned all concern with political affairs. Evidently both ᶜAbbās Qulī Khān and Intiẓām ul-Ḥukamā had written to him in the spring, stating their cases in the dispute that split the Society of Humanity, but neither was favored with a reply.[73]

Malkum's writings had been a powerful factor in acquainting

69. Concerning the lodge Bīdārī-yi Īrān, see *ibid.*, II: 43–147; Maḥmūd Katīrāʾī, *Frāmāsūnrī dar Īrān* (Tehran, 1347 solar/1968), p. 123 f., 194 f.; and Hamid Algar, "An Introduction to the History of Freemasonry in Iran," *Middle Eastern Studies*, VI (1970): 287–288.

70. Introduction to *Majmūᶜa-yi Āthār*, p. xx.

71. Ādamīyat, *op. cit.*, pp. 292–293; Rāʾīn, *op. cit.*, I: 660.

72. His obituary appeared in *The Times* for July 14, 1908.

73. Sāsānī, *op. cit.* (n. 14, above), p. 145.

Iranians with modern notions of government, and in *Qānūn* he had voiced the earliest explicit demand for an elected assembly of popular representatives. His pseudomasonic organizations had furnished a model not only for the Society of Humanity which dissolved after Muḥammad ʿAlī Shāh's coup d'état, but also for the revolutionary societies that were to restore the constitution. In these respects, then, his political career could not be said to have been a failure, despite the dissolution of the Majlis.

His emotional and active involvement in the events of the revolution, however, had been slight. From Rome he had contented himself with the activity he frequently condemned as useless: exhortation and encouragement, and little resulted from his contacts with Amīn us-Sulṭān and Muḥammad ʿAlī Shāh except the receipt of comforting flattery. Clearly the assertion that it was the turn of the people of Iran had been seriously meant. And in death, Malkum now completed his withdrawal from involvement in Iran by abandoning his expedient profession of Islam. Contrary to all Muslim usage, he willed that his body be cremated,[74] and the ashes bore witness to all the ambiguities of his life.

74. *Ibid.*

CONCLUSION

THE POSTHUMOUS CAREER of Mīrzā Malkum Khān has been on the whole more glorious and freer of taint than the actual events of his life. To the West he has been known chiefly from the brief but laudatory references to him in the works of E. G. Browne, particularly his *Persian Revolution of 1905–1909*;[1] in much of Iranian historiography he has been seen as a courageous and patriotic pioneer of modernism.[2] It might almost be said that his trickery lived on after him, registering a final success by suppressing or excising the discreditable aspects of his career. He has been remembered above all as the publisher of *Qānūn* and the author of treatises on modern political, economic, and legal concepts; the episode of the lottery concession has received less attention and, more important, the shallowness of his thought, based frequently on considerations of expediency and expressed with much posturing and charlatanry, has almost completely escaped notice. Westernization has come to be thought of as both salubrious and inevitable, and therefore the individual held to be among the intellectual initiators of the process has almost automatically acquired heroic status.

Probably the most enthusiastic promoter of Malkum's posthumous fame has been the historian Firīdūn Ādamīyat, who concedes that Malkum was "greedy and enamoured of money" yet attributes to him a whole series of virtues which more than make up for this minor blemish.

1. E. G. Browne, *Persian Revolution of 1905–1909* (Cambridge, 1910), p. 32 f.

2. See, for example, Mahdī Malikzāda, *Tārīkh-i Inqilāb-i Mashrūṭīyat* (Tehran, 1327 solar/1948), I: 225–227; Sayyid Ḥasan Taqīzāda, *Tārīkh-i Avāʾil-i Inqilāb-i Mashrūṭīyat* (Tehran, 1328 solar/1949), p. 40; and Bozorg Alavi, *Geschichte und Entwicklung der modernen persischen Literatur* (Berlin, 1964), p. 64 (Malkum is described as a "historically significant personality who exercised a great influence on the intelligentsia of the period through his ceaseless political and cultural activity," and "intellectual initiator of the revolution").

Ādamīyat contends that with his weighty treatises, Malkum strove for more than fifty years for the establishment of a popular government in Iran, and for thirty years after his death no Iranian had anything fresh to say on political matters, and was constrained to repeat Malkum's ideas.[3] Indeed, not only in Iran but in the whole of Asia there were few among Malkum's contemporaries who could be compared with him in the depth of his political philosophy and the extent of his modern learning.[4]

Some of Malkum's contemporaries accorded him ridiculously high rank. Ẓill us-Sulṭān wrote that "without any exaggeration, he is like Aristotle and Plato,"[5] an absurdity echoed by the dervish Ḥājjī Pīrzāda Nāʾīnī in a lengthy piece of doggerel written after an encounter with Malkum in London.[6] The Russian envoy in London, de Staal, in more muted vein, wrote to his superiors in St. Petersburg that Malkum presented "the strange combination of a cunning oriental and an emeritus philosopher."[7] Malkum left a favorable impression of his intelligence on Wilfred Scawen Blunt who, after meeting him for the first time, came away "more convinced than ever of the superior intelligence of the Eastern mind."[8]

Other contemporaries, better acquainted with Malkum, were far more critical. Iʿtimād us-Salṭana confided many outbursts against him to the pages of his diary[9] and thought *Qānūn* a "worthless and despicable rag."[10] Even Amīn ud-Daula, a faithful collaborator and correspondent of Malkum, had a clearly ambivalent attitude towards him: in several letters he exhorts Malkum to abandon his posturing and to make specific proposals for reform,[11] and in his memoirs (not originally intended for publication) he calls Malkum the equal of Amīn us-Sulṭān in greed and compares the rivalry of the two men during Nāṣir ud-Dīn Shāh's visit to London in 1889 to "wild beasts fighting over prey."[12]

3. *Fikr-i Āzādī va Muqaddima-yi Nihḍat-i Mashrūṭīyat* (Tehran, 1340 solar/1961), pp. 99–100.

4. *Andīshahā-yi Mīrzā Āqā Khān Kirmānī* (Tehran, 1346 solar/1967), pp. xii–xiii.

5. *Tārīkh-i Sargudhasht-i Masʿūdī* (Tehran, 1325 lunar/1907), p. 125.

6. *Safarnāma*, ed. Ḥāfiẓ Farmānfarmāyān (Tehran, 1343 solar/1964), I: 320–321.

7. Meyendorff, ed., *Correspondance Diplomatique de M. de Staal, 1884–1900* (Paris, 1929), I: 448.

8. *Secret History of the English Occupation of Egypt* (London, 1908), p. 85.

9. See above, pp. 149, 154.

10. See the excerpt from his *Khwābnāma* in Khān Malik Sāsānī, *Siyāsatgarān-i Daura-yi Qājār* (Tehran, 1337–1345 solar/1958–1966), II: 209. (The judgment is put into the mouth of Amīn us-Sulṭān.)

11. See above, pp. 155–156.

12. *Khāṭirāt-i Siyāsī*, ed. Ḥafiẓ Farmānfarmāyān (Tehran, 1342 solar/1962), p. 146.

While the general tone of Persian writings on Malkum has been positive, critical comment is also to be encountered. The literary scholar and historian Mīrzā Muḥammad Qazvīnī referred to Malkum as "this swindling Armenian trickster," and after transcribing some of his writings remarked that "this task has incapacitated me; I must rest a while to purify my brain."[13] Maḥmūd Maḥmūd, author of a voluminous history of Anglo-Iranian relations in the nineteenth century, was one of the few to perceive that had it not been for the events of 1889, Malkum would never have published *Qānūn* and gained his reputation as a precursor of revolution.[14] Khān Malik Sāsānī devoted to Malkum a chapter of his *Siyāsatgarān-i Daura-yi Qājār* and presented a generally negative picture of him, with emphasis on his greed and charlatanry and hints at treachery and subservience to British interests.[15] Accusations of treachery are more fully developed, though hardly substantiated, by Ibrāhīm Ṣafāʾī in his pamphlet *Rahbarān-i Mashrūṭa, II: Mīrzā Malkum Khān.* Ṣafāʾī speaks of a plot to assassinate Nāṣir ud-Dīn Shāh concocted in London by Malkum and the Foreign Office, with the participation of E. G. Browne, Sayyid Jamāl ud-Dīn, and the wife of Wilfred Scawen Blunt (identified as the Sayyid's mistress)![16]

Summary attempts have been made to estimate Malkum's role in the evolution of Persian prose, and it would seem indeed that his simple, not to say declamatory, style had a distinct influence on the development of political writing and journalism.[17] Yet none of the discussions of Malkum and his life written in Persian has yet included a genuinely critical assessment of his life and ideas, nor attempted a serious evaluation of their place in the intellectual history of Iran. Merely to assert that he was among the earliest proponents of westernization hardly seems adequate. One must observe too that his writings were repetitive and banal, frequently charged with all kinds of egoism. The manner of his advocacy of westernization was exceedingly glib and confessedly based on considerations of expediency. As the Italian scholar Alessandro Bausani has observed, Malkum lacked the moral seriousness which alone could have made his thought cohesive and convincing. His liberalism and modernism came from outside Iran and were "superimposed [on the country], instead of historically evolving out of Persian soci-

13. Mīrzā Muḥammad Qazvīnī, *Yāddāshthā*, ed. Īraj Afshār (Tehran, 1342 solar/1963), VII: 132–136.

14. Maḥmūd Maḥmūd, *Tārīkh-i Ravābiṭ-i Siyāsī-yi Īrān va Inglīs dar Qarn-i Nūzdahum-i Mīlādī* (Tehran, 1328 solar/1949), V: 1225.

15. Sāsānī, *op. cit.*, I: 127–148.

16. Ibrāhīm Ṣafāʾī, *Rahbarān-i Mashrūṭa, II: Mīrzā Malkum Khān* (Tehran, 1342 solar/1963), pp. 18–21.

17. Alavi, *op. cit.* (n. 2, above), pp. 64–67; Malik ush-Shuʿarā Bahār, *Sabkshināsī* (Tehran, 1337 solar/1958), III: 374.

ety."[18] The superimposition was achieved in the first place by an equation of Islamic and Western values and concepts that rested neither upon personal conviction nor upon adequate argumentation. As a short-term measure it proved successful, and the influence of Malkum can be clearly discerned in many of the proclamations of intent made by the early constitutionalists. Yet it has in the long run condemned Iran to an unsatisfactory state of suspension between traditional values that no longer receive much more than lip service and a process of external westernization that has signally failed to produce a true regeneration of the country. Only a serious and well-informed approach to the problem of modernity, evolving organically out of comprehension of tradition and attachment to it, could have pointed the way to such regeneration. For such a task Malkum was totally disqualified; and so far as his failure is the reflection of a more general one in Iranian society, his career may be regarded as an illustration of the moral and intellectual level of Iranian modernism.

18. *Storia della Letteratura Persiana* (Milan, 1960), p. 199.

APPENDIX A

THE ATTRIBUTION OF FOUR COMEDIES TO MALKUM KHĀN

THE UNDISPUTED LITERARY TALENT of Mīrzā Malkum Khān was for long thought to include the skills of playwright. He has been regarded as the author of four comedies which are among the earliest specimens of dramatic composition in Persian, and thus thought to have served in this respect too as an innovator and agent of westernization. Three of the comedies have been published,[1] and the existence of the fourth has been deduced from a critique of the plays written by Ākhūndzāda and addressed, it was for long thought, to Mīrzā Malkum Khān.[2]

The attribution to him of the comedies is, at first sight, plausible enough and is supported by much circumstantial evidence. The first recorded dramatic performances in Iran (other, that is, than the traditional passion plays performed during Muḥarram) took place in the Dār ul-Funūn; Malkum was closely associated with the institution in its

1. *Sargudhasht-i Ashraf Khān, Ḥākim-i ʿArabistān, dar Ayyām-i Tavaqquf-i Ū dar Ṭihrān* [What befell Ashrāf Khān, the governor of Arabistān, during the days of his residence in Tehran]; *Ṭarīqa-yi Ḥukūmat-i Zamān Khān-i Burūjirdī* [The method of government of Zamān Khān of Burūjird]; and *Ḥikāyat-i Karbalā Raftan-i Shāhqulī Mīrzā va Sargudhasht-i Ayyām-i Tavaqquf-i Chand-rūza dar Kirmānshāhān nazd-i Shāhmurād Mīrzā, Ḥākim-i Ānjā* [The tale of Shāhqulī Mīrzā's journey to Karbalā and what befell him during his brief residence in Kirmānshāh as a guest of the governor, Shāmurād Mīrzā], collected together under the title *Majmūʿa-yi Mushtamil bar Se Qiṭʿa Tiʾātr Mansūb ba Marḥūm Mīrzā Malkum Khān Nāẓim ud-Daula* (Berlin, 1340 lunar/1921–1922).

2. *Sargudhasht-i Āqā Hāshim* [The tale of Āqā Hāshim]. Persian text of the letter in M. F. Akhundov (Ākhūndzāda), *Äsärläri* (Baku, 1961), II: 356–373; Azerbayjani translation in *ibid.*, pp. 232–241; Russian translation in M. F. Akhundov, *Izbrannoe* (Moscow, 1956), pp. 254–265.

early years and exercised upon its members a considerable influence, both as teacher and as initiator into the rites of masonry.[3] In the Ottoman Empire, it had been above all Armenians such as Güllü Agop (1840–1902), proprietor of the Gedikpaşa theater, and Minakyan (1832–1920), director of the Ottoman Theater, who had been responsible for the early flourishing of the Turkish drama.[4] During his residence in Istanbul from 1862 to 1872, Malkum doubtless came to know of these developments, and if he had decided to perform a similar role in Iran, by promoting drama in Persian, it would have furnished one more instance of Armenian cultural mediation between Europe and the Islamic world. Then, too, both Malkum and his father were closely acquainted with Ahmet Vefik Paşa, who not only made skillful Turkish renderings of Molière's comedies, but also built a theater in Bursa while governor of the city in 1879 and undertook to pay the actors' salaries.[5] Above all, Malkum was, as we have seen, an intimate friend of Fatḥ ᶜAlī Ākhūndzāda, whose Azerbayjani Turkish plays formed the most celebrated pieces of dramatic composition in the nineteenth-century Islamic world,[6] a copy of which Malkum received from the author during his visit to Istanbul in 1863.[7]

The four plays attributed to Malkum Khān indeed show an indebtedness to the example of Ākhūndzāda and suggest direct inspiration from his model. They betray essentially the same concern as that motivating the work of Ākhūndzāda and formulated by him as follows: "The people of Europe regard the noble art of the drama as a means for the refinement of morals. The conduct and manners of certain characters are presented in such a way as to arouse ridicule and enable the spectators to draw a useful moral lesson."[8] In the same way that Ākhūndzāda ridicules corrupt, superstitious, and ignorant individuals, particularly those belonging to the governing class, so too in the Persian comedies attributed to Malkum fictitious provincial governors are portrayed

3. See Abūl Qāsim Jannatī-ᶜAṭāʾī, *Bunyād-i Namāyish dar Īrān* (Tehran, 1334 solar/1955), p. 59; ᶜAlī Naṣīrīān, "Naẓarī ba Hunar-i Namāyish dar Īrān," *Kaweh*, new series, I: 2 (Khurdād 1342/May 1963), 117–118. Significantly enough, the performances were staged by Armenians. See Muḥammad Ḥasan Khān Iᶜtimād us-Salṭana, *Rūznāma-yi Khāṭirāt*, ed. Īraj Afshār (Tehran, 1345 solar/1966), p. 692. Clerical objections ultimately caused them to cease (G. N. Curzon, *Persia and the Persian Question* [London, 1892], I: 494).

4. Metin And, *A History of Theatre and Popular Entertainment in Turkey* (Ankara, 1963–1964), pp. 67–74, 78.

5. *Ibid.*, p. 74, and see above, p. 71.

6. M. F. Akhundov, *Komediyalar* (Baku, 1962).

7. See Ākhūndzāda's report of his journey to Istanbul, in Mīrzā Fatḥ ᶜAlī Ākhūndzāda, *Alifbā-yi Jadīd va Maktūbāt*, eds. Ḥamīd Muḥammadzāda and Ḥamīd Ārāslī (Baku, 1963), p. 78.

8. Letter to Mīrzā Ḥusayn Khān dated September 1868 in *ibid.*, p. 109.

in a variety of humiliating and laughable circumstances. The plays are, however, considerably inferior to those of Ākhūndzāda, and, with one exception, appear never to have been performed.[9] Their author can have known little or nothing of dramaturgical technique. Characters are made to recite long accounts of events that have occurred offstage and to perform various actions not generally witnessed in the theater. Thus, in the play *Ḥikāyat-i Karbalā Raftan-i Shāhqulī Mīrzā* (The story of Shāhqulī Mīrzā's journey to Karbalā), the hero is robbed of his trousers by Ṭāʾūs, a prostitute recommended to him by the governor of Kirmanshah and is obliged to take refuge in the lavatory. He is rescued by his servant who, to avoid further scandal, escorts him from the city disguised in female dress. Such grossness of humor is absent from the plays of Ākhūndzāda. Similarly, the Azerbayjani playwright would not have included in any of his comedies so technically impossible a scene as that occurring in act three of *Sargudhasht-i Ashraf Khān, Ḥākim-i ᶜArabistān* (What befell Ashraf Khan, the governor of Arabistan), where two characters are made to converse on horseback. It seems clear that the author conceived of the drama as another genre of written literature, with no idea of the exigencies of performance on the stage.

The first publication of any of the plays took place in 1908, when *Sargudhasht-i Ashraf Khān* appeared as a feuilleton in a Tabriz fortnightly journal, the *Ittiḥād*. This journal was the organ of the Anjuman-i Ittiḥād, one of the constitutionalist societies of the city.[10] The text was taken from a manuscript in the possession of Sayyid Ḥasan Taqīzāda, then prominent in the constitutionalist movement.[11] Publication began in the first number, which appeared on Ṣafar 2, 1326/March 6, 1908, was interrupted for issues fourteen and fifteen, and finally completed in number eighteen, dated Rabīᶜ uth-Thānī 26/May 28. This printing of the play bore no indication of authorship, and the last installment was concluded with the words "written by the lowliest and most abject one, in Tabrīz, on Jumādī ul-Ukhrā 12, 1319/January 25, 1902," presumably copied from the manuscript. The *Ittiḥād* survived for only three more numbers, its last issue appearing on Jumādī ul-Ūlā

9. The exception is *Ṭarīqa-yi Ḥukūmat-i Zamān Khān-i Burūjirdī* which was performed at the Rūdakī Hall in Tehran in 1348 solar/1969, and advertised as the work of Malkum. See Firīdūn Ādamīyat, *Andīshahā-yi Fatḥ ᶜAlī Ākhūndzāda* (Tehran, 1349 solar/1970), p. 68, n. 75.

10. See E. G. Browne, *The Press and Poetry of Modern Persia* (Cambridge, 1914), p. 34. The same author in his *Literary History of Persia* (Cambridge, 1942), IV: 463, falsely implies that more than one play appeared before the coup d'état of June 1908: "Three more plays, written at a date unknown to me, by the late Prince Malkom Khān, formerly Persian minister in London, were partly published as a feuilleton (*pā-waraq*) in the Tabriz newspaper *Ittiḥād* (Union) in 1326/1908."

11. See prefatory note to the Berlin edition cited in n. 1, above.

12, 1326/June 12, 1908, for the coup d'état of Muḥammad ʿAlī Shāh in that month brought about the dissolution of the Majlis and the suspension of all constitutionalist newspapers. It was thus impossible to proceed to the serialization of the other plays.

It was not until 1340 lunar/1921–1922 that another edition appeared, this time in Berlin at the Kāvīānī press of Kāẓimzāda Īrānshahr, under the title of *Majmūʿa-yi Mushtamil bar Se Qiṭʿa Tiʾātr Mansūb ba Marḥūm Mīrzā Malkum Khān* (Collection containing three dramas attributed to the late Mīrzā Malkum Khān). According to a prefatory note by the editor, Sayyid Javād Tabrīzī, the text was based on a manuscript of the plays found in the collection of Baron Friedrich Rosen, a diplomat with some scholarly interests who had spent a number of years in Iran. Rosen's chief period of residence in Iran extended from 1890 to 1898, and throughout these years Malkum was absent in Europe. It is unlikely that Rosen should have made his acquaintance after returning to Europe at the end of his term at the legation in Tehran: in his otherwise diffuse and anecdotally rich memoirs he makes no mention of Malkum.[12] Hence Rosen cannot be supposed to have vouched for the validity of the attribution to Malkum. He had most probably acquired his manuscript of the plays as one of several anonymous copies circulating in Tehran and learned from Iranian acquaintances that they were thought to be the work of Malkum.[13] This lack of certainty is reflected in Sayyid Javād's note when he appeals to common knowledge of Malkum as the author of the plays: "as is well-known, this collection of plays was written by the late Prince Mīrzā Malkum Khān, son of Mīrzā Yaʿqūb of Isfahan." Uncertainty is further evident in the title given to the collection.

Despite these misgivings implicit in the Berlin edition, biographers of Malkum and historians of recent Persian literature have had no hesitation in ascribing the plays to him, regarding them as one more instance of his revivifying influence on Persian letters.[14] In particular,

12. *Oriental Memoirs of a German Diplomatist* (London, 1930).

13. The statement of Guseini Abul'fas ("Eschë Raz ob Avtore Pervykh Persidskikh Pyes," *Narody Azii i Afriki*, 1965:6, p. 143) that "as is well known, after the death of Malkum Khan, his archive was sold off and evidently turned up in Iran, where Dr. Rosen bought a part of the books" is entirely unfounded. Some of Malkum's correspondence was donated by his widow to the Bibliothèque Nationale (see bibliography); the fate of the remainder and of his library is unknown.

14. E. G. Browne, *A Literary History of Persia*, IV (Cambridge, 1924): 463; introduction by Muḥīṭ Ṭabāṭabāʾī to *Majmūʿa-yi Āthār-i Mīrzā Malkum Khān* (Tehran, 1322 solar/1943), p. xlii; Jannatī-ʿAṭāʾī, *op. cit.* (n. 3, above), p. 60 (he reprints *Ṭarīqa-yi Ḥukūmat-i Zamān Khān-i Burūjirdī* on pp. 5–27 of the second part of his work); Jan Rypka, *Iranische Literaturgeschichte* (Leipzig, 1959), p. 348; Alessandro Bausani, *Storia della Letteratura Persiana* (Milan, 1960), p. 845; D. S. Kommissarov, *Ocherki Sovremennoi Persidskoi Prozy* (Moscow, 1960), p. 32; M. Rezvani, *Le Théâtre et la*

a number of Soviet scholars have seen in them additional evidence for the salubrious influence exercised upon Malkum by Ākhūndzāda, "the great Azerbayjani materialist thinker."[15] It must be conceded that since Malkum's interest in the alphabet question may have been aroused by Ākhūndzāda, and in any event unfolded in collaboration with him, it has been only natural to assume the existence of a similar discipleship in the sphere of the drama. Interest in the plays, however, has not been confined to the Soviet Union. Translations have been made not only into Russian,[16] but also French,[17] Danish,[18] and most recently Italian,[19] accompanied, in all cases except the last, by partially inaccurate biographical sketches of Malkum.

It was not until 1956 that doubt came to be cast on the attribution of the plays to Malkum. In an article based on documents preserved in the Ākhūndzāda archive in Baku, two Azerbayjani scholars, A. E. Ibrahimov and H. Mämmädzadä, came to the conclusion that the comedies had been wrongly ascribed to Malkum and were in fact the work of a hitherto unknown writer, Mīrzā Āqā of Tabriz.[20] Other than the widely current assumption that Malkum had written the plays and their attribution to him by the Berlin edition, the only evidence for his

---

Danse en Iran (Paris, 1962), p. 136; ᶜAlī Aṣghar Shamīm, *Īrān dar Daura-yi Salṭanat-i Qājār* (Tehran, 1342 solar/1963), p. 332 (the London edition of the plays mentioned by Shamīm is entirely imaginary); Bozorg Alavi, *Geschichte und Entwicklung der modernen persischen Prosaliteratur* (Berlin, 1964), pp. 65, 68 (according to whom Malkum wrote the plays "while in exile, in Cairo and elsewhere"); H. Kamshad, *Modern Persian Prose Literature* (Cambridge, 1966), p. 14 (who assumes that Malkum wrote the plays while in Istanbul, "where he got in touch with the circle of Persian reformers already in exile," these being left unidentified).

15. See especially A. M. Shoitov, "Rol' M. F. Akhundova v Razvitii Persidskoi Progressivnoi Literatury," *Kratkie Soobshcheniya Instituta Vostokovedeniya*, IX (1953): 61.

16. Of one play only, *Sargudhasht-i Ashraf Khān*: Ya. A. Eingorn, "Komediya Mirzy Mal'kom Khana 'Proisshestvie s Ashraf Khanom, Gubernatorom Arabistana,' " *Byulletin' Sredne-Aziatskogo Gosudarstvennogo Universiteta (Tashkent)*, 16 (1927): 102–120.

17. Of all three plays contained in the Berlin edition: A. Bricteux, "Les Comedies de Malkom Khan: Les Mésaventures d'Achraf Khan; Zaman Khan, ou le Gouverneur Modèle; Les Tribulations de Chah Qouli Mirza," *Bibliothèque de la Faculté de Philosophie et de Lettres de l'Université de Liège*, fasc. LIII (1933).

18. Of two plays, *Sargudhasht-i Ashraf Khān* and *Ḥikāyat-i Zamān Khan*: Arthur Christensen, "To Iranske Komedier fra Kadjarernes Tid," *Studier fra Sprog- og Oldtidsforskning*, fasc. 178 (Copenhagen, 1938).

19. Of all three plays in the Berlin edition: Gianroberto Scarcia, *Mirza Aqa Tabrizi: Tre Commedie* (Rome, 1967).

20. "Mirzä Mälkümkhana Aid Hesab Ädilän Pyeslärin Äsl Müällifi Haggında," *Nizami Adına Ädäbiyat vä Dil Institutunum Äsärläri* (*Ädäbiyat Seriyası*), IX (1956): 161–169.

authorship had consisted of a letter from Ākhūndzāda addressed, it was thought, to him, criticizing the numerous deficiencies of the plays.[21] On examining the original of the letter in the Ākhūndzāda archive, the two scholars realized that Malkum had not in fact been the recipient of the letter. The letter opens with the formula: "My dear brother Mīrzā Āqā, may God lengthen your life!"[22] Ākhūndzāda had coined for Malkum the flattering title of Rūḥ ul-Quds, "the Holy Spirit," and consistently addressed him by it in his correspondence;[23] it is unlikely that he should have deviated from the habit on this one occasion. Moreover, "Āqā" never formed part of Malkum's appellation, but its occurrence in the opening formula of Ākhūndzāda's letter, in conjunction with the title "Mīrzā," indicates that it must be regarded here as a name. These considerations have been overlooked by those who assumed the plays to have been written by Malkum and were thus obliged to regard "Mīrzā Āqā" as a formula by which he might have been addressed.

The letter of criticism was dated June 28, 1871, and sent to Mīrzā Āqā, first secretary of the French Embassy in Tehran: Ākhūndzāda took care to record the address on the copy he made which is now preserved in the archives bearing his name.[24] It is established that Malkum Khān was never employed by the French Embassy in Tehran, and in June 1871 he was in any event still in Istanbul, not to return to Iran until the spring of the following year.[25]

Of equal importance is the internal evidence supplied by the letter itself. Before proceeding to enumerate specific points of criticism in the four plays, Ākhūndzāda deems it necessary to provide their author with a brief description of the physical appearance of a theater.

> A theatre is a tall and spacious building inside which there are boxes [literally, small cells—*ḥujrahā-yi kūchik*], arranged in upper and lower tiers and running around three sides of the building, all facing the fourth side. The local people—nobles, tradesmen, artisans, men and women, all who are inclined—pay an entrance fee and then enter the building, sitting either in the boxes or on chairs affixed to the ground, and looking towards the fourth side of the building. . . . Then those skilled in the art of drama, whom the Europeans call "actors," each attired in a certain manner, emerge to enact a predetermined story, while the spectators listen to their discourse.[26]

21. See note 2 above.

22. Akhundov, *Äsärläri,* II: 356.

23. See Ākhūndzāda's letter to Jalāl ud-Dīn Mīrzā in *Alifbā-yi Jadīd va Maktūbāt,* p. 176.

24. Facsimile of the address, in Russian and Persian, in Ibrahimov and Mämmädzadä, *op. cit.,* p. 166.

25. See above, p. 96.

26. Akhundov, *Äsärläri,* II: 356–357.

It is obvious that Malkum, if he had been the author of the plays, would have had no need of instruction in such elementary details: from Paris as well as Istanbul doubtless he had acquired a reasonable familiarity with the structure of theaters.

The falsity of the attribution of the four comedies to Malkum becomes even more apparent from an examination of the letter which prompted Ākhūndzāda's critical reply. In a note accompanying the manuscript of the plays, sent to Ākhūndzāda for his perusal, Mīrzā Āqā remarks that "although I have never had the good fortune to attain to your felicity-bestowing presence, I have constantly heard of the noble and praiseworthy qualities and characteristics of your excellency, which indeed are unceasingly on every tongue, and have inwardly cherished a sincere devotion to you."[27] This letter was written in Rabīᶜ uth-Thānī 1288/June 1871, and cannot possibly have been written by Malkum who had met Ākhūndzāda in Istanbul in 1863 and engaged in a warm and friendly correspondence with him ever since his return to the Caucasus.[28]

Mīrzā Āqā supplies autobiographical information in a second letter to Ākhūndzāda which further precludes his identification with Malkum.

> Your servant goes by the name of Mīrzā Āqā, and comes from the city of Tabriz. From earliest childhood I conceived a desire to learn the French and Russian languages, and in fact I have gained enough knowledge of French to acquit myself in that tongue, whether in speech, writing or translation. I also have a slight acquaintance with Russian. After serving for a number of years at the royal teachers' training college [*muᶜallimkhāna-yi pādishāhī*] and other posts in Baghdad and Istanbul . . . I have been working now for almost seven years as First Secretary at the French Embassy in Tehran.[29]

Clearly, none of this corresponds to the career of Mīrzā Malkum Khān, other than the acquisition of a knowledge of French.

In the first letter of Ākhūndzāda and also in a note appended to the manuscript of the plays sent to him and now preserved in Baku, Mīrzā Āqā relates how he came to compose them under the influence of Ākhūndzāda's Azerbayjani Turkish comedies.

> One day I was sitting talking with some companions in a friend's house. Our conversation turned on the ability of rhetoric skillfully to control allusions and figures of speech. Then our host rose and brought us the plays written by the respected man of letters, Mīrzā Fatḥ ᶜAlī Ākhūndzāda, in the Azer-

27. Letter reproduced in facsimile and partially translated into Azerbayjani, in Ibrahimov and Mämmädzadä, *op. cit.*, pp. 164–165; Persian text given in *Alifbā-yi Jadīd va Maktūbāt*, pp. 391–392.

28. See Chapter Four above.

29. Facsimile and partial translation in Ibrahimov and Mämmädzadä, *op. cit.*, pp. 164–165; Persian text in *Alifbā-yi Jadīd va Maktūbāt*, pp. 389–390.

bayjani tongue. His beautiful, sweet and simple words, each like a precious pearl, passed from hand to hand, and like earrings adorned the ears of all who heard them. Since such works are a means for the education of the people, and for guiding them on the path of progress, I decided, ignoring my manifest lack of talent, to imitate his style, and thus it was that I came to write in the Persian tongue these four tales, each consisting of four scenes [*majlis*].[30]

It is probable that the friend who showed Mīrzā Āqā Ākhūndzāda's Azerbayjani plays was the Qajar prince, Jalāl ud-Dīn Mīrzā, to whom the author had entrusted the task of finding a Persian translator.[31] In fact, Mīrzā Āqā appears first to have considered rendering Ākhūndzāda's plays into Persian, but seeing himself unable to retain the freshness and vigor of the Azerbayjani in his version, decided instead to try his hand at an original composition.[32] Ākhūndzāda's plays ultimately found a skillful translator in Mīrzā Jaᶜfar Qarājadāghī, whose Persian version possibly became even more renowned than the original.[33]

This evidence, presented for the first time in 1956 by Ibrahimov and Mämmädzadä, must be considered conclusive, and the attribution of the four comedies to Mīrzā Malkum Khān can no longer be regarded as justifiable. The conclusions of the two Azerbayjani scholars, nonetheless, have met with skepticism. The Soviet orientalist, D. S. Kommissarov, in a footnote to his *Ocherki Sovremennoi Persidskoi Prozy*, (Moscow, 1960), remarks that the material adduced by them is interesting, but not conclusive,[34] and in the body of his text he insists on claiming that "following Akhundov's [Ākhūndzāda's] method of critical realism, Mīrzā Malkum Khān wrote several plays."[35] It is unfortunate that Kommissarov does not elucidate the nature of his reservations. Jan Rypka appears to have been similarly reluctant to incorporate the results of Ibrahimov and Mämmädzadä's research into his *Iranische Literaturgeschichte* (Leipzig, 1959), and merely repeats the current assumption that "he [Malkum] wrote plays."[36] In a footnote he refers to the article of the Azerbayjani scholars, sayings that "possibly some of the plays are not by Malkum Khān."[37] It is not, however, a question of distinguishing between plays which have been falsely attributed to

30. Ibrahimov and Mämmädzadä, *op. cit.*, p. 168.

31. See his letter to Jalāl ud-Dīn Mīrzā dated 1870 in *Maktūbāt*, p. 182.

32. See his first letter to Ākhūndzāda in *ibid.*, p. 391.

33. See Ākhūndzāda's letter to Qarājadāghī, expressing his satisfaction with the translation, in *ibid.*, pp. 204–210. The translation was first lithographed in Tehran in 1291 lunar/1873. A list of later editions and translations from the Persian into English, French and German, is given by Rypka, *op. cit.* (n. 14, above), p. 593.

34. P. 32, n. 14.

35. *Ibid.*, p. 32.

36. P. 348.

37. *Ibid.*, p. 348, n. 16.

Malkum and others of which he was in fact the author: all four belong together, and all came from the same pen.

The only other work in which notice has been taken of Ibrahimov and Mämmädzadä's conclusions is an article by the Italian scholar, Gianroberto Scarcia, published in May 1967, and entitled "Malkom Khān (1833–1908) e la Nascita del Teatro Persiano Moderno."[38] He summarizes their evidence and arguments and appears to accept the soundness of their thesis, though refraining from doing so explicitly. Instead of treating Mīrzā Āqā Tabrīzī as the author of the plays, he is content to refer to a "pseudo Malkom Khān" as their author.[39] Any reservations he may have had about the validity of Ibrahimov and Mämmädzadä's findings have now evidently been resolved, for his own translation of the three plays contained in the Berlin edition is clearly entitled *Mīrzā Āqā Tabrīzī: Tre Commedie.*[40]

Additional evidence for the falsity of the attribution to Malkum, together with further information on the true author of the plays, Mīrzā Āqā Tabrīzī, was supplied by another Azerbayjani scholar, Guseini Abul'fas, in an article published in 1965.[41] He anticipates the hypothesis being advanced, in answer to the thesis of Ibrahimov and Mämmädzadä, that Malkum on this occasion chose to use a pseudonym to conceal, even from Ākhūndzāda, his authorship of the plays. This possibility Abul'fas refutes by referring to the fact that Mīrzā Āqā requests of Ākhūndzāda that he keep the plays and their authorship secret until authorized by him to reveal their existence. If he had been using a pseudonym in the first place, such a request would have been superfluous.[42] To this may be added the observation that Malkum had been in correspondence with Ākhūndzāda since 1864 and was exchanging letters with him on the alphabet question at precisely the same time that Mīrzā Āqā wrote from Tehran.[43] It is inconceivable that Malkum should have maintained a dual correspondence with Ākhūndzāda, using both his own name and a pseudonym, and arranging for letters bearing the latter to be mailed from Tehran. The handwriting of Mīrzā Āqā's letters is, moreover, easi-

38. The article appeared in *Oriente Moderno*, XLVII (1967): 248–266.

39. See n. 18 above.

40. Published in Naples in 1969.

41. Abul'fas, "Eschë Raz ob Avtore Pervykh Persidskikh Pyes," *Narody Azii i Afriki*, 1965:6, 142–145. The contents of the article have been described by Hubert Evans in "An Enquiry into the Authorship of Three Persian Plays Attributed to Malkom Khan," *Central Asian Review*, XV (1967): 21–25.

42. Abul'fas, *op. cit.*, p. 143.

43. Abul'fas is wrong in his assertion (*ibid.*, p. 143) that Malkum had visited Tiflis several months before the receipt of Mīrzā Āqā's letter: his visit came in March 1872. See above, pp. 97–99.

ly distinguishable from the more elegant and delicate *nastaʿlīq* generally affected by Malkum in his correspondence.

The late Saʿīd Nafīsī, the celebrated Iranian scholar and man of letters, fully accepted the findings of Ibrahimov and Mämmädzadä, which were evidently communicated to him by Abul'fas. Curious to discover more about Mīrzā Āqā Tabrīzī, he came across a further work of the hitherto unknown author which supplies confirmation of his existence and a somewhat fuller account of his life. He wrote to Abul'fas:

> I have always suspected that Malkum Khān was not the author of these plays, and I am happy that your letter has confirmed the justice of my doubts on the question. I am in a position to inform you that Mīrzā Āqā Tabrīzī was still alive in 1921, and wrote in his own hand a book entitled *Risāla-yi Akhlāqīya* [Treatise on ethics], which is now preserved at the Central Library of Tehran University.[44]

The manuscript contains biographical information suggesting the identity of its author with Ākhūndzāda's correspondent: the work is by one Mīrzā Āqā Tabrīzī, who learned French from foreigners and taught them Persian in return, thus earning the title of "Mīrzā"; he traveled to Baghdad and Istanbul before later returning to Iran.[45] The handwriting of the manuscript appears, from examples illustrating the article of Abul'fas, to be identical with that of the letters to Ākhūndzāda.[46]

The identity of the author of *Risāla-yi Akhlāqīya* with the writer of the four plays formerly ascribed to Malkum is not, however, essential for establishing the true authorship of the plays. The evidence advanced by Ibrahimov and Mämmädzadä is in itself adequate and decisive. It remains, then, only to examine how the attribution of the plays to Malkum came to arise and to receive wide and unquestioning credence.

Malkum himself, it seems, must be acquitted of all responsibility in the matter. It is true that he was still alive when the first publication of *Sargudhasht-i Ashraf Khān* took place in the *Ittiḥād* of Tabriz. There is, however, no indication that he authorized or was even aware of the attribution. He was ailing at the time and died soon after, at Lausanne on July 13, 1908—that is, three and a half months after the play had begun to appear.[47] It is unlikely that in the course of this period he should have received a copy of the newspaper and thus had an oppor-

44. *Ibid.*, p. 144. Apparently, the works of Mīrzā Āqā now are being prepared for publication in Baku, in Persian, and in Azerbayjani translation (*ibid.*, p. 145).

45. *Ibid.*, p. 144.

46. Plate facing *ibid.*, p. 144.

47. See above, p. 258.

tunity to repudiate authorship of the comedy. The possibility, of course, cannot be entirely excluded that Malkum came to know of the appearance of the play in *Ittiḥād,* and wrote a letter dissociating himself from it, but that the contents of the letter never became known, either because of his death soon after or because of Muḥammad ᶜAlī Shāh's coup d'état with its resultant disruption of journalistic activity.

As for the Berlin edition of 1922–1923, it might be thought that Malkum's widow was in a position to deny her husband's authorship of the plays on seeing them attributed to him. Princess Malkum survived her husband for a number of years I have been unable to determine, but it is certain that she lived at least until February 1924, for it was then that she donated a collection of her husband's correspondence to the Bibliothèque Nationale.[48] It is possible that she failed to learn of the existence of the Berlin edition; that she did so, but was unwilling to deplete her husband's posthumous fame; or that she was genuinely ignorant of the matter and supposed Malkum to have written the plays.

An explanation for the attribution of the comedies to Malkum has to be sought elsewhere than in his or his widow's negligence or complicity. It should first be noted that although Malkum did not write the plays, there are certain of his works which contain what might be called dramatic elements. He wrote a number of dialogues, quite lively in content and divided into scenes (majlis) after the manner of a play. Such are, for example, *Rafīq va Vazīr* (Our friend and the minister), dealing with administrative and governmental reform;[49] *Shaykh va Vazīr* (The shaykh and the minister), devoted to discussion of the alphabet question;[50] and *Sayyāḥī Gūyad* (A traveler's narrative), which might be summarized as a critique of the state of learning and literature in Qajar Iran.[51] Indeed, the realistic and vivid tone of these dialogues, together with their polemical content, render them of superior dramatic worth to the somewhat banal farces of Mīrzā Āqā Tabrīzī. It is, then, comprehensible that readers acquainted with Malkum's dialogues should have assumed him to be the author of the plays as they circu-

48. See her letter pasted in the front of Supplément Persan 2340, dated February 24, 1924. Officials of the Oriental Manuscript Room at the Bibliothèque Nationale cite the continued existence of Malkum's widow as the reason for their refusal to permit the documents to be microfilmed. If Princess Malkum were still alive, she would now be well into her thirteenth decade (assuming her to have been about twenty when she married Malkum in 1864). A letter to the address supplied by the Bibliothèque Nationale as hers has failed to evoke any response.

49. See *Majmūᶜa-yi Āthār*, pp. 53–72, and pp. 00–00 above.

50. See *Kullīyāt-i Malkum*, ed. Hāshim Rabīᶜzāda (Tabriz, 1325 lunar/1908), pp. 87–124; and pp. 93–95 above.

51. *Ibid.*, pp. 187–212.

lated in anonymous manuscript, or accepted their attribution to him as accurate after they had appeared in print.[52]

The content of Mīrzā Āqā Tabrīzī's plays, moreover, is entirely compatible with Malkum's attested social and political attitudes and suggests certain parallels with his writings. In three of the comedies provincial governors are placed in ridiculous and shameful situations, and Malkum also frequently expressed his contempt for this segment of the ruling class. Thus, in *Uṣūl-i Madhhab-i Dīvānīān* (Principles of faith for government officials), a work intended as a bitter attack on Amīn us-Sulṭān, he has the following to say:

> Every wretch who possesses a patch of ground or a bit of wealth, he [Amīn us-Sulṭān] must strip bare with a thousand lying promises in accordance with that variety of swindling known in government terminology as "an offering to the presence" [*taqdīm-i huḍūr*], and then, with a filthy scrap of paper known as "the universally obeyed decree" [*farmān-i jahānmutāᶜ*], he appoints him as governor of some wilderness or other, until a few days later he is dismissed with ignominy, and some other idiot is found to take his place.[53]

The fates of Shāhqulī Mīrzā, Zamān Khān, and Ashraf Khān in the plays of Mīrzā Āqā Tabrīzī are little better than the ignominious career thus depicted by Malkum.

In one play, moreover, *Ṭarīqa-yi Ḥukūmat-i Zamān Khān-i Burūjirdī* (The method of government employed by Zamān Khān of Burūjird), one of the heroes is an Armenian arrack seller, who on occasion makes exclamations in Armenian: if Malkum had been the author, it might be thought that he were paying homage to his ancestry.

The most important consideration for an understanding of the false attribution is the general currency of anonymous literary composition in Qajar Iran. Work critical of existing social and political conditions was inevitably productive of danger for its author, and only anonymity could procure a partial guarantee of safety. Such work, moreover, could not be entrusted to a printing press; reproduction had to be done laboriously by hand, and in this process of copying out anonymous manuscripts, it was almost inevitable that false or uncertain attributions of authorship should come to be made. For example, toward the end of the century the celebrated preacher Sayyid Jamāl ud-Dīn Iṣfahānī composed a little work entitled *Ruʾyā-yi Ṣādiqa* (The veracious dream), in which he prophesied an awesome fate in the hereafter for the chief

52. Something of the same confusion between dramatic and pseudodramatic forms is visible in Rypka's statement that "he [Malkum] wrote plays, or better to say, political pamphlets in dialogue form" (*op. cit.* [n. 14, above], p. 348).

53. *Kullīyāt-i Malkum*, p. 255.

cleric of Isfahan, Āqā Najafī; the governor of the city, Ẓill us-Sulṭān; and other notables. The work was first printed in St. Petersburg by friends of the author in seventy anonymous copies which were then forwarded to Iran and formed the basis of further, handwritten copies.[54] The claim has been made that the true author of the work was not Sayyid Jamāl ud-Dīn, but his associate, Mīrzā Naṣrullāh Malik ul-Mutakallimīn. This claim appears improbable, although it may be that Malik ul-Mutakallimīn had some subordinate share in the composition of the book.[55] The anonymity of the work precludes absolute certainty.

Anonymity for long prevented the true authorship of the masterly Persian translation of Morier's *Hajji Baba* from being known: rather than Mīrzā Ḥabīb Iṣfahānī, it was thought to be his fellow exile in Istanbul, Shaykh Aḥmad Rūḥī, who had accomplished the feat.[56]

As a final example may be mentioned the *Siyāḥatnāma-yi Ibrāhīm Bayg* (The travels of Ibrahim Beg) by Zayn ul-ᶜĀbidīn Marāgha'ī, a kind of Gulliver's travels through Iran. The work appeared at intervals in three volumes, and it was only on publication of the third in Istanbul in 1909 that the author saw fit to reveal his identity. He was not immediately believed, for being a man of little education and literary background he was thought incapable of producing a work which is both fluent and compelling, despite its occasional naiveté.[57]

Mīrzā Āqā Tabrīzī likewise considered it expedient to retain his anonymity. The manuscript he sent Ākhūndzāda for his examination was anonymous,[58] and there is no record of his acknowledging authorship of the plays to anyone else. This may in part have been due to the discouraging effect of Ākhūndzāda's strictures on his efforts. With Mīrzā Āqā Tabrīzī remaining thus silent, it is easily imagined how those who may have chanced upon his work should have attributed it to one of established fame whose writings also circulated in anonymous, handwritten copies—that is, to Malkum. Of all the anonymous works circulating in the late nineteenth and early twentieth centuries, those of Malkum were at once the most numerous, the most widely known, and the most effective. It is indeed probable that his tracts on governmental reform written in the early 1850s, copied and circulated without men-

54. Sayyid Muḥammad ᶜAlī Jamālzāda, *Sar au Tah-i Yak Karbās* (Tehran, 1334 solar/1955), I: 93.

55. Mahdī Malikzāda, *Tārīkh-i Inqilāb-i Mashrūṭīyat-i Īrān* (Tehran, 1327 solar/1948), I: 81.

56. Kamshad, *op. cit.* (n. 14, above), pp. 21–23.

57. Browne, *Literary History of Persia*, IV: 467. The German translator of the work, Walther Schulz, evidently regarded the work as autobiographical and took the fictitious hero of the story, Ibrahim Beg, as its author. See his preface to *Ibrahim Begs Reisebuch über Persien* (Leipzig, 1903).

58. Ibrahimov, Mämmädzadä, *op. cit.* (n. 20, above), p. 167.

tion of the author's name, initiated this genre of literature in Qajar Iran and associated him with its subsequent diffusion.

That there existed something of a general tendency to ascribe to Malkum various anonymous works is attested not only by the case of Mīrzā Āqā Tabrīzī's plays, but also by two other false attributions. The first printed collection of his treatises, published by Hāshim Rabīᶜzāda in 1908, contained a piece entitled *Risāla-yi Ghaybīya* which dealt with the necessity of law and the essential identity of Islamic and European legal concepts.[59] Malkum wrote from his sickbed in Rome disavowing authorship of the treatise and protesting against its inclusion among his works. While pleading for the exercise of greater care in the compilation of any future collection, he nonetheless conceded the existence of similarities in style and content between the anonymous treatise and many of his own writings.[60] Another false attribution, that of the treatise *Inshāllāh, Māshāllāh* by Mīrzā Āqā Khān, took longer to discover, and doubts surrounding the matter have only recently been dispelled.[61]

Thus it was that Mīrzā Āqā Tabrīzī's choice of anonymity for long cost him his rightful fame as an early Persian playwright. For Malkum, however, even if the plays can no longer be taken as evidence of his dramaturgical talent, they still perform a service: to demonstrate the extent of his renown as a skilled and versatile writer of sociocritical literature.

59. *Kullīyāt-i Malkum*, pp. 57–69. The treatise was reprinted by Muḥīṭ Ṭabāṭabāʾī in *Majmūᶜa-yi Āthār-i Mīrzā Malkum Khān*, pp. 1–16 (of appendices), with a warning note on the falsity of its attribution to Malkum (p. xlix).

60. Text of the letter given in *Majmūᶜa-yi Āthār*, pp. 2–3 (of appendices).

61. The work is a bitterly satirical attack upon religion, composed in reply to a treatise written by the leader of the Shaykhī sect, Ḥājjī Muḥammad Karīm Khān Kirmānī. See Firīdūn Ādamīyat, *Andīshahā-yi Mīrzā Āqā Khān Kirmānī* (Tehran, 1346 solar/1967), pp. 52–53; and Yaḥyā Daulatābādī, *Tārīkh-i Muᶜāṣir yā Ḥayāt-i Yahyā* (Tehran, n.d.), I: 160.

APPENDIX B

A Traveler's Narrative

THE FOLLOWING TRANSLATION is offered as a specimen of Malkum's style as essayist.* It cannot be regarded as strictly representative of his work, for unlike most of his treatises and essays, it has little to say on political and economic matters. His writings on such topics, however, have been adequately summarized and discussed in the foregoing chapters, and a reading of them *in extenso* would prove tedious. *A Traveler's Narrative* is, by contrast, a lively treatment of the subjects it sets out to discuss, despite obvious literary shortcomings, and is inspired throughout by an acute sense of satire.

The piece constitutes a sustained attack on two classes of men: poets and men of letters and religious scholars. Government officials, physicians, and astrologers all receive passing blows, but are not on this occasion the chief objects of satire. It is regrettable that the exact date of composition of the essay is unknown, for the views on traditional poetry and eloquence expressed in it form one of the earliest protests against that subordination of content to form which characterized much of Persian letters in the Qajar period. The establishment of the Qajar dynasty had followed by a few decades the formation of the Isfahan school of poetry, which aspired to imitation of the classical masters, particularly the panegyrists of the Seljuq period.[1] When the Qajar court was established in Tehran and came to function as a new center of patronage, the school of Isfahan transferred to the capital, and the imprint of its ideals can be

* The translation is based on the text entitled "Sayyāḥī Gūyad," in *Kullīyāt-i Malkum*, pp. 187–212.

1. See Malik ush-Shuᶜarā Bahār, "Bāzgasht-i Adabī," *Armaghān*, XIII (1311 solar/1932): 441–448; XIV (1312 solar/1933): 57–69.

seen on most Persian poetry until late in the nineteenth century. The poetry in imitation of classical masters produced by men such as Saḥāb (d. 1808), Ṣabā (d. 1822), and even the greatest of the school, Qāʾānī (d. 1854), was for the most part forced and unconvincing; the search for rhetorical ingenuity became frantic and sometimes took the poet beyond the bounds of comprehensibility. It is verse such as this that Malkum ridicules by means of the rhymed absurdities the poets in his piece recite. Later in the nineteenth century, the transformation of Persian poetry began with the introduction of political and social concerns into the corpus of accepted poetic themes and the subordination of form to content, of word to meaning. Although Malkum never tried his hand at verse, in this essay he foreshadows some of these developments which were to revivify Persian poetry.

The view of the ulama expounded at length in this piece is of great interest for revealing Malkum's sincere opinion of that class. He ridicules even their title of "learned men" (*ʿulamā*), preferring instead to coin the word *jahlmandān* (ignoramuses) as a more appropriate designation. Their concern with points of ritual and branches of the law (*furūʿāt*) is depicted as inherently absurd, and they are accused of having divided the community into warring sects merely for the sake of selfish interest. They do the bidding of kings by proclaiming their self-seeking wars to have religious sanction and, while turning a blind eye on the failings of the powerful, visit all their harshness on the weak. All objections to their misdeeds they silence by denouncing the protestor as an infidel, and their minds are closed to all new knowledge, particularly that emanating from non-Muslim sources.

Although the justice of many of Malkum's accusations, once shorn of polemical exaggeration, may be accepted, it is nonetheless clear from the piece that he was impatient with the whole apparatus of traditional culture and religious learning. With his background of European education and his concern for a radical westernization of Iranian life, he could have had little sympathy for a class which, in the nature of things, was bound to absorb and elaborate a transmitted body of learning (*naql*) and to cultivate a knowledge of Arabic.

The class nonetheless has its uses, even for a reformer such as Malkum, for he suggests that they form the best support for the honor of the nation and are capable of rendering "unlimited services to people and to state." They need, however, one to guide them (*murabbī nadārand*), "to reduce their affairs to order, and regulate and determine the tasks they are to fulfill." It is clear from other evidence that Malkum himself aspired to the position of "guide" of the ulama and hoped to direct their attention away from *furūʿāt* to matters he considered more pressing. It is by no means certain that this would have resulted in truer service by the ulama to the cause of religion: Malkum's profession of belief that "the perspicuous faith of Islam is perfect and the best of all paths for men to follow," rings as hollow as all his other utterances on the matter.

Malkum's view of the ulama has anticipated certain more recent attitudes toward them. His mocking of their heavily Arabicized speech bears comparison with Jamālzāda's depiction of a shaykh in his celebrated story *Fārsī Shikar Ast* (Persian is sugar-sweet).[2] The shaykh expresses himself with greater grammatical accuracy than the figures in Malkum's piece, a fact which doubtless reflects Jamālzāda's superior command of Arabic. It is also of interest to note that the complaint that the ulama devote excessive attention to minor matters of ritual and the details of ablution still is heard frequently in Iran.

Despite the interest of its contents and the satirical verve apparent in its wording, the essay is weak and unconvincing in its structure. It lacks the masterly coherence and control that alone would qualify it to rank with masterpieces of Persian satire such as the work of ʿUbayd Zākānī (d. 1371). There is no real transition from one episode to the next, and the ending is abrupt and unexpected. Too many characters make their brief appearances, and not all have a clearly defined function. Thus, the narrator, his friend, and the "ill-mannered youth" are all positive figures, observing and criticizing the lunacy around them, with no apparent difference of outlook or belief. This structural weakness is less apparent in Malkum's shorter dialogues, *Rafīq va Vazīr* and *Shaykh va Vazīr*, where a clearly circumscribed topic is discussed by only two persons.

The translation is inevitably free at those points where it was necessary to construct whole sentences of nonsense approximately corresponding to those in the original. Those sentences which in the text are written in a barbarous pseudo-Arabic are marked with an asterisk in the translation.

I once had occasion to witness a sublime and wondrous gathering in one of the cities of Iran, which I attended in the company of a friend. Not long had passed after my arrival before a certain dignified *ākhūnd*[3] joined our gathering and settled himself down in the place of honor. An hour later, a person adorned in costly garments with embroidered hems entered the room and took his place beside the ākhūnd. With an earnest frown on his face, he exchanged the customary greetings and compli-

2. *Yakī būd, yakī nabūd,* 5th ed. (Tehran, 1339 solar/1960), pp. 22–37.

3. *Ākhūnd*: one distinguished by dress and possession of religious learning, or pretension thereto, as a member of the religious classes.

ments with all present and then, to all appearances, subsided in an ocean of thought.

I asked my friend: "Who is this lofty personage?"

He replied: "Our host, one of the gentry of this city."

Soon after arrived another person, who was wearing a white robe decorated with silver thread, over his robe, a cloak, and on top of the cloak, a coat of squirrel fur. Instead of trousers, he had chosen to clothe his legs in a nondescript, dark blue undergarment. He sat down directly facing our host. Then came another guest, a man of impudent bearing, with a fur hat set at a jaunty angle on his head, clad in military attire and a green cloak with golden epaulettes. He went and stationed himself next to the ākhūnd.

It was at this point that I saw our host suddenly emit a roar of such dimensions that I feared for myself and turning to my friend requested an explanation.

He replied: "Our respected host was simply calling for his water pipe."

Soon I saw a host of servants rush in and jostle each other with such abandon that the guests were almost trampled underfoot. I was waiting for the imminent collision when I observed the ākhūnd angrily preparing to quit the gathering. He had arisen and was beginning to deliver a furious oration.

Our host, slightly unknitting his brow, addressed him in conciliatory tone and finally succeeded in seating him anew. The ākhūnd replied with a strange mixture of ceremonially polite and intentionally offensive phrases. The gentleman in the white robe took the side of our host, but the guest who was clad in a green cloak took up the cudgels for the ākhūnd, and an hour passed in pleasant conversation between them.

I was not well acquainted with their manner of expression and therefore asked my friend to explain the substance of the dispute. His reply was as follows: "The reason for the ākhūnd's attempted departure was the laxity of his host's servants in bringing him his accustomed water pipe. This aroused his anger and caused him to arise and prepare to leave. And his parting words were: 'May God have mercy on past generations! I spit on times such as these!'

"Then our host responded: 'Patiently to forebear is a duty for you. Exert yourself in patience, I beg of you! Do you not constantly recommend this lofty quality to us? How can it befit your spiritual dignity to be filled with such pride that you find delay in the simple matter of a water pipe to be quite intolerable? You consider yourself an exemplary model for all men and invite us to learn pleasing morals and conduct from your person, but is obedience truly incumbent on us? In what chapter of the law is it stipulated that you should always receive your water pipe before all others, never once having to wait?'

"The ākhūnd replied: 'If you imagine yourself to have acquired some dignity from service to the state, I too have earned much honor from service to the Sacred Law.[4] Disrespect shown to me is tantamount to disrespect of God's Law, let none gainsay it! And if this matter is not spelled out in the lawbooks, it is nonetheless present in the Glorious Qur'ān. To honor the believer is to revere the values of religion. Did not the Prophet say: "The learned among my people are as the Prophets of the Children of Israel"? You have not, like me, expended toil and trouble and the light of your eyes in the dark corner of a madrasa! Come now, tell us, what worthy service have you performed for government and people to deserve all this pomp and grandeur? What have you done but cause your depredations to descend throughout the land and usurp the people's heard-earned wealth? All you have to show for your efforts is a manner of speech befitting your station and the joy and glee of foreigners that the affairs of our land go according to their desires!' "

The gentleman in the white robe, who was evidently an accountant in government service, turned to the ākhūnd and said: "Respected sir! You have let your anger pass beyond all reasonable bounds. Now you saw fit to mention madrasas; tell us, pray, who builds madrasas for you and your like? Who pays the cost of your dignity and rank? You who claim to be a servant of the effulgent Law of God, tell us honestly, what service have you performed? What flawless, well-argued book have you composed to remain as a monument in time to come? How many thousand traditions of the Prophet do you know by heart? With how many Arab masters have you studied the Glorious Qur'ān, its recitation and interpretation? How many thousands of the straying and lost have you led to the haven of true guidance? What service, indeed, have you performed other than this, that you have divided our Twelver Shiʿi community, which once was one, into two parties, and called them Shaykhī and Uṣūlī?[5] You have forced these wretches to contend with

4. Compare with this fictitious statement the words of Mullā Muḥammad Ṣāliḥ Burghānī (d. ca. 1850), addressed to the governor of Qazvin: "Rule and rank last as long as your appointment by the king; after your dismissal, the pleasures you enjoyed are exposed to loss. But the ulama are constantly in the presence of the Creator. As soon as you and your like see us, you act with humility and submission to us, treating us with respect. . . . This, then, is a divine power, and superior to all other pleasures" (Muḥammad b. Sulaymān Tunukābunī, *Qiṣaṣ ul-ʿUlamā* [Tehran, 1304 lunar/1885], p. 64).

5. The Shaykhīs, a sect established by Shaykh Aḥmad Aḥsā'ī (1154/1741–1241/1826). The most distinctive feature of his teaching was the doctrine of a "fourth

and condemn each other; you have severed the ties of love and fraternity between them. And this, so that 'guides' and 'elders' might constantly be in demand and all kinds of hostility continuously erupt.

"Tell me, what mosque have you built, what madrasa established? And what unknown *imāmzāda*[6] have you discovered and honored with a worthy tomb?

"Now you say that disrespect shown to you is tantamount to dishonoring the Sacred Law, but this you have yet to prove. You are not yourself the law; you claim only to be a *mujtahid*,[7] so tell us clearly what you mean. As for what God has ordained, His commands are general in scope; specific provisions may freely be discussed. Why should you alone qualify for the rank of 'believer' and of 'scholar'; cannot we also aspire thereto? Or are you of those believers and learned men whom God has mentioned in His Book?[8] And as for the saying of the Prophet—may the peace and blessings of God be upon him—that 'the learned among my people are as the Prophets of the Children of Israel,' we will know that it refers to you when you transform your walking stick into a snake and when you restore the dead to life! Only then will you qualify as one of the learned intended by the Seal of Prophets!"

On hearing this, the military man laughed and said: "Glorious and Exalted is God Almighty! See what a pass we have reached! His excellency the clerk, who always spells Āshtīān[9] with an ᶜ*ayn* and a *ṭā*, has taken it on himself to explain a Qurᵓānic verse, and started to mumble

---

pillar" (*rukn-i rābi*ᶜ) of the faith, that is, an intermediary between the community and the Hidden Imam, whose existence tends to lessen the absoluteness of the Occultation. Shaykh Aḥmad was denounced as an infidel by a number of the ulama of Qazvin (see Tunukābunī, *op. cit.*, pp. 31–32). On his life, see the work of his son, ᶜAbdullāh b. Aḥmad Aḥsāᵓī, *Sharḥ-i Ḥālāt-i Shaykh Aḥmad ul-Aḥsāᵓī* (Bombay, 1310 lunar/1893). A concise description of his teachings is given by Henri Corbin in "L'Ecole Shaykhie en Théologie Shiᶜite," *Annuaire de l'Ecole des Hautes-Etudes (Section des Sciences Religieuses), année 1960–1961*, pp. 1–60.

The Uṣūlīs: the mass of the Twelver Shiᶜi community, those who held to the principles (*uṣūl*) of jurisprudence authoritatively expounded for the Qajar period by Āqā Muḥammad Bāqir Bihbihānī (1117/1705–1208/1803). Clashes between the Uṣūlīs and Shaykhīs repeatedly occurred in a number of Iranian cities, especially Tabriz and Kirman, down through the early years of the twentieth century. See Aḥmad Kasravī, *Zindagānī-yi Man* (Tehran, 1340 solar/1961), p. 22; and Gianroberto Scarcia, "Kerman 1905: la 'guerra' tra Šeiḫī e Bālāsarī," *Annali del Istituto Universitario Orientale di Napoli*, XIII (1963): 186–203.

6. *Imāmzāda*: a relative or descendant of one of the Twelve Imams, as well as the tomb enshrining his remains.

7. *Mujtahid*: for a definition, see p. 14 above.

8. Malkum is presumably alluding here to the verse "truly among His bondsmen the wise [or learned, ᶜ*ulamā*ᵓ] fear God" (Qurᵓān, 35:28).

9. Āshtīān, a village near Arāk in northwest Iran, properly spelled with *alif-madda* and *tā*, not ᶜ*ayn* and *ṭā*.

about 'general' and 'specific.' My dear sir, it is quite enough that you should scrawl out your illegible *siyāq*,[10] be innocent of all the principles of accountancy, unable to perform the simplest arithmetic, and yet hold the position of chief accountant in the land! To manage the accounts while quite incapable of accountancy is indeed a staggering feat. 'Deduct therefrom' is the extent of your learning; 'the lofty ministry,' your only adornment. Come now, leave aside 'general' and 'specific!'

"Besides, the meaning of the *ḥadīth* is not what you imagine. Comparison does not imply complete identity between objects or persons compared. If the ulama are the best of men in their seeking of proximity to God, in learning and in wisdom, it is enough to justify the comparison. Then, too, consider this: the Prophets of the Children of Israel were issuing a challenge, were laying claim to prophecy. They performed miraculous deeds only to bear witness to their claim. If you should imitate Pharaoh and deny the word of God, then will it be a duty for the ulama to bring forth miracles and to turn a stick into a snake!"

All this brought his excellency the accountant to a pitch of fury, and he replied: "Your true calling is that of a poet! Now nonchalance and carelessness may be part of the poet's profession, but they should not always be on display. It is no cause for surprise that when they wish to enumerate the true servants of the state, they write: Mīrzā the mouthful, Mīrzā the fragment, Mīrzā the particle, Mīrzā the drop and Mīrzā the invisible.[11] In youth such persons are sensualists and libertines, but in old age they set themselves up as sages and preceptors. Their talents lie in patching words together, and when they come to compose history, it becomes all too clear that the sum of their knowledge is the four dynasties of ancient Iran. Were you to ask them what celebrated persons were alive in the first year of the reign of Parvīz, and what great events befell at that time, they would be unable to give you satisfaction. Out of all the occurrences in the history of the world, they are content to be familiar with the tale of Rustam and Isfandiyār[12] and what passed between Khusrau and Shīrīn.[13] Of prosody, rhyme, and rhetoric, they know nothing, and of the poetry and literature of foreign peoples they are entirely unaware. Whenever they cannot fit a verse to its proper

10. *Siyāq*: a system of notation traditionally used in accountancy, based upon abbreviated forms of the Arabic words denoting numerals.

11. The meaning of this statement is obscure. It may be that here the accountant wishes to belittle his adversary's profession: the ranks of the military, as entered on the payroll, range from "mouthful" to "invisible," and thus all represent insubstantial quantities.

12. Two heroes of the Iranian epic tradition.

13. The hero and heroine of a romantic episode frequently celebrated in Persian verse.

meter, they pass it off as a 'pleasing pause.'[14] Any weird fancy that is contrary to the rules of both Persian and Arabic they regard as proof of the utmost eloquence. Despite all this, they are not content with a stipend of 300 *tomans* and a hundred *kharvārs* in kind!"[15]

When the ākhūnd saw the turn that affairs had taken, he said: "Gentlemen! I have abandoned all my complaints, and so now leave each other in peace." The guests asked and granted each other forgiveness, and the gathering dispersed.

Leaving that seat of argument and dissension, I emerged into the street and fell into the clutches of sundry classes of madmen, each one separately of perverse disposition and each afflicted with a different species of lunacy. Some hoped to cure the sicknesses of the body by the use of magic formulas. Others wished to deduce the fate of men from the conjunction and disposition of the planets. Still another group was of the belief that language was invented not for the purpose of conveying ideas, but for the construction of rhyming phrases and other devices for squandering men's time.

This latter species of lunatic was celebrated among the commonalty for its wordy blabbering. In strict adherence to their beliefs, the members of this group paid no attention to meaning, whether in speech or in writing. They considered obscurity of speech the highest degree of accomplishment and spent most of their life in the study of rare and uncommon words. When they listened to someone speaking, it was not in order to grasp the purport of his speech; rather they were on the lookout for some new and unfamiliar word that he might utter.

Because of their innate stupidity, whenever one of them knew twenty different words for one meaning, instead of using only one, he would employ all twenty in succession, considering eloquence to repose in peculiarity of expression. All their energy and attention were devoted to striving after the utmost degree of obscure complexity.

The more incomprehensible a statement was, the more luster it gained in their eyes, and if they wished to praise the accomplishments of some writer, they would say: "That rascal is so eloquent that none can understand his writings."

Because they reckoned rhymed prose to be the finest of all literary artifices and had no purpose in their writings other than the production of rhymes, they would frequently string together whole lines of nonsense, just for the sake of rhyme.

14. "Pleasing pause" (*sakta-yi malīḥ*): a poetic licence consisting in a pause in the meter of a verse, corresponding to the rest in music.

15. *Kharvār*: a unit of measure equivalent to 300 kilograms.

Whenever the word *vāṣil* (arrived) occurs in their compositions, after it you will find *hāṣil* (obtaining); all beings (*vujūd*) are generous (*dhī-jūd*); dispositions (*mizāj*) are invariably effulgent (*vahhāj*). A word in isolation they clearly thought as tasteless as dough; it had to be rhymed with another in order to ferment. Every wretch who was qualified by some adjective had another affixed to him for all eternity. Any falsity or lie (*durūgh*) had to be like the darkened sky (*bi-furūgh*); to serve and to bear (*khidmat*) without trouble and care (*ẓahmat*) was quite out of the question, and whosoever's rank was lofty and high (*ʿālī*), his rank was sublime as the sky (*mutaʿālī*).

They had certain inherited words which all the idle blabbers recorded and unvaryingly used in their correspondence. Thus even when cholera was raging, they would write: "Your noble missive arrived at the best and fairest of times"; and none thought of asking them: "You unjust blabberer! If cholera is the fairest of times, then what is the worst?"

According to the custom prevalent in correspondence up to this day, in all their communications they wrote as follows: "We submit that our real concern is your effulgent disposition. Should you intend to inquire after our condition, we enjoy the blessing of health and are busied with praying for your well-being. We suffer from no manner of misfortune, except separation from the pleasures of conversation. We entertain great hope that such may soon be allotted us and come within our grasp."

They had written books which even after a second earnest attempt at understanding left the reader confused and uncertain as to their meaning. I have myself read a hundred of their books and not found a single new idea in any of them. When your glance fell on the page, you would encounter a Joseph lost in the well of the dimple on the chin; the moth of the heart was melting on the fire of love; and a snake-like tress was twisting round the cheeks of the beloved. In every line a goblet was being drained; the arrows of the eyelashes were being fitted into the bow of the eyebrows; and with the polo stick of the tresses the hearts of the lovelorn were being snatched up.[16]

I saw ten thousand panegyric odes which all in one manner and style began with the spring. Then, racing back and forth between mountain and plain, sea and river, after a thousand adventures, the poets arrived in the patron's presence. Then, from his eyelashes to his horse's tail, all would be praised in a flurry of rhyme. After limitless and unbounded extravagances, they would finally petition the cerulean vault to halt the course of time that the life of their patron might be eternal.

Whatever tyrant they praised, inevitably the wolf and the sheep

16. All stock images in the vocabulary of Persian lyrical poetry.

would practice fraternal love from the auspicious effects of his justice, and in awe of his anger, amber would no longer stretch out the hand of aggression against straw.

They told lies in praise of every scoundrel, spinning together extravagancies a lunatic would not dare repeat. But when these blabberers recited them, none thought of objecting, rather everyone said together: "How true!" All this, I failed to understand. Was it that they had contrived some meaning for the poet's words that had never occurred even to him?

Once I chanced on the most celebrated of this species in a garden where they had convened a gathering. They were busy praising each other with the most elevated flattery and making a show of their art and talent with the most awesome extravagance. One of them was particularly celebrated among his fellows for his facility in coining rhymes and in conceiving unlikely turns of phrase. As his eye fell on me, he said:

> Truly the world is now my darling, for now from the fourfold clime,
> The caravan has arrived before visage of imperious speech!

He had hardly delivered himself of the second hemistich when the blabberers began to exclaim: "Well done! A masterpiece! What a mind! Truly you are the mother and father of all eloquence! Mercury, the celestial scribe, in hopeless envy of your turn of speech, casts away his meteorite quill! Venus dances enraptured on the throne your pen has furnished! The world is reborn from the life-giving drops shed by the bounteous raincloud of your fancy!"

Upon hearing the lavishing of so much praise, another of the blabberers thought good to make his contribution. He said: "Indeed your excellency has spoken well. Your humble servant, too, has an offering to make which he trusts will be worth the hearing:

> Be swift as the soul, but not swift-footed;
>   swallow a hundred morsels, yet never chew.
> Thou art not that body, thou art a seeing eye;
>   be free of the body, thou hast beheld the soul,
> The animal spirit knows naught but sleep;
>   men's bodies are but shade and shadow.
> My mother of invention grieves at her own decease;
>   she suffers the pangs of labor, as the lamb is
>   born of the ewe.

The participants in the gathering came close to fainting, such was their joy and so intense their pleasure. From every side arose murmurs of approval, and all were astonished at the profound wisdom of the blabberer's utterances. Someone swore by the heads of all those present that never had any diver thus penetrated the ocean-depths of meaning.

Meanwhile, another of the poets had firmly secured his hat, and adopting a heroic stance he began to intone:

> Lofty tree of Kayanid stock! Spread copiously
> your seed; no harm can result.
> Triumphant shall I be in every warlike clash;
> in sleep and in waking, like heroic Rustam
> and swift-paced Bīzhan.[17]
> The champion turns black to white and white to
> black; puts up a shield to all your arrows.
> He makes captive the emperor of the world;
> enslaves unto himself the tongue of praise.

Not pausing to let the gathering express its appreciation of this piece, yet another rhymster sprang up and with a wealth of exaggerated gesture began to wail:

> O blood of my liver, trickling forth from the phoenix!
> Who in this earthly abode is beyond thy gaze?
> When the steed of thought enters the land of heat,
> the swift-turning heavens begin to melt.
> The firmament revolves, unceasingly alert; the light of
> guidance is concealed within the serpent's skin.
> Life he has gained from that pre-eternal spread; but
> the friend averts his gaze, and passes on.
> The dust of the world settles on the mouth of heaven;
> the rich banquet is gathered up.
> Every jewel that the stone's jaws emit, is like a
> tooth from the mouth extracted.

At this point, one of the blabberers who had particularly high standards and had not yet seen fit to praise any of the works recited, drew a scroll of paper out of his belt and, with much pride and complacency, began to read the following:

"The lofty-soaring falcon of talent and learning adorned thus its tongue, that perpetual diminishment of fine and noble speech was contrary to the pearl-like drops of the fresh and verdant quill of growth, and the resourceful scribe, throughout the revolution of days and nights, brought forth gems of bright and glowing truth.

"The finely prancing meteors of fate stood unjustly accused in that feast of fine speech and eloquence. Truth, forsooth, shone like a

17. Two more heroes from the epic tradition.

gleaming tooth; nor could the eye perceive aught uncouth. The virgin bride of speech, groomed by the comb of thought, emerged from the veil of men's imagining into the broad hall of eloquence, and there, with all manner of sweet scent, and still sweeter sentiment, the cheek of that cherished idol was made pure and free of sorrow and gloom, of smoke and fume. With the auspicious blessings of noble quality, all hewn from the mine of honor, she snatched the desire of her heart from the jaws of the dragon of time. There, in the springtime of her youth, in the fourth clime of the terrestrial globe, she gave utterance to her fivefold eloquence, arising from the six directions of thought and mounting to the seventh heaven of fame and fair renown."[18]

The complacent blabberer was preparing further to slacken the reins on the steed of eloquence, so that it might gallop beside the swift-flying bird of subtle and diaphanous thought, when some ill-mannered youth of distraught aspect leaped up from his corner and tore aside the curtain of modesty and shame.

"O blabbering idiots!

"What mean you by so much absurdity? Why this earnest intent to squander your time and cause your fellows pain and discomfort? Is time your deadly enemy? Shall men's thoughts always turn on empty words? Why torment our wretched people who would gladly know what it is you have to say? Where is the lofty-soaring falcon? And who is the virgin bride of speech? Why not express matters in such a way that your words are clear to yourselves and instructive to others?

"Obscure verbiage and rhyming phrases have no charm: your effort is wasted and your pride misplaced. Anyone who commands a wide vocabulary can render his speech so complex and obscure that no intellect may comprehend him. Yet true eloquence does not reside in obscurity. A good style of composition derives from clarity of thought and results in ease of comprehension; it does not come from the studied obscurity of those absurd writings you take as model and authority.

"Have you never sifted the fair from the ugly in their works, never asked the ancient versifiers and chroniclers: 'O shameless scribe! O honorless poetaster! O fraudulent fool! Why squander your time on these absurdities and afflict mankind with worthless, empty words? What sense is there in this, that you waste twenty years of precious life in learning endless words and then ponder three days over a line of rhyming nonsense?'

18. To mention the numerals four, five, six, and seven in successive lines of verse was a much practiced artifice in classical Persian poetry. So stylized did the practice become that mere mention of the numeral served to indicate associated objects: thus "four" alluded to the four elements, or the four humors of the body; "five," to the five senses; "six," to the six directions; and "seven," to the seven heavens of the traditional cosmology.

"Now you claim to worship the ancients in all regards; why not observe, then, their rules in what you write? In all matters you refer to their pronouncements as final proof and evidence; yet in the art of composition—the true area of their excellence over later generations—you flout their basic rules! They insisted on clarity of expression and ease of understanding; you strive for obscurity and extravagance. In all tongues, expression is subordinate to meaning; but you defy the principles of composition approved by all mankind and make meaning dependent on expression.

"All too often you go beyond what needs to be said simply for the sake of having a rhyme. Do you not see how blind it is to regard obscurity as the highest feat of the written word? Every lunatic knows that the real task of a writer is not to hinder comprehension. His words should be as clear, concise, relevant, and coherent as possible. His meaning should be expressed in such a manner that it is capable of retaining stylistic excellence in any language into which it is rendered.

"From childhood on you have been accustomed to mere blabbering and are unaware of the ugliness of all you write. But were you to read your writings translated into other tongues and beheld the mere ideas, stripped of the adornment of rhyme, then truly would you understand what nonsense it is you write! When foreigners read your writings, they wonder how it is that you pass as sane.[19]

"As for the viceregents of good fortune,[20] no class of men ever benefited from the common people as they have done, nor has any people suffered on account of its great and noble ones as ours has done. Yet, instead of being thankful for the toil others endure that they may enjoy their ease, they strive only to multiply their pain and care. For the sake of no conceivable advantage they bring down every day a new disaster on the people. They send abroad the goods we need ourselves and pur-

19. This section of Malkum's piece invites comparison with an episode occurring on pp. 51–64 of a novel by the contemporary Iranian writer, Fereidoun Esfandiary, entitled *The Identity Card* (New York, 1966). A quintessentially Iranian gathering of complacent poets and their uncritical admirers is portrayed with convincing and economic skill. The poets recite verse of lofty and elevated tone but banal and outworn content, which all lavishly applaud. The tranquil atmosphere of the flawlessly formal ceremony is shattered by the hero of the novel, like Malkum's "ill-mannered youth," who when invited to appreciate the works recited abruptly declares that poetry is dead and embarks on a eulogy of modern science.

The nonsense verse Malkum has his poetasters recite is also reminiscent of some of the pieces in *Vaghvagh Sāhāb* by Ṣādiq Hidāyat and Masᶜūd Farzād (Tehran, numerous editions).

20. "The viceregents of good fortune" (*khulafā-yi iqbāl*): a sarcastic term by which Malkum evidently intends to denote the government of Iran, or the ruling class as a whole.

chase in exchange luxuries for their narrow, selfish pleasure. They trade our rice for paper flowers and to obtain a cubit of four-eyed[21] granite part with a hundredweight of silk. They buy dog skins from the West for their weight in silver and sell our whole cotton crop for a fistful of earth!

"As for our religious scholars, instead of studying the souls of men, they investigate the methods of cooking *kūkū*[22] and halva. Were you to ask them concerning the immortality of the soul, they would respond with an exposition of the finer points of ritual ablution. And should some unbeliever request from them a proof of prophecy, they would offer him the principles of ethical behavior. Though the perspicuous faith of Islam is perfect and the best of all paths for men to follow, the ignorance and stupidity of this herd has hidden the principles of God's law beneath a mass of petty rules and secondary concerns, such that the truths of this noblest of faiths remain unknown to most nations of mankind. They have imposed on men all kinds of minor duty that are of no use in spreading the faith or securing the public good, and in elaborating them they have spent years in argument and dissension.

"If someone were to say that four thousand years ago, in a certain village, a certain shaykh's donkey spoke so many words to his master, these respected ignoramuses[23] would immediately gather their books together and dispute interminably whether the ass in question, at the time of speaking, was facing west or east.

"I have seen as many as three hundred different books, all contradicting one another, on the approved manner of washing one's hands and performing ablution after an act of nature. One said that the right hand has to be washed first of all, and another claimed that if you started with your left foot, you went beyond the pale of the faith. Another of these idiot scholars maintained that whosoever offers a greeting in squint-eyed style[24] is an apostate and deserving of death. Yet another had succeeded in establishing that whoever fails to remove his stockings

21. "Four-eyed" (*chahār-chashmī*): by the use of this term, here and at other points in the piece, Malkum appears to mean "European." Because the designation "squint-eyed" is used in a contextually similar sense, it may be that the two terms are intended to refer to two European nations. We may conjecture that the English are the "four-eyed," and the Russians the "squint-eyed," for later in the piece Malkum implies that but for the "fanatic rage of the ignoramuses," the "squint-eyed" would have entirely absorbed Iran.

22. *Kūkū*: a kind of omelette, usually filled with spinach or other vegetables.

23. "Ignoramuses": thus I render Malkum's coinage *jahlmandān* (sing., *jahlmand*), composed of *jahl* (ignorance) plus suffix *-mand*, and intended as the counterpart of *dānishmand* (learned: *dānish* [learning, knowledge] plus suffix *-mand*).

24. See n. 21 above.

at a certain hour of the day, will burn in hellfire for all eternity.[25]

"For two thousand years these learned men have spent night and day discussing the attributes of a certain king of the West. One advanced the theory that the monarch in question sprouted horns from his forehead. Another pointed out that his parentage was unknown. Some said that he was an exceedingly ascetic man and an ineffably just ruler, while others attempted to prove by sheer weight of verbiage that he was the most cruel and vicious of warriors. All parties wrote books in defence of their assertions.[26]

"Another task of the learned ignoramuses was from time to time to please their compassionate overlords by drowning the nations of the world in blood and making them fodder for the sword. This they saw fit to call jihad.

"They did not examine the affairs and objects of this world in accordance with their true and obvious nature; rather, the basis of their investigations was what had been said concerning them. Realities men had observed with their own eyes, they deemed unworthy of credence, but any absurdity they read in some rotting book they would immediately believe. If, for example, some idiot read in a book that another idiot had forty years before proclaimed the sun to be triangular in shape, it would be impossible to persuade him of its circularity. Anyone who expressed doubt concerning the truth of the written word was, without delay, stamped an unbeliever.

"Merely on account of some virtue allegedly possessed by an ancient writer—one quite irrelevant to the point at issue—they would deny the plainest facts. Any wisdom they claimed to reside in some unintelligible phrase they would explain by repeating: 'Truly God is omnipotent!'

"Such people it is who still regard themselves as the legitimate heirs of all worldly wealth and the apportioners of eternal felicity."[27]

25. Malkum is here alluding to a conflict of views on a certain detail of the ritual ablution: whether it is necessary to wash the bare feet or simply pass moistened hands over one's stockinged feet (the practice known as *masḥ* from Qurʾān, 5:6).

26. The "king of the west" to whom reference is made is Alexander the Great, sometimes identified with the figure of Dhūl Qarnayn, "the Possessor of Two Horns" (Qurʾān, 18:33 ff.). In traditional Persian literature Alexander is depicted not so much as a warrior and conqueror as a seeker after ultimate truths, who finally discovers the "water of life" in the mountains of Qāf, on the farthermost edge of the world. See art., "İskender Nâme," *Islâm Ansiklopedisi*, fasc. 52 (Istanbul, 1951).

27. "Heirs of all worldly wealth": presumably in the sense that the ulama would take charge of the estates of those who died intestate, and possibly too in the sense that sums of money contributed for religious or charitable purposes (*zakāt*, *ṣadaqa*, *khums*, etc.) would be entrusted to them. "Apportioners of eternal felicity": in the sense that they arrogated to themselves the judgment of the blessed and the damned.

One day I was sitting in a room with a group of these ignoramuses when that same ill-mannered youth whose acquaintance I had made at the previous congress of lunatics and who clearly never lost an opportunity to be impolite, interrupted the learned discourse, saying: "The four-eyed nation has made more progress in all manner of wondrous art and industry than the squint-eyed people."

He had hardly completed his utterance when one of the ignoramuses leaped two feet in the air and said:

"Refinement of the form imprinted on man's character depends on the permanence of the souls of the community. Innovation and deficiency are suspended for it has been said *'asceticism and self-denial in things small yet great shall cause you loss of selfhood.' By virtue of this irrefutable proof, he is accursed and an infidel!"

The youth replied: "No, you are the infidel!"

Here I interjected: "He is right. He understands and expresses matters better than you are able. You imagine learning and scholarship to consist in complexity of expression and try to reduce all factual knowledge to a play of words."

The ignoramus began to scream: "The degree of conduct and behavior, the excellence of formality and favor, result in the succession of man's allotted fate. For as Platakunos, who hailed from the most luminous of cities and was one of the most accomplished pupils of Buqmatinos, once had occasion to remark: *'each scent is affected by a body and each body affected by a scent.' Therefore, because of the descent of intelligences, which necessitates composition of the body and the merging of all souls, the simple body cannot receive subtle, immaterial result. I thus conclude that the soul is immortal and you are an infidel!"

The youth replied: "It may well be that the soul is immortal and that I am an infidel. But this you should know for certain, that the use of obscure and unfamiliar words and the mention of a few Greek philosophers are no proof of real knowledge. Appeal to every Platakunos and Buqmatinos in the world; still your words will be meaningless and absurd! Your God-given natural tongue is capable of expressing any thought or idea, and if you were truly learned you would exercise your talent in that tongue. But your true aim is not to acquire and transmit learning. Rather, with a show of knowledge, you try to adorn or conceal your one true accomplishment—the science of deception. It is for this that your speech is deliberately obscure!"

The eloquent ignoramus exclaimed in fury: "*'We have made a promise to those who disbelieve!' The corporeal treachery of innate disposition and the guile of nature have proven the qualities of the carnal self. For the greatest of all bounties is the tongue of our ancestors, and likewise the supreme exemplar of rhetoric manifest to all men is traced out in the bonds of the generous one of eternal essence. Hence it is clear that the peoples of the occident have borrowed their sciences from our ocean of learning.[28] Aeons and eras will pass before they ascend from the lowest depths of ignorance to the lofty degree of intelligence!"

The youth retorted: "It is precisely because of claims such as these that you remain devoid of all true learning. Your pride and complacency cause you to stay ignorant of the state of other peoples and the progress they achieve. You have restricted the learning of mankind to a few books of the ancients which you imagine can never be surpassed. The falsity of this belief is apparent to all possessed of true insight. The wisdom of the Creator and Sustainer has disposed our powers of intellect in such manner that progress is continuous and perpetual. It is the most signal instance of His creative power that He has inclined the intellect of man to unceasing progress, and this inclination alone secures our superiority over the animal realm. You wish nonetheless to make of the slight and insubstantial knowledge of the ancients, together with the whole mass of their absurdities, the ultimate limit of human progress! The worst of it is that you know nothing even of what they knew!

"Once you have committed to memory some obscure name or unknown word, you imagine yourselves to be a compendium of all learning and accomplishment. But this you should know: that if you and all your kind should join forces and come together, a mere schoolboy of four-eyed race could worst you all in argument.

"For a thousand years you have been pretending to the possession of intelligence, yet never have you uttered a word to justify your pretension. The most learned among you, exerting their minds to the utmost, are capable only of repeating what has been said ten thousand times before.

"The truth of the matter is that you excel only in consuming the people's wealth."

The accomplished ignoramus, beside himself with rage, glared threateningly at the youth and shouted incoherently: "*May the curses of God be upon infidels and His wrath upon these cursed wretches! *Infidels, unbelievers! Denunciation of abomination! Paper blackened with the deeds of the heretics! The evil and vicious encompassed by damnation! By the Omnipotent One, you have surpassed all unbelievers in unbelief and become an unbeliever even in their eyes, unbeliever!!"

28. Malkum's insertion of the claim that "the peoples of the occident have borrowed their sciences from our ocean of learning" in a passage of nonsense, uttered by a figure of absurd and unlimited ignorance, is an interesting indication of his own attitude to the claim. If he himself seriously asserted the sciences and institutions of modern Europe to be the long-forgotten achievement of the Muslims themselves, it was for tactical purposes that he explicitly confessed. See above, pp. 14, 180.

The youth said: "This manner of speech neither lessens my unbelief, nor adds to your degree of learning. If what you say is true, express yourself in such a way that even if we cannot understand you, at least you should be able to understand yourself, instead of thus wasting a lifetime on empty words. If you had ever engaged in serious study, you would not have become the laughing-stock of the people, nor would our nation have been thus humiliated at the hands of foreigners. You who claim to be the educators of the people and their guides upon the path—your duty is not done merely by mounting the pulpit to make a show of piety and asceticism! In every respect you must aid and protect the people. Lay the foundations for prosperity; shorten the hand of the tyrant and oppressor; deliver the people of the Prophet from the grasp of the infidel. To show people how to wash and ostentatiously to tell one's beads are not fit occupations for the exponents of the Law of God!"

When the ignoramus heard these words, he bade farewell to all restraint and patience, the flame of his anger leaped ever higher and, loudly intoning the *takbīr*,[29] he lifted his stick to bring it down on the head of that shameless, cursed wretch and give him his just reward.

But the eloquent youth saved his skin by nimbly quitting the gathering, and the champion of the faith was left victorious and unchallenged on the field of battle.

I too left the assembly, and outside I encountered another pack of ignoramuses who were dragging some wretch along in the most ignominious fashion. I asked one of them who the man was and what offence he had committed.

He replied: "The vile, accursed wretch was so full of vice and so forgetful of the rites of religion that not only did he associate with the unbelievers, but even learned their language. Today he was reading a book in the four-eyed tongue, and so we are preparing to chastise him that none other may commit the same abomination."

I proceeded on my way and beheld another man groaning helplessly as his feet were bastinadoed, invoking God, the Prophet, and the Imams as he pleaded for mercy. In amazement and full concern for the wretch's fate I went forward and asked the ignoramuses who were standing there loudly condemning him: "Who is he, and what is his offence?"

They answered: "We found the mother of corruption[30] in his pocket; now we are inflicting the penalty prescribed by law."

29. *Takbīr*: pronunciation of the words *Allāhu Akbar*. Their use here by the "ignoramus" as he raises his stick signifies his belief that the youth is an enemy of the faith and that chastisement of him will constitute jihad.

30. "The mother of corruption" (*mādar-i fasād*, cf. Arabic *umm al-khabāʾith*): an epithet commonly applied to wine.

I had still not recovered from my astonishment at their reply when I saw another youth being dragged along in fetters. I inquired the nature of his crime from one of the ignoramuses. After repeated and emphatic denunciation of him as an unbeliever, he answered: "This accursed fellow is a Sufi[31] and an unbeliever. He does not believe all that he reads and is convinced that most of the ancient historians were liars. In addition, he has been heard on several occasions to say that the sun never rises in the west."

I said to my friend, in whose company I still was: "Glorious and Exalted is God Almighty! What kind of creatures are they that they have no fear of God? They commit all the proscribed and forbidden acts, in public and in private, but they torture and torment these powerless wretches on account of some minor slip, some simple human weakness! They pass over altogether the sins and errors of the great and deem the lowly and defenseless deserving of every kind of harshness. Thus they become partners of the viceregents of good fortune inflicting on others the punishment they themselves deserve. Truly I am astounded! How is it that God, the Lord of the Worlds, permits such people to exist and thrive?"

My guide and friend warned me against my audacious thoughts and said in awesome tones: "Seek not the secrets of the unseen world beyond, and question not the wisdom of God's decree! Put not such trust in your own mind and reason! Some benefit follows on every harm, and every error contains the seeds of its own correction. If a thing appears ugly to you, then hasten to give your fellows fair advice, that it may be remedied. Yet what do men truly know of ugly and of fair? The wisdom of the Peerless Creator is not of such low degree that one ignorant like you should be able to examine the destinies of the world.

"The existence of these ignoramuses, which you deem void of use and profit, is productive of numerous beneficial effects, one hundredth

31. Sufis were frequently thought in Qajar times to be unbelievers because of the antinomian tendencies some of them displayed. Clerical hostility to them was particularly marked early in the period. Sayyid Muḥammad Bāqir Bihbihānī prided himself on the title *ṣūfīkush*, "Sufi killer" (see Tunukābunī, *op. cit.* [n. 4, above], p. 148); and his eldest son, Āqā Muḥammad ᶜAlī Bihbihānī, encompassed the death of two prominent members of the Niᶜmatullāhī order, Nūr ᶜAlī Shāh and Maᶜṣūm ᶜAlī Shāh (see Muḥammad ᶜAlī Tabrīzī Khiyābānī, *Rayḥānat ul-Adab* [Tehran, 1326 solar/1947], II: 245–247).

Partial justification for the view of Sufis held by the ulama is supplied by the testimony of a number of European observers, who compared the state of belief of Sufis they encountered to that of European freethinkers (J. B. Fraser, *Narrative of the Residence of the Persian Princes in London in 1835 and 1836* [London, 1838], I: 231; Arthur de Gobineau, *Les Religions et Les Philosophies dans l'Asie Centrale* [Paris, 1865], ch. v; A. Sepsis, "Quelques Mots sur l'Etat Religieux Actuel de la Perse," *Revue de l'Orient*, III [1844]: 107–109).

part of which the human mind cannot grasp. Without this class, how could the nation survive and prosper? Even if they have deviated completely from their true and original path of conduct and fallen from that high position of respect they ought duly to command, it remains a fact that their very turbans are a better protection for the realm than all the 'victorious brigades'[32] put together.

"If the oppressors have still not stretched out their hands in every direction, the only reason is their fear of the fanatic rage of the ignoramuses. Or else by now the squint-eyed would have done their worst.

"For the honor and respect of our nation, no better support and prop than these ignoramuses can be imagined. Alas, there is none to guide them, none to reduce their affairs to order, to regulate and determine the tasks they are to fulfill. There is no doubt that they could render unlimited services to people and to state. Worldly concerns and care for livelihood keep them constantly distracted; yet even now they are the source of much benefit to the nation. It is only the unseemly actions of a few that have brought the whole class into disrepute, for among the ignoramuses are to be found persons who, by their high moral qualities, more than compensate for the failings of their fellows. These reputable ignoramuses, even though few in number, are a source of pride for all humanity: pious, learned, godfearing, protectors of the oppressed, upholders of the faith, deadly enemies of wrong belief, truthful in speech, free of all human failings, and adorned with every virtue."

I said: "Up to now I have encountered no one endowed with qualities such as those you mention."

My friend replied: "The good and noble in every class are always absent from public view. They shun the crowd whenever possible and have no desire to put themselves on display. If these truly learned men whose sole aim is the truth and who are worthy of implicit faith and trust were to put their wares up for public sale, what would be left to distinguish them from the ignoramus mass?"

As we were speaking thus, my eye fell on an ignoramus who was seated with his devotees and engaged in expounding the principles of justice and the requirements of the law. A merchant on whose face piety and honesty were clearly written entered the assembly and began talking to the ignoramus in a humble, pleading fashion.

Their conversation became protracted, and, advancing stealthily in such manner as to remain unnoticed, I gave ear to their words and recorded them in my notebook.

32. "Victorious brigades" (*afvāj-i qāhira*): the term by which the Iranian army was conventionally designated in Qajar chronicles, irrespective of the fortunes of battle.

The merchant was saying: "By your blessed head, if I did not need it, I would never mention the matter. True, at the time when I entrusted the five hundred tumans to your excellency, I had no need of them, but recently I have come into straitened circumstances. If you do not now kindly return the money, I will stand disgraced!"

The ignoramus replied: "The acquisition of property once obtained is quite impossible, for partnership is dependent on the severance of rational objections and secondary ideas. The proof of this is that possession needs manifest support, just as vision requires effulgent light and brilliance."

The merchant said: "All that your excellency says is true and to the point, but your servant is in urgent need. Please give instructions that my deposit be returned."

The ignoramus responded: "Our guides in matters of the faith have always considered disaster as a form of recurrent blessing, and, having regard for the axiom that *'the deprived are secure against being led astray,' they conclude that denial of witness devolves upon cloistered learning. Were it not so, why should our souls, which may be likened to lightning flashes, be restricted, stable, and composite all at once?"

To which the merchant answered: "Sir, the truth of the matter is, I cannot understand your idiom. I have several creditors awaiting me; my mind is distraught; I must go. So permit me to receive my money and take my leave."

The ignoramus replied: "*'Words are more precious than glittering treasure.' It is therefore incumbent on you to subject the accursedness of stupidity to the star of good fortune."

The merchant exclaimed: "My lord and master, I beg of you! A thousand tasks await me!"

The ignoramus resumed: "*'He who confines your property is the best of righteous men.' It is as if you wished to thin the martyrs' ranks!"

The merchant protested: "My dear sir, what do you mean to say? To what end have you delayed me here from morning until now? Is it so lengthy and difficult an affair to restore to people the money they entrusted to you? Tell them to bring my money, and I'll be gone about my business."

The ignoramus responded: "*'Deceit with facility, the reward for ignorance.' Hearken to this fragrant counsel, for the wise have said. . . ."

The merchant exploded: "I spit on the tombs of all the wise and all their cursed sires! What game is this you wish to play? I did not come that you might rejoice at my wretched plight."

The ignoramus gravely said: "*'Anger, anger upon anger, ruins man's affair.' The advice of scholarly investigators has been in all cases, and on all bases, *'whatever you take from God's servants, a small share for yourself.' "

The merchant cried out: "You idiot! What are all these words? You hope by this idiotic drivel to cheat me of my money? By God Almighty, until I have every last *dīnār*,[33] I'll leave you not in peace!"

The ignoramus replied: "Refutation of accusation! Denial of attribution! *'We shall beat you in fury!' Legal penalty, plentifully applied!"

The merchant shouted in despair: "Truly you are mad! Your brain has suffered damage! What is it you have to say? Why will you not return my money?"

The ignoramus then declaimed: "O cursed dog! O filthy wretch, impure, unclean, through and through! You dishonor the treasurer of the Sacred Law, impute evil to ignorance-dispelling light! Thrash the abominable infidel! Torment and chastise the hell-bound apostate!"

The master's obedient disciples, in a fine fit of anger, set on the merchant from every side and expelled the guiltless wretch, bleeding and half-dead, from their lofty midst. The unfortunate merchant staked all that he had upon his claim, but wherever he turned, he was thrust away, with nought to show for his troubles but fresh beatings and chastisement.

33. *Dīnār*: a monetary unit equivalent, in the Qajar period, to one thousandth of a *qirān*, and in present-day Iran to one hundredth of a rial.

APPENDIX C

Qānūn, Number Fourteen

THE FOLLOWING SPECIMEN of *Qānūn* may be taken as typical of the middle period of the journal. Although bearing no date, it may be presumed to have been published in the spring of 1891, for it contains an allusion to the article attacking Malkum in the official gazette *Īrān* that appeared in March of that year. Its contents bear the stamp of Malkum's inimitable style, and the fictitious letters it contains are intended to convey the impression that all are united in support of Malkum: the army is on the brink of revolt, the ministers are all disgusted with Amīn us-Sulṭān, and even the royal family cannot withhold its sympathy from the author of *Qānūn*. Of particular interest is Malkum's manner of indirect attack upon the shah: it is implied that he is totally helpless and has irrevocably abandoned the control of affairs to his chief minister. Malkum doubtless wished thereby to arouse Nāṣir ud-Dīn Shāh's indignation and to incite him to dismiss Amīn us-Sulṭān. It was, however, against Malkum that the royal fury continued to be directed.

QĀNŪN

Number Fourteen *Union - Justice - Progress* *Subscription: Adequate Intelligence*

We can convey to all supporters of the Law[1] the happy tidings that nowadays all manner of thoughts are astir in Iran. Utterances are being

1. Malkum's use of the words *qānūn* and *ādamīyat* in his journal is deliberately ambiguous: they might convey either their general senses of "law" and "humanity"

made and courageous deeds performed that a few years ago none would have thought possible.

According to reliable information, a group of army officers and commanders has unanimously submitted the following declaration to the guardians of the state:

O guardians of the state!

To what chaotic and miserable condition you have reduced Iran! Why do you thus harass our wretched people? What law, what faith can justify all this jailing, torturing, killing, and plundering? How much longer are we soldiers to cause misery to our people at your behest? What shame and humiliation we suffer at your hands as reward for our obedience and endurance: see in what scandalous way you have made of our military ranks and salaries a source of disgrace to the nation! You must think us entirely devoid of shame and honor to appoint your lowliest domestic servants not only over us, the commanders of the army, but over the minister of war, the offspring of the shah himself.[2] There are men among us whose ancestors, for fourteen generations, have sacrificed themselves in the service of the state, and now, without the slightest qualm, you force them, for the sake of a few filthy *shāhīs'*[3] salary, to go and kiss the shoes of some dirty youth in your *ābdārkhāna*[4] seventy times a day! Until today, we have been completely blind and unaware of our rights and duties. We imagined that the salaries we begged out of you with a thousand humiliations [literally, cuckoldries], you had somehow inherited from your fathers and that you bestowed them on us as an act of grace. But now we realize that our salaries are taken from the taxes which we, the people of Iran, pay for the protection of our rights and which you scandalously misuse to make prisoners of our nation. That time is past when we thought you to be our lords and masters and, deceived by your promises, subjected the property, life, and faith of the nation to your idiotic vagaries! The roaring flood of your oppressive

respectively, or, more narrowly, designate his newspaper and the secret society that undertook its distribution, the League of Humanity. In order to retain some sense of ambiguity in English, I have translated the words in question and spelled them with capital letters.

2. The minister of war was Kāmrān Mīrzā Nā'ib us-Salṭana, third son of Nāṣir ud-Dīn Shāh and governor of Tehran.

3. *Shāhī*: a unit of currency equivalent, in the Qajar period, to one twentieth of a *qirān*.

4. *Ābdārkhāna*: the room or outhouse in which a servant prepares coffee, tea, sherbet, or a water pipe for his master and his guests. Amīn us-Sulṭān's father was, of course, Nāṣir ud-Dīn Shāh's *ābdār*, the servant entrusted with these tasks, and Malkum's repeated references to the *ābdārkhāna* are intended as a reminder to all of Amīn us-Sulṭān's lowly origin. It is implied that with his appointment to the premiership, the ministry has in effect been transformed into an *ābdārkhāna*.

deeds, the laments of the people, and the voice of Law have finally awakened us. Now we well understand that the Compassionate Lord did not create us for slavery to such as you! Now we are fully aware that, in accordance with the Law of God, we soldiers must be protectors of the people's rights, instead of ravening beasts unleashed by you to torture and trample underfoot our brothers in religion and fellow countrymen, at your whim and pleasure! Now we clearly realize that all this wretchedness of Iran is due to our apathy, neglect, and lack of union! We warn you that we have grasped the meaning and power of union, and we have become Men.[5] We are no longer alone, that you might continue to incite us against each other and make us the executioners of our people. Henceforth, instead of being your lowly slaves and the torturers of the nation, we shall be the proud servants of the people of Iran and protectors of the rights of all true Men. We shall still sacrifice our lives, but it will be for the sake of our human rights, not for the shameful rule of injustice which you regard as your eternal fief! Awake, o guardians of evil, for we soldiers have become Men!

One of the ministers of Iran, who has wasted his life in service to the state and the desire for its progress and advancement and who now in utter disgust eagerly awaits his death, has written a brief description of the present state of Iran. He says in conclusion:

"Do not imagine that the men who rule the state themselves gain any benefit from the ruinous situation created by their stupidity. It is true that they appear to enjoy many privileges, but in reality they, and all who follow in their wake, are the most wretched of us all. Which of our ministers can sleep tranquilly at night? What king other than our shah is imprisoned by servants and a prey to [material] needs? Everyone knows that this monarch, whose doorman is meant to be Darius and whose bodyguard reputedly consists of Khusrau and Alexander,[6] trembles in fear by night and day, is surrounded by executioners and has more difficulty supporting his family than his humblest servant! Were ever the children of some black slave in America as poor and distraught as the progeny of Fatḥ ʿAlī Shāh?[7] Is there anyone in the land who has suffered more oppression than the children of ʿAbbās Mīrzā?[8]

5. On the implications of the phrase "to become a man" (*ādam shudan*), see above, p. 229.

6. An allusion to the fulsome epithets bestowed on Nāṣir ud-Dīn Shāh in panegyric poetry, in official documents and court chronicles.

7. Fatḥ ʿAlī Shāh had a particularly numerous progeny. For a full account of his reproductive achievements, see Aḥmad Mīrzā ʿAḍud ud-Daula, *Tārīkh-i ʿAḍudī*, ed. Ḥusayn Kūhī Kirmānī (Tehran, 1327 solar/1948), *passim*.

8. That is, ʿAbbās Mīrzā, the eldest son of Fatḥ ʿAlī Shāh who predeceased his father in 1833.

Is there any humiliation and degradation[9] that has not constantly been visited on the brothers of the present shah?[10] As for his sons, ask them themselves: what hellish hovels they must go to in order to pay with their liver's blood for a crust of bread graciously bestowed on them by the servants of the *ābdārkhāna*! And what should I say concerning the sufferings endured by that noble being who has had the misfortune to see himself designated heir to the throne in this day and age? You must surely be aware that there is not a peasant in the whole of Iran who is at such a loss to secure his daily bread as this high-born prince! Where can one openly declare that in this same province of Azerbayjan where the appointees of the *ābdārkhāna* waste the salaries of twenty brigades on frivolous amusement, the future king of Iran does not even have a decent room in which to sit? It is because of things such as this that I say all one can do is to spit and then go and leave them all behind."

No, your Excellency. One must remain to become a Man, and by the propagation of Humanity to deliver one's progeny and nation from this ocean of catastrophe.

Another minister writes:

"It was well said that one should fear a government that has no shame. See the lengths to which their unprincipled shamelessness has gone! The guardians of the realm now sit and forge blatant lies about well-tried servants of the state, lies which, as any child can see, prove only their stupidity and will end in their disgrace. Ask any of the celebrated European travelers whether he has ever encountered among some savage tribe a whore who would thus knowingly encompass her own disgrace by inventing transparent lies? A set of men who have made themselves the fountainhead of all the vices in the world, who continually surround themselves with mountainous heaps of scandal and disgrace—how dare they cause personal accusations to be printed in a newspaper![11] If the men of Law should wish to publish and reveal the deeds of these authors of Iran's misfortune, which one of them would

9. Malkum uses the expression *pīsī vārid kardan*, a colloquialism meaning "to trouble, to vex, to expose to disgrace" (see Muḥammad ᶜAlī Jamālzāda, *Farhang-i Lughāt-i ᶜĀmmīyāna* [Tehran, 1341 solar/1962], p. 46). *Pīsī* literally signifies leprosy, and Malkum's use of the expression is intended to emphasize the helpless and undignified state in which the shah's brothers find themselves. Much of the effectiveness of *Qānūn* resided in the unprecedented literary use of vulgarisms such as this.

10. Among the brothers of Nāṣir ud-Dīn Shāh, ᶜAbbās Mīrzā Mulkārā had a particularly disturbed career. He spent thirty years in exile in Baghdad under British protection, and, although later able to effect a reconciliation with his brother and return to Iran, he was constantly regarded with distrust and suspicion. See his autobiography, *Sharḥ-i Ḥāl*, ed. ᶜAbd ul-Ḥusayn Navāʾī (Tehran, 1325 solar/1946).

11. Doubtless an angry allusion to the article published, by royal command, in the journal *Īrān*. See above, p. 180.

ever dare, crouching in the corner of his stable, to show his head and face the stench of scandal and disgrace? But for such revelations there is no need: the pens of Humanity will pay no attention to the vices of these foremost scoundrels of the age. It is better to entrust their punishment to the just verdict of the people of Iran."

A high-minded prince writes as follows:

"O men of Law! We members of the royal house are sincerely gratified at your efforts and intentions. The true meaning of service to the state and gratitude for favor received is precisely that which your eloquent pen sets forth. A thousand congratulations on your sense of honor and learning! The Qajar dynasty will be in your debt for all eternity! Even the blind can see that under present circumstances our monarchy is doomed. But none of us has dared to express the truth of the matter clearly, and it is you who has carried off the ball of manly courage. Continue to write, and write in harsh, straightforward terms, for our sleep of apathy is too deep to be dispelled by normal speech. Our monarch, as everyone is aware, is tired and imprisoned in his ābdār-khāna. It is as if he has abdicated and handed Iran over to these vicious rogues. If there is anything that can bring us to our senses, it is the whiplash of eloquent discourse. If today the monarch does not appreciate your manner of speaking the truth, be sure that the rush of events will soon prove, and his own imperial intuition confess, that the men of Law are the true well-wishers of the monarchy. So write on, noble servants of the state, write on! For our only hope lies in the popular enthusiasm that the spirit of Humanity has brought forth in the land of Iran."

O exalted prince!

We are performing our duty of service to the state; what are you doing? You can perform a thousand deeds for the salvation of the ship of state; why do you sit thus idly? You should have realized by now that although the foundation of the monarchy used to be the idiocy of the people, its preservation will henceforth be possible only through following the dictates of justice and the principles of Humanity. Who is better equipped than you to propagate those principles? Instead of waiting for the efforts of others to reform affairs, show some zeal yourself, and be the vanguard and protector of Humanity. You have no excuse for delay in assuming this sacred task: all men of conscience are prepared [to help you], and the methods of propagation are inscribed in the breast of every self-respecting man. In accordance with these methods, and, using your intelligence and skill, gather together the Men you see around you, and attract them to your circle. Then appoint the more accomplished among them to be Trustees of Humanity[12] and encourage them in turn to found as many new circles as possible. Do not hesitate, for if you now grasp the grandeur of your destiny, you can without difficulty, by the spark of your words and the model of your example, kindle the light of Humanity in this realm, attain your highest goal and be a source of pride to Men until the end of time.

A respected merchant whose spirit soars high on account of Humanity writes from Tabriz:

"You can have little idea how the ministers of Tehran fear *Qānūn* and Humanity. They open everyone's letters, and anyone who has so much as glanced at *Qānūn* is arrested and asked why he has become a Man. The wise ones of Tehran seem to think they are extirpating the very names of *Qānūn* and Humanity from Iran, and they still imagine that *Qānūn* is a newspaper the contents of which become useless and outdated if it fails to arrive by post. They have not yet realized that if *Qānūn* comes by post or muleteer, today or next year, its contents will always be fresh. The more strictly it is prohibited, the more effective will be its ideas. Now the best present which can be brought from abroad is a page of *Qānūn*. Thanks to the measures of those wise men, the saddlebags of travelers and the pockets of pilgrims are stuffed to overflowing with copies of *Qānūn*. The day before yesterday, one of my partners found a thousand copies of *Qānūn* at the bottom of a crate of sugar that had just been brought from the customs. A trader in Salmās[13] found two hundred copies in a roll of broadcloth. What need, then, for new laws [to prevent the entry of *Qānūn*]? The copies which are already circulating among men of insight are enough to resurrect a graveyard. You can scarcely imagine how well some of our accomplished and learned men explain and expound on the principles of Humanity. Their commentary on each line of *Qānūn* is enough to fill a book. One of the great *mujtahids* openly says that the reading of *Qānūn* is the alchemy of union. The devil of disunity connot penetrate the house where a page of *Qānūn* is to be found.[14]

"In short, men's thoughts are in a remarkable state of turmoil, and how, indeed, might it be otherwise? Did the people of Iran ever take an oath to lie abjectly beneath the kicks of a pitiless bunch of ruffians? The spirit of Iran everywhere bears witness that soon this edifice of

12. On the *Auṣiyā-yi Ādamīyat*, see above, p. 233.

13. A city in Azerbayjan, situated between Tabriz and Lake Riḍāʾīya.

14. This sentence is deliberately phrased to sound like a religious pronouncement, as if it were actually taken from the *fatvā* of a *mujtahid*.

tyranny shall collapse, and the banner of divine justice shall be hoisted throughout the realm."

Answers

H.A. It has been sent. Always inform us of arrival.

M.ᶜA. The injustice committed against your own person you may naturally forgive. But as for the injustice inflicted by the wild beasts[15] of the state on your brothers in Humanity—to avenge it is incumbent on every Man.

A.T. Send more to the *ᶜatabāt*.

A.O. The words of the vultures[16] are not worthy of attention.

Sh.M. Consider these two brigades already prepared to sacrifice themselves for Humanity.

S.D. God is greatest!

Declaration of the Guardians of the Victorious
Ābdārkhāna

O people of Iran, what senseless words are these you now see fit to utter? Law, union, the protection of rights—what does all this mean? What law could be better than the sword of our executioners? What rights could be clearer than ours to enjoy your slavery? If you really wish, like other peoples, to reform and order your affairs anew and if—may God forbid—the people of Iran are to gain some honor and respect, then what is to become of our proprietary rights over you and your consecrated duties of servitude to us? Have not the vultures of our treasury explained to you a thousand times that whatever you have—life, property, religion, honor—all belongs to us? These shameless people who have started to speak of law are such unlettered idiots that we have been unable to find a particle of meaning in all the words they write, despite our learning and intelligence. It is for this very reason that in our tender concern for your welfare we anxiously seek to prevent your eyes from alighting on their writings. We do not doubt that with your sincere and slavish devotion to our angelic selves you will never look for unity, for unity is disbelief according to the norms by which we rule. If you wish to be sensible, you should exert yourselves to the utmost to be as far apart from and as hostile to each other as possible. It is in particular necessary for some of you to be Babis so that we can rip open their stomachs as a warning to others and confiscate their property with a plausible excuse. It is also highly desirable for you to be

15. *Jānvarān*: the counterpart, in Malkum's terminology, of *ādamān* ("men"), designating Malkum's enemies, Amīn us-Sulṭān and those who carried out his instructions.

16. *Lāshakhūrān*: another term denoting Malkum's adversaries.

divided into a number of parties such as Shaykhī,[17] Mutasharriᶜ,[18] Shiᶜi, Sunni, and Dahrī,[19] which insult, curse, and torment each other. For then you become quite oblivious of your human rights, and without any trouble we can mount you like asses and load you with the burdens of disgrace to our heart's desire. Do not imagine that we will fail to appreciate your self-sacrificing services. Be sure that if ever you are as talented as Qāʾim Maqām and serve the state as faithfully as he did, or if you are as skillful and devoted in restoring the fortunes of the monarchy as Mīrzā Taqī Khān,[20] without delay we shall ungrudgingly extend to you the same manful treatment we did to them. And if, God forbid, one of you should still persist in idle talk despite these oaths of ours, then know for certain that he shall immediately be marked as an ingrate, a traitor, and an infidel.

Of course, in your hearts you will in all justice agree that all the duties we assign you in your slavery correspond precisely to that Islam which we have produced especially for our own protection. Who observes the principles of our Islam better than we ourselves? See how firmly we have silenced your *mujtahids* and caused them humbly to submit to the raging beasts who are our servants! See how powerfully and thoroughly we have extirpated every trace of just practice and equitable behavior throughout the well-guarded land [of Iran]![21] Is there anyone who has ever sold the rights of the state and the means of livelihood of the people so cheaply to foreigners as we have done? The scandal and disgrace of bribes, the drunken arrogance of power, the invention of all kinds of foul sport, the squandering of the Muslims' treasury,[22] was ever there an age in which these evils were more flourishing? How is it possible that despite all these manifest bounties you are not night and day engaged in praying for the perpetuation of our wise and skillful rule? If, in accordance with the customs of this lofty institution, the beasts of state should plunder at their will your rights and all your possessions and reduce you to a state of abject beggary worse than

17. See p. 282, n. 5 above.

18. Mutasharriᶜ: one who binds himself to strict observance of the religious law (*sharīᶜa*), in contradistinction to the Sufi who might exhibit antinomian tendencies.

19. Dahrī: approximately, "materialist," "believer in eternal time." The word was originally applied to crypto-Manicheans, but its sense was later expanded to include any kind of heresy or disbelief.

20. Here, as in his letter to *The Times* of March 16, 1891 (see p. 180), Malkum is again attempting to identify himself implicitly with two ministers who had given their lives for the sake of reform.

21. *Mamālik-i Maḥrūsa*: the conventional designation for Iran in official documents and chronicles, here intended satirically.

22. In order to arouse religious feeling, Malkum uses the expression *bayt ul-māl*, the term by which the treasury of the Islamic state was designated in the lifetime of the Prophet, instead of the usual *khazāna*.

that of any savage tribe, why should you grieve and sorrow? Do you not see how strictly we have forbidden the newspaper *Akhtar*[23] to say a word on matters such as these? And if we are able to expel you from your homeland whenever we choose, without interrogation, and to cut off your ear and nose and head without a trial, then what cause is there for surprise? Do you not know that our Bounteous Lord has created your entire being solely for our pleasure? So, o people of Iran, instead of following the path of error and seeking out the laws of God, try to appreciate our acts of compassion to our subjects, and ponder on your inherently slavish state. Be proud that we have made of the land over which Jamshīd[24] used to reign a blot on the history of the age and thus proven and recorded the extent of your dignity and honor. In gratitude for this bounty, fall upon the earth and kiss those *gīva*'s[25] of the blessed ābdārkhāna which have trampled under their filthy heels such a nation as Iran and aroused the wonder of all mankind!

In reply to this proclamation of the present rulers of Tehran, the Spirit of Humanity cries out in tones that penetrate to every corner of the earth:

"O Iran of lofty fortune! It is not your allotted portion in this world to suffer the disgrace of slavery now imposed upon you! For centuries you were the throne on which the glory of Humanity reposed; why should you today lie buried in the graveyard of abjection? Where are those lions of heavenly lineage who bequeathed as a trust to your virtue and honor, glory and felicity in this world and the hereafter? Arise, o champion of wounded heart, for the days of darkness are at an end, and the sun of knowledge has illumined the world from East to West."

23. On the vicissitudes of *Akhtar*, see above, pp. 186–187.

24. A legendary king of pre-Islamic Iran, generally equated with Solomon.

25. *Gīva*: A kind of canvas shoe, with a sole made of pieces of rag pressed together, commonly worn by peasants in Iran.

BIBLIOGRAPHY

I: PRIMARY SOURCES

Published works of Malkum Khān

Aqwāl ᶜAlī. London, 1303 lunar/1885. (In "reformed" script.)

Dürub-u Emsal-i Müntehabe. London, 1303 lunar/1885. (In "reformed" script.)

Gulistān. London, 1303 lunar/1885. (In "reformed" script, with preface by Malkum.)

Kullīyāt-i Malkum. Edited by Hāshim Rabīᶜzāda. Tabriz, 1325 lunar/1908. (Containing thirteen treatises including one, "Risāla-yi Ghaybīya," falsely ascribed to Malkum.)

Kullīyāt-i Malkum. Tehran, 1326 lunar/1909. (Containing three treatises.)

Mabdaʾ-i Taraqqī, Shaykh va Vazīr. Tiflis, 1325 lunar/1908.

Majmūᶜa-yi Āthār-i Mīrzā Malkum Khān. Edited with introduction by Muḥīṭ Ṭabāṭabāʾī. Tehran, 1327 solar/1948. (Containing thirteen treatises, including "Risāla-yi Ghaybīya.")

Namūna-yi Khaṭṭ-i Ādamīyat. London, 1303 lunar/1885.

Nidā-yi ᶜAdālat. Tehran, n.d.

"Persian Civilisation." *Contemporary Review* LIX (1891): 238–244.

Qānūn. 42 issues. London, 1890–1898.

Uṣūl-i Madhhab-i Dīvānīān. Tehran, n.d.

"Uṣūl-i Taraqqī." Edited by Firīdūn Ādamīyat. *Sukhan* XVI (1345 solar/1966): 70–73; 131–135; 250–254; 406–414; 481–489; 622–630.

*Unpublished works of Malkum Khān**

Manuscript collection dated 1295 lunar/1878 containing eleven treatises, Central Library, University of Tehran, 3257.

Risāla-yi Farāmūshkhāna. Malik Library, Tehran, 3116; Kitābkhāna-yi Millī, Tehran, 149 a.f.

* The work in the Bibliothèque Nationale entitled *Tadhkirat ul-Ikhvān* listed by Blochet (*Catalogue des Manuscrits Persans,* IV: 299) as one of Malkum's treatises was not in fact written by him. It consists of an anonymous Persian translation of an Arabic work on freemasonry (Supplément Persan, 1992).

Unpublished treatises in the possession of Firīdūn Ādamīyat, Tehran. (Not seen by me.)

Documents and letters

PUBLISHED

Ākhūndzāda, Fatḥ ᶜAlī. *Alifbā-yi Jadīd va Maktūbāt*. Edited by Ḥamīd Muḥammadzāda and Ḥamīd Ārāslī. Baku, 1963.
Mahdavī, A. and Afshār, Īraj, eds. *Majmūᶜa-yi Asnād va Madārik-i Chāp Nashuda dar bāra-yi Sayyid Jamāl ud-Dīn-i Mashhūr ba Afghānī*. Tehran, 1342 solar/1963.
Meyendorff, A., ed. *Correspondance Diplomatique de M. de Staal, 1884–1900*. 4 vols. Paris, 1929.
Ṣafāʾī, Ibrāhīm, ed. *Asnād-i Siyāsī-yi Daurān-i Qājārīya*. Tehran, 1346 solar/1967.

UNPUBLISHED

Bibliothèque Nationale, Paris. Collection of letters received by Malkum and donated by his widow in 1924. Supplément Persan, 1986, 1987, 1988, 1989, 1990, 1991, 1995, 1996, 1997. (Blochet, *Catalogue des Manuscrits Persans* IV: 284–291.)
Derelioğlu Collection, Hoover Institute. Letter of Âlî Paşa to Haydar Efendi dated Muḥarram 1279/July 1862.
Rāpurt-i Shakhṣī ki Dau Daraja az Farāmūshkhāna-rā Ṭayy Karda Ast. Kitabkhāna-yi Millī, Tehran, 1397.
United Kingdom. Diplomatic Correspondence Preserved in Public Records, Office, London. F.O. 60/487, 497, 637.

II: SECONDARY SOURCES

Works in Persian (including Tajik) and Arabic

Ādamīyat, Firīdūn. *Amīr Kabīr va Irān*. Tehran, 1334 solar/1955.
———. *Andīshahā-yi Mīrzā Āqā Khān-i Kirmānī*. Tehran, 1346 solar/1967.
———. *Andīshahā-yi Mīrzā Fatḥ ᶜAlī Ākhūndzāda*. Tehran, 1349 solar/1970.
———. *Fikr-i Āzādī va Muqaddima-yi Niḥḍat-i Mashrūṭīyat-i Īrān*. Tehran, 1340 solar/1961.
———. "Se Maktūb-i Mīrzā Fatḥ ᶜAlī." *Yaghmā* XIX (1345 solar/1966): 363–366.
Afshār, Īraj. "Asnād Marbūṭ ba Farrukh Khān." *Yaghmā* XVIII (1344 solar/1965): 583–591.
———. "Tiligrāf dar Īrān." *Savād au Bayāḍ*. Tehran, 1344 solar/1965, pp. 228–239.
Akhundov, M. F. (Mīrzā Fatḥ ᶜAlī Ākhūndzāda). *Maktubho*. Dushanbe, 1962.
Āl-i Aḥmad, Jalāl. *Gharbzadagī*. Tehran, 1341 solar/1962.
Amīn ud-Daula, Mīrzā ᶜAlī Khān. *Khāṭirāt-i Siyāsī*. Edited by Ḥāfiẓ Farmānfarmāyān. Tehran, 1341 solar/1962.
Arfaᶜ ud-Daula, Mīrzā Riḍā. *Īrān-i Dīrūz*. Tehran, 1345 solar/1966.

al-ʿAzzāwī, ʿAbbās. *Tārīkh al-ʿIrāq bayn Iḥtilālayn.* 8 vols. Baghdad, 1373 lunar/1953–1954.

Bahār, Malik ush-Shuʿarā. *Sabkshināsī.* 3 vols. Tehran, 1337 solar/1958.

Bīdābādī, Muḥammad ʿAlī. *Makārim ul-Āthār dar Aḥvāl-i Rijāl-i Daura-yi Qājār.* Isfahan, 1337 solar/1958. vol. I. (Only volume issued.)

Chahārdihī, Murtaḍā Mudarris. *Zindagānī va Falsafa-yi Sayyid Jamāl ud-Dīn-i Afghānī.* Tehran, 1344 solar/1955.

Daulatābādī, Yaḥyā. *Tārīkh-i Muʿāṣir yā Ḥayāt-i Yaḥyā.* 3 vols. Tehran, n.d.

Farāhānī, Adīb ul-Mamālik. *Dīvān.* Edited by Vaḥīd Dastgirdī. Tehran, 1312 solar/1932.

Hāshimī, Muḥammad Ṣadr. *Tārīkh-i Jarāʾid va Majallāt-i Īrān.* 4 vols. Isfahan, 1327–1328 solar/1948–1950.

Hidāyat, Riḍā Qulī Khān. *Rauḍat us-Ṣafā-yi Nāṣirī.* 10 vols. Tehran, n.d.

Ḥikmat, ʿAlī Aṣghar. *Pārsī-yi Naghz.* Tehran, 1323 solar/1944.

Humā, Nāṭiq. "Naẓar Āqā va Nāmahāʾī az Ū." *Rāhnamā-yi Kitāb* XII (1348 solar/1969): 662–673; XIII (1349 solar/1970): 52–63.

Iqbāl, ʿAbbās. *Mīrzā Taqī Khān Amīr Kabīr.* Tehran, 1340 solar/1961.

———. "Sharḥ-i Ḥāl-i Marḥūm Ḥājj Mullā ʿAlī Kanī." *Yādgār* IV (1326 solar/1947): 72–78.

Iṣfahānī, ʿImād ud-Dīn Ḥusayn. *Tārīkh-i Jughrāfiyāʾī-yi Karbalā-yi Muʿallā.* Tehran, 1326 solar/1947.

Iʿtimād us-Salṭana, Mīrzā Muḥammad Ḥasan Khān. *al-Maʾāthir va-l-Āthār.* Tehran, 1306 lunar/1889.

———. *Mirʾāt ul-Buldān-i Nāṣirī.* 4 vols. Tehran, 1924–1297 lunar/1877–1880.

———. *Rūznāma-yi Khāṭirāt.* Edited by Īraj Afshār. Tehran, 1345 solar/1967.

Jamālzāda, Sayyid Muḥammad ʿAlī. *Sar au Tah-i Yak Karbās.* 2 vols. Tehran, 1327 solar/1948.

Jannatī-ʿAṭāʾī, Abūl Qāsim. *Bunyād-i Namāyish dar Īrān.* Tehran, 1344 solar/1955.

Katīrāʾī, Maḥmūd. *Frāmāsūnrī dar Īrān.* Tehran, 1347 solar/1968.

Khūrmūjī, Muḥammad Jaʿfar. *Ḥaqāʾiq ul-Akhbār-i Nāṣirī.* Edited by Ḥusayn Khadīv-i Jam. Tehran, 1344 solar/1965.

Kirmānī, Mīrzā Āqā Khān. *Hasht Bihisht.* n.p., n.d.

Kirmānī, Nāẓim ul-Islām. *Tārīkh-i Bīdārī-yi Īrāniān.* Tehran, 1332 solar/1953.

Lisān ul-Mulk, Mīrzā Muḥammad Taqī Sipihr. *Nāsikh ut-Tavārīkh.* Tehran, n.d.

Lohuti, Abulqosim (Abūl Qāsim Lāhūtī). *Kulliyot.* 6 vols. Dushanbe, 1963.

Luṭfullāh Khān, Shaykh. *Sharḥ-i Ḥāl va Āthār-i Sayyid Jamāl ud-Dīn-i Asadābādī Maʿrūf ba Afghānī.* Tabriz, 1327 solar/1948.

Maḥmūd, Maḥmūd. *Tārīkh-i Ravābiṭ-i Siyāsī-yi Īrān va Inglīs dar Qarn-i Nūzdahum-i Mīlādī.* 8 vols. Tehran, 1328 solar/1949.

Malikzāda, Mahdī. *Tārīkh-i Inqilāb-i Mashrūṭīyat.* Tehran, 1327 solar/1948.

Mukhbir us-Salṭana, Mahdī Qulī Khān Hidāyat. *Khāṭirāt va Khaṭarāt.* Tehran, 1329 solar/1950.

———. *Safarnāma-yi Tasharruf ba Makka-yi Muʿaẓẓama az Ṭarīq-i Chīn va Zhāpun va Amrīkā.* Tehran, n.d.

Mulkārā, ᶜAbbās Mīrzā. *Sharḥ-i Ḥāl.* Edited by ᶜAbd ul-Ḥusayn Navāʾī. Tehran, 1325 solar/1946.

Mustaufī, ᶜAbdullāh. *Sharḥ-i Zindagānī-yi Man yā Tārīkh-i Ijtimāᶜi va Idārī-yi Daura-yi Qājārīya.* 2 vols. Tehran, 1341 solar/1942.

Muᶜtamad, Maḥmūd Farhād. *Mushīr ud-Daula Sipahsālār-i Aᶜẓam.* Tehran, 1326 solar/1947.

Nāʾīnī, Ḥājjī Pīrzāda. *Safarnāma.* Edited by Ḥāfiẓ Farmānfarmāyān. 2 vols. Tehran, 1343 solar/1964.

Najafqulī, Ḥusām Muᶜizzī. *Tārīkh-i Ravābiṭ-i Īrān bā Dunyā.* Tehran, 1325 solar/1946.

Nāṣir ud-Dīn Shāh. *Safarnāma.* Tehran, 1343 solar/1946.

———. *Safarnāma-yi Farang.* Tehran, 1308 lunar/1890.

Naṣīrīān, ᶜAlī. "Naẓarī ba Hunar-i Namāyish dar Īrān." *Kaweh* (new series) I:2 (Khurdād 1342/May 1963), 116–118.

Qāʾimmaqāmī, Jahāngīr. "Chand Sanad Marbūṭ ba Tārīkh-i Farāmūshkhāna dar Īrān." *Yaghmā* XVI (1342 solar/1963): 404–405.

———. "Ravābiṭ-i Ẓill us-Sulṭān va Mīrzā Malkum Khān." *Barrasīhā-yi Tārīkhī* III:6 (Bahman-Isfand, 1347/January–February, 1969), 83–120.

Rāʾīn, Ismāᶜīl. *Anjumanhā-yi Sirrī dar Inqilāb-i Mashrūṭīyat-i Īrān.* Tehran, 1345 solar/1966.

———. *Farāmūshkhāna va Frāmāsūnrī dar Īrān.* 3 vols. Tehran, 1348 solar/1968.

———. *Ḥuqūqbigīrān-i Inglīs dar Īrān.* Tehran, 1348 solar/1968.

———. *Īrānīān-i Armanī.* Tehran, 1349 solar/1970.

Riḍā, Rashīd. *Tārīkh al-Ustādh al-Imām ash-Shaykh Muḥammad ᶜAbduh.* 2 vols. Cairo, 1349 lunar/1930.

Saᶜādat-Nūrī, Ḥusayn. "Naẓar Āqā va Amīr Kabīr." *Rāhnamā-yi Kitāb* VI (1342 solar/1964): 445–450.

Ṣafāʾī, Ibrāhīm. *Rahbarān-i Mashrūta: II, Mīrzā Malkum Khān; XVIII, Shaykh ur-Raʾīs; Serī-yi Duvvum, II, Atābak.* Tehran, 1342–1345 solar/1963–1966.

Sarābī, Ḥusayn ibn ᶜAbdullāh. *Makhzan ul-Vaqāyiᶜ.* Tehran, 1344 solar/1966.

Sāsānī, Khān Malik. *Siyāsatgarān-i Daura-yi Qājār.* 2 vols. Tehran, 1337–1345 solar/1958–1966.

———. *Yādbūdhā-yi Safārat-i Istānbūl.* Tehran, 1345 solar/1966.

Sayyāḥ, Ḥājj. *Khāṭirāt-i Ḥājj Sayyāḥ yā Daura-yi Khauf va Vaḥshat.* Edited by Ḥamīd Sayyāḥ. Tehran, 1346 solar/1967.

Shamīm, ᶜAlī Aṣghar. *Īrān dar Daura-yi Salṭanat-i Qājār.* Tehran, 1342 solar/1963.

Sharaf ud-Dīn, Qahramān Mīrzā. "Yak Silsila Asnād-i Tārīkhī yā ᶜIlal-i Vāqiᶜī-yi Jang-i Duvvum-i Rūs-Īrān." *Sharq* I (1320 solar/1931–1932): 253–257; 318–331; 439–440; 564–567; 625–632; 669–672.

Shaykh ur-Raʾīs, Abūl Ḥasan Mīrzā. *Ittiḥād ul-Islām.* Bombay, 1312 lunar/1894.

Tabrīzī, Sayyid Javād, ed. *Majmūᶜa-yi Mushtamil bar se Qiṭᶜa Tiʾātr Mansūb ba Marḥūm Malkum Khān Nāẓim ud-Daula.* Berlin, 1340 lunar/1921.

Taymūrī, Ibrāhīm. *ᶜAṣr-i Bīkhabarī yā Tārīkh-i Imtiyāzāt dar Īrān.* Tehran, 1336 solar/1957.

———. *Taḥrīm-i Tanbākū yā Avvalīn Muqāvamat-i Manfī dar Īrān*. Tehran, 1328 solar/1949.
Yaghmāʾī, Iqbāl. "Madrasa-yi Dār ul-Funūn." *Yaghmā* XXIII (1348 solar/1969): 143–149.
Ẓill us-Sulṭān, Masᶜūd Mīrzā. *Sargudhasht-i Masᶜūdī*. Tehran, 1325 lunar/1907.

Works in Turkish (including Azerbayjani)

Akhundov, M. F. (Mīrzā Fatḥ ᶜAlī Ākhūndzāda). *Äsärläri*. 3 vols. Baku, 1961.
———. *Komediyalar*. Baku, 1962.
Akhundov, Nazim. *Azärbayjan Satira Zhurnalları*. Baku, 1968.
Barkan, Ömer Lutfi. "Kânûn Nâme." *İslam Ansiklopedisi* VI: 185–196.
Baykara, Hüseyin. *Azerbaycan'da Yenileşme Hareketleri*. Ankara, 1966.
Çark, Y. *Türk Devleti Hizmetinde Ermeniler*. Istanbul, 1953.
Dünyada ve Türkiyede Masonluk. Istanbul, 1965.
Fuat, Ali. "Münif Paşa." *Türk Tarih Encümeni Mecmuası* I (1930): 1–16.
Galib, Mehmet. "Tarihden bir Sahife: Âlî ve Fuad Paşaların Vasiyetnameleri." *Tarih-i Osmani Encümeni Mecmuası* I (1329 lunar/1911): 73–84.
Gövsa, İbrahim. *Türk Meşhurları Ansiklopedisi*. Istanbul, n.d.
Hatämi, H. *Mühajir Iran Gazetlärinin Müstämläkäjilik vä Imperializm Aleyhinä Mübarizäsi*. Baku, 1964.
Ibrahimov, A. E. and Mämmädzadä, H. "Mirza Malkumkhana Hesab Ädilän Pyeslärin Asl Muallifi Haggında." *Nizami Adına Ädäbiyat vä Dil Institutunun Äsärläri* (Ädäbiyat Seriyası) IX (1956): 161–169.
İnal, Mehmed Kemal. *Osmanlı Devrinde Son Sadrıazamlar*. Istanbul, 1940.
Koçaş, Sadi. *Tarih Boyunca Ermeniler ve Türk-Ermeni İlişkileri*. Ankara, 1967.
Köprülü, Orhan. "Fuad Paşa." *İslam Ansiklopedisi* IV: 672–681.
Kuntay, Mithat Cemal. *Namık Kemal Devrinin İnsanları ve Olayları Arasında*. 4 vols. Istanbul, 1944.
Levend, Agah Sırrı. *Türk Dilinde Gelişme ve Sadeleşme Safhaları*. Ankara, 1949.
"Masonluk Tarihinden Notlar." *Türk Mason Dergisi* I (1951): 29–32.
Tanpınar, Ahmet Hamdi. "Ahmet Vefik Paşa." *İslam Ansiklopedisi* I: 207–210.
Tansel, Fevziye Abdullah. "Arap Harflerinin Islahı ve Değiştirilmesi Hakkında İlk Teşebbüsler ve Neticeleri." *Türk Tarih Kurumu: Belleten* XVII (1953): 224–249.
Tanzimat: Yüzüncü Yıldönümü Münasebetile. Istanbul, 1940.
Yurtsever, A. Vahap. *Mirza Ahuntzadenin Hayatı ve Eserleri*. Ankara, 1950.

Works in other languages

Aali Pacha (Âlî Paşa). "Testament Politique." *La Revue de Paris* XVII (1910): 505–524.
Abul'fas, Guseini. "Eshchë Raz ob Avtore Pervykh Persidskikh Pyes." *Narody Azii i Afriki*, 1965:6, 142–145.
Afghānī, Jamāl ud-Dīn. "The Reign of Terror in Persia." *Contemporary Review* LXI (1892): 238–248.

Akhundov, Mirza Fatali (Mīrzā Fatḥ ʿAlī Ākhūndzāda). *Izbrannoe.* Edited by Aziz Sharif. Moscow, 1956.

Alavi, Bozorg. *Geschichte und Entwicklung der modernen persischen Literatur.* Berlin, 1964.

Algar, Hamid. "An Introduction to the History of Freemasonry in Iran." *Middle Eastern Studies* VI (1970): 276–296.

———. *Religion and State in Iran, 1785–1906: The Role of the Ulama in the Qajar Period.* Berkeley and Los Angeles, 1969.

Alieva, Dilara. *Iz Istorii Azerbaydzhansko-Gruzinskikh Literaturnykh Svyazei.* Baku, 1958.

And, Metin. *A History of Theatre and Popular Entertainment in Turkey.* Ankara, 1963–1964.

Bausani, Alessandro. *Storia della Letteratura Persiana.* Milan, 1960.

Benjamin, S. G. W. *Persia and the Persians.* London, 1887.

Berkes, Niyazi. *The Development of Secularism in Turkey.* Montreal, 1964.

Bertel's, Ye. E. *Iz Istorii Popytok Reformy Arabskogo Alfavita, I: Mal'kom Khan.* Leningrad, 1928. (Not seen by me.)

Blunt, W. S. *Diaries.* London, 1932.

———. *The Future of Islam.* London, 1882.

———. *Secret History of the English Occupation of Egypt.* London, 1903.

Braginskiy, I. and Kommissarov, D. S. *Persidskaya Literatura.* Moscow, 1963.

Bricteux, A., trans. "Les Comédies de Malkom Khan: Les Mésaventures d'Achraf Khan; Zaman Khan, ou le Gouverneur Modèle; les Tribulations de Chah Qouli Mirza." *Bibliothèque de la Faculté de Philosophie et de Lettres de l'Université de Liège,* fasc. LIII (1933).

Brosset, M., trans. and ed. *Collection d'Historiens Arméniens.* 3 vols. St. Petersburg, 1874.

Browne, E. G. *A Literary History of Persia.* Vol. IV. Cambridge, 1924.

———. *The Persian Revolution of 1905–1909.* Cambridge, 1910.

———. *The Press and Poetry of Modern Persia.* Cambridge, 1914.

Cahen, Claude. "Amīn." *Encyclopaedia of Islam,* new edition. I: 437.

Chardin, J. *Voyages en Perse et Autres Lieux de l'Orient.* 3 vols. Amsterdam, 1711.

Christensen, A. "To Iranske Komedier fra Kadjarernes Tid." *Studier fra Sprog- og Oldtidsforskning* fasc. 178 (1938).

Curzon, G. N. *Persia and the Persian Question.* 2 vols. London, 1892.

Daniel, Norman. *Islam, Europe and Empire.* Edinburgh, 1966.

Davison, R. H. "The Question of Fuad Paşa's Political Testament." *Türk Tarih Kurumu: Belleten* XXIII (1959): 119–136.

———. *Reform in the Ottoman Empire, 1856–1876.* Princeton, 1963.

della Valle, P. *Viaggi di Petro della Valle il Pellegrino Descritti da lui Medesimo in Lettere Familiari all'erudito suo Amico, Mario Schipano.* Rome, 1668.

Dieulafoy, Jane. *La Perse, la Chaldee et la Susiane.* Paris, 1887.

Donaldson, D. M. *The Shi'ite Religion.* London, 1933.

Dzhafarov, D. *M. F. Akhundov.* Moscow, 1962.

Eingorn, Ya. A. "Komediya Mirzy Mal'kom Khana, Proisshestvie s Ashraf

Khanom, Gubernatorom Arabistana." *Byulleten' Sredne Aziatskogo Universiteta (Tashkent)* 16 (1927): 102–120.

Evans, Hubert. "An Enquiry into the Authorship of Three Persian Plays Attributed to Malkom Khan." *Central Asian Review* XV (1967): 21–25.

Feuvrier, J.-B. *Trois Ans à la Cour de Perse.* Paris, 1899.

Fouad Pacha (Fuad Paşa). "Testament Politique." *La Revue de Paris* III: 4 (October–December, 1896), 126–135.

———. "Political Testament." *Nineteenth Century* LIII (1903): 190–197.

Fraser, J. B. *Narrative of the Residence of the Persian Princes in London in 1835 and 1836, together with an Account of their Subsequent Adventures.* 2 vols. London, 1838.

———. *Travels in Koordistan, Mesopotamia etc.* 2 vols. London, 1849.

Frechtling, L. E. "The Reuter Concession in Persia." *Asiatic Review* XXIV (1938): 518–533.

Fyzee, A. A. A. *Outlines of Muhammadan Law.* Oxford, 1955.

Gobineau, A. de. *Les Religions et les Philosophies dans l'Asie Centrale.* Paris, 1865.

Greaves, R. L. *Persia and the Defence of India, 1884–1892.* London, 1959.

Greenfield, James. *Die Verfassung des persischen Staates.* Berlin, 1904.

Hanway, J. *An Historical Account of the British Trade over the Caspian Sea.* 2 vols. London, 1762.

Haweis, H. R. "Talk with a Persian Statesman." *Contemporary Review* LXX (1896): 74–77.

Hayit, Baymirza. *Turkestan im zwanzigsten Jahrhundert.* Darmstadt, 1956.

Ilyin, Ye. "Iz Istorii Masonstva v Persii." *Drevnosti Vostochnye: Trudy Vostochnoi Kommissi Imperatorskogo Arkheologicheskogo Obshchestva.* Moscow, 1908, pp. 17–20.

Ivanov, M. S. *Iranskaya Revolyutsiya 1905–1911 Godov.* Moscow, 1957.

Jäschke, G. "Die türkisch-orthodoxe Kirche." *Der Islam* XXXIX (1964): 95–129.

Kamshad, H. *Modern Persian Prose Literature.* Cambridge, 1966.

Kasumov, M. M. "Bor'ba M. F. Akhundova Protiv Religii Islama." *Trudy Instituta Istorii i Filosofii Akademii Nauk Azerbaydzhanskoi SSR* III (1953): 70–101.

———. "Mirovozzrenie M. F. Akhundova." *Trudy Instituta Istorii i Filosofii Akademii Nauk Azerbaydzhanskoi SSR* VII (1955): 70–101.

Kazem Beg, Mirza. "Bab et les Babis." *Journal Asiatique* VIII (1866): 196–252.

Kazemzadeh, F. *Russia and Britain in Persia, 1864–1914.* New Haven, 1968.

Keddie, N. R. *An Islamic Response to Imperialism: Political and Religious Writings of Sayyid Jamal ad-Din "al-Afghani."* Berkeley and Los Angeles, 1968.

———. "Religion and Irreligion in Early Iranian Nationalism." *Comparative Studies in Society and History* IV (1962): 265–295.

———. *Religion and Rebellion in Iran: The Tobacco Protest of 1891–1892.* London, 1966.

Kedourie, Elie. *Afghani and ʿAbduh: An Essay on Religious Unbelief and Political Activism in Modern Islam.* London, 1966.

Kommissarov, D. S. *Ocherki Sovremennoi Persidskoi Prozy.* Moscow, 1960.
Lambton, A. K. S. "The Tobacco Régie: Prelude to Revolution." *Studia Islamica* XXII (1965): 119–157.
———. "Secret Societies and the Persian Revolution of 1905–1906." *St. Anthony's Papers* IV (1958): 43–60.
Lewis, Bernard. *The Emergence of Modern Turkey.* Oxford, 1961.
Lockhart, L. *The Fall of the Safavid Dynasty and the Afghan Occupation of Persia.* Cambridge, 1958.
Mantran, Roger. "Baġdād a l'Epoque Ottomane." *Baġdād: Volume Special Publié a l'Occasion du Mille-deux-centième Anniversaire de la Fondation.* Leyden, 1962, pp. 314–326.
Mardin, Şerif. *The Genesis of Young Ottoman Thought.* Princeton, 1962.
Martin, Bradford G. *German-Persian Diplomatic Relations, 1873–1912.* 's-Gravenhage, 1959.
Meinhardus, O. F. A. *Christian Egypt, Ancient and Modern.* Cairo, 1965.
Mismer, Charles. "L'Islamisme et la Science." *Revue de la Philosophie Positive* XXX (May–June, 1883): 432–438.
———. "La Régénération de l'Islam." *Revue de la Philosophie Positive* XXXI (September–October, 1883): 283–289.
———. *Soirées de Constantinople.* Paris, 1870.
———. *Souvenirs du Monde Musulman.* Paris, 1892.
Nāṣir ud-Dīn Shāh. *The Diary of H.M. the Shah of Persia during his Tour through Europe in A.D. 1873.* Translated by J.W. Redhouse. London, 1874.
Olivier, G. A. *Voyage dans l'Empire Othoman, l'Egypte et la Perse.* 3 vols. Paris, 1802.
Osmanova, E. G. and Shukurova, M. Sh. *Ocherk Istorii Sovetskoi Tadzhikskoi Literatury.* Moscow, 1961.
Pahlen, K. K. *Mission to Turkestan.* New York and Toronto, 1964.
Pakdaman, Homa. *Djamal-ed-Din Assad Abadi dit Afghani.* Paris, 1969.
Piemontese, Angelo. "Per una biografia di Mīrzā Malkom Xān." *Annali, Istituto Orientale di Napoli.* New series XIX (1969): 361–385.
Polak, J. E. *Persien, das Land und seine Bewohner.* 2 vols. Leipzig, 1865.
Rabino, H. L. "Une Tentative de Reformes en 1875." *Revue du Monde Musulman* XXVI (1914): 133–135.
Ramazani, Rouhollah. *The Foreign Policy of Iran, 1500–1941.* Charlottesville, 1966.
Rawlinson, Sir H. *England and Russia in the East.* London, 1875.
Rezvani, M. *Le Théâtre et la Danse en Iran.* Paris, 1962.
Rypka, Jan. *Iranische Literaturgeschichte.* Leipzig, 1959.
Sanjian, A. K. *The Armenian Communities in Syria under the Ottoman Dominion.* Cambridge, Mass., 1965.
Scarcia, Gianroberto. "Malkom Khān (1833–1908) e la Nascita del Teatro Persiano Moderno." *Oriente Moderno* XLVII (1967): 248–266.
———, trans. *Mīrzā Āqā Tabrīzī: Tre Commedie.* Naples, 1967.
Seth, Mesrob J. *History of the Armenians in India.* London, 1897.
Shoitov, A. M. "Rol' M. F. Akhundova v Razvitii Persidskoi Progressivnoi

Literatury." *Kratkie Soobshchenie Instituta Vostokovedeniya* IX (1953): 58–65.
Sykes, Sir P. *History of Persia.* 2 vols. London, 1963.
Tavernier, J.-B. *Voyages en Perse.* Edited by Vincent Monteil. Paris, 1964.
Wolff, Sir H. D. *Rambling Recollections.* London, 1908.

Newspapers and Periodicals

Bombay Gazette
Bulletin du Grand Orient de France: Suprême Conseil pour la France et les Possessions Françaises
The Illustrated London News
Madras Times
Le Monde Maçonnique
Pall Mall Gazette
The Queen
The Times

INDEX

ᶜAbbās, Shah, 1, 2
ᶜAbbās Āqā, 254
ᶜAbbās Mīrzā, 4, 13 n. 47, 27 n. 38, 103, 302
ᶜAbbās Qulī Khān. *See* Ādamīyat, ᶜAbbās Qulī Khān Qazvīnī
Ābdārbāshī, 165, 196
Ābdārkhāna, 196, 198, 239, 301, 303, 306
ᶜAbduh, Muḥammad, 215
Abdülaziz, Sultan, 72, 75
Abdülhamid, Sultan, 71 n. 54, 186, 203, 214, 217–218
Abovyan, Khachatur, 79
Abul'fas, Guseini, 272–273
Ādam, 226, 229
Ādamīyat, ᶜAbbās Qulī Khān Qazvīnī, 248–250, 253–258
Ādamīyat, Firīdūn, 260–261
ᶜ*Adlīya*, 102. *See also* Ministry of Justice
Administrative reform, 26, 27–33, 34, 48, 67, 105–107, 108
Afghānī, Sayyid Jamāl ud-Dīn. *See* Asadābādī, Sayyid Jamāl ud-Dīn
Afghans, Afghanistan, 3, 24, 54, 131, 201, 213
Afshār, ᶜAskar Khān, 25
Agha Khan, 225
Agop, Güllü, 265
Ahvaz, 136
Ājūdānbāshī, Mīrzā Ḥusayn Khān, 35
Akhbār-i Vaqāyiᶜ, 185
Akhtar, 186–187, 216, 308
Ākhūndzāda, Mīrzā Fatḥ ᶜAlī, 77, 158, 159, 161, 215, 219, 226, 264–268, 271–272; and alphabet reform, 82–92; and westernization, 78, 80; as playwright, 80, 85, 86, 265–270; attitude to religion, 79, 80–81, 84, 85, 91–92; attitude to Russian government, 81; biography of, 78–80; critique of plays attributed to Malkum, 269–270, 276; death, 99; hatred of Arabs and Islam, 37, 81, 91–92; relations with Malkum, 78, 81, 84, 86–99, 128; relations with Mīrzā Ḥusayn Khān Sipahsālār, 83, 85; relations with Mīrzā Yūsuf Khān Mustashār ud-Daula, 140–141; visit to Istanbul, 82–84. Works: *Story of Monsieur Jourdain*, 80; *Three Letters of the Indian Prince, Kamāl ud-Daula*, 81, 92, 96, 98
ᶜAlā us-Salṭana, Mīrzā Muḥammad ᶜAlī Khān, 174, 176, 178, 210 n. 18
Aleppo, 2
ᶜAlī Khān, Mīrzā, 88
Âlî Paşa, Mehmed Emin, 7, 60–61, 61 n. 16, 65–66, 67, 70, 73, 76–77, 83, 188
"ᶜAlī Shāh," Ẓill us-Sulṭān, 50
Alifbā-yi Bihrūzī, 149 n. 85
Alison, 115
Alphabet reform, 7, 8, 68, 78, 82–97, 140, 149, 158–162, 219, 221, 250
America, 93, 244, 251, 302
Amīn, 231–232, 249
Amīn-i Ḍarb, Ḥājj Muḥammad Iṣfahānī, 201–202
Amīn ud-Daula, Mīrzā ᶜAlī Khān, 49, 118, 166, 171–172, 191 n. 17, 201–203, 206, 233, 244, 250; and alphabet reform, 158–159; as minister of posts, 199–200; as prime minister, 242–243; relations with Malkum, 146–149, 150–157, 204, 261
Amīn ud-Daula, Mīrzā Farrukh Khān Ghaffārī, 24–25, 119, 126, 127
Amīn us-Sulṭān, Mīrzā ᶜAlī Aṣghar (Atābak), 65, 156, 176, 181, 194, 200–204,

210, 211, 239, 242, 259, 261, 275, 300; ancestry, 164–165; and secret agreement with Russia, 152; assassinated, 254; dismissal from premiership, 241; initiated into freemasonry, 251–253; journey to Arabia via Japan, 251; letter to Mīrzā Ḥasan Shīrāzī, 213; relations with Malkum, 165–167, 171–173, 177–178, 188–189, 196, 243–244; relations with Society of Humanity, 253–254; resumes premiership, 243
Amir Ali, 140 n. 44
Amīr Kabīr, Mīrzā Taqī Khān, 4, 6, 16, 20, 21, 26, 30 n. 52, 66, 181, 185–186, 307
ᶜAmūoghlī, Ḥaydar, 254
Anatolia, 1, 3, 127
Andreini, Enrico, 10 n. 37, 15 n. 52, 53 n. 158
Anglo-Asiatic Syndicate, 169–170, 173–174, 176, 182
Anīs ud-Daula, 123
Anjuman-i Ḥuqūq, 257
Anjuman-i Ittiḥād, 266
Anṣārī, Shaykh Murtaḍā, 210
Antioch, 125
Antippa, Mūsā, 125
Antwerp, 167
Anglo-Iranian Treaty of 1919, 134
Anzalī, 113, 117, 123
ᶜArab, Mullā Ṣāliḥ, 122
Arab Iraq, 56–57, 62, 96, 101, 202
Aras river, 2, 124
Arfaᶜ ud-Daula, Mīrzā Riḍā Khān "Dānish," 149, 167
Ârifî Paşa, 74
Armenians, 1–5, 10, 18, 21, 40, 64, 66, 79, 89, 128, 144, 164 n. 7, 241, 265, 265 n. 3, 275
Asadābādī, Sayyid Jamāl ud-Dīn, 99, 179 n. 57, 201–202, 203, 205–215, 219–220, 224, 226, 237, 262
Ashkhabad, 194, 234
Asia, as antithesis of "progressive" Europe, 11–13, 80, 99, 179–180, 241
ᶜ*Askarīya*, 102
Assyrians, 5, 21
Astarābād, 132
Astrakhan, 132
ᶜ*Atabāt*, 53, 56–58, 64, 101, 208, 218, 224, 225 n. 23, 234, 306
Attock, 131
ᶜAun al-Mamālik, Mīrzā Ibrāhīm Khān, 253
Azalīs, Azalism, 215–216, 221–224, 227
Azerbayjan, 1, 78, 124, 142, 144, 164, 239, 251, 254, 257, 303
Bâb-ı Âlî, 7, 60, 65
Bābīs, Babism, 11, 46, 58–59, 213, 215, 216 n. 40, 221–225, 306. *See also* Azalīs and Bahāᵓīs
Baghdad, 46, 56, 58, 60, 61, 62, 101, 119, 194, 223, 270, 273
Bahāᵓīs, 224, 224 n. 87, 225
"Bahāᵓullāh." *See* Nūrī, Mīrzā Ḥusayn ᶜAlī
Bahrayn, 136
Baku, 268
Balkhī, Sayyid Burhān ud-Dīn, 70
Baluchistan, 131
Banks, banking, 110, 110 n. 35, 112, 116, 125, 135; Bank of England, 117, 169; Imperial Bank of Persia, 165
Basra, 211
Bausani, Alessandro, 282
Bavānātī, Mīrzā Muḥammad, 204
Bebek, 76
Belgium, 120, 167
Berge, Adolf, 80
Berlin, 51, 119, 151, 166; Congress of, 148, 151
Bestuzhev-Marlinskiy, A. A., 80
Bihbihānī, Āqā Muḥammad Bāqir, 57
Bismarck, 148, 151, 151 n. 98
Blonnet, 52–53
Blunt, Wilfred Scawen, 11, 11 n. 1, 95, 104, 179, 206, 222, 261, 262
Bodenstedt, Friedrich, 79 n. 2
Bombay, 66, 182 n. 61, 194, 225, 234
Bombay Gazette, 182 n. 61
Britain, 73, 163
British policy in Iran, 3, 23–24, 28, 53–54, 114–115, 119, 121, 123, 124, 127–134, 135–139, 144, 151–152, 157, 163–165, 172
Browne, E. G., 172 n. 39, 187, 210, 218–219, 234, 260, 262
Brussels, 119, 250
Buddhism, 80
Bukhara, 54, 112, 163, 235 n. 50
Burghānī, Mullā Muḥammad Ṣāliḥ, 282 n. 4
Bursa, 265
Burūjird, 146
Bushire, 136, 158, 201

Cadogan, A. C., 169
Cairo, 63, 65
Calcutta, 182 n. 61
Cardoël, Buzie de, 168–171, 173, 174, 176, 182, 183
Cargill, W. W., 169
Carlsbad, 141, 251–253
Caspian Sea, 3, 132, 138
Caucasian Social Democratic Party, 254

Caucasus, 1, 34 n. 74, 78, 79, 91, 127, 162, 248, 257, 270
Central Asia, 53–54, 127, 136, 191
Chavchavadze, Aleksandr, 79
China, 251
Christians, Christianity, 10, 11, 13, 17, 64, 65, 70, 94, 164, 179–180, 246
Cloëte, Laurence, 169, 169 n. 29, 170
Committee of Union and Progress, 73
Concessions, 19, 100, 108, 112, 114–125, 134–135, 163, 167, 200; Liquor concession, 147; Lottery concession, 65, 168–184, 194, 218–219, 242, 242 n. 12, 256, 260; Reuter concession, 113–125, 134, 147, 163, 168, 211; Tobacco concession, 165, 192, 210–213
Constitutional government, 48, 184, 236–237, 247
Constitutional Revolution, 38, 40, 50, 94, 200, 214, 236, 238
Contemporary Review, 179
Cotte, Edouard, 115–118
Curzon, G. N., 142, 145, 172 n. 39
Cyprus, 215
Cyrillic alphabet, 93, 95, 161

Dār ul-Funūn, 20, 21, 25, 39, 49, 185, 244, 264
Dār ush-Shūrā-yi Kubrā, 105
Darbandī, Sayyid Fāḍil, 209
Darbār-i aᶜẓam, 105–106, 236–237, 238
Dāʾūd Khān, Mīrzā, 4
Dāvīd Khān, 203
Deccan, 130
Dekabrists, 80, 81
Derby, Lord, 136
Dīvān-i maẓālim, 69
Dīvānkhāna, 102, 105, 113
Diyarbekir, 59
Dolgorukiy, 6
Dolgorukov, 164
Donish, Ahmad, 78
Dorn, Bernard, 80
Dürûb-u Emsâl-i Müntehabe, 159

Echmiadzin, 1
Educational reform, 20, 32
Egypt, 4, 63, 185, 201, 217, 234, 251
Erzurum, 4

Fālasīrī, Sayyid ᶜAlī Akbar, 211
Falkenhagen, von, 124
Fanā, 80
Farāmūshkhāna, 12, 21, 36–53, 55, 62, 65, 69, 70, 92, 99, 124, 126, 129, 140, 146, 161, 188, 189, 192, 201, 203, 207, 209, 213, 222, 226, 228, 229, 231, 243 n. 15, 249, 251, 255
Farīd ul-Mulk, Mīrzā Muḥammad ᶜAlī Khān, 159, 203
Farmānfarmā, ᶜAbd ul-Ḥusayn Mīrzā, 242
Farmānfarmā, Ḥusayn ᶜAlī Mīrzā, 131 n. 7
Fars, 144, 158
Fārsī Shikar Ast, 280
Fatḥ ᶜAlī Shāh, 37, 57 n. 3, 129, 130, 302
Fikret, Tevfik, 192 n. 20
Firīdūn (son of Malkum), 65, 218 n. 59, 243, 243 n. 14
Foreign Office, 128, 152, 175, 262
France, 15, 18, 114, 129, 130, 191, 251
Freemasonry, 9, 12, 24–25, 35, 36–40, 45, 49, 50, 51, 61, 71, 99, 114, 125–126, 142, 206, 225 n. 90, 228, 243, 252–253, 257–258. Lodges: Clémente Amitié, 140 n. 42; Etoile du Bosphore, 71, 72; Proodos, 71, 125–126; Reveil de l'Iran, 45, 51, 258; Ser, 71; Sincère Amitié, 24, 114, 126, 142; Union d'Orient, 72; Unsterblichkeit, 51. *See also* Grand Orient
Freethinking, 8, 79, 216
French policy in Iran, 52
French Revolution, 47, 71
Fuad, Reşad, 75
Fuad Paşa, 65, 67, 70, 72–76, 83, 85, 188
Furūghī, Mīrzā Dhakā ul-Mulk, 203, 203 n. 78

Galib, Mehmet, 73, 76–77
Ganja, 79
Garrūsī, Ḥasan ᶜAlī Khān, 64, 118
Gasprinskiy, Ismail, 78
Gedikpaşa theater, 265
Geneva, 188
Georgia, Georgians, 79, 133, 164
Germany, 120, 151, 167
Ghulām Riḍā, Ḥājjī Mīrzā, 249
Gilan, 113, 117, 249
Gobineau, Comte Arthur de, 36, 52
Gorchakov, 120, 123
Grand Orient: of France, 24, 51, 52, 71, 142, 258; of Greece, 125
Granville, Lord, 119, 121, 136, 137
Greece, 73, 125
Greeks, 89
Guizot, 16 n. 54
Gulistān, 93, 159, 219
Gurgan, 132
Gwalior, 130

Ḥabl ul-Matīn, 247, 257
Habsburg Empire, 185
Hagopian, 3
Hajji Baba, 276

Ḥakīm-Ilāhī, Mīrzā Ja^c^far, 49, 50 n. 142, 53
Hâmit, Abdülhakk, 192 n. 20
Ḥaqā'iqnagār, Mīrzā Ja^c^far, 49
Hāshim, Mīrzā, 23 n. 18
Hasht Bihisht, 224 n. 86
Hatt-ı Hümayûn, 67
Haweis, Rev. H. R., 179
Hay'at-i Daulat, 105
Haydar Efendi, 59
Ḥaydar Khān, 204
Henriette, Princess, 64, 141, 219, 274
Herat, 23, 54, 131, 234
Hidāyat, Riḍā Qulī Khān, 26, 35, 49
Hidden Imam, 219–220, 221, 222, 231
Ḥikāyat-i Karbalā Raftan-i Shāhqulī Mīrzā, 266
Ḥikmat, 49
Hikmet, Mustafa, 74
Humanity, pseudoreligion of, 11, 228–230
Hürriyet, 89, 90, 93, 187–188
Ḥusām ul-Mulk, 233
Ḥusām us-Salṭana, 23, 54
Ḥusayn Khān, Mīrzā, Sipahsālār, 10, 128, 129, 140, 153, 163, 233; and Reuter concession, 113–114; as ambassador in Istanbul, 59, 70, 83, 85; as prime minister, 96, 101–107; dismissed from premiership, 123; early life, 66–67; relations with Malkum, 62–63, 66, 96–97, 99, 104–107, 124
Ḥusaynzāda, Ākhūnd Mullā Aḥmad, 91
Hyderabad, 132

Ibrāhīm (father of Amīn us-Sulṭān), 164–165
Ibrahimov, A. E., 268–273
Iḥtishām ud-Daula, Sulṭān Uvays Mīrzā, 50, 51
Iḥtishām us-Salṭana, Mīrzā Maḥmūd Khān, 250
Illustrated London News, 121, 163, 168
India, 3, 5, 9, 111, 127, 130, 131, 132, 133, 136, 152, 182, 191, 201, 225, 233
Inshāllāh, Māshāllāh, 277
Intiẓām ul-Ḥukamā, Mīrzā ^c^Alī Khān, 257–258
I^c^rāb, 82, 83, 87, 93
Iran, 1–3, 13, 15, 18, 20–22, 34, 36, 37, 42, 44, 51, 86, 93, 96, 100, 101, 107, 108, 111–112, 113, 119, 120, 123, 125, 127, 129, 130–136, 139, 142, 163, 164, 179–180, 190, 193, 200, 205, 206, 209, 211, 214, 224, 235, 240, 241, 258, 265, 275, 277, 304, 305, 308
Īrān, 180, 300
Iranische Literaturgeschichte, 231
Īrānshahr, Kāẓimzāda, 267
Isfahan, 1, 3, 57, 136, 138, 144, 145, 156, 206 n. 3, 215, 216, 234, 267, 278
Iṣfahānī, Mīrzā Ḥabīb, 55, 276
Iṣfahānī, Sayyid Jamāl ud-Dīn, 275
Iskandar Khān, 10, 204
Islam, 37, 64, 75, 140, 164; attempted secularization of, 90, 207; expedient appeals to, 9, 13, 14, 15, 17, 38, 40–41, 75–76, 84, 89, 91, 140, 179–180, 188–189, 207, 216, 230–231; expedient conversion to, 6, 7, 9; "reform" of, 7, 12, 13, 37, 59, 80, 92, 207; "renaissance" of, 7, 8, 13, 37–38, 59
Islamic law, 14, 42, 172–173; attempts to equate with European law, 14, 29, 31, 139–141, 190–191, 207–208, 277; codification of, 31, 191, 191 n. 17
Ismā^c^īl, Shah, 221
Ismā^c^īl Pāshā, 63 n. 22
Istanbul, 7, 9, 24, 27, 51, 54, 59, 62, 63–66, 70, 71, 78, 82, 83, 86, 88, 92, 93, 94, 97, 100, 103, 104, 105, 114, 116, 118, 119, 125–126, 128, 140–142, 146, 148, 161, 186–187, 189, 206, 207, 213–215, 217–218, 220–222, 224, 225, 234, 265, 269, 270, 273, 276
Italy, 178, 243, 256
I^c^timād us-Salṭana, Mīrzā Ḥasan Khān, 23, 47, 114 n. 55, 148, 149, 154, 199, 202, 205, 261
Ittiḥād, 266, 273–274
Ittiḥād ul-Islām, 226 n. 102
Ismir, 2
İzzet Molla, Keçecizade, 72

Jalāl ud-Dīn Mīrzā, 37–38, 47, 48, 50, 53, 92, 96–97, 271
Jamālzāda, Muḥammad ^c^Alī, 280
Japan, 113, 251
Java, 5
Jews, 89, 115, 163, 211
Jilva, Mīrzā Ḥasan, 49
Julfa: Old, 1, 2, 124; New, 1, 2, 3, 5, 144, 156

Kabul, 131
Kalāt, 136
Kanī, Mullā ^c^Alī, 47, 122
Karbala, 56, 58, 101
Kars, 1
Kārūn river, 136–139, 164, 165
Kasravī, Aḥmad, 248
Kazem-Beg, Mirza, 80
Kāẓimayn, 56, 101
Kemal, Namık, 89, 93, 94, 159
Kennedy, 202

Kerr, Lord Charles, 169
Khālid Bey, 181
Khānaqīn, 55
Khiva, 54, 112
Khorasan, 54, 204, 233
Khurramshahr, 136
Khuzistan, 136, 144
Kirman, 215–216
Kirmānī, Mīrzā Āqā Khān, 51, 161, 194, 197, 212–213, 214, 215–225, 227, 234, 277
Kirmānī, Mīrzā Riḍā, 237
Kirmānī, Nāẓim ul-Islām, 50, 52 n. 153
Kirmanshah, 45, 53, 202, 234, 249, 266
Kommissarov, D. S., 271
Kurds, Kurdistan, 57, 144

Lāhūtī, Abūl Qāsim, 45, 234–235
Lausanne, 273
Le Monde Maçonnique, 125
League of Humanity, 161, 192, 223, 226, 228–236, 239–240, 249
Legal reform, 102, 105, 107, 190–192. *See also* Islamic law
Lewis, Sir Charles, 169, 173, 175–177
London, 10, 11, 24, 25, 51, 65, 80, 99, 100, 108, 114, 118, 119, 120, 121, 124, 126, 127–134, 139, 141, 143, 149, 156, 158, 159, 161, 165, 166–168, 170–171, 173, 175, 178, 188, 189, 194, 201–203, 205, 206, 209–210, 213, 215, 216, 220, 233, 239, 243, 261, 262
Luristan, 144, 146

Madras Times, 182
Maḥallātī, Ḥājj Sayyāḥ, 203
Maḥmūd Maḥmūd, 262
Majd ul-Mulk, 49
Majlis-i Mashvarat-i Vuzarā, 105–106
Majlis-i Shaurā-yi Millī (Majlis), 236, 250, 251, 253, 254, 258–259, 267
Majlis-i Tanẓīmāt, 30, 35, 106
Majlis-i vuzarā, 30, 31, 35, 106
Majmūʿa-yi Mushtamil bar Se Qiṭʿa Tiʾātr, 267
Malayir, 249
Malījak, 156
Malik ul-Mutakallimīn, Mīrzā Naṣrullāh, 276
Malkum Khān, Mīrzā, Nāẓim ud-Daula: ancestry, 5; and alphabet reform, 8, 82, 86–95, 158–162; and Babism, 58–59, 221–225; and constitutionalism, 236–237; and Constitutional Revolution, 238, 247–248; and lottery concession, 168–184; and publication of *Qānūn*, 187–205; and Reuter concession, 113, 116–121, 124–125; and testament of Fuad Paşa, 73–76; and testament of Âlî Paşa, 76–77; appointed ambassador to Italy, 244; appointed consul-general in Egypt, 63; appointed counsellor at Iranian embassy in Istanbul, 64; appointed envoy to Britain, 99, 118; as envoy to Britain, 10, 127–174; as *mutarjim-i humāyūn*, 23; as teacher and interpreter at Dār ul-Funūn, 20, 21, 22; as writer of Persian, 235–236, 262, 279; assessments of, 260–263; attitude to Britain, 128–134, 137–139; attitude to France, 129, 130; attitude to religion, 9–15, 17, 64, 82, 89, 92, 97–99, 179–180, 207, 220, 228–229; attitude to Russia, 130–134, 139, 155; attitude to ulama, 28–29, 51, 69, 208–209, 208 n. 13, 210–213, 236, 279–280; attitude to westernization, 12, 14, 17, 18, 28, 33, 68, 75, 76, 82, 89, 94, 107, 179–180, 191, 246, 279; banished to Arab Iraq, 55; birth, 1; criticizes conduct of Marv campaign, 55; dies in Switzerland, 258; dismissed from Iranian embassy in London, 174; establishes farāmūshkhāna, 36–53, 55, 122; expelled from Baghdad, 59; falsely attributed with four comedies, 264–277; granted *Nishān-i Humāyūn*, 103; granted title of Nāẓim ud-Daula, 148; granted title of Nāẓim ul-Mulk, 103–104; his daughters, 65–66; his son, 65; in Istanbul, 62–77; in Tiflis, 97–99, 104; introduces telegraph to Iran, 12, 17, 25, 26, 40; Iranian delegate to Congress of Berlin, 148; leaves Iranian embassy in Istanbul, 65; marriage, 10, 64–65; masonic activities, 24–25, 61, 71, 99, 125–126; member of Iranian delegation to Paris, 24, 119; messianic pretensions, 226; proclaimed Jesus reincarnate, 220–222; proposals for administrative reform, 27–33, 35, 69–70, 105–107, 134–135, 153, 236–237; proposals for economic reform, 32, 100, 108–114; proposals for educational reform, 32, 135; proposals for financial reform, 69–70; proposals for Iranian foreign policy, 128–134, 137–138; proposals for legal reform, 105; proposals for military reform, 31–32, 34, 69; pseudoautobiographic account, 11, 46, 119 n. 72; reinstated at Iranian embassy in Istanbul, 66; relations with Abūl Ḥasan Mīrzā Shaykh ur-Raʾīs, 225–227; relations with Ākhūndzāda, 78, 81, 84, 86–99, 104, 268; relations with Amīn ud-Daula, 146–149, 152, 157; relations with

Amīn us-Sulṭān, 165–167, 171–172, 177, 194, 196–197, 251–253; relations with Mīrzā Āqā Khān Kirmānī, 215–225; relations with Mīrzā Ḥusayn Khān Sipahsālār, 62–65, 66, 85, 103–107, 113; relations with Mīrzā Yūsuf Khān Mustashār ud-Daula, 139–141; relations with Muḥammad ᶜAlī Shāh, 256–257; relations with Muẓaffar ud-Dīn Shāh, 143–144, 239–241, 245–246; relations with Nāṣir ud-Dīn Shāh, 22, 25, 27, 63, 124, 152–153, 155–156, 178, 197–198, 202; relations with Sayyid Jamāl ud-Dīn Asadābādī, 206–215; relations with Wolff, 165, 170; relations with Ẓill us-Sulṭān, 5, 144–146, 149–150, 156–157, 256; reputation for magic, 22; retains Ottoman nationality, 70, 97; return visits to Iran, 148–149, 155; "special adviser" to Mīrzā Ḥusayn Khān, 96, 103–107, 113; studies in France, 15–17; takes Ottoman nationality, 65; titled *Rūḥ ul-Quds*, 95–96, 99, 219, 269; view of Asia, 109–111; wills his body to be cremated, 259. Works: *Daftar-i Qānūn*, 190–191; *Dastgāh-i Dīvān*, 68–70, 105; *Ḥarf-i Gharīb*, 16, 105, 113, 137; *Ishtihārnāma-yi Auliyā-yi Ādamīyat*, 239–240; *Kitābcha-yi Ghaybī yā Daftar-i Tanẓīmāt*, 27–33, 34, 35, 48, 68, 105, 106, 107, 189, 190; *Mabdaʾ-i Taraqqī*, 67; *Namūna-yi Khaṭṭ-i Ādamīyat*, 161; *Naum va Yaqẓa*, 17; *Nidā-yi ᶜAdālat*, 245–247; *Persian Civilisation*, 179–180, 190–191; *Pūlitīkhā-yi Daulatī*, 67, 76, 129–134, 135; *Rafīq va Vazīr*, 33–34, 75, 94, 274, 280; *Risāla-yi Farāmūshkhāna*, 39–41; *Sayyāḥī Gūyad*, 274, 278–299; *Shaykh va Vazīr*, 67, 91, 93–95, 274, 280; *Tanẓīm-i Lashkar va Majlis-i Idāra*, 34–35, 69; *Uṣūl-i Ādamīyat*, 229–231; *Uṣūl-i Madhhab-i Dīvānīān*, 197, 275; *Uṣūl-i Tamaddun*, 16, 108–113, 108 n. 26, 120, 137

Malkum, Takrān, 144 n. 60

Mämmädzadä, H., 268–273

Marāghaʾī, Zayn ul-ᶜĀbidīn, 276

Marjaᶜ-i taqlīd, 210, 212

Marv, 54–55, 135–138

Mashhad, 215, 225, 233, 234

Mashīz, 215

Mazandaran, 113, 234, 249

Mazzini, 185

Mecca, 218, 233, 251

Meclis-i şura-yi devlet, 67

Mecmua-ı Fünun, 187

Messianism, 222

Meşveret, 73

Midhat Paşa, 101

Mikāʾīl Khān, 10, 169, 170, 173–174, 177, 178–179, 182, 183, 204

Military reform, 13 n. 47, 27 n. 38, 31–32, 34–35, 67, 69, 102–103, 105, 113

Minakyan, 265

Mining, 114, 116, 135

Ministries, institution of, 26; Ministry of Finance, 102; Ministry of Foreign Affairs, 88, 102, 114, 134, 151–152, 166, 188–189; Ministry of Justice, 102, 105; Ministry of Pensions and Endowments, 102, 106; Ministry of War, 102; Ministry of Works, 106

Mirabeau, 17, 18

Mīrzā Āqāsī, Ḥājjī, 6, 22

Mismer, Charles, 7, 8, 13, 86

Molla Näsräddin, 248

Montenegro, 77

Morier, James, 276

Moscow, 80, 123

Muḥammad ᶜAlī Āqā, 24

Muḥammad ᶜAlī Pāshā, 4, 17, 185

Muḥammad ᶜAlī Shāh, 253–259, 267, 274

Muḥammad Āqā, 115

Muḥammad Khān, 204

Muḥammad Khān, Āghā, 164

Muḥammad Riḍā, Mīrzā, 35

Muḥammad Shāh, 6, 7, 22

Mühbir, 89, 90, 187

Muᶜīn ul-Mulk, Mīrzā Muḥsin Khān, 114–115, 118, 125–126, 129, 141–142, 186–187, 203, 233, 245

Mujtahid(s), 14, 57, 145, 200, 212, 236, 246, 305, 307

Mukhbir ud-Daula, 233

Mukhbir us-Salṭana, 215 n. 45

Mulkārā, ᶜAbbās Mīrzā, 171, 191 n. 17, 303 n. 10

Munich, 201

Münif Paşa, Mehmed, 72, 82, 83, 84, 86, 88, 159, 187, 206, 218

Munshībāshī, Mīrzā Muḥammad Khān Qazvīnī, 248

Münster, Count, 151

Murray, Charles Augustus, 23

Muscat, 131

Mushīr ud-Daula, Mīrzā Jaᶜfar Khān, 26, 27, 35

Mushīr ud-Daula, Mīrzā Yaḥyā Khān, 166, 191 n. 17, 233, 248

Mushtāq ᶜAlī Shāh, 215

Mustashār ud-Daula, Mīrzā Yūsuf Khān, 99, 139–141, 140 n. 42, 142, 204

Mustaufī, ᶜAbdullāh, 107

Mustaufī ul-Mamālik, Mīrzā Yūsuf, 69, 122
Mu^ctamad ud-Daula, Farhād Mīrzā, 122, 123
Mu^ɔtaman ul-Mulk, Mīrzā Sa^cīd Khān, 47, 65, 66, 68–69, 123–124, 153
Muẓaffar ud-Dīn Shāh, 49, 142–144, 146, 237, 239–246, 250, 256

Nabī Khān, 97
Naci Efendi, Yahya, 7
Nadīmbāshī, Ḥājjī, 255, 257
Nādir Shāh, 56
Nafīsī, Sa^cīd, 273
Nahj al-Balāgha, 159
Nā^ɔib us-Salṭana, Kāmrān Mīrzā, 156, 166, 196, 203–204, 248
Nā^ɔīnī, Ḥājjī Pīrzāda, 261
Najaf, 56, 101
Najaf Qulī Khān, Mīrzā, 125, 186, 217
Najafī, Āqā, 145, 276
Najīb Pāshā, 58
Najmābādī, Shaykh Hādī, 48, 50, 201, 208, 233
Nakhjavan, 1
Nāma-yi Khusruvān, 92
Napoleon I, 130, 151
Napoleon III, 24
Naqī, ^cAlī, 25
Narīmān Khān, 24, 141, 147
Nāṣir ud-Dīn Shāh, 7, 37, 46, 102–103, 105–107, 136–137, 159, 164–165, 172, 186, 192, 195, 199–202, 204, 209, 211, 243; and Dār ul-Funūn, 20; and execution of Amīr Kabīr, 6; and farāmūshkhāna, 38–39, 42, 48–49, 52–53; and Reuter concession, 117, 121–124; assassinated, 237–239, 262; first journey to Europe, 118–119, 120–122, 126, 136, 146, 163; religiosity of, 101; relations with Malkum, 12, 22, 25–27, 62, 69, 75, 76, 113, 128, 135, 148–150, 172, 174, 197–198, 210, 219, 240, 255, 300; third journey to Europe, 163, 166–168, 261; visit to Arab Iraq, 96, 101
Nāṣir ul-Mulk, 152, 233
Naṣrullāh Khān, Mīrzā, 203, 243, 245
Naẓar Āqā, 21, 21 n. 5, 141–142, 147, 209 n. 18, 244–245
Nāẓim-i Daftar, Mīrzā Muḥammad Khān, 47
New Oriental Bank Corporation, 169
New Ottoman Society, 89
Nice, 178
Nicolson, Sir Arthur, 137, 155, 165
Niẓām-i Jadīd, 103
North Africa, 191, 251
Notting Hill Gate, 159
Nūbār Pāshā, 4
Nūkha, 78
Nūrī, Mīrzā Āqā Khān, 6, 15, 20, 23, 26, 30
Nūrī, Mīrzā Ḥusayn ^cAlī ("Bahā^ɔullāh"), 58, 59

Ocherki Sovremennoi Persidskoi Prozy, 271
Oriental Printing Company, 192
Ornstein, 211 n. 27
Ottoman Scientific Society, 72, 82, 83–84, 87, 88, 91
Ottoman Theater, 265
Ottomans, Ottoman Empire, 1, 27, 57, 59–62, 67, 70, 73, 76, 85, 86, 88, 89, 94, 103, 114, 125, 129, 148, 208, 212–213, 217, 224, 225, 265

Pan-Islamism, 187, 224, 226 n. 102
Paris, 15, 17, 24, 25, 65, 73, 80, 119, 126, 139, 141, 166, 243, 245, 270; Treaty of, 24, 53
Persian Gulf, 131, 133, 136, 137
Persian Investment Corporation, 169–170, 172 n. 39, 173, 174, 175, 176, 177, 178, 182
Persian Revolution, 218, 260
Perso-Russian War, Second, 131
Peter the Great, 69, 75, 132
Poona, 225
Poti, 85 n. 30
Press: Arabic, 185; Azerbayjani, 248; Persian, 185–187, 247–248; Turkish, 76, 93, 185–188
Punjab, 131

Qā^ɔānī, 279
Qā^ɔim Maqām, Mīrzā Abūl Qāsim, 181, 307
Qajars, Qajar dynasty, 3, 5, 57, 101, 144, 208, 225, 278, 304
Qānūn (the concept of secular law), 29, 31, 67, 190–192, 191 n. 20, 207, 224
Qānūn (Malkum's newspaper), 9, 22, 29, 37, 59, 74, 94, 111, 141, 162, 167, 177, 180, 184, 187–205, 207, 208 n. 13, 209, 211–213, 215, 216–217, 219, 223, 224, 225 n. 23, 226–228, 230, 231, 233, 234, 237–239, 241, 244, 247–248, 249, 259, 260, 261, 300–308
Qarājadāghī, Mīrzā Ja^cfar, 271
Qavām ud-Daula, 156, 172, 173, 174, 175
Qazvin, 141, 149, 204, 234, 248, 257
Qazvīnī, Mīrzā Muḥammad, 262
Qum, 53

Qushūn, 102
Quṭūr, 148

Rabīᶜzāda, Hāshim, 277
Railways, 114–115, 116–117, 120, 122, 123, 135, 147, 154–157, 164; Caspian Sea-Persian Gulf, 116; Iskenderun-Basra, 67; Tehran-Shāh ᶜAbd ul-ᶜAẓīm, 114–115, 154
Ramz-i Yūsufī, 140
Rasht, 117, 120, 215, 257
Rawlinson, Sir Henry, 116 n. 62
Redcliffe, Lord Stratford de, 71
Refutation of the Materialists, 208
Republicanism, 47–48
Reşid Efendi, 68
Reşit Paşa, Mustafa, 71
Reuter, Baron Julius von, 113–125, 164–167
Reuter, George, 164
Revue de Paris, 74, 76
Riḍā Khān, Mīrzā, 24
Risāla-yi Akhlāqīya, 273
Risāla-yi Ghaybīya, 277
Risāla-yi Majdīya, 49
Rıza, Ahmet, 74
Rıza, Paşa, 218
Roman alphabet, 93, 95, 161
Rome, 177, 238, 244, 245, 248, 251, 252, 257, 277
Rosen, Baron Friedrich, 267
Rothschilds, 112, 164, 167
Rousseau, Jean-Jacques, 5
Rūḥ ul-Islām, 140–141
Rūḥī, Shaykh Aḥmad, 215, 276
Rumeli Hisar, 65, 72
Rūmī, Maulānā Jalāl ud-Dīn, 45 n. 122, 79, 80, 96
Russia, 3, 54, 73, 76, 78, 80, 85, 120, 201, 202, 204, 251, 257
Russian policy in Iran, 3, 4, 23, 46, 103, 113, 119, 120, 121, 123, 124, 127, 128, 130–134, 135, 136, 137, 139, 151, 152, 164, 165, 171–172
Ruʾyā-yi Ṣādiqa, 275–276
Rūznāma-yi Vaqāyiᶜ-i Ittifāqīya, 185–186
Rypka, Jan, 271

Ṣabā, Mīrzā Maḥmūd Khān, 49, 279
Saᶜd ud-Daula, Mīrzā Javād Khān, 250
Saᶜdī, 93, 159, 250
Sādiq Khān, 254
Ṣafā, Ḥājjī Mīrzā, 70
Ṣafāʾī, Ibrāhīm, 262
Safavids, 1–3, 56
Saḥāb, 279
St. Petersburg, 76, 80, 120, 121, 123, 127, 137, 138, 155, 167, 175, 261, 276
Salisbury, Lord, 138, 183
Salmās, 305
Samarra, 56, 210–212
Ṣanīᶜ ud-Daula, 254
Sanua, James, 228 n. 2
Sarakhs, 137, 138
Sargudhasht-i Ashraf Khān, Ḥākim-i ᶜArabistān, 266, 273
Sāsānī, Khān Malik, 53, 65, 262
Sassoons, 164
Savalan, 114
Sayfullāh Mīrzā, 50
Scalieri, 71, 125 n. 98, 126
Scarcia, Gianroberto, 272
Scotland, 167–168, 171, 174
Secret societies, 12, 38, 40, 45, 235, 247
Selim III, Sultan, 67, 71, 103
Serbia, 77
Shāh ᶜAbd ul-ᶜAẓīm, 202
Shams ul-Aṭibbā, Sayyid Riḍā, 53
Sharīᶜa. *See* Islamic law
Shaṭṭ al-ᶜArab, 136
Shaykh ur-Raʾīs, Abūl Ḥasan Mīrzā, 225–227
Shaykhīs, Shaykhism, 215, 277 n. 61, 282 n. 5
Shiᶜis, Shiᶜism, 14, 45, 56–57, 58, 70, 75–76, 208, 212, 213, 220, 221, 224, 230
Shiraz, 211, 234
Shīrāzī, Mīrzā Ḥasan, 210–214, 217, 235
Shīrāzī, Mīrzā Ṣāliḥ, 185
Shujāᶜ, Shah, 131
Shushtar, 136
Şinasi, 187, 192 n. 20
Sind, 130, 131
Sipahsālār. *See* Ḥusayn Khān, Mīrzā, Sipahsālār
Sipahsālār, Mīrzā Muḥammad Khān, 55
Sipihr, Mīrzā Muḥammad Taqī Lisān ul-Mulk, 49
Sistan, 131
Siyāḥatnāma-yi Ibrāhīm Bayg, 276
Siyāsatgarān-i Daura-yi Qājār, 262
Smith, R. M., 145
Society of Humanity, 248–251, 253–259
Sollogub, Vladimir, 80
Spain, 93
Spanish Inquisition, 98
Staal, Baron de, 139, 152, 155, 175, 261
Strousberg, 114
Suavi, Ali, 88, 90 n. 42, 187
Ṣubḥ-i Azal, 215, 222, 223
Suez Canal, 185
Sufis, Sufi orders, Sufism, 38, 45, 79, 80, 221, 229, 230, 234, 296 n. 31

Sulaymānīya, 58
Sulṭānīya, 26
Ṣūr-i Isrāfīl, 245 n. 22, 247–248
Switzerland, 258
Syria, 3, 4, 251

Ṭabāṭabā'ī, Sayyid Muḥammad, 50–51
Ṭabāṭabā'ī, Sayyid Ṣādiq, 50–51, 201
Tabriz, 1, 26, 124, 142, 204, 239, 266, 270, 273, 305
Tabrīzī, Mīrzā Āqā, 268–272, 276–277
Tabrīzī, Muḥammad Ṭāhir, 186
Tabrīzī, Sayyid Javād, 267
Takvîm-i Vakâyi, 185
Talibov, 78
Tamaddun, 247
Tanzimat, 27, 66–67, 82, 105, 128
Taqallub: Ṭarḥ-i Jadīd, 257
Taqī Khān, Mīrzā. *See* Amīr Kabīr, Mīrzā Taqī Khān
Taqīya, 46
Taqīzāda, Sayyid Ḥasan, 266
Ṭarīqa-yi Ḥukūmat-i Zamān Khān-i Burūjirdī, 275
Tasvir-i Efkâr, 187
Tavernier, Jean-Baptiste, 2
Tehran, 12, 20, 37, 59, 88, 96, 99, 100, 101, 103, 104, 108, 114, 115, 117, 118, 120, 121, 122–126, 128, 129, 138, 146, 147, 151, 153, 155, 156, 161, 163, 165, 170, 173, 176, 181, 183, 187, 190, 192, 195, 198, 199, 201, 203, 205, 209, 211, 213, 215, 217, 223, 234, 235, 241, 242, 248, 257, 267, 269, 272, 278, 305, 308
Telegraph, introduction of to Iran, 12, 17, 25, 26
Tercümân-ı Ahvâl, 187
The Spirit of Islam, 140 n. 44
The Times, 172 n. 39, 174, 176, 180, 219
Theater: Azerbayjani, 80, 85, 265, 270; Persian, 265 ff., 265 n. 3; Turkish, 265
Tholozan, Dr., 48
Thomson, W. T., 136
Tiflis, 66, 79, 80, 81, 83, 85, 88, 93, 97, 98, 99, 104, 123, 140, 149, 150, 164, 174, 248
Tigris, 136
Tilsit, Treaty of, 130
Tolstoy, L., 79
Topçubaşı, Arakel Bey, 64
Transcaspia, 119, 153
Tunis, 77
Turkey, 162, 179, 201. *See also* Ottoman Empire
Turkistan, 132
Turkomans, 54
Turkumānchāy, Treaty of, 34
Turshīz, 204

Ulama, 69, 145, 208–209, 224, 234, 236, 246–247; and alphabet reform, 89–90; and farāmūshkhāna, 41, 43, 47, 48, 50; and Reuter concession, 122; and tobacco concession, 210–214; and westernization, 28–29, 89; of ᶜatabāt, 101, 225 n. 23
Uṣūlīs, 283 n. 5
Uzbeks, 54

Vāḍiḥ, Mīrzā Shafīᶜ, 79, 79 n. 2
Valī, Sayyid, 203
Valle, Pietro della, 2
Vefik Paşa, Ahmet, 7, 71–72, 187, 265
Venice, 3
Victoria, Queen, 120
Vienna, 119, 141, 244
Volga, 3
Voltaire, 8
Vuthūq ud-Daula, 134

Wallachia, 77
al-Waqā'iᶜ al-Miṣrīyya, 185
Westernization, 11, 12, 13, 15, 17, 18, 28, 75–76, 78, 82, 90, 118, 144, 179–180, 189, 191, 216, 246, 260, 262
Wilhelm, Kaiser, 151
Winston, 155
Wolff, Joseph, 163
Wolff, Sir Henry Drummond, 125, 138–139, 163–167, 169–171, 173, 175, 176, 181 n. 60, 242 n. 12, 243–244

Yak Kalima, 139, 204
Yaᶜqūb Khān, Mīrzā, 5, 6, 7, 8, 9, 11, 11 n. 42, 13, 15, 20, 37, 53–54, 53 n. 158, 62, 72, 86, 96, 144, 148, 267
Yazd, 144, 233
Yusufian, Boghos, 4

Zagros, 131
Zākānī, ᶜUbayd, 280
Zand, Karīm Khān, 56
Zāyanda Rūd, 1
Zayn ul-ᶜĀbidīn, Ḥājjī Mīrzā, 50
Ẓill us-Sulṭān, Masᶜūd Mīrzā, 5, 144–146, 148, 149–150, 156–157, 158, 166, 182 n. 61, 196, 206, 206 n. 3, 215, 256, 261, 276
Zinovyev, 133 n. 14, 152
Zoroastrians, 215–216
Zühdü Paşa, 218